The Power of Writing

DAVID W. CHAPMAN
Samford University

PRESTON LYNN WALLER
McLennan Community College

Mayfield Publishing Company
Mountain View, California
London • Toronto

Library of Congress Cataloging-in-Publication Data
Chapman, David W.
    The power of writing / by David W. Chapman and Preston Lynn Waller.
      p.   cm.
    Includes index.
    ISBN 1-55934-138-6
    1. English language — Rhetoric.   I. Waller, Preston Lynn.
    II. Title.
    PE1408.C48   1993
    808'.042 — dc20

                                                        93-21676
                                                          CIP

Manufactured in the United States of America

10 9 8 7 6 5 4 3 2 1

Mayfield Publishing Company
1280 Villa Street
Mountain View, CA 94041

Sponsoring editor, Janet M. Beatty; production editor, April Wells-Hayes; copyeditor, Margaret Moore; text designer, Joan Greenfield; cover designer, Steve Naegele; cover image: © Ralph Wetmore/Tony Stone Images; art editor, Jean Mailander; art director, Jeanne M. Schreiber; manufacturing manager, Martha Branch. The text was set in 10/13 Galliard by Thompson Type and printed on 50# Finch Opaque by the Maple Vail Book Manufacturing Group.

Acknowledgments and copyrights continue at the back of the book on page 366, which constitutes an extension of the copyright page.

Preface

Most people write for the same reason they balance their checkbooks, drive their cars, or read their newspapers. Writing allows them to control the circumstances of their lives. Unfortunately, many students enter a composition classroom believing that writing is a special talent possessed by a few gifted individuals. As long as they see writing as something that *other* people do, they cannot develop their own abilities to write. We wrote *The Power of Writing* to show students how *they* can use writing to get things done.

For this reason, *The Power of Writing* is written *to* students and *for* students. We address the student directly from the first page in order to communicate clearly that writing is something they can do. We want them to see the potential of writing for organizing experience, clarifying thinking, discovering new ideas, communicating information, arguing a debatable issue, investigating a problem — to explore the full range of uses for writing in their lives.

In writing this book, we have tried to concentrate on the essential elements of writing. These are not the old "basics": lectures on the qualities of good writing, for instance. Telling students what they should do when they write has little effect on their actual performance. Nobody learns to swim sitting on a beach towel. *The Power of Writing* immediately immerses the student in the activity of writing. Part I: Writing Strategies helps students to explore their ideas, develop a focus, and revise in light of purpose and audience. Part II: The Aims of Writing leads students through specific assignments in writing to discover, inform, analyze, persuade, and investigate. Part III: Editing provides students with essential information on mechanics and style. Even in this section, we engage the students in the process of editing rather than getting bogged down in hair-splitting discussions of grammatical terms.

We are under no delusion that this textbook, or any textbook, should be the focus of a composition course. At one time, administrators and even some composition teachers might have pointed to the textbook as the best explanation of what the composition course entailed. Most of us now point to our classrooms, our conferences with our students, and our students' papers as the best representation of what we can accomplish in such a course.

Given a focus on student–teacher interaction as the foundation of the composition course, what part should a textbook play in the development of student writing? As a minimum, a textbook shouldn't get in the way. When students have invested large sums of money in an oversized text, their teacher feels almost compelled to spend time explaining the book, diverting attention from the students' own work. Because *The Power of Writing* was written to be read by students, we have avoided unnecessary jargon and theoretical justification for our approaches. Although our book is based on sound rhetorical theory — for instance, emphasizing a process approach to writing and encouraging collaborative activity — we do not feel that students in an introductory writing course should spend time figuring out the difference between topics and *topoi* or comparing Aristotle's views on argument to those of Stephen Toulmin. Many books aim to train new composition teachers. We don't believe a student textbook should serve that purpose.

We have strived, then, to make *The Power of Writing* a textbook that works for the teacher. Students get the necessary background information they need from the textbook so that class time focuses on working with the students' own writing. If students are struggling with a particular problem, the instructor can refer them to a section of the text that will provide helpful information in a clear, easy-to-understand format. The book's many activities will help the class as a whole explore new ideas and consider new approaches. The tone of the book is encouraging to students, especially those who often ignore independent reading assignments.

The Power of Writing . . .

- Empowers student writers

    Students learn how to use writing to improve their personal, professional, and academic lives. Writing is not treated as an end in itself but as a means of achieving individual and social goals.

- Recognizes student diversity

    American higher education has become increasingly open to students of different ages, cultures, educational backgrounds, and career goals. *The Power of Writing* emphasizes the importance of cultural background and heritage and the role that communication plays in developing mutual understanding and respect.

- Encourages collaborative activity

    Composition scholars have become increasingly aware of the social nature of all writing. *The Power of Writing* encourages group brainstorming, peer review, and other collaborative writing activities. Many of the activities take place in Discovery Groups set up to explore alternative approaches and to examine issues critically instead of merely to give pat answers.

- Acknowledges professional writing concerns

  The Power of Writing will appeal to those students who have an interest in professional writing situations. For instance, students are often asked to write for situations they could encounter on the job. Sections on conducting field research and preparing graphics recognize the need for these skills in many practical writing situations.

- Appeals to reluctant writers

  The friendly tone of the text and the use of illustrations and examples are appealing to the student who may be unprepared for college-level reading or who lacks motivation. High-interest reading selections are used throughout. The visually interesting format encourages independent reading of the textbook.

- Provides information on writing with a computer

  Students are encouraged to see the computer as more than a fancy typewriter. As well as considering word processing applications, "Byte-Size Bulletins" provide information on modems, printers, electronic mail, databases, style programs, and many other subjects of interest. Instead of being relegated to an appendix, word processing information is placed in the context where it is most needed. We discuss databases in a chapter that considers library research and explain spell checkers in a chapter on editing. Since the emphasis is on the potential uses of computers, even students who do not use a word processor will find the information timely and relevant.

- Is informed by composition theory and research

  Although *The Power of Writing* is not laden with rhetorical jargon, it does rely on the results of composition research for its approach to student writing. For instance, the emphasis on collaboration in writing is based on recent studies showing the importance of collaboration to students' intellectual development. Writing assignments are also sequenced, beginning with short writing-to-discover activities and leading progressively to the more challenging tasks of writing to persuade and to investigate. Wherever possible, the editing activities are designed to represent writing in context rather than to focus on individual sentences. Rather than simply treating language as a static object, the "Language Notes," which instructors may find useful as "mini-lessons," engage the class in becoming conscious of their own language customs and habits. Critical thinking is encouraged throughout the text. The text itself becomes open to question in the "Critical Moments" section at the end of each chapter. In other words, the text is student centered, process oriented, and collaboratively based.

This book on writing—indeed, any current book on writing—would not have been possible without the work of that generation of writers and scholars who decided that freshman composition is something more than a momentary distraction on the way to more important things. Although they represent a variety of approaches and opinions, I have no doubt that this book was influenced by Janet Emig, James Britton, Gary Tate, Edward P. J. Corbett, Winifred Horner, Frank D'Angelo, Peter Elbow, Donald Murray, Janice Lauer, James Kinneavy, and many others who wrote the books and articles that were the inspiration of all the subsequent work that has gone on in rhetoric and composition.

More immediately, we wish to thank our students at Texas Tech University, McLennan Community College, and Samford University who contributed, directly and indirectly, to *The Power of Writing*. Our understanding of what works in a writing classroom was produced in the context of collaborating with hundreds of students on the writing assignments for our classes.

We also want to express our appreciation for those people who carried this work from concept to reality. Ruth Holt and Bonnie Siler worked tirelessly on manuscript preparation. Sharon Kenan and Alan Berecka often found our literary needles in the library haystack. Lissette Carpenter, Charles Workman, Janice Lasseter, David Roberts, David Dedo, and many other colleagues provided their support. Patricia E. Connors, Memphis State University; Deborah Core, Eastern Kentucky University; Robert Cosgrove, Saddleback College; Jeannie Simms Dobson, Greenville Technical College; Janice Neuleib, Illinois State University; W. S. Newman, DeKalb College; and Nell Ann Pickett, Hinds Community College offered many valuable comments and suggestions that have made this a better book than the one we started to write.

We have been fortunate to work with a publisher that believes in the integrity of authors rather than in books written by committee. To all our friends at Mayfield Publishing—Tom Broadbent and April Wells-Hayes and Julianne Rovesti, among others—many thanks! And most of all, to Jan Beatty, who believed in the project from the beginning and watched over it to the end, goes our inestimable sense of gratitude for a job well done.

Finally, we want to recognize the support of our families. Our wives, LuAnn and Bonnie, have borne with patience the litany that begins "I can't _____; I'll be working on the book." We also want to recognize our children—Luke, Jennifer, Michael, Bobby—who didn't contribute anything but will be thrilled to have their names in a book.

Contents

CHAPTER 5 *Writing to Inform*   83

CHAPTER 8   *Writing to Investigate*   196

CHAPTER 11 *Editing for Style*   326

Exercises

PART I

Writing Strategies

CHAPTER 1

Getting Started

WHY DO WE WRITE?

A few years ago on a business trip I was treated rudely and unprofessionally by the ticket agent of a major airline. In a letter to the company, I politely, but firmly, protested the way the agent had handled my request. I described the behavior of the agent and the company policies which had been violated. I noted that I was a frequent traveler and that such behavior would discourage my future use of that airline. A few weeks later I received a letter of apology from one of the corporate managers and a coupon toward the purchase of my next flight. The courteous response of the airline convinced me that they were genuinely concerned about the quality of their service, and I now frequently request to fly on this airline.

As my experience with the airline indicates, we frequently write in response to a personal need. Through writing we conduct business, explain new procedures, influence others, and respond to problems — but in every case, we write to satisfy a human need to communicate. Without a means of communication with others, we would often be helpless victims of our circumstances. It is important, then, to see the ability to write, *and write well,* as a way of exercising control over the circumstances of our lives. In this course you will not only learn to write well, but also learn how to use writing to think through ideas, resolve misunderstandings, and argue effectively for your point of view.

WRITING IN A COMMUNITY

What image does the word *writer* bring to mind for you? Many people visualize a man in a frock coat furiously dipping his pen into an ink pot and dashing off line after line. Others see a tired journalist in a wrinkled shirt, pecking away at her typewriter in the middle of the night. Such Hollywood depictions of writers have served to reinforce the notion that only "gifted" people are able to write well. In reality, writers are not a special breed of people. In a technologically advanced society, such as our own, everyone needs the ability to read and write well. However, we shouldn't measure writing ability by some exalted notion of the "great" writer. *You are successful as a writer when you have communicated clearly to a community of readers.* This community may be the school you attend, the business where you work, or an organization you have joined. Your writing might be a report for a history class, a letter to the editor, a suggestion for improving your workplace, or a poem about the death of a friend. In every case, you will want to be able to communicate your thoughts, feelings, and ideas with purpose and clarity.

By enrolling in this class, you have immediately become a member of a community of readers and writers. This community will be valuable to you in two ways. First, your own ideas will be challenged by people who may have a very different perspective on the world than your own. Your writing will become sharpened and focused as you work to help them understand your own thoughts on a subject. Second, other students will become a resource to you for ideas and approaches. Because it's important for you to gain perspective on your work from classmates, we have included many suggestions for collaborative activity in this book. We hope that you will take advantage of these opportunities to gain insight from other students who are facing the same tasks you are.

Writing in the Presence of Others

As the Hollywood stereotype of the lonely writer indicates, we often think of writing as a solitary act. It is true that many writers prefer to be alone when they write, usually in a quiet place free from noise and other distractions. Unfortunately, most writing takes place under less than ideal conditions. The novelist or poet may have the luxury of writing in a secluded mountain retreat, but most writing takes place on the job—in crowded offices, often under the pressure of a deadline. As you work on your writing for this course, you may often have to work under stressful conditions. You may have to write in the spare moments you have on campus or even on a break period on the job. You may find yourself writing late at night or early in the morning. As difficult as these situations can be, they should be considered good preparation for the challenges of most real-world writing. A poet and a physician, William Carlos Williams always kept a typewriter set up at his office so that he could work on his poems between patients. I know one woman who placed a typewriter on a tall counter so that she could work on her college papers between household duties without having to sit down. With determination, writing can be done in almost any situation.

On the other hand, if you can control your writing environment, you should take every opportunity to do so. You know the atmosphere most conducive to your work. If you're sharing an apartment with other people, you may want to find a room where you can close the door and get some time to yourself to work on your writing assignments. If home is too busy, you may need to work at the library or even a quiet café. As a college freshman, I found a lounge area that was open for students on the top floor of a high-rise building. Not only was it quiet, but I also found the view from that altitude to be inspirational. If you are enterprising, you can find a time and a place that will work for you.

EXERCISE 1.1   Your Writing Environment

Pair off with another student in your class to discuss your writing habits. After asking these questions, write a one-page summary of your partner's writing habits.

1.   Where do you like to write?

2.   What time of the day is best for your writing?

3.   What distracts you from doing your best work?

4.   Do you like absolute quiet or some noise in the background?

5.   What kind of furniture and surroundings do you like to have when you write?

6.   What instrument or equipment do you use for writing? For instance, do you prefer pencil or pen? Do you have a favorite pen you like to use? Do you write on notebook paper? legal pad? stationery? Do you type?

7.   Have you ever used a word processor? Do you compose on the word processor, or do you use a word processor only after you've finished a handwritten draft?

8.   Do you like to write? Would you prefer to write a story you've made up, a description of something that really happened to you, or a report about something you've read?

Most people prefer to write when they are alone. They find it easier to concentrate when no one else is around. However, even if you are alone when you write, writing is never really a solitary act. For one thing, most of us are always thinking about the way someone else would respond to our writing. In working on a school assignment, we are usually trying to produce the kind of writing the teacher expects. If we are writing on a job, we are trying to impress our supervisor or our co-workers. Our awareness of how these people will read our work often determines what we say and how we say it.

Writing Influenced by Language and Culture

Besides our intended readers, many other factors influence what we have to say when we write. Some of these factors are so obvious that we tend to ignore them. For instance, the language you will use to write your papers in this course will be

BYTE-SIZE BULLETIN: WRITING ON A WORD PROCESSOR

Throughout this book you will find brief explanations about how a computer might be used to improve your writing performance. If you have access to a personal computer, we encourage you to take advantage of this technology. We call these explanations "Byte-Size Bulletins" because the memory capacity of a computer is measured in units called **bytes**. Even if you are not currently using a computer, you will find "Byte-Size" informative; and in all likelihood, you will write on a computer at some point in your career. Nearly all businesses have made computers available to their employees for writing and for storing data in electronic form.

When using a computer to write, you usually use word processing **software**, a program which enables you to add, delete, and change text in a document. The physical computer, on the other hand, consists of **hardware** such as the following:

a **monitor** (works like a television screen for displaying the information you type on the keyboard)

disk drives (computer programs are stored on disks; a disk drive can "read" these disks in the same way that a cassette player can read a cassette tape)

a **mouse** (used for drawing, editing text, and giving commands; not all computers have a mouse)

a **central processing unit,** or **CPU** (the electronic circuits that are the "brains" of the computer)

a **keyboard** (similar to that found on a typewriter, but with some additional keys for operating the software)

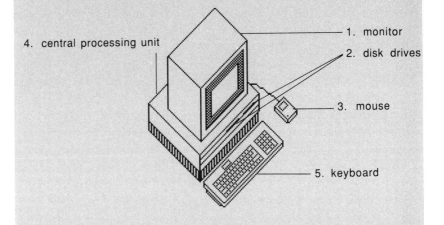

In addition to the computer, a **printer** is also necessary to make "hard copies" of your work.

The computer offers several advantages over an electric typewriter. Because you are entering your words in electronic form on the screen, you can add, delete, or change words without fussing with correction tape or fluid. On a word processor, you can enter new paragraphs in the middle of a document without having to retype the entire paper. The word processor automatically "pushes" the text forward to make room for the new words you are entering. You will find that revising your writing is much easier on a word processor.

You may want to gain access to a computer for the writing you will be doing in this course. Many schools have computer labs that are available for student word processing. You should find out about the availability of such labs on your campus. If you don't already own a computer, you might want to consider making such a purchase. You may be able to buy a computer at a discount price through your school. A computer can be used for personal financial records, for electronic communication, and for many other purposes. But if you used your computer only for word processing, it would still be a wise investment.

English. Your ability to write well, then, will be determined by your knowledge of the language, your past reading experiences, your vocabulary, your level of confidence, and other factors related to your competence in using the language. If English is not your native tongue, you may be intensely aware of the difficulties of expressing yourself in this language. You may occasionally be frustrated when writing because you can't think of the right word to use for the particular meaning you have in mind. Even if English is your first language, you will be affected by regional differences in language use. For instance, a picnic in one part of the country might include *sodas* to drink and *rolls* for the hamburgers. In another area, these same items might be referred to as *pop* and hamburger *buns*. Your decision to use "soda" or "pop" is so unconscious that it might be said that your language is choosing you, rather than you choosing it.

Of course, you will often want to make conscious decisions about the kind of language that is appropriate for a particular occasion. You might, for instance, say "soda" in everyday conversation, but use the term "carbonated beverage" if you were trying to be more precise or formal. One advantage of written language over conversation is that we have the opportunity to think about which word will best convey the meaning that we intend. We also think about the "tone" we are conveying with our words. Using words like *mendacity* for *lying* or *obstinate* for *stubborn* is a little like putting on dress clothes. *Mendacity* is not a better word than *lying*, but it may be a more appropriate word in some formal writing.

EXERCISE 1.2 You and Your Language

We often have a choice about which word we choose to fit a particular situation. In the following sentences, choose the word you would most likely use in casual conversation.

1. I (dived, dove) into the water.

2. She remained (poised, cool) under pressure.

3. The shirt had (loud, bold) colors.

4. He was stopped by a (cop, policeman).

5. There was a lot of (hype, publicity) surrounding the game.

6. I was (nervous, frightened) when we went rapelling.

7. I was (nervous, frightened) as we waited for the test results.

8. The jury thought the witness's testimony was (incredible, unreliable).

9. Her smile was (radiant, warm).

10. Your altitude is determined by your (attitude, outlook).

Discuss as a class or in small groups how you make decisions about which word is appropriate for a certain situation.

These differences in language suggest even more significant influences on your writing and thinking—cultural differences. Take the word *family*, for instance. Whom do you think of as members of your family? For some people, "family" brings to mind a small group of people:

Mom

Dad

brothers/sisters

husband/wife

children

For many people, family includes stepparents and stepchildren as well. But in all of these cases, the reference is to the "immediate family," or what sociologists call the "nuclear family." Before World War II, many people described their "family" this way:

Grandma	Grandpa
aunts	uncles
cousins	nephews
nieces	Mom
Dad	brothers/sisters
husband/wife	children

In our time, it is less likely that we will know our distant relatives well. Some may live in distant cities. We may never have seen some of them. Consequently, we tend to think of them as "relatives" instead of "family." Few people today would mention the names of aunts and uncles if asked to name the members of their family. The range of possibilities suggested by this one word shows how deeply we are affected by our cultural identity.

In addition to family background, many Americans enjoy an ethnic heritage as well. Will Rogers, the famous "cowboy comedian," was proud of his Cherokee ancestry. When he encountered socialites who bragged that their forefathers had come over on the *Mayflower*, Rogers liked to remind them that his ancestors were waiting to meet their boat. Unlike Will Rogers, the vast majority of us cannot lay claim to being native Americans. The ethnic diversity of this country, expressed in different languages, customs, traditions, and beliefs, has sometimes been a source of friction among competing groups. However, most Americans celebrate their differences as well as their common allegiance to American ideals of justice and liberty for all. The Irish were once a persecuted minority in this country, but now St. Patrick's Day is a celebration for all Americans. The publication of Alex Haley's *Roots* was a major cultural event in the seventies, in part because it reminded many black Americans of their noble African heritage. Certainly, ethnic tensions still exist in our country, but more and more Americans recognize the richness of diverse customs and traditions.

EXERCISE 1.3   Language and Culture

Our cultural diversity is evident in our language as well as in our customs. What countries or groups contributed the following words to our language? (Look up the origin of these words in a college dictionary.)

hamburger	America
Cinco de Mayo	dungaree
klutz	algebra
Santa Claus	yam
Oklahoma	dojo

Sometimes we may be tempted to think of cultural differences as communication barriers. "How can someone from a radically different background from my own ever really understand what I am trying to say?" we may think. But one function of language is to produce just this kind of understanding. Through our words, we can give others insight into our own special world of thought and feeling. We allow them to glimpse a way of thinking and acting that may be entirely different from their own. This is a fundamental purpose of communication—to develop mutual understanding and a sense of community.

In *Lives on the Boundary*, Mike Rose writes about his struggles to make it academically as an Italian-American growing up in South Los Angeles. His parents were not well educated, and when Rose was placed in classes for "slow" students due to a clerical error, they never thought to challenge this placement or even to inquire into the reasons for it. Rose describes the difficulties he and many other students face in college this way:

> The students are taking their seats in the large auditorium, moving in two streams down the main aisles, entering from a side exit to capture seats in the front. You're a few minutes late and find a seat somewhere in the middle. There are a couple of hundred students around you and in front of you, a hundred or so behind. A youngish man walks onto the stage and lays a folder and a book on the podium. There are track lights above him, and in back of him there's a system of huge blackboards that rise and descend on rollers in the wall. The man begins talking. He raises his voice and taps the podium and sweeps his hand through the air. Occasionally, he'll turn to the moving boards and write out a phrase or someone's name or a reference to a section of the textbook. You begin writing these things down. He has a beard and smiles now and then and seems wrapped up in what he's talking about.
>
> "These are the social facts that are reflected in the interpretations we make of them," says the man on the stage and then extends his open hand toward the audience. "Now, this is not the place to rehearse the arguments between Kantian idealists and Lockean realists, but . . ." You're still writing down, ". . . reflected in the interpretations we make of them . . . ," and he continues: "But let us stop for a moment and consider what it means to say 'social fact.' What is a fact? And in considering this question, we are drawn into hermeneutics." . . .
>
> People are taking notes and you are taking notes. You are taking notes on a lecture you don't understand. You get a phrase, a sentence, then the next loses you. It's as though you're hearing a conversation in a crowd or from another room — out of phase, muted. The man on the stage concludes his lecture and everyone rustles and you close your notebook and prepare to leave. You feel a little strange. Maybe tomorrow this stuff will clear up. Maybe by tomorrow this will be easier. But by the time you're in the hallway, you don't think it will be easier at all.

Most of us can probably identify with the feelings of inadequacy that Rose depicts in this passage. The anonymity of large lecture classes, the struggle to understand words and ideas that are unfamiliar to us, the intimidation of college professors who seem to be demanding more than we can possibly achieve — these are obstacles faced by most students as they enter college. In *Lives on the Boundary*, Rose uses language powerfully to convey the problems faced by millions of Americans in our educational system. By developing your language skills in this course, you will be learning ways to make your voice heard and to allow others to understand your individual concerns.

HOW DO I GET STARTED?

The Space Needle in Seattle, with its towering arches and disk-shaped observation deck, is one of the best-known attractions in that city. A monument to futurist architecture, this graceful tower stretches 607 feet above the city and is anchored in tons of concrete 30 feet below its surface; and yet, this entire project began as a simple sketch on the back of a napkin. Most great achievements begin with similar humble beginnings. Kurt Vonnegut planned *Slaughterhouse Five* on the back of strips of wallpaper. William Faulkner sketched out the relationships among the characters in one of his novels on the walls of his home. Whenever you begin planning to write, you should keep these principles in mind:

1. Write while you are thinking.

   Many people like to begin planning mentally before they write anything down. A more effective strategy is to write down your thoughts as they come to you. This way you have a record of your ideas that you can refer back to as you begin your first draft. Many writers carry a notebook or journal with them for recording thoughts that come to them at odd moments during the day.

2. Write down all of your thoughts.

   Don't try to evaluate your ideas until you have completed the planning phase. Sometimes, ideas that seem ridiculous at first can lead to a breakthrough in understanding. Early designs for airplanes usually imitated the flapping wings of birds; it was only when someone got the idea of a fixed wing — a ridiculous thought at first — that modern aviation was born.

3. Write brief phrases instead of long sentences.

   As your ideas begin to take shape, you will want to write in complete sentences and paragraphs. During the planning phase, however, make brief notes (words or phrases) that suggest the idea you have in mind.

METHODS OF PLANNING

Planning is usually one of the most enjoyable parts of the writing process. Think of the planning phase as "window shopping" with your mind. You are considering all the possibilities for what you want to do in the paper. You can explore new ideas, test preconceived notions, and try to state your own feelings more clearly. E. M. Forster, the great English novelist, once wrote, "How do I know what I think until I see what I say?" You may find yourself surprised by some of the things you have to say as you begin the planning phase. Because your writing may take unexpected turns, your first attempt at writing down ideas is frequently referred to as a "discovery draft."

Listing

One of the easiest ways to get started with your writing is to make a *list*. Let's suppose you've been asked to write about a hobby that you enjoy. As you think over your interests, you come up with the following list:

playing softball

watching TV

Pictionary

dancing

going to movies

country music

Mexican food

motorcycles

Notice several things about this list. First, all the activities are described in a word or two. Reading this list, we have no way of knowing whether the writer likes to prepare Mexican food or simply enjoys eating it. However, since the list is for the writer's benefit, it's not important that someone else understand the full meaning of every item on the list. Second, the writer has made no attempt to evaluate which of these activities would be appropriate for a paper on hobbies. Is "watching TV" too ordinary an experience to make an interesting paper? Is "country music" really a hobby, or is it more like an amusement? At some point, the writer will want to raise these questions, but they shouldn't interrupt the flow of thought at this time. The most important thing about this list is that it provides a foundation for the writer's later work. By compiling a list, the writer immediately sees results from the mental effort that goes into planning the paper.

EXERCISE 1.4 Listing

Prepare a list of five to ten items on *one* of these topics:

a frustrating or embarrassing experience

a time when you were frightened

a time when someone helped you out

an experience that didn't turn out the way you expected

a time when you got in trouble for something you didn't do

a childish prank or practical joke

Clustering

Another strategy for planning is *clustering*. A cluster is simply a way to organize related ideas during your planning phase. Place the topic you want to write about in the center of a blank piece of paper and draw a circle around it. Related ideas are connected to the center with lines. For each of these related ideas, provide further examples and illustrations. Suppose you have decided to write about playing softball at a family reunion. You might make a cluster diagram that looks something like the one in Figure 1.1.

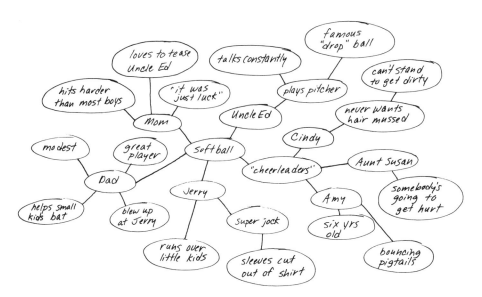

FIGURE 1.1: Clustering

One of the advantages of clustering is that it indicates the relationships among the ideas you are considering. In the cluster diagram in Figure 1.1, the players and spectators are all connected to the main idea — playing softball at a family reunion — and the characteristics of each of the participants are indicated on the branching lines. In some cases, these strands of thought may become the paragraphs of the completed essay.

EXERCISE 1.5 **Clustering**

Choose *one* of the following options as a clustering activity.

1. Select a family event that you can recall vividly and create a cluster diagram to describe the roles played by various family members.

2. Select one of the items from the list you created for exercise 1.4 and explore it further by making a cluster diagram.

Questioning

If you are writing about an activity or an event, you may want to organize your thinking the way a reporter does. Every event can be described by considering the *5 W's and an H:*

Who?

What?

Where?

When?

Why?

How?

Suppose you have decided to write a paper about a terrifying event in your life. Maybe you were lost in a strange part of town and convinced that you were being followed. Here is an application of the 5 W's and an H to your situation:

Who?

Who was following you?

Who did you think was following you?

Who knew where you were?

What?

What were you doing in this part of town?

What about this part of town scared you?

What would you have used to defend yourself?

Where?

Where did you get lost?

Where were you going?

When?

When did you first know you were lost?

When would someone have noticed you missing?

When did you start feeling like you were being followed?

Why?

Why did you get lost?

Why did you think someone was following you?

Why didn't you call someone to come get you?

How?

How did you discover who was following you?

How did you deal with this person?

How did you get back home?

As you can see, the basic six questions are only a starting point. You will have to determine how to apply these questions to your particular situation. By asking these questions, however, you have a systematic method for exploring the nature of any event.

EXERCISE 1.6 Questioning

Try out the questioning method either in a small group or individually by choosing *one* of the following options.

1. Form a small group with other members of your class. Imagine that you are the Discipline Committee at your college. You are going to hear the case of a student who has been accused of destroying furniture in the Student Center. Using the 5 W's and an H, prepare a list of specific questions to ask this student.

2. Using the 5 W's and an H, prepare a list of specific questions about an event in your own life. Write out the answers to these questions.

Cubing

A cube is, of course, a six-sided object. The purpose of cubing is to see a topic from many different sides. Too often our thinking falls into predictable patterns, into "mental ruts." For instance, in playing a game with dice, we always look to the top of the dice to determine the number we have rolled. We could, if we chose, use the number on the bottom of the dice to determine our roll, or even the number on the side closest to us. Cubing forces us to consider our subject from six different angles. Sometimes the results can be bizarre, but frequently cubing leads to original thinking and startling conclusions. Before you can begin cubing, you must think of a subject you would like to explore (or you may have one assigned to you).

1. Describe/define it.
    Use all five senses to describe a physical object. If your subject is an abstraction, like "friendship" or "depression," try to come up with a definition for it.

2. Compare/contrast it.
    What is your subject like? What is it unlike? List the similarities or differences.

3. Associate it.
    This is similar to the psychiatrist's technique of free association. You simply list everything that comes to mind when you think of this subject. Where would you expect to find it? How does it relate to other people, places, or things?

4. Analyze it.
    What are its parts? features? historical developments? subsystems? ingredients?

5. Apply it.
    What is its purpose? Is it harmful? helpful? both? How is it made? caused? ruined? stopped? cured? solved?

6. Argue for/against it.
    Who doesn't like it? Why not? Who likes it? Why? What do you think of it?

Let's suppose you have chosen "eyeglasses" as the subject of your cubing activity. You might produce a chart of ideas that would look like this:

Eyeglasses

1. Describe/define it.
    Lenses — round, curved, hexagonal. Frames — wire, plastic, combination. Colors — black, brown, clear, mixed, gold wire, some bright colors. Designer — Sophia Loren, Calvin Klein. Corrective. Sunglasses. Bifocals. Leave marks on your nose. Eyes look funny when you take them off.

2. Compare/contrast it.
    Second set of eyes. "Four eyes." "Cat's eye" glasses. Thick lenses = "Coke bottle bottoms." Contact lenses are invisible eyeglasses. Binoculars. Magnifying glass. Shades. Visors. "Specs." Accessory. Ornament for the face. Almost like jewelry.

3. Associate it.

    Stereotypes. People with glasses are nerds. Intellectuals. Businessmen. Tycoons. Yuppies on TV wear aviator glasses. Revolutionaries like horn rims. Dan Akroyd. Blues Brothers made black frames the rage. Athletes. Goggles — Jabbar and Dickerson. Librarians. Old people. Snobs. (Peering over the glasses.)

4. Analyze it.

    Lens and frame. Bridge across the nose. Nose pads. Hinges. Ear pieces. Straight, curved, and half circles. Straps. Compromise between strength and light weight. Once considered mark of weakness. Now fashionable. Plastic, metal, glass.

5. Apply it.

    Used for nearsighted, farsighted, astigmatism. Wear when reading, driving, doing close work. Breaking someone's glasses is a malicious act. Ophthalmologists. Optometrists. Opticians. 9–5 doctors. Eye charts. Machine with lenses. New computer analysis. Choosing frames. Old, established stores. "While-you-wait" places at the mall.

6. Argue for/against it.

    Contacts are better. Actually help your eyes. Look more natural. Fashions don't affect them. Don't get broken or lost as easily. Eyeglasses are better. No hassle to put them on. No danger of infection. No hunting on your knees for them. Stylish. Some people can't wear contacts. (Can't stand people who blink constantly.)

The process of cubing will often suggest several different directions for your writing. In the preceding example, the writer might choose to write about eyeglass fashions, compare retail eyewear stores, or argue the merits of contacts versus eyeglasses. One advantage of the cubing exercise is that it often suggests several interesting approaches to the subject.

EXERCISE 1.7 Cubing

1. Choose *one* subject from the areas listed below and explore it thoroughly, using each of the six cubing activities. Try to work rapidly. Spend about three to five minutes on each "side" of the cube.

    Object: a toy, a vehicle, a building, a tool

    Activity: a sport, a craft, a public event, a crime

    Organization: a government, a club, a business, a service

2. Go through the cubing activities on a subject that interests you.

Looping

As with all the planning activities we have considered, looping is a method of writing down your thoughts as they occur to you. Three basic steps make up the looping process:

1. For 10 minutes write down all of your thoughts on your subject. This part of the process is called "freewriting," and the idea is to let your mind roam freely over the subject. Write continuously for the entire 10 minutes. If you are momentarily stumped, repeat the last word or phrase you wrote until you can go on.

2. Review what you have written. What is the most interesting idea that came out of your freewriting? Is there anything here that is original or unexpected? Write down a sentence that summarizes this idea. It may take the form of a statement or a question.

3. Use this idea as the subject of another freewriting activity. As you can see, the idea of looping is to refine your thoughts and sharpen your point of view. You make a complete "loop" by returning to an earlier idea and expanding on it.

In the following example, a student named Lenny uses the looping method to clarify his thoughts on being a father. His "First Thoughts" are rambling and disconnected, but they serve a valuable function in stimulating his thinking and exploring his feelings. When he addresses the subject again (in another loop), his ideas are more sharply focused.

Freewriting: Children
(First Thoughts)

As a guy, I've always been a little afraid of kids. I was the youngest in my family so I never really knew how to act around them. Babies were the worst. It seems like women just know how to hold them and how to make them happy, but I'm all thumbs. I'm always afraid I'm going to hurt them or drop them. If you don't watch it, their heads flop around and stuff. Anyway, I was pretty unsure of myself when our kids came along. My dad never did much with us as babies. I'm sure he never changed a diaper in his life. Now, I don't think it's unmanly to change a diaper; I just don't like doing it, and I know that's pretty selfish of me, of me, of me, of me. OK, so part of it is I have to learn how to be something that I've never seen. I can't be like my dad, but how am I going to be? It's like we're having to invent our family. I know one thing. I love Adam. And I think that's what's going to make it work for us. It's not like I'm doing things just for Connie, though it is for her, too. I'm doing it for my son, because I want to be needed by him.

After completing his "First Thoughts," Lenny has a much clearer conception of what he wants to say about children. He hadn't realized before he began to write how his role as a father was defined in contrast to that of his own father. What came as an afterthought in the first loop becomes the focus of the second loop. He now knows that he wants to contrast his father's approach to parenting with his own.

Freewriting: Fathers and Sons
(More Focused)

I have always looked up to my dad. He always seemed to know how to do anything. I can remember when the car would start acting up, and Dad would say, "Must be the alternator going out." And I would think, "How in the heck does he know?" But he was always right, or just about always. So it was natural that I tried to do everything just like my dad would. He taught me a lot of things. Sometimes he rode me pretty hard. He never let me do a sloppy job. I remember once I was painting the porch, and he got mad at me because I would dip my paintbrush in the bucket and then wipe it all off on the side of the can so I wouldn't drip any. "You gotta use that brush like a scoop," he said. He jerked the brush out of my hand and showed me how to twist the brush as I took it out of the can. He slapped a big bunch of paint on there and then worked it out across the boards. He could work that brush down a wall in no time. That was my dad.

But there are some things I didn't learn from my dad. He never was one to fool with little children. I remember he told me one time that he told my mom she was in charge of the "women's work" when they got married. He was proud that he had settled the issue at the start of their marriage. "Women's work," of course, consisted of things like cooking and tending to babies. I'm sure a lot of people would think my dad was a real louse for saying that, but he wasn't a bad guy, and he really loved my mom. He just grew up in a different world. His parents had lived on a farm. Farming was hard work — sometimes sunup to sundown work. There was always time for men to be with the children until they were old enough to work themselves. And women didn't work outside the home back then. The house/field division of labor maybe made sense in that time. Wrong or right, that was my father's world.

But my world is different. Right now, Connie is working full-time while I go to school. I am usually around Adam more than she is. Sometimes it's hard for me being around the baby so much. I think maybe mothers were built so that crying babies don't bother them as much. But I don't think anybody likes changing dirty diapers. I don't think it's ultimately a matter of who is "cut out" for this kind of work. Things need to be done and sometimes that means I'm the one to do it. I know sometimes my dad thinks I've gone soft. He never says it, but I can tell by the look in his eye, and that hurts. But what keeps me going is not what dad expects, or what Connie expects of me. It's Adam. When I see those little blue eyes staring up at me, I know he trusts me, and I want to do everything I can to deserve that trust.

As this looping process illustrates, the first freewriting activity has no particular purpose in the beginning. The writer is simply exploring feelings about children. However, in the process of writing about children, he discovers his real concern — how fathers relate to their children. This becomes the subject of the next freewriting activity. It is important not to equate freewriting with the first draft of an essay. Freewriting is usually random, disconnected, and fairly incoherent writing. The purpose of freewriting is to discover a purpose statement, not to serve as the basis for a finished essay. In the preceding example, very little of the material in the first freewriting activity is repeated in the second. As the looping process continues, the writing does become more focused and organized, but such coherence is not typical of first attempts at freewriting.

EXERCISE 1.8 Looping

Select one of the following options to practice the looping process.

1. Write your own description of a mother's role or a father's role in a family. Then reread what you have written and identify the most interesting idea you've uncovered. You may even want to see what idea in your writing was most interesting to other students in the class. Complete the looping process by writing on the same subject again, focusing on your most interesting idea.

2. Choose one of these general themes as the subject of your initial freewriting. Then write down the most interesting idea that appears in your writing. Freewrite again using this statement as your guide.

    emotions

    time

    annoyances

    money

    working

    responsibility

Specialized Forms of Planning

You may discover other strategies that help you get started with writing projects. If you do a particular kind of writing frequently, you might generate a list of questions that will allow you to consider the subject systematically. For instance, if you have to write incident reports on your job, you might include questions such as these:

Who was involved? Describe them. How old were they?

Have they been cited previously? How many times? What was the nature of the infraction?

CALVIN AND HOBBES © 1992 Watterson, Universal Press Syndicate

What action was taken? Were all parties informed of this action?

As we look at specific forms of writing in part II of this text, you will find additional strategies for approaching these writing assignments.

KEEPING A JOURNAL

Many writers find it helpful to record their ideas in a journal. The journal provides a place to work through your problems, experiment with new forms of expression, and develop your writing skills. Unlike a diary, a journal is not a mere record of the day's events. Instead of simply telling about what happened in your day, you will want to give your reaction to important events or ideas that occurred to you. Compare these two journal entries:

September 5 (Reggie)

I overslept and missed my first class. Biology was pretty boring. I really don't understand anything he is talking about. I got a hamburger for lunch and barely made it to work on time. We had to unload a lot of heavy stuff, and I was really tired when I got home. I need to read my history assignment, but I am sure I'll fall asleep before I finish it. Not much happened today.

September 5 (Mark)

They hired a new guy at work this week. He's nice enough, I guess, but he really gets on my nerves. He has this little laugh — "ah-huh, ah-huh" — that comes out about every two minutes. He sits next to me, so I can't get away from him, and he's always asking questions. "I can't get this circuit tester to work — ah-huh, ah-huh. Can you — ah-huh, ah-huh — help me?" I know I really appreciated the guys that helped me out when I was new, so I try to show him stuff, but he's not always real quick on the uptake. I must have shown him ten times where to put the probes. I wish the guy was mean and nasty, then I could tell him to get lost.

But he just keeps looking at me like a lost puppy. "Have you seen my — ah-huh, ah-huh — work orders? I think — ah-huh, ah-huh — I lost them." So I spend ten minutes looking for his work orders (he left them in the break room — don't ask me why he took them on break), and then the boss chews me out for getting behind on my work.

Reggie's journal entry is little more than a summary of the day's activities. Such entries are not only boring to read, but they are also usually tedious to write. Mark's entry, on the other hand, concentrates on one subject and describes his reaction to his circumstances. Mark not only tells us about his co-worker, but also tries to explain why he finds him so irritating. Frequently, you will come to a clearer understanding of your own thoughts and feelings in the process of writing a journal entry like Mark's. Here are some suggestions for things to write about in your journal:

personal events that are meaningful to you

your *reactions* to people around you

memories of past events that have made an impact on you

conversations you want to remember

questions that occur to you

your personal *achievements* and *failures*

your reaction to *public events* in the news

your response to *books* or *articles* you have read

descriptions of *trips* you take

special occasions you are celebrating

Don't think that everything you record in your journal has to be a major event. A conversation with your grandmother probably has more significance for you than a political revolution in a distant country. On the other hand, you will find your journal more interesting if you do more than simply record everyday occurrences. Try to make your own writing assignments. For instance, you might try to decide what is your most valuable possession, what country you would most like to visit, or the excuses people give for their bad habits. Try to challenge your mind as you write in your journal.

Write your journal entries rapidly. Don't worry about spelling and grammar as you write, and don't try to second-guess yourself or to judge the quality of your writing. Since you are making these entries on a regular basis, you need to be able to write quickly and efficiently. If you decide to use a journal entry as the basis for a more formal paper, you can clear up any spelling or grammar problems at that time.

EXERCISE 1.9 **Journal Assignment**

Discuss these questions with your teacher:

1. What kind of a notebook should I use for my journal?

2. How often will I be required to make entries in my journal?

3. How long should the average journal entry be?

4. Should I start each entry on a new page?

5. Will I be asked to share my journal entries with others in the class?

6. Should anything be written in my journal other than the daily entries (e.g., class notes, early drafts of assignments)?

7. What should I do if I forget to make an entry in my journal?

8. Should I bring my journal with me to class?

9. How often will the journals be collected?

10. How will the journals be graded?

11. Are some topics too personal to be included in the journal?

WRITING ASSIGNMENT **A Memorable Experience**

Step one   Using the list you developed in exercise 1.4, write about an event in your life. Your ultimate purpose in writing about this event is not only to describe your behavior, but also to explain to your reader something about yourself. Why did you act or respond the way you did? Your writing will be a "discovery draft," an exploration in writing of your thoughts and reflections. You should write the draft quickly without worrying about your style. As you work on further revisions, you will want to look carefully at these issues, but your initial purpose is simply to get your thoughts on paper.

Step two   After completing your first draft, read your paper aloud or share copies of it with classmates or with some trusted friends. (See "Responding to Writing," in chapter 2, for more details about effectively responding to your classmates' writing.) You may want to use the questions below to guide your discussion, but you should raise your own questions about the paper as well. Where did you have difficulty expressing your ideas? Did you communicate the ideas and feelings that you intended? You may want to ask for reactions to specific ideas or to particular sections of the paper. Here are some questions for your readers to consider:

1. Explain in one sentence what happened to the writer. Was the description clear? What else would you like to know about what occurred?

2. Would you have acted or reacted the same way? What kind of person is the writer based on what you learned in reading about his or her experience?

3. Does the writer concentrate on a single event, or are there several incidents described? Could the paper be focused more effectively? If so, how?

LANGUAGE NOTE: THE WRITER'S TOOLS

Every writer finds certain "desktop" resources to be helpful in the writing process. A good **college dictionary** is a must. Invest in one that has over 100,000 entries. After all, the dictionary will be a lifelong resource for you—for checking your spelling, looking up definitions, finding out about the origin of words, and providing other important items of information.

Another useful tool is the **thesaurus**. A thesaurus lists words related in meaning. For instance, if you looked up *difficult*, you would find *hard, tough, arduous, toilsome, laborious, onerous,* and *burdensome*. Of course, a thesaurus can't tell you which word is appropriate for the particular sentence you are writing, but it does suggest a range of possibilities. A thesaurus can be especially helpful when you are trying to recall a particular word that you think would be perfect for the meaning you have in mind. By consulting the thesaurus, you often find that "just right" word.

Many writers like to keep a **grammar handbook** nearby when they are writing. The handbook is a compendium of information about writing. For instance, a handbook may suggest when numbers should be written out (e.g., twenty-one) and when they should be left in Arabic numerals (e.g., 1,248). It can explain the difference between *effect* and *affect, infer* and *imply,* and many other common concerns.

A writer may want to keep other books handy as well, such as an **atlas**, an **encyclopedia**, a **style guide**, or an **almanac**, depending on the kind of writing to be done. Incidentally, many of these sources are now being offered in computerized form. Information that used to require several volumes of print can often be stored on a compact disc or accessed through an electronic database.

4.   What would you recommend the writer add to this paper in the next draft? What would you recommend be left out?

Step three   Continue writing and revising, based on your readers' comments and your own sense of what you want to say. Before submitting a final draft for evaluation, be sure you have met these requirements:

- Your writing is focused on a main idea.

- You use specific details rather than generalizations to reinforce your main idea.

- You show originality in your treatment of this idea. (If everything you write seems too obvious, most people will not find it interesting to read.)

- You have carefully edited your writing for readability, correctness, and style (see chapters 9–11).

- You have met all the requirements of your instructor, including headings, titles, page margins, page numbering, and spacing.

THE CRITICAL MOMENT

Presumably, the reason you are going to college is to get an education. But just what is education? Is being educated simply a matter of memorizing certain facts and formulas? Or does it also imply the ability to investigate topics and to solve problems? Too often we speak of education as though our minds were simply containers for the facts that are to be "crammed" into them. Although being educated does require knowing certain facts, most of us would agree that it includes much more than this. An educated person should be able to determine which facts are important in a given situation and should be able to use those facts to make decisions. This ability to sort through evidence and to make independent judgments is often called critical thinking. And the ability to think critically should be the hallmark of a person with a college education.

As you read about important ideas, listen to lectures, and participate in discussions, you will be developing your critical thinking abilities. Don't simply accept everything you hear or read, but examine ideas carefully and explore their implications.

To encourage you to begin this process of critical thinking, we have included at the end of each chapter a "Critical Moment" section that asks you to consider some of the issues raised by that chapter. The questions presented in the "Critical Moment" section are not those that can be answered simply or definitively. They are a chance for you to exercise your own critical abilities on an issue of importance.

Not every book you read will suggest you take a moment for critical reflection, but we hope that such an approach will become a habit for you. Don't just settle for getting a college degree. Develop the habits of mind that will give you a college education. Begin by thinking through your response to these questions:

1. Why do most employers value a college degree?

2. What other reasons are there for going to college besides financial ones?

3. What do you hope to learn from reading this book? How can you get the most out of it?

Focusing

WRITING FOR A PURPOSE

Many of the techniques we used for getting started in chapter 1 can help us to tap into our capacity for creative thinking. Through freewriting and brainstorming, we are able to generate ideas quickly and make connections. This kind of thinking often produces a rich collection of material for writing, but it often takes a rather jumbled form. Even when using a more structured form of inquiry such as questioning or cubing, we still need to weed out the ideas that don't contribute to our basic purpose for writing. When we move from jumbled lists of information to a more coherent sense of purpose and organization, we are *focusing* our writing.

Although it is possible that the purpose of your writing will be clear from the outset, most writers find that such purpose emerges through the process of writing. You begin with some vague notion of what you want to say, and, as you write, you come to a clearer understanding of your purpose. You then write another draft that expresses that purpose more clearly.

You will also be aided in this process of focusing your writing by the comments of your readers. One way we find out how successful we have been in communicating our purpose in writing is to test our drafts on various readers. At the end of this chapter, you will find some tips for using group response to help you improve your writing.

Discovering Your Purpose

In reviewing the information you have created during a brainstorming session, you should be looking for a purpose that will help organize your thinking and direct your writing. Suppose you have generated the following list of thoughts about medicines:

taking "purple medicine" for colds

yucky medicines

bribes ("You can have some ice cream if you take your medicine.")

inhalers for my asthma

getting pills caught in my throat

medicines (good) versus drugs (bad)

forms: pills, capsules, syrups, caplets, suppositories

men in white coats behind tall counters

pestle and mortar (which is which?)

categories: pain relievers, sore throat, cold, skin medication, eye wash, medicines-for-things-nobody-wants-to-talk-about

side effects

cost of medicines

Obviously, you need to organize these ideas in order to write about them. How you organize them will depend on your sense of purpose. On any given topic, there are many different approaches you could take. In thinking over the preceding list, you might decide to write about the way your parents treated you for a cold when you were a child, how you feel when you go into the drugstore to get a "medicine-that-nobody-wants-to-talk-about," or the confusion between appropriate and inappropriate drug use in our society.

Let's say you are interested in writing about how your parents treated you for a cold. You want to recapture some of the suffering and some of the fear you experienced. You will want to keep some of the ideas from your earlier list, but now that you have a specific purpose, you will think of other ideas you wish to add.

purple medicine

coughing, runny nose, stuffed up head

running a fever

difficulty breathing

bitter medicines

bribes

cold baths

parents whispering

talking on the phone with the doctor

going to the Emergency Room

getting an I.V.

the playroom

the nurses

mother staying with me

This list clearly has more sense of direction and purpose than the first. In fact, you might be inclined to dive in and begin writing a draft at this point, but you probably would be better served to organize your thoughts into groups before making that step.

1. Coming down with a cold
    Symptoms: cough, runny nose, stuffed up head
    Treatment: purple medicine, Tylenol

2. Getting bronchitis
    Symptoms: difficulty breathing, high fever
    Treatment: bitter medicines, cold baths

3. Going to the Emergency Room
    Dad calling the doctor
    Wrapping me up in a blanket and carrying me out to the car
    Going into a little room with a curtain and machines all around
    Crying and screaming as they gave me the I.V.
    Mom and the nurses comforting me
    Mom sleeping in my room
    Feeling better and going to the playroom

As you can see, once you decide on your purpose for writing, the random list of thoughts can turn into a fairly coherent and organized development of your topic.

You may be wondering, though, how a writer decides on a purpose. This can happen in various ways. Sometimes it is simply a matter of following your own interests and inclinations. Henry James once wrote that his novel *The Portrait of a Lady* began with his vision of a single character that excited his imagination. From that point on, everything else — setting, plot, other characters — began to fall in place. You also may want to write about a person who has made an impression on you. Often writers remember a particular moment from the past that is so vivid it seems to just have occurred — the sounds of a restaurant or a particular expression on their mother's face or the smell of a campfire — and everything else that occurred at that time begins to flood their memory.

Sometimes your purpose in writing is defined by others. You are told to explain the influence of population density on aggressive behavior in animals. You are asked to prepare a report of your committee's findings on groundwater pollution.

Often purpose is defined by your own needs. You write a letter to an old friend to find out what has happened in her life. You send a notice to your employees about a change in policy concerning vacation leave. You write a poem about your great-aunt Dortesha to be read at her 100th birthday celebration.

As the preceding examples indicate, you do not always need to have a clear sense of purpose in order to begin writing. You may begin writing because you are attracted to a particular idea, because you are troubled by a feeling you have had, or because you have been given an assignment. Frequently, your purpose will often emerge during the process of writing and brainstorming. In fact, we are sometimes more productive as writers if we *begin* writing without knowing exactly where we are going. Sometimes we are more open to alternative ideas and solutions if we haven't already decided exactly what we want to say in our writing. But however and whenever you arrive at a purpose, it is absolutely crucial that you have one. Without a sense of purpose, you can never know what to include in your writing and what to leave out. You won't know how to organize your writing or when you have finished. In other words, you cannot *focus* your writing without having a purpose in mind.

EXERCISE 2.1 Finding the Purpose

Which of the following paragraphs express(es) a clear sense of purpose? What is it?

1. It is never a simple process to construct the definition of an abstract concept. Indeed, justice is an intangible ideal that escapes the ease of a concrete definition. One aspect of justice is certain. It is indeed relative. For this reason, we can never begin to realize the hopes of the future until we have laid to rest the ghosts of our past.

2. For six days and seven nights, Rome became a raging inferno. Fire destroyed houses and shops, palaces, and temples. Some people rushed to the tombs of the dead to escape the flames; others perished in a vain attempt to save their household belongings. Meanwhile, Nero watched the burning city from the Tower of Maecenas and made plans to rebuild the city according to his own design. Although Nero cannot be directly implicated in the great fire that destroyed Rome, there is little doubt that the disaster fit conveniently into his plans for the city.

3. I am writing to tell you just how I feel about the so-called service I got at your store. After waiting forever to get anybody to help me, I finally got some nitwit who probably hasn't ever had a job before — and with good reason! Mr. Good-for-Nothing tells me that I need one thing for the job I was doing when it was totally the wrong part. Now what am I supposed to do?

Stating Your Purpose

Because having a clear sense of purpose in writing is so crucial, you may want actually to write out your purpose statement at some point. The statement that conveys your purpose for writing is often referred to as a **thesis**. The word *thesis* came from a Greek word that means to "assume a position." When you write a thesis for an essay, you are essentially saying, "This is where I stand" or "This is how I see it." Here are some typical thesis statements:

For most contemporary Americans, television has replaced religion as the "opiate of the masses."

You don't go to Dockers' Grill because the food is good or because you want to play billiards; you go because you want to be seen.

Although it is not as popular with his critics, most readers would agree that Dickens's last work, *The Mystery of Edwin Drood*, is also his best.

For someone writing a dictionary, claustrophobia might be defined as the "fear of being in confined places"; for those of us who suffer from it, claustrophobia is an invisible hand that clutches at our throat every time we enter a crowded lobby or watch the doors close in front of us in an elevator.

A thesis can serve as a guiding beacon when dozens of thoughts begin to crowd into your head in the midst of writing a draft. As you begin to write, you may find yourself drifting away from your original purpose. At this point, you must either revise your thesis with the new purpose in mind or eliminate any material that doesn't contribute to the original thesis.

You may also find that your purpose becomes more refined as you write. Your original thesis may be a general statement:

A recording can never capture the thrill of actually being at a concert.

As you write, you may come to a more specific statement of your purpose:

Attending a concert, even a poor one, is always more exciting for me than hearing a recording because I feel connected to the band and the audience in a way that can occur only during a live performance.

EXERCISE 2.2 **Purpose Statements**

Brainstorm a list of ideas on one of the following topics, and then write three possible purpose statements for a paper you would write on the topic.

going to the doctor or dentist

staying at the home of a friend or relative

making something for the first time (food, clothes, crafts, building project, etc.)

performing in a musical group

going someplace for the first time (courthouse, amusement park, bowling alley, concert, museum, cemetery, workplace, etc.)

So far, we have discussed the thesis simply as a planning statement, but you may be wondering how (and if) the thesis should appear in your draft. The answer is generally "yes." How and where it appears differs according to the kind of writing

WRITING FOR A PURPOSE **31**

you are doing. If you are writing a business proposal, your statement of purpose should be clear and immediate:

> Proposal: NorthCentral Telecommunications should merge its accounting and investment offices into a single department.

In an essay, a thesis is often stated near the beginning of the paper. What is the thesis statement in the following paragraph?

> "Free" trips to Hawaii, "gold" credit cards, supplemental insurance poli-cies — thousands of Americans fall prey every day to such scams. They innocently put up hundreds of dollars to guarantee their reservations on a trip to Hawaii; only the tickets never come, and the company making the offer mysteriously goes out of business. The gold credit cards, for which they have paid up to $200, prove to be memberships in a buying club carrying overpriced merchandise. And even though the supplemental insurance policies cost only a few dollars a month, the coverage is so limited that most financial advisers consider them a waste of money. With so many schemers intent on bilking the public, all consumers should be aware of the kinds of scams they may encounter and how they can protect themselves.

The final sentence in the paragraph is the thesis. It lets the reader know basically what to expect in the remainder of the paper — a survey of various scams and some suggestions for consumers who want to keep themselves from being cheated. Typi-cally, the thesis comes near the end of the paper's introduction. The opening sen-tences create interest and a context for the information to follow. By the end of the introduction, the reader expects to know the overall purpose of the paper.

However, in an informal essay, you may want to imply your purpose rather than state it directly. For instance, you would not want to begin an essay about the tragic loss of a family member this way:

> In this essay I will explain how the death of my sister was a devastating emo-tional experience for me.

Such a bald statement of purpose is likely to make the writer appear cold and unfeeling. In some cases the reader will need to understand the thesis intuitively rather than overtly, but the purpose of the writing should still be apparent to the reader.

Throughout the paper, the reader needs to be reminded of the writer's purpose and to understand how subsequent paragraphs relate back to that purpose. The reader almost subconsciously responds to these orienting phrases the way a fan at a football game occasionally glances at the clock to see how far the game has pro-gressed. If we were to extract just the orienting phrases from a paper, they might look like this:

One of the most popular scams . . .

Another scam frequently used is . . .

The "free" vacation scam is one of the oldest . . .

Other scams include . . .

Although thousands are victimized by scams every year, a little common sense can prevent most of them.

The first thing you can do to protect yourself is . . .

Whenever you are in doubt about an offer, you should also . . .

Finally, the Better Business Bureau advises you to . . .

The orienting phrase serves as a transition from one idea to another, and it frequently introduces the main topic of the paragraph.

As well as using orienting phrases, you might want to consider more formal ways of indicating your purpose. Of course, the title of your paper is the first method of orienting the reader. For informative writing, the title should usually tell something about what your purpose is as well as your general subject. For instance, instead of merely titling your paper

Scams

your reader would be better served if you indicated your purpose:

Scams, Schemes, Lies, and Fraud:
The Consumer's Guide to Self-Defense

EXERCISE 2.3   Identifying Thesis Statements

Identify the thesis statements in the following paragraphs.

1.   How would you react if you learned that one of your best friends had recently contracted HIV? Would you comfort and provide support for this person? Or would you turn away from your friend? We would all like to believe that our friends can depend on us during the hard times of life and that they can rely on us for strength, help, and advice. But, in the case of AIDS victims, many times the very institutions of our society which are supposed to provide comfort and support seem more eager to condemn than to console. Religious institutions throughout our country must become more sensitive to the moral issues surrounding the AIDS epidemic and must take a more active role in taking care of the emotional, psychological, and physical needs of both AIDS victims and their families.

2.   Go into any consumer electronics store. Look around at the wide array of entertainment electronics available to the public today. Now think of the TVs, VCRs, and CD players which continually amuse you and your buddies. When was the last time you sat down with a friend and played a game which did not involve gadgets from the world of

Nintendo or Sega? When was the last time your family spent a day without the television set interrupting your conversations? Clearly, we are a generation that has bartered away its natural creativity and personal relationships for a few cheap electronic thrills.

3. Tax credits for the cost of child care in families in which both parents work are unfair because they penalize families in which the mother or father has chosen to make a full-time occupation of caring for and training the children. Governmental policies which provide economic advantages to households in which there are already two incomes, but place a greater tax burden on those family units least able to afford it because one parent is not working for a paycheck, are shortsighted and actually destructive. Although legislators may believe they are encouraging economic growth by such tax laws, they are, in fact, limiting the very freedoms on which our society is based.

WRITING FOR RESULTS

Knowing your purpose is a crucial first step toward focusing your writing. However, *knowing* your purpose is not the same thing as *achieving* it. Most of us probably have defended our writing at one time or another by declaring to a reader, "That's not what I meant!" However, blaming the reader for our failure to be clear or convincing will not improve our writing.

The cost for failing to achieve our purposes in writing can be high. Ultimately, most of us would like the things we write to make a difference to those around us. Writing can be hard work, and we generally like to see results from our labors. If you are going to be successful in getting results from your writing, you need to understand the three most important factors in any writing situation: your personal credibility, your knowledge of the subject, and your knowledge of the readers.

Your Personal Credibility

How interested would you be in reading an article about "Succeeding in Business" written by the chief executive officer of a bankrupt savings and loan operation? How much faith would you put in a report about hazardous waste issued by a chemical manufacturer that had been cited repeatedly for illegal dumping? One of the first questions we tend to ask ourselves whenever we read anything is how *credible* is the source of the information. We may think that only people who are nationally prominent—legislators, scientists, famous authors, and so on—have enough credibility to speak out on the issues. We naturally look to the secretary of state for information about foreign affairs. We would expect Michael Jordan to have more insight into professional basketball than an amateur player.

It is a mistake, however, to think that only well-known people have a right to be heard on important issues. If you are a parent, you probably know more about

"Strange how all six of your previous employers left the 'C' out of the word 'excellent'."

the cost and availability of child care in your neighborhood than the secretary of state. If you want to know if professional basketball is more interesting to watch now than it was 10 years ago, would you ask Michael Jordan or a casual viewer? Isn't a spectator more of an authority on the entertainment aspect of the game than a player? You don't have to be a celebrity in order to be an authority on those ideas and issues that directly affect your life.

One of the most basic factors affecting your credibility is your personal integrity. People listen to and respect the views of people they can trust. If your readers know that you are biased or seeking personal gain, they are unlikely to trust your judgment or respect your opinion. Since our readers may not know us personally, our credibility frequently comes from the way we present our information. If we use inflammatory language or "loaded" words, our readers may suspect us of trying to "slant" the information to serve our own purposes. Compare the credibility of these two writers based on the way they present their ideas:

Suzanne

Nobody thinks women's athletics are important. But they are. Women have just as much right as men to be athletes. I wanted to be on the volleyball team, but there weren't enough spots for everyone who wanted to play. The problem is that men

All of us are aware of people who speak differently from ourselves. One person may call a particular piece of living room furniture a "couch." Another may call the same piece of furniture a "sofa." One person may pronounce the word *cement* with an accent on the first syllable (SEE-ment) and another with the accent on the second syllable (suh-MENT). In general, we do well to tolerate each other's differences and respect those who speak in ways different from our own.

It is important to recognize that those who use language in unusual ways inevitably draw attention to the way they are speaking. Writers use this property of language to their advantage when they are creating characters in a story. For instance, if the deputy in a western novel tells the marshal that he "best skeedaddle over to the waterin' hole," we may smile at the homespun quality of the language. Poets frequently play with the meanings of words and express ideas in unusual ways. When Shakespeare writes, "that which we call a rose / By any other name would smell as sweet," he expresses the common truth that the name given to something doesn't determine its quality.

Failure to conform to the conventions of language may also interfere with communication. Those who say, "He brung me a letter," or "We was tired," will typically be considered less credible sources of information than those who use the standard forms, "He brought me a letter," and "We were tired." The standards for written English are even more exacting than those applied in oral situations. Whenever your writing will be made public, strive to make it conform to standard written English unless you will benefit from drawing attention to your word choices instead of to the meaning you wish to convey.

are afraid that women could be better athletes than men. If women were given an equal shot at it, they could be just as good as the men are.

Rosita

Although support for women's athletics has increased, male athletes continue to receive the majority of funding at most schools. The Title IX Amendment, passed by Congress in 1972, prohibited discrimination against athletes based on their sex. One result of this legislation was increased support for women's athletics at the college level. However, a survey of 203 Division I colleges during 1990–91 revealed that male athletes at most schools receive twice as much scholarship money as women (Lederman). The result of these policies is that many deserving women athletes will be unable to participate in varsity sports. (Lederman, Douglas. "Men Outnumber Women and Get Most Money in Big-Time Sports Programs." *Chronicle of Higher Education* 8 Apr. 1992: A3, 37, 40.)

Rosita supports her point of view with factual information that she has collected about women's sports, but her style of writing establishes her credibility as well.

She states clearly the point she is trying to prove, and her writing sounds objective and reasonable. On the other hand, Suzanne's point is not entirely clear. Is she arguing for competition between men and women athletes ("men are afraid that women could be better athletes")? Or does she want increased support for women's athletics at her college? If the latter is the case, she should indicate the inequities in the present system. For instance, if she demonstrates that fewer women than men are allowed to play intercollegiate volleyball, she can make a strong case that the system is biased against women.

EXERCISE 2.4 **Finding Sources of Information**

What sources of information would be available on each of the following topics? Which ones would be most credible? Discuss as a class or in small groups the sources you would use.

international students on campus

local tourist attractions

the quality of food in the cafeteria

the safety of a particular intersection in town

the availability and quality of apartments near campus

Your Knowledge of the Subject

The more you can find out about your subject, the more likely you are to convince your readers that your ideas should be respected. Which of these two writers is more convincing in assessing the impact of Robert Kennedy's life?

Reggie

Robert Kennedy's reputation is really overinflated. He probably never would have even been in office without the famous Kennedy name. He rode his brother's coattails into the White House administration, but that hardly qualifies as a personal achievement.

Anita

Although Robert Kennedy often sacrificed his own political ambitions to help in his brother's campaigns, he made many contributions to our nation in his own right. As counsel to the Senate Rackets Committee, he relentlessly fought the corruption in the Teamsters. As attorney general, he crusaded for civil rights, providing federal protection for the Freedom Riders and for James Meredith, the first black student to attend the University of Mississippi. Of course, the legacy is incomplete. In all likelihood, Robert Kennedy would have gone on from his victory in the California primary to have become the next president—if an assassin's bullet had not cut his life short in 1968.

Although it is possible to side with Reggie if we are already convinced that he is right, most objective readers will be swayed by the superior evidence provided in Anita's report.

We can become knowledgeable about a subject in several ways. Some knowledge is derived from your own experience. If you have restored an antique car, you already have an "insider's" view of this process. Perhaps you make quilts or race dirt bikes or work in an Italian restaurant. You can speak with some authority about your area of expertise.

Many of the subjects you will want to write about in college will require you to go beyond your existing field of knowledge. Make it your goal to be forever listening, reading, discussing, and writing, in an effort to continue your intellectual and social growth. In chapters 4–8, we will consider various ways of investigating an unfamiliar topic. The more you understand of your subject, the more you can express yourself clearly, forcefully, and convincingly.

Your Knowledge of the Readers

As well as establishing your personal credibility and being well informed, understanding your readers is essential to effective communication. Do not assume, for instance, that everyone will be interested in what you have to say. We are bombarded by so many messages every day that it is easy to ignore those that don't seem relevant to us. Compare the effectiveness of the following memos in presenting information in a way that is helpful to the reader:

Memo 1:

Date: November 9, 1993

To: All Employees

From: Don Brueckner, Office Manager

Subject: Pre-Admission Review

Please be advised that certain changes are now in effect in regards to the admission procedures for hospital admittance. The patient or his or her attending doctor must send a completed Request for Pre-Admission Review to the insurer on the approved form before the start of an inpatient hospital confinement or, in the case of an Emergency Confinement, within 48 hours of the start of such confinement, not counting any day of a weekend or a legal holiday. For this purpose, only Saturday and Sunday will be deemed a day of the weekend.

Memo 2:

Date: November 9, 1993

To: All Employees

From: Don Brueckner, Office Manager

Subject: Pre-Admission Review

Before being admitted to the hospital, you should have your doctor complete the Request for Pre-Admission Review. These forms are available in my office. If you fail to complete the Pre-Admission Review, your benefits will be reduced by $300. In the event you are admitted to the hospital on an emergency basis, you should have your doctor call the Pre-Admission Review Unit within 48 hours. The toll-free number for this call is printed on the back of your health insurance ID card. The *Guide to Employee Health Benefits* contains a complete description of pre-admission review procedures. If you need more information, contact my office at 555-2413.

Both of these memos indicate the need for a pre-admission review, but the first does so in language that is unnecessarily complicated and tedious. The first memo is more precise about the period of time allowed for the pre-admission review, but every writer has to make decisions about how much detail is necessary to make the point.

The second memo is written in language that directly addresses the reader ("If you fail to complete . . .") and which keeps the reader's use for this information foremost in mind. Instead of providing exhaustive details about the procedures, the reader is referred to another publication for more complete information. Sentences and paragraphs are kept short so that the memo can be read easily and quickly. The reader is warned of the consequences of failure to complete the review procedures, and this warning helps to underscore the importance of this information. As this memo demonstrates, effective writing responds to the needs and interests of the reader.

WRITING FOR AN AUDIENCE

When you begin writing a paper, you may not be thinking about an audience at all. At this stage, you are toying with ideas, trying to establish your purpose, and exploring your topic. But as *what* you have to say becomes clearer, you will want to think more about *to whom* you are writing. Of course, if you are submitting a paper to a teacher to be graded, you will be concerned to meet the expectations and standards of that teacher. It would be a mistake, however, to think that your teacher is applying arbitrary standards that have no relevance outside of the classroom. In all probability, your teacher is assessing the paper according to standards derived from his or her knowledge of what would make such writing successful in other contexts. For instance, if you write a business letter in this class, your evaluation usually depends on the probable success of that letter in a real business transaction.

Although every writing situation presents certain unique demands, it is possible to generalize about some of the more common situations you may encounter. In the following sections, we want to consider three common audiences: a specific person, a defined group, and a general audience.

Writing for a Specific Person

You may find it easiest to write when you have a specific person in mind, such as a family member or a close friend. When writing to someone you know well, it is easy to refer to common experiences and shared acquaintances without having to provide the kind of full explanation an "outsider" would require. In fact, a letter written to a close friend may be difficult for an outsider to understand because so many of the references have a private meaning.

However, you will frequently need to write to people who are strangers to you. You may be asked to cooperate with other people on a business venture, or you may have to seek information from a government office. In these situations, you can still assume several things about your audience. You know that the reader wants you to be *clear* about your request. You know that the reader wants your request to be *concise*. No one wants to wade through a confusing and wordy letter to find out what the writer wants. You can be sure that the reader will appreciate a *courteous* letter. Even when you are protesting unfair treatment, you should maintain a professional and businesslike tone in your writing. By observing these three "C's," you will help ensure that your letter is effective in securing the intended response.

EXERCISE 2.5 **Audience Awareness**

In the following excerpts, how aware do the writers seem of an audience? What parts of these passages might confuse someone who did not know the particular situation of the writers?

1. [I] observed extrodanary dexterity of the Indians in jumping from once cake of ice to another, for the purpose of Catching the buffalow as they float down. [M]any of the cakes of ice which they pass over are not two feet square. The Plains are on fire in View of the fort on both sides of the River. (William Clark)

2. It is all hurry and bustle to get things in order. It's children milk the cows, all hands help yoke these cattle the d---l's in them. Plutarch answers "I can't. I must hold the tent up, it is blowing away." Hurray boys. Who tied these horses? "Seneca, don't stand there with your hands in your pocket. Get your saddles and be ready." (Amelia Stewart Knight)

3. I proposed a living chain of Jews to carry shells from the depot and load them on streetcars at the west end station. The streetcars could carry them through the center of Budapest to the eastern end of the line where German Army units could move them to the front line. My idea worked. We made a living chain of them, six or eight kilometers long, to carry the shells from the depot to the station. Then dozens of streetcars, one after the other sped across Budapest to meet Zehender's men in the east. The guns blazed away. (Adolf Eichmann)

EXERCISE 2.6 **Bob's Novelties**

You have received notice that the Street Department is going to resurface the road in front of your shop, Bob's Novelties. You are concerned that you may lose a substantial amount of business because customers will be unable to get to your shop while the road is under construction. List the questions you would include in a letter to the director of the Street Department.

Writing for a Defined Group

Sometimes your writing will be directed toward a group of people. In general, as your audience expands, your writing will become less personal. A memorandum to be distributed to an office is unlikely to have the same familiar tone as a letter to a good friend. By thinking about your readers, you can make important decisions about what to include in your writing and what to leave out. If you were giving directions to other students for a meeting to be held on campus, you probably would need to give only the name of the building and the room number. However, if you were giving directions to an out-of-town speaker for the same meeting, you would have to give much more elaborate directions—how to get to campus, where to park, how to find the building, and so on. If you are not sure how much your audience knows about your subject, you generally should err on the side of telling too much rather than too little.

EXERCISE 2.7 **The Health Fair**

Imagine that you have been placed in charge of advertising a health fair to be held at a local shopping mall. Doctors and nurses will be present to answer questions and to provide free health screenings. Physical therapists will provide information about the treatment of sports injuries and rehabilitation programs. Children will be given information about dental care and provided with free toothbrushes and floss. Emergency medical services will demonstrate their equipment and explain how to provide first aid for common injuries.

How would you adapt your message for these different groups:

a handbill to be distributed at local daycare facilities and preschools

an announcement to be published in a newsletter for senior citizens a poster to be displayed in local high schools and recreation centers

a direct-mail advertisement to all local residents

As well as assessing the knowledge of your audience, you will want to consider their attitude toward your subject. If your audience is enthusiastic about your subject, you may only need to explain what they need to know. If your audience is indifferent or hostile to your subject, you will have to earn their trust and good will.

When the Declaration of Independence was first being considered by representatives from the various colonies, there were many bitter disputes about the wording of the document. Northerners were often at odds with Southerners, landowners argued with merchants, radicals opposed conservatives. It was Benjamin Franklin who managed to unify these diverse groups by observing that all who signed the document, no matter where their particular sympathies lay, were committing treason against the British crown. "We must indeed all hang together," reasoned Franklin, "or, most assuredly, we shall all hang separately." As Franklin brought together warring factions by appealing to their common interest, you will have to find the common ground you share with people who may have interests and ideas quite different from your own. Frequently, we find such common ground by noting that we are members of the same *community*. Although we may disagree over methods, we want our businesses to be successful, our neighborhoods to be clean and safe, and our community to thrive. Your job is to indicate how your proposals can lead to these generally accepted values. In chapter 7 we will consider the appeals necessary for successful persuasion, but it is important to realize that all communication requires a measure of good will between the source of the message and the audience.

EXERCISE 2.8 The Campus Speaker

1. Assume that you are a member of a student committee that invites speakers on campus. Think of someone (or a representative of a particular group) whose views would be controversial. What groups would be likely to oppose your choice? What "common ground" would you stress in dealing with the opposition?

2. Meet in a small group to discuss one of the statements below. What common ground can you find with those opposing your position? (If everyone in your group agrees, think of an individual or a group that would logically oppose your position. How would you find common ground with them?)

    a. Students should attend school all year round. It is expensive and wasteful to leave school buildings vacant in the summer. Similarly, teachers should not get paid for 12 months when they work only nine. Finally, students would learn more if the school year were longer and their studies were not interrupted by the long summer break.

    b. Children under 18 should not be allowed to purchase records and tapes with obscene lyrics on them. After all, we don't allow those who are underage to attend porno-graphic movies. Songs advocating drugs, sex, or violence are an unhealthy influence on children. Allowing those who are at an impressionable age to hear these songs contributes to the breakdown of society.

c. Congress passed a law in 1965 prohibiting billboard displays on rural interstate highways. Such a law robs businesses in rural areas of needed revenue and deprives travelers of useful information. Besides, isn't it a little hypocritical to support the idea of cutting through the countryside with four lanes of concrete and asphalt, all loaded with diesel-belching trucks, and then to disapprove of a few billboards?

Writing for a General Audience

Sometimes you may be writing for people you do not know well or those you do not know at all. Even though you are unfamiliar with this audience's knowledge about your topic and their attitude toward it, you can still make some general assumptions.

First, you can safely assume that your writing should be *clear*. Even the best of readers will become discouraged if they read a sentence or a paragraph several times and can't determine its meaning. In chapters 9–11, we will offer specific suggestions for making your writing clearer and easier to read.

Second, most writing for general audiences should be *interesting*. By "interest-ing" we don't mean that everything you write should sound like a best-selling novel, but it should appeal to the reader. Think of a news article of the kind you would read in *Newsweek* or the morning paper. Even if the reporter presents the news without embellishment, he or she has generally taken pains to write in well-struc-tured sentences, to place important ideas at the beginning of the story, and to write in an active style. Journalists can't guarantee that every reader will find the news pleasant to read, but they do strive to make it as interesting as possible. Similarly, you should strive to make your writing appeal to your readers.

Third, good writing should be *fair* to the audience and to the sources of information. All communication is based on trust and mutual respect. If you mis-represent your sources or slant the information you have to further your own interests, you undermine that trust.

EXERCISE 2.9 Doublespeak

Language that intentionally misleads the reader is often referred to as "doublespeak." Dou-blespeak is often used by leaders in government and business when they attempt to avoid responsibility for their own actions. See if you can translate these examples of doublespeak into ordinary language:

revenue enhancement

pre-owned vehicle

substandard housing

correctional facility

uncontrolled contact with the ground (used in reference to airplanes)

RESPONDING TO WRITING

Because most of us are unsure about how an individual reader will respond to our thoughts, we often want to try out our ideas on someone we can trust to be helpful and honest. In this class, your instructor may set up writing groups for this purpose. Even if you're not part of a formal group, you generally will find it helpful to seek out the advice of a trusted friend to respond to your writing.

Sometimes you may be called on to respond to other students' written work. At first, you may feel uneasy when talking about their writing, fearing that you will offend them by appearing judgmental or overly critical. However, by keeping a few simple ground rules in mind, you can avoid many of the pitfalls in responding to another person's writing.

1. Listen carefully to what is being said.

    One way to indicate your respect for another person's writing is to listen to it carefully. If the paper is being read aloud, you may want to take notes as you listen so that your mind doesn't wander. If you have time, you may want to hear the paper read twice—the first time for general meaning and the second time to take notes about your specific concerns. Even if you have a copy of the paper to read, make notes that will guide your discussion of the paper.

2. Respond as if you were the intended audience.

    When possible, try to imagine how the intended reader would respond to the paper. You could begin your comments by saying, "If I were your boss . . ." or "If I had never read this book before . . . ," to indicate the basis for your response.

3. Make observations rather than evaluations.

    Perhaps the most common response after someone has finished reading a paper is "I thought it was good" or "I didn't like it." Instead of making evaluative comments, begin by simply making observations about what the writer did in the paper. Before judging how well someone has communicated, it is good to agree on what has been communicated. Here are some sample remarks of this kind:

So there were three main parts to the paper: how to choose a daycare facility based on price, location, and quality of care.

As well as word processing capabilities, computers offer many possibilities for communication. You may want to print your most recent draft and circulate copies to your writing group. Their suggested revisions can be easily incorporated into the paper, whether you need to delete weak sections from the paper or add new information. Word processors make it simple to add, delete, or move existing text as you revise your paper. If other members of your writing group are using the same kind of computer, it may be possible simply to exchange disks instead of bothering with paper copies.

Some computers are joined together on **networks** that allow one computer to send messages to and receive messages from another computer. By entering the appropriate commands, you can have your draft sent electronically to another computer where it can be read and critiqued by another student. Some personal computers are hooked up to large **mainframe** computers. By using **electronic mail** (or "e-mail" as it is popularly known), you can send messages to other locations, either on your campus or, in some cases, in different parts of the country or world. Using these large networks, you could find out what a student in Maine thinks about your paper on acid rain or even what a student in Brasilia thinks about your paper on deforestation in the Amazon.

Another way to communicate with a personal computer is through the use of a **modem**. The modem allows you to use the telephone line to send messages to other computer users. Computer messages are sometimes posted on electronic bulletin boards that are open to the public.

Many people are just beginning to realize the potential of the computer for communicating with other people, but these changes are rapidly transforming the way we think about the world. Just as long-distance telephone communication has become an accepted part of modern life, computers are rapidly creating a global community for print communications.

I thought the waiter always kept the whole tip, but you said that where you worked everybody shared the tips equally. I had never heard that before.

You were so funny when you described living in a small town. I grew up in a small town, but I can see how it would have been strange for you when you saw the cars parked at an angle on Main Street.

4. Ask questions if you don't understand.

One of the ways you can be most helpful to a writer is by noting that something has confused you. We often write about subjects that are very familiar to us, and we forget that other people might not know what a "scone" is or when to use a "shim." Of course, it's possible that the intended audience for the paper may know these terms, but it doesn't hurt to raise the question.

In the beginning, you said that most people spend too much for a car. Did you ever explain why they do?

I was confused when you said, "Blue eyes are really colorless." What makes them blue?

At one point in the paper, you said that Mike was the meanest person at Westmont High. Later you said he was always helping people out. I don't understand how the same person could be so different.

5. Test the writer's observations against your own experience.

 All of us can easily fall into the trap of thinking that everyone else shares our feelings about people and places. Suppose you are listening to a paper in which the writer claims that most people would rather eat in a casual atmosphere rather than go to an elegant restaurant. If you love going to fine restaurants, you might want to question this statement. However, you should offer your experience as an alternative view rather than accusing the writer of being wrong.

6. Encourage the writer by your comments.

 Writing is not easy, and all of us appreciate some encouragement when we are struggling to express an idea. Don't go on a "fault-finding expedition" with another person's paper. When you have finished responding to the paper, the writer should be thinking about ways to improve the paper—not ways to dispose of it. If you think many of your comments are being interpreted as "attacks" on the writer, make an extra effort to show your approval for the writer's accomplishments.

 On the other hand, simply telling the writer that the paper is "good" or "splendid" isn't necessarily an encouragement. The writer may think you are just trying to be polite. If the paper really is splendid, you should explain what makes it so good. By observing these marks of excellence, you will be reinforcing the writer's good habits and rewarding the effort that went into preparing the paper.

If you are the writer whose work is being evaluated, you can help this process go smoothly. If your paper is being presented orally, read your work loudly and clearly. After you finish reading, give your group an adequate amount of time to review their notes and collect their thoughts. As comments are being made, don't be defensive about your work. You may not necessarily agree with what others have to say, but if you seem angry or argumentative, you may miss out on valuable commentary that could help you improve your writing (and your grade). Finally, you can encourage response by asking questions about your work. If you think your writing may be confusing at some point, ask your group if it is. If you think you've given too much detail on some minor point, ask the group's opinion. When a group works together well, the writer of a paper should hear comments the way a hungry diner hears a waiter explaining the house specialties. When a group works poorly, the writer hears comments the way a sullen defendant hears charges read against him or her by a prosecuting attorney. Your response to the comments being made can dramatically affect the atmosphere in the group.

EXERCISE 2.10 Responding to "My Brother"

Read the following student paper, and then form a small group to answer the questions that follow it.

My Brother

Eddie despises change. In fact, if someone tries to change his routine, he rebels   1 completely. Eddie has only one friend besides his immediate family. This friend of his is named E.L. Wherever Eddie is, E.L. can be found somewhere close by. Besides me, E.L. is the only other person that knows all of Eddie's deepest secrets. If someone who has never met Eddie before, and did not know anything about him met him, they would probably never know that there was something different about him. Eddie, to most strangers, just appears to be a young teenager that is a loner. The fact is, Eddie is much more than that. Eddie is an autistic savant, and his best friend E.L. is imaginary.

My little brother Eddie is sixteen years old and is an autistic savant. That is to say, my brother is a highly intelligent person, he just doesn't have the ability to express his intelligence like most other people. Somewhere between his brain, where an intelligent idea is created, and his mouth, the idea is lost. Eddie realizes that he has a problem, he realizes that he is different from other kids, and these realizations sometimes put him in a deep depression. Depression is okay for most people because they can express their feelings, think about their feelings, and then they deal with them. Eddie can't do that.

My brother is about five-feet, seven-inches tall and is built like a football player. He has the body that every girl, in her right mind, would be insanely jealous of. The boy is very lean, and has very defined muscles. What makes me sick is that he has never worked out a day in his life, his awesome body comes naturally to him. Eddie having this strong body however, does have one downfall; he doesn't know his own strength. When depressed, Eddie goes through extreme bouts of frustration. During these bouts, he's done everything from running away from home, to slamming me into a wall and dislocating my shoulder. Normally, Eddie isn't a violent person. In fact, Eddie normally is very timid, docile, and very protective of me. Eddie doesn't like seeing me around people he's not familiar with. Until he's comfortable with the idea, and feels sure that this new person is no threat to us, he will stick very close to me and watch closely every move this new person makes.

Eddie has his good days and his bad days like everyone else. The only difference is Eddie's bad days last for months, and they're beginning to outweigh the good days. When Eddie becomes depressed or upset about something, he regresses. That is to say, he closes himself off from the rest of the world and will not communicate with anyone. When Eddie does this, the doctors consider him "severely autistic." The frustrating part is that there is so little known about this condition that there is really nothing we can do when Eddie goes into one of these phases.

I love my brother and of course, so do my parents but as my parents say we have got to live our own lives. Eddie is becoming too difficult to handle and he is becoming an obsession in our own lives. My family and I have been struggling with a very difficult decision that has to be made. We have to decide if the best thing for Eddie isn't institution- alization. What Eddie feels, I feel.

Activity

1. What causes Eddie to be depressed? What is the author's relationship with Eddie?

2. How might someone respond to this paper who has never heard of autism? How might someone respond who has an autistic person in his or her family?

3. Select a sentence from the paper that you felt was particularly effective in helping you to understand the frustrations of raising an autistic child. Explain why you chose this sentence. Then choose a sentence that was particularly difficult to read. What interfered with your ability to understand this sentence?

4. Were any of the ideas in the paper unclear? Were any of them contradictory? What else would you like to know about Eddie?

5. From what you read in the paper, do you think Eddie's parents would be justified in sending him to an institution?

6. Is the writer ready to edit this essay to be turned in as a final paper, or does it need more substantial revision? What would you encourage the writer to do with the paper at this point?

EXERCISE 2.11 Group Response to Writing

Bring something you have written to share with a small group in your class. Remember to follow the guidelines for group work given in this chapter:

1. Take notes as you read the paper or hear the paper read to you.

2. Discuss how different people or groups might respond to this paper.

3. Make observations about the paper rather than evaluations. What was the main point? What passages were particularly effective? Observation statements often begin by ex- pressing your personal reaction to the paper:

    I was surprised when you said _____ .

    I was intrigued when you explained _____ .

    Did you mean to sound angry when you said _____ .

4. Ask questions about things you don't understand or would like to see explained more fully.

5. Use your own experience either to confirm or contradict the author's point of view.

6. Tell what you think the author should do next with the paper. Remember that a success- ful conference should encourage the author to want to write more.

WRITING ASSIGNMENT Current Issues

Step one   Make a list or a cluster of ideas on one of the topics listed in exercise 2.8, part 2, or one of your own choosing. Consider various arguments you have heard and evidence that would support or contradict those arguments.

Step two   Write a draft setting forth your position on the issue. Write quickly and don't try to second-guess your judgments at this point. Remember that you are free to experiment with different approaches, or even to change your position entirely, as you revise this draft.

Step three   Review your draft (either on your own or in a small group) and answer these questions:

1.   Write one sentence that sums up your position on the issue.

2.   What evidence have you presented (from observation, experience, reading, or discussion with others) that supports your position?

3.   What arguments would someone opposing your position be likely to raise? How would you answer that person?

4.   How could you improve this paper in your next draft? (For instance, do you need to get more information, reorganize the paper, refute opposing arguments?)

Step four   Keep alternating between writing drafts and reflecting on what you have written until you have clearly focused your paper.

Step five   Before submitting your final paper, answer these questions:

1.   Have I *disagreed* with the opposition without sounding *disagreeable*? Have I kept the tone of my paper calm, reasonable, and well informed?

2.   Have I placed my arguments in logical order? Does one lead clearly to the next?

3.   Do I maintain my position throughout? Are my arguments consistent with one another?

4.   What person or group probably would disagree with me? How would they react in reading this paper?

5.   Have I edited my paper carefully for errors in spelling, punctuation, and grammar?

THE CRITICAL MOMENT

When you begin writing, you should focus your attention primarily on what you have to say. Later, as you begin to think about presenting your writing to others, you will naturally want to consider how they might respond. In some cases, you may feel some tension between your own views and what is popular or socially acceptable. For instance, you may feel that animals should never be used for laboratory experiments, but you recognize that many of your readers support this practice.

1. Should you modify your own position to win a better reception from your audience?

2. Should you belittle or demean those who are not sympathetic to your viewpoint?

3. If you represent the minority position on an issue, do you have to present a stronger argument than someone who sides with the majority?

CHAPTER 3

Revising

In the first two chapters, we considered how to get started with our writing and how to adapt our ideas to fit a particular audience. We also discussed ways to focus our ideas by testing them on a group of trusted friends. The third step is to prepare those ideas for a wider public.

MAKING TIME FOR REVISION

As we saw in the previous chapter, the response of other people is an important first step in revising your paper. Your first attempt at writing on any subject may be uncertain and a bit awkward. This is true of even the best writers. The French poet Nicolas Boileau once commented, "For every four words I write, I strike out three." Although Boileau's strategy may seem extreme, good writers are constantly revising their work. In fact, most writers refer to their first attempt on any subject as a "rough" draft, one that will need substantial revision before it is ready for others to read.

Unfortunately, many people think of revision as some superficial changes made at the last minute—adding a comma here, correcting a misspelling there. In this chapter, we consider more fundamental changes in the content of your writing. While revising a draft, you may decide to eliminate entire paragraphs, move sections of your paper around, or even begin writing again from an entirely different point of view. In the process of revising, you may find it helpful to return to some of the strategies that we discussed in the chapter on "Getting Started" in order to develop a new line of thought that has emerged during the revision process. Only when you are confident that you have accomplished your basic purpose in writing should you begin to correct errors in grammar, diction, and spelling. It hardly makes sense to

CALVIN and HOBBES © 1989 Watterson, Universal Press Syndicate

spend time crafting an individual sentence if that sentence is ultimately jettisoned in a subsequent revision. When you are confident that what you've written genuinely expresses your intention and effectively communicates to your audience, you can begin correcting your errors and improving your style. These important matters are treated in chapters 9–11, on "Readability," "Correctness," and "Style."

Often the revision process will require several drafts, as you try out different approaches. If you have submitted your writing to others for review, you will often want to incorporate their suggestions into subsequent drafts. Frequently, there is a temptation to spend the majority of our time thinking about our paper before we write anything. A more successful strategy is to write quickly, getting down the ideas as they come, and then reserve plenty of time to revise the rough draft before putting it into final form.

THE REVISION GUIDE

It is often helpful to have some questions to guide our revision process. These three simple questions can help us consider what we have accomplished and what needs further development:

1. What do I like about what I have written?
2. What do I want to change?
3. How will I change it?

The following example shows how a student wrote about a difficult experience in her life. After brainstorming several topics, she decided to write about being in the hospital. Read the following draft, and analyze what the writer has done well and what might be added or changed.

Draft 1

A Painful Experience

by Karen Vanderburg

Where am I? What happened? Just as I awoke, the nurse made   1
her way towards me. I was informed that I was in recovery and the
surgery went well. I faded in and out of consciousness. I asked for
Bobby, but the nurse said, "No one is allowed in recovery."

I had never had a surgery before this one. I had been X-rayed at
a minor emergency clinic when I fell out of a tree in the fourth grade,
but it turned out that I had not broken any bones. About an hour
before I went into surgery, my family arrived. When Mom arrived,
she refused to enter the room until Bobby left. They have a bad past
history. I told Bobby that he didn't have to leave. He said, "I'll go to
keep peace. You need your mom now. I'll be back before your
surgery."

The interns soon came for me. My anxiety and fear began building. They took me down to the "prep" room. Kay went into the room
with me. I knew what was about to come—the I.V. An I.V. is worse
than a regular needle because it is jabbed into the soft part of your
hand, directly into a vein, and then it stays there.

The nurse pushed my cot on wheels through the enormous green
doors. I felt like a helpless child as I lay there on my back with the
doctor and nurses towering over me. My tears and fears grew. My
doctor patted my hands and said, "You'll be okay, big girl."

After the surgery, it was time to return to my room. I was still   5
mad at Mom for driving Bobby out of my room. It was quite some
time before I was able to forgive her.

Like most drafts, "A Painful Experience" is neither splendid nor terrible. Revising this paper is a little like panning for gold. We look for the "nuggets," the ideas
that are interesting and well expressed, and we discard the "gravel," the wasted
words and irrelevant ideas.

Let's begin with our first revision question. What do we *like* about this draft?
We may like a description, a clever phrase, an insight into someone's character, or
an interesting idea. Often in looking back at a first draft we may discover that the
most interesting idea wasn't even foremost in our minds as we began writing. Karen
set out to write about a surgery, but she discovers that her relationships—with the
hospital staff, her family, and her boyfriend—are clearly more important than the
surgery itself. In the next draft, she decides to focus on these relationships. Instead
of simply writing about "going to the hospital," she wants to concentrate on her
need for emotional support during this traumatic experience. This movement from
a general notion of the subject to a specific purpose is a genuine "re-vision."

The second revision question asks us to consider what we *don't* like about the draft. In Karen's second paragraph, she brings up a trip to a minor emergency clinic in the fourth grade. This former experience doesn't seem relevant to her current surgery, and it does nothing to explain her need for emotional support during this time. Consequently, she decides to leave it out.

Karen discussed the paper with some friends, and they were confused by several things in the paper. They liked the idea of beginning the paper when she woke up from surgery, but they felt she needed to let the reader know when she began to "flash back" to the earlier events. They felt she needed to let the reader know who Kay was (even though they assumed she was Karen's sister). Most of all, they wanted to know what happened to Bobby. He promises to return before the surgery, but he never appears in the story again. Karen realized in talking with her friends that she had assumed too much about what her readers would know, and she promised to make some of the details clearer.

The third revision question follows naturally from the other two. Karen knows she wants to change the paper to focus more on her relationships during the hospital stay. She will expand the paper to include more about her mother, Kay, Bobby, and the hospital staff. She will also eliminate the mention of her visit to the minor emergency clinic.

Draft 2

A Painful Experience

by Karen Vanderburg

Karen liked the sense of disorientation in the opening paragraph and made only minor changes.

Where am I? What happened? Just as I awoke, a nurse made her way towards me. I was informed that I was in recovery and that the surgery had gone well. I remember fading in and out of consciousness. I kept asking for Bobby, but the nurse said, "No one is allowed in recovery."

Karen begins to focus on her relationship with Bobby.

The last time I had seen Bobby was about an hour before the surgery. He doesn't like hospitals, and I knew it hadn't been easy for him to come. Somehow that made it more special that he had come — I knew he must really care about me.

Responding to her group's concerns, Karen includes some background information on Bobby.

We had been dating on and off for about a year. Bobby wasn't a great talker, but he always thought of something we could do. He seldom called. He would arrive, unannounced, in his '67 emerald-green Cougar and ask if I wanted to go to the park or a ballgame or a movie. Normally, I would have said "no." If a guy wants to ask me out, he could at least have the courtesy to call ahead of time. But Bobby didn't mean to be rude — he just never thought ahead about anything. I might as well get mad at a puppy for spilling its water dish as to be mad at Bobby for not being more responsible. It was just his way. And, to be honest, I suppose his Tom Cruise good looks made it pretty easy to forgive him.

He had arrived at the hospital early that morning. He sat on the edge of the bed and held my hand. He tried to make conversation, but it didn't go well. After a few words, we would lapse into silence, but not an awkward one. He made me feel peaceful, calm.

About an hour before I went into surgery, my mother and sister   5
showed up. Mother had just finished the night shift. Kay had picked up Mom after she dropped her little boy off at the daycare. When Mom arrived, she refused to enter the room until Bobby left. They have a bad past history. I told Bobby that he didn't have to leave. He said, "I'll go to keep peace. You need your mom now. I'll be back before your surgery."

I honestly wasn't sure why I needed my mother. She tried to be comforting, but I could see the worry in her eyes. She even managed to make me feel guilty. I could almost hear her saying, "I told you to take care of your colon. I told you not to eat all those greasy french fries." Mothers seem instinctively to believe that all problems could be prevented if children would only eat their vegetables.

At least, Kay was there. We hadn't seen much of each other since she moved out, but we were still best friends as well as sisters. She knew better than to ask me how I was doing. Instead, she talked about Joshua getting into the cabinets, and how Mike would talk in his sleep, and about her friend Liz who had just managed to wreck her third car this year. She made me feel like I was at a slumber party instead of in a hospital.

Bobby still hadn't returned when the nurse came for me. Mom promised she would tell the nurse on duty to send him to the "prep" room, but it was Kay, not Bobby, who held my hand as the nurse pushed me down the corridor. It was Kay who joked that she had seen the surgical nurse on "America's Most Wanted." And it was Kay who stroked my hair as the nurse jabbed the I.V. into my arm.

Soon, even Kay was gone. The nurse pushed my cot on wheels through the enormous green doors. I felt like a helpless child as I lay there on my back with the doctor and nurses towering over me. My tears and fears grew. My doctor patted my hands and said, "You'll be okay, big girl."

The next thing I can remember is waking up in the recovery   10
room. Where was Bobby? Why wasn't he here? I lashed out at Mom when she came in. "Why did you send him away? Why didn't you tell him to come to me?"

I still hadn't seen Bobby when Kay came up the morning after the surgery. She told me that Mom didn't like Bobby because she

The conflict between Bobby and Karen's mother is obviously important. Karen also introduces a few details about her sister Kay.

Karen provides further insight into her relationship with her mother.

Kay becomes a much more important figure in the revision than in the original.

This paragraph is powerful in conveying Karen's sense of helplessness. She keeps it much as it was in the first draft.

At her group's urging, Karen expands on her confrontation with her mother after the

BYTE-SIZE BULLETIN: REVISING ON A WORD PROCESSOR

When revising your paper on a word processor, you will want to learn the **commands** that allow you to make changes in your rough draft. The commands that you give will vary depending on the particular word processing program that you are using. All word processing programs, however, should allow you to accomplish these basic functions:

Insert new text   This is the simplest function to perform. Simply move the cursor to the point where you want to insert the new text. (The new "text" might be a single letter or a dozen pages.) The word processor will automatically "push" the existing text forward as you type in the new text.

Delete existing text   Most keyboards have a **delete** key that allows you to erase one character at a time. (On some keyboards, the **backspace** key will delete.) Other commands will allow you to delete words, lines, or longer sections of your paper.

Move text   Often you will want to move sentences or paragraphs from one section of your paper to another. In order to move text, you have to identify a **block** of text that you want moved and then indicate where you want it inserted. Block moves are sometimes referred to as **cutting and pasting**.

Finding and replacing text   The **find** or **search** function allows you to search for a particular word or phrase that you've used in the paper. If you remember that you used the word *umbrella* in a particular section of your paper, the find function will allow you to move quickly to that word. The **replace** function allows you to substitute one word for another throughout the paper. If you discover that you've misspelled the word *receive* in your paper, you can use the find function to locate each misspelling and the replace function to put in correct spelling.

After making changes in your paper, you will want to **save** these on your disk. In order to save a document, you must give it a **filename**. You might save the first draft of a paper you have written with the filename "BOBBY." As you make changes, you can continue to save them to that same file. However, when you save to an existing file, you replace the earlier version. If you want to preserve an early version of your paper, you can create a new file for the revised version and give it a new filename. For instance, you might call a revised version "BOBBY2." This way you can keep your rough draft and the revised version.

surgery and her breakup with Bobby.

didn't trust him. She knew I was in love with him, but she was pretty sure Bobby wasn't in love with me, and she didn't want to see me get hurt. In spite of this, she had talked to Bobby after I was taken to the prep room. He said he was suffocating and had to get out. I saw Bobby a few times after that, but things were never the same. I recovered from the surgery in about six weeks. I'm still recovering from Bobby.

Karen's revision has dramatically improved this paper. Instead of it being random observations about her hospital experience, she has developed a clear sense of purpose that controls what she includes in the paper. Karen might want to stop at this point, feeling that she has accomplished all she set out to do. However, this paper could still benefit from further revision. Because the paper now has a clear focus, Karen can concentrate on the details of her writing—adding dialogue, improving description, fine-tuning a phrase.

Karen uses the same revision questions to evaluate her second draft.

1. What does she like?

    She is pleased with the way she has expanded the paper to include her feelings about Bobby, Kay, and her mother. She thinks the ending effectively expresses the physical and emotional pain of this surgery.

2. What doesn't she like?

    The doctor and nurses were important to her, but she fails to describe them in the paper. She wants to add a few details to make them less "stick figures" and more like real people.

    There is too much narration and not enough dialogue. She can still recall exactly what was said in some cases, and she believes this would add more interest to the paper.

    She doesn't like the way some of the sentences read. For instance, "My tears and fears grew" sounds childish to her.

3. What will she change?

    Karen decides to add more dialogue and to describe the medical personnel more thoroughly. She thinks the title should be changed to reflect the new emphasis of the story. She will read all the sentences carefully and change them to read as smoothly as possible.

Because she had trouble thinking of a title, Karen decides to brainstorm for five minutes to think of as many titles as possible. She comes up with this list:

Over You	Where's Bobby?
Me and Bobby	Through Green Doors
Heart Surgery	Everybody Says I'm Fine
Someone to Hold My Hand	Complete Recovery
Wounds that Won't Heal	Hurting
Time to Heal	Partial Recovery

After discussing these titles with her group, Karen decides to use "Where's Bobby?" She thinks it hints at the most important part of the experience, and she likes the idea that this phrase takes on a new meaning at the end of the essay.

LANGUAGE NOTE: TITLES

Selecting a title can be one of the most important decisions you will make about a paper. Many reports are written with purely descriptive titles, such as "Installation Procedures for In-Dash Stereo Receivers" or "Preserving Data Integrity on a Magneto Optical Drive." Such titles serve to identify the type of information in the report for the reader who has already recognized a need for this information.

In other writing situations, you will want not only to suggest the subject matter of your writing, but also to create interest in it. "The Slaughter of the Dolphins" is likely to arouse more concern from the average reader than "The Impact of Commercial Fishing Practices on the Dolphin Population." You should guard, however, against titles that are too sensational ("Dolphins Extinct!") or too maudlin ("Poor Flipper Is Dead").

Also, be careful to capitalize your title correctly. Always capitalize the first and last word in the title. Capitalize most of the other words as well, with the exception of articles (*a, an,* and *the*), prepositions (e.g., *with, from, of*), coordinating conjunctions (e.g., *and, but, or*), and the *to* of an infinitive. Center the title at the top of the page, and double-space before beginning the body of your paper. Here are some sample titles as they would appear at the top of your paper:

> The Problem of Sound Pollution at Selected U.S. Airports
>
> Hit and Run: Rickey Henderson's Legendary Performances
>
> Concepts of Womanhood in the Pauline Epistles
>
> Swords and Daggers in William Shakespeare's *Hamlet*
>
> How to Make Money in a Bear Market

Draft 3

Where's Bobby?

by Karen Vanderburg

Karen adds descriptive detail and a bit of dialogue to add interest to the first paragraph.

Where am I? What happened? Just as I awoke, a nurse in *her white, starched uniform* made her way towards me. *She leaned over the metal rail and whispered, "You're fine, hon. The doctor says your surgery went real well. You should be out of the recovery room in a few hours."* I remember fading in and out of consciousness. I kept asking for Bobby, but she told me that no one was allowed in recovery.

The last time I had seen Bobby was about an hour before the surgery. He doesn't like hospitals, and I knew it hadn't been easy for him to come. Somehow that made it more special that he had come — I knew he must really care about me.

We had been dating on and off for about a year. Bobby wasn't a great talker, but he always thought of something we could do. He seldom called. He would arrive, unannounced, in his '67 emerald-green Cougar and ask if I wanted to go to the park or a ballgame or a movie. Normally, I would have said "no." If a guy wants to ask me out, he could at least have the courtesy to call ahead of time. But Bobby didn't mean to be rude — he just never thought ahead about anything. I might as well get mad at a puppy for spilling its water dish as to be mad at Bobby for not being more responsible. It was just his way. And, to be honest, I suppose his Tom Cruise good looks made it pretty easy to forgive him.

He had arrived at the hospital early that morning *in his blue jeans and sweatshirt. He was wearing socks with his Reeboks, which seemed to be his one concession to hospital formality.* He sat on the edge of the bed and took my hand in his.

"Are you all right, babe? Do you need anything?" he tried 5 lamely.

"No, sweetheart, I'm fine, really."

"If you need anything, you'll let me know."

"Sure."

We drifted into silence, staring out of the hospital window. It didn't seem important to me that we talk. I felt peaceful, calm, just knowing he was there.

About an hour before I went into surgery, Kay, my older sister, 10 showed up. I could tell something was wrong.

"Mom's out in the hallway," she said tensely.

"What's wrong?" I asked.

"She won't come in until Bobby's gone."

Mom had just finished the night shift. Kay had picked up Mom after she dropped her little boy off at the daycare. When Mom arrived, she refused to enter the room until Bobby left. I knew she didn't like Bobby, but I didn't realize she hated him this much. I told Bobby that he didn't have to leave. He said, "I'll go to keep peace. You need your mom now. I'll be back before your surgery."

I honestly wasn't sure why I needed my mother. She tried to be 15 comforting, but I could see the worry in her eyes. She even managed to make me feel guilty. I could almost hear her saying, "I told you to take care of your colon. I told you not to eat all those greasy french fries." Mothers seem instinctively to believe that all problems could be prevented if children would only eat their vegetables.

At least, Kay was there. We hadn't seen much of each other since she moved out, but we were still best friends as well as sisters. She knew better than to ask me how I was doing. Instead, she talked about Joshua getting into the cabinets, and how Mike would talk in

Again, descriptive detail allows us to picture Bobby in this situation.

Karen inserts some dialogue to show the stiffness of their conversation.

Again, Karen uses dialogue to dramatize a situation.

his sleep, and about her friend Liz who had just managed to wreck her third car this year. She made me feel as though I were at a slumber party instead of in a hospital.

Bobby still hadn't returned when the nurse came for me. Mom promised she would tell the nurse on duty to send him to the "prep" room, but it was Kay, not Bobby, who held my hand as the nurse pushed me down the corridor. It was Kay who joked about having seen the surgical nurse on "America's Most Wanted." And it was Kay who stroked my hair as the nurse jabbed the I.V. into my arm.

Karen replaces the weak line in the original, "My tears and fears grew," with a more concrete description. Adding the doctor's name is a small detail, but it also makes the event seem more real to a reader. Karen could have described the doctor's appearance, but it is his voice that best explains why she found him comforting.

Soon, even Kay was gone. The nurse pushed my cot on wheels through the enormous green doors. I felt like a helpless child as I lay there on my back with the doctor and nurses towering over me. I could feel the fear welling up inside of me. My chest felt tight, and I could feel the tears coming down my cheeks. *Dr. Manzetti* patted my hands and said, "You'll be okay, big girl." His voice was calm, soothing. It was the kind of voice that gathers you up in its arms and makes you feel that everything will be all right.

The next thing I can remember is waking up in the recovery room. Where was Bobby? Why wasn't he here? I lashed out at Mom when she came in. "Why did you send him away? Why didn't you tell him to come to me?"

Karen likes the ending and feels that adding more detail might lessen its effectiveness.

I still hadn't seen Bobby when Kay came up the morning after 20 the surgery. She told me that Mom didn't like Bobby because she didn't trust him. She knew I was in love with him, but she was pretty sure Bobby wasn't in love with me, and she didn't want to see me get hurt. In spite of this, she had talked to Bobby after I was taken to the prep room. He said he was suffocating and had to get out. I saw Bobby a few times after that, but things were never the same. I recovered from the surgery in about six weeks. I'm still recovering from Bobby.

EXERCISE 3.1 **Responding to a Rough Draft**

Read the following rough draft. Write down your response to the revision guide questions that follow the draft. Then, in a small group, discuss your individual responses to the revision guide questions.

To Help or Not to Help

by Cathy Chin

They had seen the car earlier, weaving all over the highway. They were obviously 1 drunk, and she just hoped they got off the road before they killed someone. Stan saw the car first. It was lying off the side of the road, rocking back and forth on the roof.

"Are you sure we should try to help?" I said as Stan brought the car to a stop. "I don't know anything about rescues. Maybe we should just find a phone and call someone to help."

"By that time, it might be too late. You do what you want, but I'm going to see if I can help them," Stan said as he jumped out of the car.

I sat for a moment, uncertain what to do. I didn't want to seem a coward, so I followed Stan over to the site of the accident. One boy was already out of the car. He looked like he was in shock. Stan was talking to the other boy who was wedged into the car. He was bleeding badly, and I nearly passed out when I saw the blood dripping down onto the roof lining.

Evidently someone else had seen the accident and called the police. An ambulance arrived before long, and they used the "Jaws of Life" to get at the boy who was trapped in the car.

I was still feeling guilty the next day about my hesitating to help out. I knew that if it had been my family or someone I knew, I never would have considered driving on by. I felt like I wasn't a very good person.

I talked to Stan some about it afterwards. He said not to worry, that I had a very normal reaction.

We never did hear any more about the boys who were in the wreck or what happened to them.

Revision Guide

1. What do you like about this draft?
2. What do you think needs to be changed?
3. How would you change it if you were the writer?

SPECIALIZED REVISION GUIDES

The general revision guide can be adapted for specific kinds of writing. Just as there are specialized forms of planning as we learned in chapter 1, there are also specialized revision guides, designed to aid you in revising particular forms of writing. A specialized revision guide draws your attention to the particular requirements of the assignment on which you are working. (Step four in the writing assignment that follows is an example of a specialized revision guide.) In the following chapters, you will find specialized revision guides to accompany the assignments that you are given. Although the questions will be more specific, all of these specialized revision guides follow the general pattern of assessing what you have written, deciding what needs improvement, and then making specific plans to incorporate these changes into your next draft.

WRITING ASSIGNMENT An Influential Person

All of us can recall people who have made a significant impact on our lives. Perhaps it was a teacher who believed in us when we had trouble believing in ourselves. Perhaps it was a band director or a coach who took extra time to help us out or just listen to our problems. Maybe it was a family member who supported us at a difficult moment in our lives. On the other hand, some people have had a negative impact on our lives. You may recall someone who lied to you, gave you false expectations, cheated you out of something you deserved, or hurt you in some other way. In this assignment, you are asked to describe this person and the way he or she influenced your life.

Step one   Brainstorm a list of five to seven people you would nominate for the "Greatest Influence on My Life" Award.

Step two   Select one of the people from your list and make three columns on your paper like this:

Physical appearance   Actions toward yourself   Actions toward others

In the first column, list everything you can recall about the person's physical appearance—facial features, mannerisms, energy level, body build, way of walking, expressions, clothing, and so on. In the second column, list the experiences you remember with this person. How did this person react to you? What did he or she say? Where did you go together? In the last column, list those things you observed this person do, even though you may not have been personally involved. Be as specific as possible in making your list. For instance, "constantly tapping on the ground" and "always moving something around on her desk" are more descriptive than just writing "nervous." Similarly, try to remember specific actions. "We used to play catch in the backyard" is more vivid than "We spent lots of time together."

Step three   Select two or three events that would best illustrate the character of the person you have selected. Write a draft in which you describe the events you have selected. As always, write quickly without evaluating your work or stopping to check on spelling.

Step four   After writing your first draft, answer these questions (either individually or in a group):

1. Is my purpose in writing this paper made clear to the readers—either by statement or by implication?

2. Does the person I have described seem like an individual or a type? What have I told about this person that is not common to all people of the same type (e.g., children, parents, friends, teachers, coaches)?

3. What is surprising in this draft? In what ways is the person I have described unpredictable?

4. How have I connected the different events I have chosen to include? Do they ultimately create a unified impression?

5. Have I described the person's appearance, voice, and mannerisms in sufficient detail? Have I included dialogue (if appropriate)? What else might I want to add to strengthen the impression?

6. Is the introductory paragraph effective in creating interest? Does the paper conclude strongly? Have I chosen an effective title?

7. Have I used language that is clear and vivid?

Step five   Continue writing and revising in successive drafts until every detail contributes to the purpose of your paper. Seek out someone who can provide you with informed commentary. You may have a writing group in your class, or you may want to find a reader outside the class. Many colleges have a writing center that can provide assistance as you work on your paper. Obviously, you should seek someone to *respond* to your writing. Never allow anyone to write the paper for you.

Before submitting your final paper, edit the paper carefully for mechanical errors. It is important to know your personal tendencies in this regard. If you have difficulty with spelling, then review all the words you might have misspelled and check them with a dictionary. If you mix up homonyms (such as *to* and *too* or *their* and *there*), then be on the alert for these words in your writing. Write down three errors that you have frequently made in the past, and review your paper with special attention to these problem areas.

1.   _____

2.   _____

3.   _____

You may find it useful to keep a section in a notebook for recurring errors that appear in your writing. Knowing your weak areas is the first step toward improving them.

THE CRITICAL MOMENT

This chapter has been based on the presumption that most people do their best writing when they have an opportunity to revise their work over a period of time. This contradicts a prevalent notion that writing is primarily a matter of inspiration. The Greeks pictured this as a divine act: The Muse descended from the clouds and gave words to the poet, music to the composer, and so on. What is your view on these issues?

1.   Is writing a craft that can be learned or a talent that is inherited?

2.   Why do some people write better than others?

3.   Must one be "inspired" to write well? What are the implications for writing in the workplace if this is true?

PART II

The Aims of Writing

CHAPTER 4

Writing to Discover

Most of us have had the experience of wanting to express an idea that lies just beneath the level of consciousness. What we want to say is "on the tip of our tongue," but we can't quite recall it. One of the reasons we have difficulty recalling details is because of the vast amount of information stored in our minds. However, writing can be a powerful tool for unlocking our minds and giving shape to our ideas. We have already seen how the planning strategies discussed in chapter 1 can be used to discover or "uncover" what we already know about a given topic. In this chapter we use these skills to increase our personal knowledge and to prepare for informative and persuasive writing tasks.

THE KNOWLEDGE INVENTORY

Whenever we begin thinking about a topic or writing task, it is often useful to conduct a "knowledge inventory," which is a list or map of our existing knowledge about the subject. Suppose I am considering purchasing a compact disc (CD) player. I might begin my research on this topic by listing what I currently know about CD players:

CD players

    excellent sound quality

    produced by lasers

    replaced LPs

    size of open hand

    all new recordings

    some classics not available

CD players found in some new cars

status symbol

no needle to scratch or wear the grooves

Usually in the process of writing down our ideas, we recall some facts that we had forgotten or "half-remembered." The act of writing down our thoughts can help bring some of this knowledge back to the forefront of our minds. Writing down our thoughts also allows us to be more specific. Although I knew the approximate size of CDs, it was in the act of making the preceding list that I realized they are about the size of an open hand.

As well as helping us to recall what we already know, the knowledge inventory helps us to discover what we don't know. Although I know that CDs use an entirely different approach to sound reproduction than LPs, I don't know how CDs are made or how the tracks are "read" by the CD player. My knowledge inventory can be expanded to include the questions raised as I think about the subject:

How are CDs made?

Who invented the CD?

How does a CD player work?

Can CDs be damaged by heat or cold?

How much do CD players cost?

What are the features available on a CD player?

How dependable are CD players?

Will the CD be replaced by the DAT (digital audio tape)?

The questions raised by the knowledge inventory can be as important as the facts that are discovered. Such questions will guide my research as I look up articles on CDs and talk to CD owners and salespeople. Before beginning the study of any subject, you should take a knowledge inventory to help you assess both what you know and what you need to know about the subject.

EXERCISE 4.1 Knowledge Inventory

Conduct a knowledge inventory on one of the following topics. Include your questions about the subject as well as your existing knowledge.

Where would be a good place to spend a vacation?

What is the best four-wheel-drive (high performance? family? economy?) vehicle to own?

What treatments are available for the common cold?

What are some different forms of physical exercise and the benefits of each?

Electronic mail is simply the exchange of messages — from casual chatter to formal reports — over an electronic **network**. Electronic mail, or **e-mail** as it is popularly called, combines the speed of a phone call with the accuracy of a written message. Imagine you work at the main office of Crop Dusters Life & Casualty Insurance in Des Moines, and you want to send a list of prospective customers to Dolly Richards, the manager of your branch office in Dubuque. If you call Dolly, she may be out of the office or busy with a customer. Even if she is available, you don't want to spend hours reading a list of names over the phone and verifying the phone numbers and addresses. If you are connected to the branch office with electronic mail, you can simply send an e-mail message that contains the information, and it will be waiting for Dolly when she comes in. Furthermore, if you want Sally in Sioux City and Cindy in Cedar Rapids to get the list, you can send it to the whole group simultaneously. In the coming weeks, Dolly, Sally, and Cindy can send updates over e-mail, telling about the customers they have called on and the sales they have made.

Electronic mail has a particularly important place in writing to discover. Communicating with other computer users over an electronic network can help you discover new ideas and collect information from experts. In fact, your discovery group can be totally electronic. Rather than meeting with your fellow students in the library at 7:00 p.m. to discuss current legislative decisions for an assignment in a U.S. government class, you might meet with people from different states — or even different countries — at 7:00 p.m. to discuss the implications of national policy over a computerized network.

How does one get on an electronic network? Some computers on your campus may already be tied into a network that would allow you to send messages to other computer users. Inquire about the availability of such services on your campus. If you own a personal computer, you can connect with other computer users by using your telephone line. You will need a **modem** to transfer the messages you send into a code that can be sent across the telephone lines and then decoded by a remote computer. You might also want to subscribe to a commercial service such as CompuServe or Genie that will connect you with thousands of other computer users. Through these services you can participate in an ongoing discussion about anything from science fiction novels to growing orchids. You can also telephone local **bulletin board services (BBS)** and post questions about the topic for your next assignment.

Although electronic mail might sound intimidating, you usually need to learn only a few simple commands to get started. Once you do start communicating electronically, it's easy to get hooked. Be aware, however, that you will be charged for long-distance service when using your modem just as if you were talking over the line. Commercial services also charge for **on-line** time (i.e., the time when you are connected to their service). Still, e-mail represents an exciting and economical way to connect to people all over the country, and even the world, who share your same interests or who can provide you with vital information.

DISCOVERY GROUPS

We have already seen the importance of groups in responding to our writing in chapter 2. By sharing our writing with a group, we learn where our ideas have been vague, incomplete, or unconvincing to others. The members of a Discovery Group serve not only as respondents to our writing, but also as co-investigators who can help us develop our thinking and suggest possible avenues for research.

What we are calling a "Discovery Group" has many equivalents in our society. When studying a problem or making decisions, we often rely on small groups to deliberate and arrive at some consensus. For instance, city governments are made up of several individuals representing different areas of the city. This helps to ensure that all citizens are fairly represented. The president sometimes appoints a special task force to study crime, drug abuse, health care, housing, and similar issues. The various members of the presidential commission are selected because of their knowledge and experience related to the issue being studied. Corporations frequently put together teams to handle special projects. The team members might include managers, engineers, accountants, salespeople, and others with training in specialized fields. Although these individuals have different backgrounds, they must work together as a group to accomplish their common goals.

There are several benefits in bringing together a group of people to work on a project. Obviously, many tasks require the expertise of several different people. A community deciding to build a new ballpark will certainly need the technical advice of engineers and architects, but they will also want to find out what the needs of the baseball team are, how the money can be raised to fund the project, and what local residents expect in the way of parking, seating, and services. Only by consulting all of these sources can the community successfully complete the project.

As well as knowledge gathering, groups often must iron out differences among competing factions. In building a ballpark, someone is likely to complain that the noise and traffic will be disruptive. Others may feel that the park is too expensive or that it is unfair to tax all citizens for the sake of those who will actually attend the games. Still others may complain that the ballpark is being placed in the wrong part of town. The group must look for a solution that is fair and equitable to all.

Finally, groups can stimulate interest in a subject and provoke creative thinking. Psychologists use the word *synergy* to describe the dynamic effect of group participation on individual thinking. As we hear others express their ideas, we begin reacting to what they have said and this stimulates our own thinking. In a good discussion, the synergy developed by working cooperatively is much greater than what might have been produced by the individual members working in isolation.

EXERCISE 4.2 **The Northridge Mall Problem**

Break into small groups of four to six people. Imagine that your mayor has appointed you to participate on a task force to study the following problem:

Northridge Mall has become a popular place for young people to congregate on the weekends. Especially on Friday and Saturday nights, the mall is crowded with teens roaming up and down the corridors or lounging on benches and floors. The Northridge Mall Merchants Association has complained that the presence of these young people is driving out their older customers. They note that some of the young people are "rude and disorderly" and that the mall merchants have encountered serious problems with "shoplifting and vandalism" on these nights. Furthermore, they complain of gang violence and intimidation both within the mall and in the parking lot.

For their part, students have complained that the merchants are often hostile and contemptuous toward them. Some have been asked to leave certain stores for no apparent reason. Others report being "hassled" by mall security for playing radios too loudly or other minor infractions (roughhousing with friends, dropping litter, playing in the fountain).

Parents are also upset. They, too, are worried about gangs and are concerned for their children's safety. They also believe that the mall has become a breeding ground for drug abuse and other forms of criminal behavior. They believe that the mall security is too lax in allowing these activities to go on. On the other hand, they feel that their children are sometimes unnecessarily detained because of their race or the way they dress.

As a group, answer the following questions:

1. Which of these problems are legitimate concerns? (Try to examine this question from the perspective of parents, teenagers, adult shoppers, security personnel, store owners, and other interested parties.)

2. What, if anything, can be done about them?

Write down the specific recommendations that you would make to the mayor.

WRITING TO LEARN

We can use techniques such as knowledge inventories and discovery groups to help us learn about a new subject as well as to assess our current knowledge on a topic. Writing in order to improve our understanding and retention of ideas is often called "writing to learn." Sometimes your teachers may give you specific assignments intended to help you remember or apply concepts from a course you are taking. As well as improving your performance in the course, these activities may also encourage you to make connections between the course information and your own personal concerns. Frequently, such writing-to-learn activities are collected in a journal to be reviewed by the teacher. Sometimes you may want to pose your own questions when studying for a difficult course or reviewing your reading from the textbook. By actively participating in the knowledge-making process, you will understand your subject much more thoroughly. Here are examples of the kinds of questions or prompts that you might be given as a writing-to-learn activity:

From a physics course

> Explain to your little brother why light is normally perceived as white when it is actually made up of a spectrum of different colors.

From a history course

> One of the causes of the westward migration across America in the 1800s was the innate desire of adventurous people to explore new territories. Do Americans still possess this adventurous spirit? If so, how is it manifested?

From a music appreciation course

> As well as giving pleasure to individuals, music is often a way of establishing a bond between people. From our reading, what are some examples of music that is identified with particular nations, groups, or cultures?

As you can see from these examples, writing-to-learn activities ask you to place information in a particular context. In responding to such a question, write spontaneously and rapidly. You should check with your teacher to find out exactly how such assignments will be graded, but usually the focus is on content rather than on the form of the reply.

Many times writing-to-learn activities will require you to test the ideas and assumptions of your textbook's author against your own experience. The following example is from a student writing in a journal for a sociology course.

> I am appalled. . . . I heard a cheer that is being used by a private prep school . . . at this time. It is so racist, I can hardly believe the students are allowed to use it. It goes as follows:
>
> > That's all right, that's okay!
> > <u>You</u> will work for <u>us</u> someday.
>
> They say this cheer when they play city teams. I can't believe that the administration of this school allows its students to degrade others in this way. If I were on the receiving end of this cheer, as a player or a fan, I'd be furious and want to lash out at the users of the cheer. It would hurt me deeply and then that hurt would turn to anger.
>
> The cheer <u>assumes</u> ranking and position of people from the city with no thought of city people being above the prep school.
>
> No wonder prejudice is so widespread. Kids think it's fun and cute to tear people's self-esteem apart! What a sick society.

This entry indicates the ways that racism still exists in blatant forms in everyday life. It makes clear the underlying meaning of the cheer and the social attitudes it conveys. Writing such a journal entry helps to reinforce concepts discussed in the sociology course—for example, the meaning of prejudice, class structure, social attitudes, symbolic action. It also helps to contextualize these ideas so that they become meaningful for the writer.

EXERCISE 4.3 **Tired Tots on the Fast Track**

Writing to learn is particularly effective as a way of responding to reading. We must read carefully in order to formulate our own response. As we write, we test the author's ideas and assumptions through our own experience.

Read the following article about the pressures on preschool children and respond to the writing-to-learn activity that follows it.

Tired Tots on the Fast Track

by Suzanne Fields

We've moved from a child-centered society to a work-centered one, and the children   1
are paying for it. Pushing children too fast too soon may slow them down later on.

Young children exposed to structured learning have been found to suffer more anxiety over tests, to be less creative later, and to lose the academic edge in elementary school.

A study of 120 preschoolers by the Spencer Foundation observed the effects of parental stress on the children's later achievement, and reached glum conclusions. "We forget that play is the work of childhood," Kathryn Hirsh-Pasek, professor of psychology and one of the authors of the study, told the *Chronicle of Higher Education*. "We need to have respect for children and to let them explore and learn on their own."

These sentiments are echoed by many early-childhood experts, where the issue is less that all preschool is bad than that certain kinds of preschools damage children.

"When we instruct children in academic subjects, or in swimming, gymnastics, or   5
ballet, at too early an age, we miseducate," says David Elkind, a professor of child's study [sic] at Tufts University.

"We put them at risk for short-term stress and long-term personality damage for no useful purpose. There is no evidence that such early instruction has lasting benefits, and considerable evidence that it can do lasting harm."

Then why do many preschools and kindergartens push academic achievement? The answers are both cultural and personal.

We've lost our competitive edge and in a fit of pique approaching panic, we're looking for quick fixes, starting with youngsters. High tech further confounds us, suggesting short cuts to learning via computers, even though most tots aren't ready to learn much from microchips.

A misreading of psychological theorists suggests to many parents that kids can learn almost anything as long as someone takes the time, and "the earlier the better." Such attitudes may have more to do with a parent's needs and vanities than a child's ability.

"Gourmet couples" who become parents often want to pursue their young child's   10
schooling as human extensions of their own careers.

"If John Stuart Mill could write Latin at the age of 3," says one typical overachieving parent, "by golly, so can my John Jr." . . .

Teachers complain that young children often seem more like exhausted executives than tired children, and pediatricians observe an increase in childhood depression.

Precocious kids are even said to be "burning out" at 10 or 11. Growing up is hard enough without precocious parents pouring it on.

Activity   Imagine that you have received the following letter from a longtime friend.

Dear _____,

Can you believe our little Alice is already three years old? She is our pride and joy. You should see her riding around the house on her stick "pony."

We are starting her in preschool this fall, and we wanted your opinion. Wonderland Nursery emphasizes free play, although the children do participate in some group activities. I have been leaning more toward KinderKollege. They have a highly structured curriculum that emphasizes academic performance. The supervisor at KinderKollege told me, "You get what you expect out of little children, and we expect a lot!"

As competitive as the world is today, maybe Alice needs to get started on the fast track at a place like KinderKollege.

What do you think?

Write soon,

Hattie

Write an answer to Hattie based on the information taken from the article on "Tired Tots."

Summarizing

One of the most common writing-to-learn activities is the summary. A summary condenses information—a paragraph, a section, a chapter—into a concise rendering of the major points or ideas. Obviously, you must be selective about what you include. Generally, only the author's main ideas and conclusions are included. Supporting facts and illustrations are either given briefly or omitted entirely. In a summary, unlike a review or a critique, you should not attempt to interpret the author's work or offer an alternative view. It is very important when summarizing not to distort the author's original statement in any way.

Read the following paragraph and the summary statement that follows it.

The Students' Right to Their Own Language

by Neil Postman

Another argument advanced in behalf of the poor and oppressed is the students' right to their own language. I have never heard this argument come from parents whose children are not competent to use Standard English. It is an argument . . . put forward by "liberal" education critics whose children *are* competent in Standard English but who in some curious way wish to express their solidarity with and charity for those who are less capable. It is a case of pure condescension, and I do not think teachers should be taken in by it. Like the mode of dress, the mode of language in school ought to be relatively formal and exemplary, and therefore markedly different from the custom in less rigorous places.

Summary
    Neil Postman believes that children should be required to use Standard English in school. He accuses education critics of being condescending when they suggest that students have a "right to their own language."

Because writing a summary inevitably forces you to look for the main ideas in a passage, it is a valuable aid in understanding and remembering the key points in your reading.

EXERCISE 4.4 Summary

Write a summary of the following passage in two or three sentences.

> One can usually think of . . . deprivation as falling into two broad categories. First, there is what may be called *case* poverty. This one encounters in every community, rural or urban, however prosperous that community or the times. Case poverty is the poor farm family with the junk-filled yard and the dirty children playing in the bare dirt. Or it is the gray-black hovel beside the railroad tracks. Or it is the basement dwelling in the alley.
>
> Case poverty is commonly and properly related to some characteristic of the individuals so afflicted. Nearly everyone else has mastered his environment: This proves that it is not intractable. But some quality peculiar to the individual or the family involved — mental deficiency, poor health, inability to adapt to the discipline of industrial life, uncontrollable procreation, alcoholism, discrimination involving a very limited minority, some educational handicap unrelated to community shortcoming, or perhaps a combination of several of these handicaps — has kept these individuals from participating in the general well-being.
>
> Second, there is what may be called *insular* poverty — that which manifests itself as an "island" of poverty. In the island, everyone or nearly everyone is poor. Here, evidently, it is not easy to explain matters by individual inadequacy. We may mark individuals down as intrinsically deficient in social performance; it is not proper or even wise so to characterize an entire community. The people of the island have been frustrated by some factor common to their environment.

Paraphrasing

Unlike the summary, a paraphrase attempts to retain all the ideas contained in the original statement. Consequently, a paraphrase is generally as long as or longer than the original. It is important in writing the paraphrase to be faithful to the meaning of the original version. Compare the two paraphrases that follow this quotation:

Original

To keep in the rear of opportunity in matters of indulgence is as valuable a habit as to keep abreast of opportunity in matters of enterprise. (Thomas Hardy)

Paraphrase 1

A successful person is usually one of the last people to spend money on self-gratifying pleasures, but one of the first to take advantage of an opportunity to make money or get ahead in business.

Paraphrase 2

If you don't get to have fun, the next best thing is to make money.

The first paraphrase is certainly less formal than Hardy's statement, but it accurately represents his thought. The writer of paraphrase 2, on the other hand, has distorted the Hardy quotation. Hardy never suggests that making money is a compensation for having fun.

If you encounter difficult words in writing a paraphrase, use your dictionary to look them up. Be sure, however, to identify the correct meaning for the word as it is used in the context of the sentence. The word *enterprise,* for instance, may simply mean a "project," but Hardy is referring specifically to a "business venture."

EXERCISE 4.5 Paraphrase

Choose one of the following three quotations and write a paraphrase that accurately reflects its meaning.

Necessity never made a good bargain. (Benjamin Franklin)

When a true genius appears in the world, you may know him by this sign, that the dunces are all in a confederacy against him. (Jonathan Swift)

It takes two to speak the truth — one to speak and another to hear. (Henry David Thoreau)

EXERCISE 4.6 Writing-to-Learn Skills

In dealing with a longer passage, you may use many of the writing-to-learn skills that we have discussed. Read the following passage and respond to the questions at the end.

From "Los Angeles Against the Mountains"

by John McPhee

On a February night some years ago, the Genofiles were awakened by a crash of thunder — lightning striking the mountain front. Ordinarily, in their quiet neighborhood, only the creek beside them was likely to make much sound, dropping steeply out of Shields

Canyon on its way to the Los Angeles River. The creek, like every component of all the river systems across the city from mountains to ocean, had not been left to nature. Its banks were concrete. Its bed was concrete. When boulders were running there, they sounded like a rolling freight. On a night like this, the boulders should have been running. The creek should have been a torrent. Its unnatural sound was unnaturally absent. There was, and had been, a lot of rain.

The Genofiles had two teen-age children, whose rooms were on the uphill side of the one-story house. The window in Scott's room looked straight up Pine Cone Road, a cul-de-sac, which, with hundreds like it, defined the northern limit of the city, the confrontation of the urban and the wild. Los Angeles is overmatched on one side by the Pacific Ocean and on the other by very high mountains. With respect to these principal boundaries, Los Angeles is done sprawling. The San Gabriels, in their state of tectonic youth, are rising as rapidly as any range on earth. Their loose inimical slopes flout the tolerance of the angle of repose. Rising straight up out of the megalopolis, they stand ten thousand feet above the nearby sea, and they are not kidding with this city. Shedding, spalling, self-destructing, they are disintegrating at a rate that is also among the fastest in the world. **The phalanxed communities of Los Angeles have pushed themselves hard against these mountains, an aggression that requires a deep defense budget to contend with the results.** Kimberlee Genofile called to her mother who joined her in Scott's room as they looked up the street. From its high turnaround, Pine Cone Road plunges downhill like a ski run, bending left and then right and then left and then right in steep christiania turns for half a mile above a three-hundred-foot straightaway that aims directly at the Genofiles' house. Not far below the turnaround, Shields Creek passes under the street, and there a kink in its concrete profile has been plugged by a six-foot boulder. Hence the silence of the creek. The water was now spreading over the street. It descended in heavy sheets. As the young Genofiles and their mother glimpsed it in the all but total darkness, the scene was suddenly illuminated by a blue electrical flash. In the blue light they saw a massive blackness, moving. It was not a landslide, not a mudslide, not a rock avalanche; nor by any means was it the front of a conventional flood. In Jackie's words, "It was just one big black thing coming at us, rolling, rolling with a lot of water in front of it, pushing the water, this big black thing. It was just one big black hill coming toward us."

In geology, it would be known as a debris flow. Debris flows amass in stream valleys and more or less resemble fresh concrete. They consist of water mixed with a good deal of solid material, most of which is above sand size. Some of it is Chevrolet size. Boulders bigger than cars ride long distances in debris flows. Boulders grouped like fish eggs pour downhill in debris flows. The dark material coming toward the Genofiles was not only full of boulders; it was so full of automobiles it was like bread dough mixed with raisins. On its way down Pine Cone Road, it plucked up cars from driveways and the street. When it crashed into the Genofiles' house, the shattering of safety glass made terrific explosive sounds. A door burst open. Mud and boulders poured into the hall. We're going to go, Jackie thought. Oh, my God, what a hell of a way for the four of us to die together.

The parents' bedroom was on the far side of the house. Bob Genofile was in there kicking through white satin draperies at the panelled glass, smashing it to provide an outlet for the water, when the three others ran in to join him. The walls of the house neither moved nor shook. As a general contractor, Bob had built dams, department stores, hospitals, six schools, seven churches, and this house. It was made of concrete block with steel reinforcement, sixteen inches on center. His wife had said it was stronger than any dam in California. His crew had called it "the fort." In those days, twenty years before, the Genofiles' acre was close by the edge of the mountain brush, but a developer had come along since then and knocked down thousands of trees and put Pine Cone Road up the slope. Now Bob Genofile was thinking, I hope the roof holds. I hope the roof is strong enough to hold. Debris was flowing over it. He told Scott to shut the bedroom door. No sooner was the door closed than it was battered down and fell into the room. Mud, rock, water poured in. It pushed everybody against the far wall. "Jump on the bed," Bob said. The bed began to rise. Kneeling on it—on a gold velvet spread—they could soon press their palms against the ceiling. The bed also moved toward the glass wall. The two teen-agers got off, to try to control the motion, and were pinned between the bed's brass railing and the wall. Boulders went up against the railing, pressed it into their legs, and held them fast. Bob dived into the muck to try to move the boulders, but he failed. The debris flow, entering through the windows as well as doors, continued to rise. Escape was still possible for the parents but not for the children. The parents looked at each other and did not stir. Each reached for and held one of the children. Their mother felt suddenly resigned, sure that her son and daughter would die and she and her husband would quickly follow. The house became buried to the eaves. Boulders sat on the roof. Thirteen automobiles were packed around the building, including five in the pool. A din of rocks kept banging against them. The stuck horn of a buried car was blaring. The family in the darkness in their fixed tableau watched one another by the light of a directional signal, endlessly blinking. The house had filled up in six minutes, and the mud stopped rising near the children's chins.

Activity

1. Write a brief summary of the entire passage.

2. Write three questions that you have about the passage.

3. Paraphrase the statement in boldface.

WRITING TO PLAN AND ORGANIZE

One of the principal reasons for writing in everyday life is to plan and organize activities. Many people begin their day by establishing a list of "things to do." Making a written list helps us to recognize our objectives, to establish priorities, and to keep us on track during the day.

Writing an Agenda

Similarly, in planning a meeting, we need to establish our objectives and main-tain an orderly flow of business. The leader of the meeting typically prepares an agenda that sets forth the business to be discussed. Often the agenda is circulated to the members of the organization in advance. This gives the membership an opportunity to prepare for the meeting and to be informed on the issues that will be discussed or debated. Although the exact nature of the agenda will depend on the nature of the meeting, most meetings are organized as follows:

Call to order

1. Reading and approval of minutes
2. Reports of officers, boards, and standing (permanently established) committees
3. Reports of special (appointed for a specified task) committees
4. Special orders (matters assigned a special priority)
5. Unfinished business and general orders (matters previously introduced)
6. New business (matters initiated at the present meeting)

Adjournment

The agenda is a method of discovery because it forces the group leader to think through the goals of a particular meeting and how they may best be accomplished. Having an agenda is absolutely essential to coordinating any group activity; without such a plan, the group may wander aimlessly over several topics without resolving any of them. Here is an example of a typical agenda:

Student Committee on Textbook Exchange

October 9, 1993

Call to order (Cindy Daniels, committee chair)

1. Reading of the minutes (Julio Martinez, committee secretary)
2. Treasurer's report (Aquil Abdaziz)
3. Old business
    a. Cooperative agreement signed with college bookstore
    b. Funding request still pending in Student Senate
    c. Subcommittee reports
        (1) Subcommittee to Locate Campus Facilities (T. J. Porter, chair)
        (2) Subcommittee on Textbook Exchange (Kathy Andrews, chair)
4. New business
    a. Letter of complaint from Bob's Bookstore
    b. Proposed survey on student participation (Alonzo Rosetti)
    c. Changes in buy-back policy

Obviously, an agenda is only a skeletal outline for the meeting. Some items on the agenda will simply involve updating the membership on actions that have been taken since the last meeting. Other items will require discussion and may lead to a committee vote. For instance, having heard the information from the subcommittee on facilities, the group may vote to adopt a particular location from the choices given, or they may raise questions that require obtaining more information. Many groups use a standard reference called *Robert's Rules of Order* to make sure that the group operates in a fair and orderly fashion.

EXERCISE 4.7 Agenda for Student Committee

Choose one of the following questions and develop an agenda for an upcoming meeting.

1. You are the chairperson of the Student Committee for Civil Rights. The committee was appointed by the college president after a recent outbreak of racist activities on campus: a bomb threat at Hillel (a campus Jewish organization), graffiti on campus buildings insulting various minorities, and a brutal attack on a black student by a group of "skinheads." At the first meeting, you discussed the goals for the committee and established two subcommittees: one to collect information about civil rights violations from minority groups on campus and another to obtain information from administrators, campus police, and other authorities about their policies for handling these problems. Write an agenda for the next meeting of your committee.

2. You are the chairperson of the Student Committee for Fair Voting Practices. You have received a number of complaints during the recent election. Some students have complained that ballot boxes were stuffed with fraudulent votes by an opposing candidate. Two candidates were accused of exceeding limits for campaign expenditures. Several campaign posters were placed illegally near voting booths. The winner of the hotly contested race for student body president found that his room had been vandalized after the election. Books and papers were tossed out the window, and his campaign poster was stuck to his bed with a knife. You need to establish a procedure for airing these grievances and following through on appropriate penalties. Write an agenda for your first meeting.

3. You are the chairperson of the Student Committee for Oktoberfest. You have been given $2,000 to pay for advertising, entertainers, decorations, equipment rental, and other expenses. At your first meeting, you appointed subcommittees on advertising and entertainment. At your second meeting, you need to hear their reports and make decisions about allocation of funds. Write an agenda to guide your group's work.

Writing a Discussion Outline

In some cases, groups meet solely for the purpose of discussing important issues. Such a group is not expected to make specific recommendations for action or even to issue a report. The purpose of these groups is simply to consider various views and to clarify the issues at stake. If the discussion is primarily for the benefit of the participants, it is often called a **roundtable** discussion—the roundtable suggesting that all of those attending are to participate in the discussion. If a small group of experts discuss a subject for the purpose of informing an audience, it is generally called a **panel**. The chair or "moderator" of the panel usually solicits questions from the audience and directs them to particular members of the panel. If the main purpose of the meeting is to respond to the questions of the audience, then the event may be called a **forum**. Public hearings are generally conducted as forums. Experts present information and current plans and then respond to the questions and comments of community members. A **symposium** is the most formal kind of public discussion. The experts in a symposium often read prepared statements, and discussion is usually limited to a brief question-and-answer period after all the prepared speeches have been given. In some cases, the audience may not participate at all. Instead, a designated "respondent" may be asked to react to the statements made by the members of the symposium. In practice, all of these terms are used loosely, and the title given to a particular discussion may not follow the format we have described here. If we were to arrange the various forms of discussion according to the amount of audience participation, they would appear as follows:

Most audience participation   Least audience participation

roundtable   forum   panel   symposium

Instead of an agenda, a discussion leader must prepare an outline that will guide the flow of the discussion. One of the most popular forms for a discussion outline is a **problem analysis**. When you are discussing a specific problem, the following questions are extremely useful:

Problem analysis

 I. What is the nature of the problem? (definition)

 II. What is the background of the problem? (history)

III. What are the requirements for a successful solution? (criteria)

IV. What are some possible solutions? (options)

 V. What is the best solution? (decision)

VI. How can this solution be put into effect? (implementation)

The discussion outline should not presuppose any particular solution to the problem. It is designed, rather, to discover a solution through informed discussion. The following example applies these problem analysis steps to a discussion of minimum wage laws.

Minimum Wage Laws

 I. What is a "minimum wage"?
   A. What is the current minimum wage?
   B. Must all employers pay minimum wage?
   C. Must all workers receive minimum wage (e.g., full-time and part-time)?

II. What led to our current minimum wage laws?
   A. When were minimum wage laws first enacted?
   B. Why were these laws enacted?
   C. Do other countries have similar laws?
   D. What has been the effect of these laws on businesses? on youth workers? on adult workers?
   E. What have been the changes in the minimum wage since its inception?
III. What is an acceptable level to set the minimum wage?
   A. What should be the effect on employment?
   B. What should be the effect on business profits?
IV. What are the alternatives to the current minimum wage?
   A. What would be the effect of repealing the current minimum wage law?
   B. What would be the effect of lowering the current minimum wage?
   C. What would be the effect of raising the current minimum wage?
V. What changes, if any, should be made in the current minimum wage law?
   A. What would be the effect of these changes?
   B. Do these changes meet the criteria established in considering an acceptable level of the minimum wage?
VI. How can changes (if needed) be enacted?
   A. How can public support be developed?
   B. How can congressional support be developed?

LANGUAGE NOTE: OUTLINING

Outlining can be useful at several stages during the writing process. After listing or mapping ideas, you may find it useful to prepare an informal outline that lists your major ideas and supporting details. Such an outline is for your own benefit and will be modified as you begin drafting the paper and discover other ideas that should be included.

After completing the paper, you may decide to include an outline that orients the reader to the major divisions of your paper. A table of contents is really nothing more than an outline that lists page numbers where particular items may be found. In some cases, the outline may be carried over into the paper in the form of headings and subheadings. Such headings can be useful in guiding the reader through your paper, particularly if it is long and complex.

The following two rules can guide you in preparing a formal outline:

1.   Items of the same relative importance are presented at the same level of notation. If the history of CDs is as important to your discussion as the future of CDs and if you will spend approximately the same amount of space on both areas, then both areas will be expressed at the same level, for example:

II. The history of CDs

III. The future of CDs

The following six levels of notation are commonly used as a method of indicating relative importance (although most outlines seldom go beyond the third degree of subordination):

I. . . .
    A. . . .
        1. . . .
            a. . . .
                (1) . . .
                    (a) . . .

2.   Make sure that all entries at the same level are expressed in the same grammatical form; that is, use parallelism.

Entries not parallel

Marilyn and Madonna

    I. Glamorous image

   II. Their early lives before stardom

  III. How they differ

Entries parallel

Marilyn and Madonna

   I. Similarities
      A. Sex symbols
      B. Early success

  II. Differences
      A. Public life
      B. Personal life

Parallelism is an important stylistic consideration in all writing, but it is a particularly pertinent consideration in outlines because each level of the outline *must* have at least two entries. An entry in an outline indicates that the topic will be divided into subparts, and division, of course, entails at least two parts.

Formal outlines may be expressed either in complete sentences (a *sentence outline*) or in words, phrases, or clauses (a *topic outline*). The sentence outline is usually considered more formal (and has the advantage of having complete sentences already drafted which may be used as topic sentences of paragraphs within the paper), but some teachers prefer topic outlines. Check with your instructor to see which type of outline is recommended for your class.

EXERCISE 4.8   **Discussion Outline**

Write a discussion outline on one of these questions:

Should a student newspaper refuse to publish an advertisement that offends certain groups on campus?

Should students be required to take a writing proficiency exam before graduating?

Should class attendance be mandatory?

Should parents be allowed to bring their children to class?

Should students be required to take a drug test before qualifying for federal aid?

Should colleges admit all students, even those who have only a marginal chance of success?

Follow the problem analysis steps as you organize your outline.

Discovery is one of the most exciting parts of the writing process. As we write, we discover thoughts, attitudes, and ideas that were not only unexpressed but also unacknowledged. In the act of writing comes a greater awareness of our own knowledge on a given subject and of our own stance on a given issue. But the act of discovery is a beginning rather than an end. Often we are led to investigate a subject further, to seek out additional resources of information. In the next few chapters, we will consider the ways that our ideas may be expanded and deepened through information resources.

THE CRITICAL MOMENT

When paraphrasing the words of another writer—as you often have done in this chapter—you are trying to give the reader an equivalent experience to reading the original. Some people would argue that all paraphrase is a distortion, that every word has its own precise meaning and any substitution inevitably loses some of the meaning of the original. Take a few minutes to respond to these questions:

1.   Is any word an exact synonym for another? Give some examples.

2.   Are some kinds of writing easier to paraphrase than others? What makes the difference?

3.   If paraphrase only approximates the meaning of an original, should this practice be abandoned?

Writing to Inform

We live in an Information Age. Our society generates more information each year than was produced from the dawn of time until the twentieth century. Certainly, this abundance of information can be a blessing as we learn more about ourselves and our world, but it can also be a curse as we try to search out a "needle" of information in an immense "haystack" of knowledge. Important ideas can sometimes become lost in the deluge of information. A few years after the *Challenger* exploded, a flight of the space shuttle *Columbia* was scrubbed due to a defective valve. The problem with the valve had been discovered on an earlier flight, but the technicians who discovered the problem had difficulty alerting those with the authority to replace the defective parts. Several missions actually were flown with a valve that could have burst at any moment, destroying the entire shuttle and its crew. Of course, a similar technical problem did result in the destruction of the *Challenger* in 1986. Unless information is presented in the correct form and through the appropriate channels, it might as well not exist.

Effective leaders know that access to information is power. The owner of a fast-growing chain of pizza restaurants was recently asked for the secret of his success. "I know exactly how many napkins we use," he replied. What he meant, of course, was that every aspect of the business was carefully inspected and controlled. To be an effective writer, you too must have a grasp of all the relevant information, and you must present this information in an effective format.

KNOWING YOUR READER

When was the last time you had trouble understanding something you read? It may have been a chapter from your history textbook, a letter from your insurance company, a notice from your bank, the comments on the last paper you submitted to an instructor, or a paragraph from a friend's letter. The problem may have been the organization of the document, the vocabulary used by the writer, or the complexity of the subject matter. What problems would you face as the reader of this memo in an office environment?

To: All Employees of Grimworts Industries

From: Arnold Grimworts III

Subject: Using Too Many Words in a Memorandum When a Short and Concise and Brief Message Containing Only the Main Points Probably Would Produce Almost, If Not Exactly, the Same Results

Date: April 12, 1994

It has come to my attention that there has recently been over the past few weeks an immense escalation of apparently needless memorandums in which the content of what is attempting to be communicated is completely overshadowed by inappropriate erudite phrasing of the most burdensome kind. Please render any hereinafter communiques amongst and/or between yourselves or any personage above or below yourselves in the most comprehensible manner which is possible. Limitation of excessive verbiage is to be commended in that the meat of the matter is what matters. We must get to the bare bones of things. I remain hopeful that, working alongside of each other and diligently keeping an eye to our manner of communication, we might regain our status of being one of the most productive and effective departments within our laudable organization. May our eyes be simultaneously focused on the betterment of ourselves, our colleagues, our superiors, and our company.

Most confusion in writing comes from the writer's failure to analyze what the reader of the document wants and needs. In chapter 2 we looked at the importance of considering the reader's knowledge and interests in determining what information to include. No one can be well informed on every subject. To write effectively, we must consider how much our reader is likely to know about our subject. It is useful to place readers somewhere along this continuum of understanding:

| Novice | Generalist | Specialist |

Level One: The Novice Reader

The novice reader is largely unacquainted with the subject. If you are writing about a catalyst in a chemistry experiment, the novice would be unable to explain, even on a rudimentary level, what the function of a catalyst is. Although the novice may have encountered the word before, it is only vaguely understood, if at all. In writing for a novice audience, you should avoid "talking down" to your readers. Remember that the novice's problem is being uninformed, not unintelligent. Compare these two sample passages written for novices:

1. Denis Diderot was a Frenchman. He lived in France his whole life. He was born in 1713 and died in 1784. Diderot was a rationalist. He believed that reason was the ultimate solution to every problem. Diderot was most famous for his *Encyclopédie*. The *Encyclopédie* is where we get our word *encyclopedia*. An encyclopedia is a big book that has articles about lots of different subjects.

2. Denis Diderot, a French philosopher, was one of the leading writers and thinkers during the Age of Enlightenment. His greatest work was the *Encyclopédie*, a compendium of information on natural history, science, philosophy, and art. The *Encyclopédie* was more than a compilation of factual articles. It was a critique of the existing political, religious, and military institutions in France. Because this work was so controversial, the *Encyclopédie* was suppressed by the French authorities in 1759, and Diderot spent the next 13 years working on it secretly, writing hundreds of articles with little assistance from anyone else.

Although the first version might be appropriate for young children, an adult reader would find it insulting. The writer assumes a lack of familiarity not only with Diderot, but also with common ideas such as what it means to be a Frenchman and what an encyclopedia is. The second version assumes that the reader understands basic concepts like philosophy and can recognize the relationship between Diderot's *Encyclopédie* and the modern encyclopedia.

How much information you give your reader and how you present it are determined by such factors as the reader's level of understanding, the way the information will be used, and how great the reader's desire is to learn. With novice readers, we must begin on a basic level but show respect for their ability to understand.

EXERCISE 5.1 **Describing a Task for a Novice Reader**

Write directions suitable for a novice that explain how to perform an ordinary task. You might explain how to catch a bus, mail a letter, make coffee, or use an automatic bank teller. Assume your reader has never done the task before.

Level Two: The Generalist Reader

Most writing is aimed at a generalist audience. The generalist has some background in the subject matter but doesn't work with it on a day-to-day basis. In the area of music, a generalist would have some familiarity with major composers—would know, for instance, Beethoven from Bach—and probably would understand terms such as *symphony, fugue, movement,* and *crescendo.* The generalist would be less likely to know the work of J. S. Bach's sons or to know the name of the conductor of the Cleveland Orchestra.

The generalist often reads with keen interest. Few people can pursue a career in all the areas that intrigue them. But often our love for our avocations is as strong as for our vocations. Texaco used to air commercials of a cowboy with a radio strapped to his saddle, singing along with the opera broadcast in the middle of the prairie. The image may seem incongruous, but many of us have learned to enjoy areas of interest outside our immediate work responsibilities. We buy magazines like *Sports Illustrated, Architectural Digest, Field and Stream, Country Living,* and *Motor Trend* because we want mentally to vacation from our life's work.

We also read material that is relevant to our work, but which still lies outside our main area of expertise. Even professionals in one field often have difficulty understanding the language and methods of those in a different field. This is particularly true of those working in scientific fields. Although we may think of chemists, biologists, physicists, astronomers, and other scientists as communicating easily with one another, an entomologist (specializing in the study of insects) may find articles written by organic chemists nearly unintelligible, even though the findings of those chemists have a significant impact on entomology. For instance, the entomologist will be very interested in new pesticides that are being developed by chemists. In writing for the entomologist, however, the chemist must use a generalist approach, translating technical terms into ordinary language. In an increasingly specialized world, the ability to communicate technical information to a generalist audience is highly prized.

EXERCISE 5.2 **Writing for a Generalist Audience**

The following passage was taken from an article on bats written for the *New Yorker* by Diane Ackerman. Most readers of the *New Yorker* would not have any specialized knowledge of bats. How does Ackerman make the phenomenon of "echo-location" understandable to a general audience?

> It's not hard to understand echo-location if you picture bats as calling or whistling to their prey with high-frequency sounds. Most of us can't hear these. At our youngest and keenest of ear, we might detect sounds of twenty thousand vibrations a second, but bats can vocalize at up to two hundred thousand. They do it not in a steady stream but at intervals—twenty or thirty times a second. A bat listens for the sounds to return to it, and when the echoes start coming faster and louder it knows that the insect it's stalking has flown nearer. By judging the time between echoes, a bat can tell how fast the prey is moving and in which direction. Some

bats are sensitive enough to register a beetle walking on sand, and some can detect the movement of a moth flexing its wings as it sits on a leaf.

One of the most important generalist audiences is the supervisor. Managers constantly make decisions based on the information they receive from their employees. They are seldom interested in detailed accounts of how processes work; they want to know the "bottom line": what will it cost? how quickly can it be done? what will be the results? Writing effectively for a supervisor who is only generally acquainted with your work can be some of the most critical writing in your career. Which of these two reports do you think an executive decision-maker would be most likely to understand and approve?

1. To facilitate the transfer of information between our West Coast and Midwest offices, I recommend that we purchase Quick Link II communications software and begin to send our communications over a modem rather than by our present methodology of facsimile machines. Quick Link allows the user to emulate a teletype (TTY), a DEC VT102, VT100, or VT52 terminal. Allowable data bit options are 5, 6, 7, or 8; parity may be odd, even, or none; and stop bit allowable settings are 1, 1.5, and 2. Special VT102/VT100 considerations are given if the user is currently operating in the proper emulation modes. Macro keys can cause a user-defined literal string to be transmitted or can be used to launch a script file. Clearstring, CLS, Echo, and RSTCTS statements are supported by the software. Given the estimated time which we now spend with our current facsimile interfacing, our company may realistically expect to increase the speed of our transmissions of information by at least three quarters.

2. Transmitting information between our West Coast and Midwest offices by our current fax machines is causing costly delays and expensive telephone bills. Just last week we lost an important client because our competitor, Innovative Communication Consultants, found supplies for her company in three days, whereas previously, due to our communication delays, we had taken five. If we switch to the use of a modem and a program such as Quick Link II, we will retain our customer base and also increase the pace of internal communications. Quick Link can communicate with almost any other type of computer terminal and uses standard communication software settings. To expedite the transfer of information, Quick Link's "macro keys" can be programmed so that the touch of one key can literally replace up to 30 keystrokes. Many of the most common settings and functions can be completely automated through these macros, saving our employees much time spent in keying in repetitive information. All in all, the use of a modem and Quick Link II should increase the speed of our communications by at least 75%.

Writing for a generalist audience always means making some assumptions about what is, indeed, general knowledge. If we have been performing a particular task for a long time, we may forget how many detailed steps are involved. For instance, if you have been using a computer for a while, you may forget to explain all the steps required to start an application. You may use words like *RAM* and *boot up* that are mystifying to someone without computer experience. In writing for a generalist audience, consider testing your explanation on real readers to see how well they understand the process you are describing.

EXERCISE 5.3 **Writing Directions for a Novice and a Generalist**

Write two sets of directions to your house or apartment: one set for a novice (someone who lives outside your community) and the other for a generalist (someone who knows the town, but not the streets in your neighborhood). Read your directions to your Discovery Group. Discuss the ways the two sets of directions differ.

Level Three: The Specialist Reader

Writing for the specialist presents a different set of challenges. You probably know your readers well. They are people with similar background and training to your own and with shared interests. They know the jargon of the field. They are "insiders." The challenge in writing for the specialist audience is that you must have something new to offer. You may be writing about new technological innovations, new approaches to using information, or new theories about how something works, but you must convince your reader that you have something worthwhile to add to the discussion. For instance, photographers would not want to read a basic explanation of how to set a camera's aperture and shutter speed. However, if someone invents an improvement on the single lens reflex camera, photographers will be eager to learn the advantages and disadvantages of the new system.

Most specialist writing involves research. Researchers are constantly developing and testing hypotheses. A hypothesis is simply a statement that can be tested and verified. "Milk is loaded with calcium" is a hypothesis. You can conduct a laboratory test to demonstrate its truth. "High voltage power lines create electromagnetic fields that endanger human health" is a hypothesis, and one that is being tested as this book is being written. Although we associate research with test tubes and microscopes, much research takes the form of systematic observations. For years, educators feared that permitting young children to write words that they could not spell would lead to habitual spelling errors. Recent research has shown that children who use "invented spelling" in the early grades will have no more spelling problems than children who are forced to correct every spelling error. Obviously, such research involved collecting papers from children in classes using invented spelling and from those in traditional classes over several years, counting the misspellings in each group, and tabulating the results. In this chapter, we consider the kind of research needed for a brief informative paper for a generalist or specialist audience, and in chapter 8 we will look at more involved research processes.

EXERCISE 5.4 Novice, Generalist, or Specialist?

See how many of these questions you can answer about Mexican culture and history:

1. What is the meaning of the word *Mexico?*
2. What is the difference between a *muchacho* and a *muchacha?*
3. What is celebrated at a *quiencenara?*
4. In what are *tamales* traditionally wrapped?
5. What is the Mexican seasonal greeting that is analogous to the English "Merry Christmas"?
6. What group of people built the pyramids and temples in Southern Mexico?
7. What is the English translation of *Playa del Sol?*
8. What political party is now in power in Mexico?
9. Who was the Spaniard who conquered Mexico City?
10. Who wrote *Laberinto de la Soledad?*

Now see how much you know about television programming:

1. Who played Jed Clampitt on *The Beverly Hillbillies?*
2. Who turns the letters on *Wheel of Fortune?*
3. What is the name of the captain of the Starship Enterprise on the original *Star Trek?*
4. What was the last name of the couple who were friends of Ricky and Lucy Ricardo on the original *I Love Lucy?*
5. Who was the long-time host of *Masterpiece Theatre* on PBS?
6. What Atlanta television mogul first began "colorizing" classic movies?
7. What is the name of a Boston tavern that became the title of a popular television series?
8. What couple on *General Hospital* was married during Elizabeth Taylor's guest appearance?
9. Jack Benny's television character was known for what personality trait?
10. What was Carol Burnett's signoff?

Rate yourself: If you know fewer than six of the answers, consider yourself a novice. If you correctly answered between six and eight of the questions, you qualify as a generalist. If you missed one or less, you qualify as a specialist in this field.

EXERCISE 5.5   **Writing for Different Audiences**

The following three passages, all written by biologist Frank A. Brown, contain the same basic information. Brown has studied what is popularly known as the "biological clock." We know that people often wake up at about the same time every day. Similarly, plants and animals often perform certain functions without any external cues. Brown recognizes that the information he has accumulated will need to be presented in different ways depending on the needs of the audience. Read the three passages and then try to figure out where each passage was originally published.

1.   Recent studies have provided reasons to postulate that the primary timer for long-cycle biological rhythms that are closely similar in period to the natural geophysical ones and that persist in so-called constant conditions is, in fact, one of organismic response to subtle geophysical fluctuations which pervade ordinary constant conditions in the laboratory (Brown, 1959, 1960). In such constant laboratory conditions a wide variety of organisms have been demonstrated to display, nearly equally conspicuously, metabolic periodicities of both solar-day and lunar-day frequencies, with their interference derivative, the 29.5-day synodic month, and in some instances, even the year.

2.   One of the greatest riddles of the universe is the uncanny ability of living things to carry out their normal activities with clocklike precision at a particular time of the day, month, and year. Why do oysters plucked from a Connecticut bay and shipped to a Midwest laboratory continue to time their lives to ocean tides 800 miles away? How do potatoes in hermetically sealed containers predict atmospheric pressure trends two days in advance? What effect do the lunar and solar rhythms have on the life habits of man? Living things clearly possess powerful adaptive capacities — but the explanation of whatever strange and permeative forces are concerned continues to challenge science. Let us consider the phenomena more closely.

3.   Familiar to all are the rhythmic changes in innumerable processes of animals and plants in nature. Examples of phenomena geared to the 24-hour solar day produced by rotation of the earth relative to the sun are sleep movements of plant leaves and petals, spontaneous activity in numerous animals, emergence of flies from their pupal cases, color changes of the skin of crabs, and wakefulness in man. Sample patterns of daily fluctuations, each interpretable as adaptive for the species, are illustrated in Fig. 1. Rhythmic phenomena linked to the 24-hour and 50-minute lunar-day period of rotation of the earth relative to the moon are most conspicuous among intertidal organisms.

Activity   Each of these passages was published in a different periodical. The following descriptions should help you identify where each passage was originally published.

Periodical	Audience	Characteristics
Saturday Evening Post	Novice	Focuses on human interest; uses an attention-getting introduction; is written in ordinary language
Science	Generalist	Treats issues of interest to the whole scientific community; focuses on the interpretation of scientific phenomena rather than research pro-

cedure; assumes an understanding of some
basic scientific principles

Physiological Zoology	Specialist	Presents current research in zoology; uses specialized and abstract language; presents sophisticated ideas in long and complex sentences; provides references to the work of other scholars

1.   Which periodical published the first passage? the second? the third?

2.   What clues did you find that helped you identify the original audience?

ACADEMIC WRITING

Much of the writing you do in college will be of an informative nature. You will take notes from lectures, write answers to essay questions, complete book reports, and do research projects. At times you may feel overwhelmed by all the writing you have to do. However, writing about a subject is one of the best ways to solidify your understanding of it. You will not only remember more about your subject, but you will also have a better grasp of the "big picture" than if you studied every item of information in isolation from the rest. Different types of informative writing will require different strategies for success. As you read the following pages, try to think how you might apply these skills in the classes you are currently taking.

Notetaking

We take notes for many reasons: to keep ourselves alert during a lecture or a presentation, to keep a record of the information for later review, to keep ourselves reminded of questions we may wish to raise at the appropriate time. Three principles should guide our notetaking strategy:

1.   Be selective.

Don't try to be a court reporter when you take notes. Trying to record everything your speaker says will keep you from understanding the really important points. Frequently, a speaker will include numerous examples and illustrations to clarify ideas and to keep the speech interesting. However, your notes should focus on the main points and conclusions instead of on the examples and illustrations.

2.   Be precise.

Although you should put the speaker's ideas into your own words, be sure you don't distort the information in the process. Saying the United States pursued a policy of "mutually assured destruction" during the Cold War is not the same thing as saying our country pursued a policy that "virtually assured destruction." Especially as time goes by, your notes will be more difficult to understand. On crucial points be sure to express the idea as precisely as possible.

3. Be critical.

    If your only purpose in coming to class is to record what the teacher says, you can be replaced by a tape recorder. As you listen, mentally test the ideas you are hearing against your own prior knowledge and experience. What are the speaker's assumptions? What are the possible implications of the points being made? Be wary of generalizations. If someone says, "All life is sacred," we may be inclined to agree. Does this mean that we should never harm rattlesnakes, cockroaches, fleas? Is vegetable life included as well? Of course, it's not generally appropriate to interrupt a speaker when you have such a question, but you may get an opportunity to speak up during a discussion period, and you'll be ready. It should be mentioned, however, that being critical is not an excuse for being rude. Raise questions out of a genuine sense of inquiry, not as a way of being antagonistic or of bringing attention to yourself.

Good notes can be an extremely valuable resource. Frequently, ideas are communicated orally long before they are printed. Your notes may represent the "state of the art" on the subject under discussion.

Essay Questions

The tests you take in college usually fall into two categories. Objective questions test your recall of specific names, dates, events, theories, and so on. Essay questions ask you to use such knowledge to identify causes, explain effects, predict trends, find implications, or perform other kinds of analysis. Some students are intimidated by essay questions because they seem too subjective. Other students relish essay questions because they think they can slide by with an inadequate knowledge of the subject if they write well. Both of these views are mistaken. Although essay questions are more open ended than objective questions, your instructor will expect you to demonstrate your knowledge of the subject as you write and to build a convincing argument for your view. Most instructors are quick to spot a "snow job." On the other hand, an essay exam does not force you to accept language that may not be clear to you (as might be the case on a multiple-choice exam). Because the essay format allows you to explain your position thoroughly, it is probably the most "objective" examination.

Many students score poorly on essay examinations because they do not answer the question being asked. Read the question below and think about what you would be required to do in order to provide an adequate answer.

After World War II, the United States often played the role of "policeman of the world." U.S. troops were frequently called on to intervene in Third World

countries. In the post–Vietnam War era, the United States has been more reluctant to commit troops abroad and has relied more on diplomatic efforts to influence foreign policy. Compare the U.S. role in two international crises — one before and one after the Vietnam War. What differences do you see in U.S. foreign policy during these two crises? Did the Persian Gulf War signal a return of the United States to a more militaristic foreign policy?

As this example indicates, essay questions are often complex, providing a context for the questions and suggesting specific lines of development. To answer this question successfully you must:

Describe the U.S. role in an international crisis that occurred between 1945 and 1965 (when the Vietnam War began to escalate).

Describe the U.S. role in an international crisis between 1975 and 1991 (end of the Vietnam War to the Persian Gulf War).

Compare the way the United States approached each of these crises.

Consider the effect of the Persian Gulf War on U.S. foreign policy.

If you discuss only one international crisis, you can expect a low grade, even though your analysis of that event is brilliant. If you discuss two crises — for instance, the Korean War and the Iran hostage crisis — but fail to make comparisons in diplomatic approaches, your grade will also suffer. And if you make a penetrating comparison of these two crises, but fail to discuss the impact of the Persian Gulf War, again, you can expect less-than-satisfactory results. The message here is that you must read the question carefully and organize your answer using the structure suggested by the essay question.

EXERCISE 5.6 Responding to an Essay Question

Read the following essay question, which might appear on an exam in a nursing class, and the opening paragraphs of three student answers to it. Meet with your Discovery Group to discuss which student seems to be taking the correct approach to answering the question.

Essay Question

In this class, we have examined changes changes over the past 40 years in birthing and prenatal care. In this essay, discuss society's changing expectations of expectant mothers. Consider the following questions in your writing: (1) How has public discussion of pregnancy changed? (2) What has been the changing role of the father in the birthing experience over the past 40 years? (3) How has medical aid to the pregnant woman, such as the administration of anesthetics, changed? Make sure that your essay discusses the subject from a historical perspective, examining changes since the early 1950s.

1. Pregnancy isn't anything like it used to be. People's ideas about pregnancy have totally changed. People used to think pregnancy was something bad, but that isn't necessarily true any more. I think most depend upon pregnancy from their parents. If their parents didn't think pregnancy was good, they probably won't either. The father's attitude during pregnancy can be particularly important to . . .

2. Throughout pregnancy the childbearer must follow appropriate procedures in order to avoid unwanted complications. If the childbearer does not ingest the proper nutrients, the fetal mass will, in all probability, suffer negative consequences. The fetal mass is constantly at risk from viruses, radiological factors, pharmaceuticals, and other teratogens that could result in congenital malformations such as . . .

3. Although we count our ages from our day of birth, much of our development as human beings can be traced to the nine months prior to actual birth. In the 50s pregnancy was treated almost as an illness. Even the word "pregnant" was considered virtually obscene; people said a woman was "P.G." or "in a family way." She was frequently exhorted to "take it easy" because most people believed that any kind of strenuous activity might harm the baby. In the final months women were often confined to the home. Similarly, labor and delivery were also guarded from the public view. Even the father of the child was sent off to the waiting room during childbirth. And since the mother was commonly anesthetized during labor, this left only the hospital staff to greet the newborn. However, methods of prenatal care and birthing changed dramatically in the eighties . . .

Book Reports

Another frequently required form of academic writing is the book report. Often your instructor will give you specific guidelines for what to include in the report. Be sure to identify clearly the name of the book and its author and other publication information. In reporting on a nonfiction book, you usually will be asked to summarize the book's contents. (Reporting on fiction presents special demands, which we will discuss in chapter 6.) If it is a long report, you may do this on a chapter-by-chapter basis. In a short report, you will have to talk about the book as a whole or major sections of it. In some cases, you will be asked to conclude with a brief evaluation of the book's worth and quality. You probably will want to comment on the author's knowledge of the field and how successful the book is in accomplishing the purpose for which it was written.

There is always a temptation to write a book report without carefully reading the book. Of course, such an approach short-circuits the purpose of the assignment, which is to give you in-depth knowledge in one area of the subject. Furthermore, you are likely to be graded down if your report sounds as though it could have been written after reading the book jacket and scanning the table of contents.

EXERCISE 5.7 **Evaluating a Book Report**

Read the book report assignment below, and evaluate the report by Shanique that follows it. Meet with your Discovery Group to discuss how well she has followed the assignment guidelines.

Assignment

After reading Jonathan Kozol's *Illiterate America*, discuss the causes of illiteracy in America and the remedy that Kozol recommends.

Shanique's Book Report

Illiterate America by Jonathan Kozol (Garden City, NY: Doubleday, 1985)

Kozol presents some truly amazing statistics in his book: one-third of our nation's population is functionally illiterate, a large percentage of our high school graduates lack sufficient skills in reading, and our nation is continually falling behind other countries in literacy levels. And from all the predictions we hear, the problem is bad and getting worse. Perhaps no other problem except drug abuse has received so much national attention as the "literacy crisis."

One of the main reasons we are hearing so much about this subject is the publication in 1985 of Jonathan Kozol's book, *Illiterate America*. Of all the books published during the 1980s, perhaps no other book got so many Americans up in arms as this one.

One reason Kozol's book is so effective is that he doesn't take his subject lightly. As he states in his introduction, "My feelings on this subject are too strong to be contained within an understated work" (xvii). Kozol's book is anything but understated. From the first chapter, where the author piles statistic upon statistic to make clear the seriousness of the problem, to the last chapter, where he sets out worst-case and best-case scenarios, Kozol's writing appeals to the audience's emotions, especially to their feelings for the underprivileged.

However, there are times where Kozol's sympathy for underprivileged people leads him viciously to attack politicians in a way that seems to do little good. To Kozol, the literacy problem is a political problem. He seems to believe that if we had better leaders (defined here as leaders who agree with Kozol) we would have no illiterates in society. In fact, Kozol goes so far as to accuse politicians of deliberately causing and maintaining the literacy crisis: "Illiteracy in any land as well-informed and wealthy as the U.S.A. in 1985 is not an error. It is not an accident. There is no way that it could be an accident or error" (89). He goes on to tell us that we should question politicians when they tell us that they want Americans to read. Kozol doesn't seem to think that innovations in technology will be much help either. Only "humanists" can solve the literacy problem in Kozol's mind. Because Kozol seems so "anti" everybody who doesn't see things his way, many readers may be turned off by his arguments.

Even though the bias in *Illiterate America* is sometimes irritating, Jonathan Kozol's 5 work is easy to read. I especially enjoyed the stories Kozol put in about people who had failed to learn to read in school. Though some people might condemn Kozol for getting a little out of hand in his politics, it is nice to read something where the author really knows what he believes. I think *Illiterate America* is one of the most important books of the 1980s, a book which got everybody's attention about one of the most important social problems in our country.

Using Quotations

Often you will be asked to use quotations as you prepare academic reports. Notice how the quotations in the book report in exercise 5.7 add interest and depth to the student report. Here are some of the main reasons you will need to use quotations in your papers:

1. When the source's authority is needed

    We often use quotations to establish the authority behind our conclusions. When we quote statements made by politicians, business leaders, media analysts, and other experts, we are demonstrating the reliability of our information. Particularly on controversial or highly contested subjects, a quotation may be crucial in making your point. Although a paraphrase is fine when you are presenting routine information, the exact words of your source are the most convincing demonstration of proof you can present. If you want to make the point that a president's environmental policies have been under attack, you might want to quote one of his critics. For instance, when former President Bush went to the Grand Canyon to tout the success of his antipollution program, Al Gore remarked, "Anyone who sees George Bush as the 'environmental president' at the Grand Canyon ought to look closely for Elvis, alive and well, rafting by on the Colorado River."

2. When the precise wording is important

    We sometimes quote because we believe that a paraphrase would distort the subtle shades of meaning found in the original. For instance, dictionary definitions are often quoted because the exact wording is important in establishing the meaning of the word. We also would be likely to quote technical procedures, legal documents, government regulations, and other complex statements, especially those concerning the law.

The exact wording of such legislative documents is so important that your entire paper may hinge upon a quotation. You may remember the furor aroused by the wording of the proposed Equal Rights Amendment, which stated that "equality of rights under the law shall not be denied or abridged by the United States or by any state on account of sex." While proponents of the amendment argued that the wording would guarantee women rights not specifically granted in the Fourteenth Amendment, opponents countered by stating that women would lose current benefits in areas such as working conditions, alimony, and child support. In fact, several revisions to the amendment were proposed, such as the following:

Neither the United States nor any state shall make any legal distinction between the rights and responsibilities of male and female persons unless such distinction is based on physiological or functional differences between them.

Equality of rights under the law shall not be denied or abridged by the United States or by any state on account of sex. The provisions of this article shall not impair the validity, however, of any laws of the United States or any state which exempt women from compulsory military service, or from service in combat units of the armed forces; or extend protections or exemptions to wives, mothers or widows; or impose upon fathers responsibility for the support of children; or secure privacy to men or women, or boys or girls; or make punishable as crimes rape, seduction or other sexual offenses.

In writing a paper concerning the history of the Equal Rights Amendment (or any other legislation, for that matter), you certainly would want to quote the wording of the document with which you are dealing.

3. When the original wording provides dramatic emphasis

Some statements are worth quoting because they add freshness and originality to your writing. These could be proverbial statements ("Less is more."), literary quotations (Shakespeare: "There is more in heaven and earth, Horatio / Than are dreamt of in your philosophy."), or other well-turned phrases (Jesse Jackson: "What does it matter if we have a new book or an old book, if we open neither?"). In your reading, always be alert for vivid quotations that will enliven your writing.

Although there are many reasons to include quotations in your writing, be selective in what you choose to quote. Quotations can interrupt the flow of your writing and make reading your paper more difficult. Too many quotations in a paper are somewhat like a roomful of people all talking at once — it's hard to follow any single conversation. Generally, you should keep your quotations short. Notice how Shanique introduces a quotation carefully and then uses it to make a point:

One reason Kozol's book is so effective is that he doesn't take his subject lightly. As he states in his introduction, "My feelings on this subject are too strong to be contained within an understated work" (xvii). Kozol's book is anything but understated.

By using quotations selectively and keeping them short, you can help the reader stay focused on your main ideas.

EXERCISE 5.8 When to Use Quotation and Paraphrase

Read the following essay, written by Barbara Ehrenreich and published in *Time* (October 15, 1990). In your Discovery Groups, discuss which statements might be quoted and which might be paraphrased in a report on U.S. involvement in the Middle East. For those you would quote, explain which of the preceding reasons would justify the need for a word-for-word quotation.

The Warrior Culture

In what we like to think of as "primitive" warrior cultures, the passage to manhood   1
requires the blooding of a spear, the taking of a scalp or head. Among the Masai of eastern Africa, the North American Plains Indians and dozens of other pretechnological peoples, a man could not marry until he had demonstrated his capacity to kill in battle. Leadership too in a warrior culture is typically contingent on military prowess and wrapped in the mystique of death. . . .

All warrior peoples have fought for the same high-sounding reasons: honor, glory or revenge. The nature of their real and perhaps not conscious motivations is a subject of much debate. Some anthropologists postulate a murderous instinct, almost unique among living species, in human males. Others discern a materialistic motive behind every fray: a need for slaves, grazing land or even human flesh to eat. Still others point to the similarities between war and other male pastimes—the hunt and outdoor sports—and suggest that it is boredom, ultimately, that stirs men to fight.

But in a warrior culture it hardly matters which motive is most basic. Aggressive behavior is rewarded whether or not it is innate to the human psyche. . . . And war, to a warrior people, is of course the highest adventure, the surest antidote to malaise, the endlessly repeated theme of legend, song, religious myth and personal quest for meaning. It is how men die and what they find to live for. . . .

More tellingly, we are unnerved by peace and seem to find it boring. When the cold war ended, we found no reason to celebrate. Instead we heated up the "war on drugs." What should have been a public-health campaign, focused on the persistent shame of poverty, became a new occasion for martial rhetoric and muscle flexing. . . .

Now, with Operation Desert Shield, our leaders are reduced to begging foreign powers   5
for the means to support our warrior class. It does not seem to occur to us that the other great northern powers—Japan, Germany, the Soviet Union—might not have found the stakes so high or the crisis quite so threatening. It has not penetrated our imagination that in a world where the powerful, industrialized nation-states are at last at peace, there might be other ways to face down a pint-size Third World warrior state than with massive force of arms. Nor have we begun to see what an anachronism we are in danger of becoming: a warrior nation in a world that pines for peace, a high-tech state with the values of a warrior band.

WRITING ASSIGNMENT A Recent Innovation

Think of a recent innovation in your field of study, in your workplace, in education, or in daily life. (You might consult some recent magazines in your field of interest for ideas.) Follow these steps as you complete the assignment:

Step one   Take a knowledge inventory as you begin your search. What do you already know? What do you need to know?

Step two   Locate a book or an article on your subject and take notes to use in your report. If you don't already have a book or magazine that would be helpful, read up on your subject at your local library.

Step three   Think about an appropriate audience for this information and write a discovery draft with that audience in mind. What would this audience already know about the subject? What will they need to know? What ideas might be new and unfamiliar to them? What terms will need definition and explanation? How can the information be most usefully organized? Keep in mind that your audience is probably different from that of the author who wrote your book or article.

Step four   Make copies of your draft for your Discovery Group. Ask the group to respond to these questions:

1.   Is the information presented clearly?

2.   Is the information presented in a way appropriate for the audience? Does the writer talk down to the audience? Could the information be made more interesting?

3.   Is additional information or explanation needed?

4.   Are quotations used appropriately?

Step five   Revise your paper in light of the suggestions made by your group. Be sure to indicate clearly your source(s) of information. Submit a final draft that has been carefully edited. You may also be required to submit your notes and earlier drafts of your paper.

PROFESSIONAL WRITING

The writing you do in school is excellent preparation for the demands of writing on the job. In your work, you will often need to gather information from various sources for memos and reports. The ability to work independently to define a task, to collect appropriate data, and to organize information effectively is one of the hallmarks of a professional.

Résumés

One of the first documents you will prepare in seeking employment is a résumé. The résumé summarizes your education, work experience, and job qualifications. In a very real sense, it represents you to prospective employers. You should prepare the résumé carefully in order to give yourself the best possible representation.

Although there are many ways to organize a résumé, because the purpose of the résumé is to explain your qualifications to an employer, it should be organized so that it highlights your unique talents. For instance, if you have a strong G.P.A., make sure this stands out on your résumé. If you have won recognition for campus leadership, place this information near the top of your résumé. If your work experience is stronger than your educational background, it is perfectly acceptable to begin with your work experience and then give your educational background. In other words, you need to plan the résumé strategically to put your skills in the best light.

Here are some general principles that will make your résumé easy to read and attractive to an employer:

1. Make sure headings stand out.

   Résumés are read quickly. You want to make sure that the employer can find information at a glance.

2. Use white space to increase readability.

   A crowded résumé discourages the reader. It is better to have a longer résumé than to crowd too much onto a page. Better yet, be more selective about what you include.

3. Use reverse chronological order.

   Employers are naturally more interested in your last school or your last job than one that you had six years ago. Begin with the most recent event and work backward.

4. Provide explanations when necessary.

   Don't assume that your employer knows that Sigma Tau Delta is an English honor society and not a fraternal organization. Don't simply give the names of your former employers. Give your job title and briefly describe your duties.

5. Personal information is not required.

   You do not need to provide your employer with information about your age, race, physical characteristics, marital status, parental responsibilities, or any other information that is not directly relevant to your job qualifications. Most employers will not raise these issues, knowing that such information can be discriminatory.

6. Proofread your résumé carefully.

   A typographical error or a misspelling may suggest to an employer that you are careless about your work. Before printing your résumé, be sure to proofread carefully to eliminate errors and to verify all the information.

EXERCISE 5.9 Evaluating a Résumé

Read the résumé on the facing page. In your Discovery Groups, discuss the strengths and weaknesses of this résumé.

ANTHONY MARQUIZ

8986 Ridgepoint Boulevard
Alleby, NH 13092
Home Phone: (603) 276-0349
Job Objective: To find fulfilling job in which I can further my skills

Education

Sapulpa Junior High	Principal: Harold Peck
Melanta, Vermont	Graduated: 1985
(802) 313-4763	Studied English, Math, etc.

Received Best Center on Football Team award in 1985.

Rosemont High School	Principal: Roberta Wright
Seneca, MA	Graduated: 1989
(413) 847-0827	Took college-track courses

Honored for athletic and academic endeavors as sophomore in 1987.

Acalde Community College	President: Dr. Owen
Laner, NH	Currently enrolled
(603) 897-9675	Attending 5 courses a week

Have completed the following courses: HIS 312, HIS 313, NUR 346, BUS 219, ACC
113, MAT 222, MAT 311, REA 266, NUR 117.
Current G.P.A.: 2.3

Employment

Belford Herald Times	Supervisor: Jody Massey
Belford, Vermont	Began: June 1, 1982
(802) 417-0926	Terminated: August 19, 1983

Delivered newspaper on bicycle. Route covered approximately 6 miles.

Sammy's Auto Parts and Repair	Owner: Sammy Stallings
Seneca, MA	Began: Sept. 1, 1988
(413) 847-9274	Terminated: Dec. 16, 1988

Stocked parts for GM, Ford, and Chrysler vehicles, inspected cars and trucks for emission
standards, changed batteries and alternators, assisted in minor automotive engine repair.

Hotshot Pizza House	Supervisor: Tommy Denman
Laner, NH	Worked summers, 1991 & 1992.
(603) 927-8763	Plan to work again summer of 1993.

Delivered pizzas hot to residential customers, business customers, and students. Prepared
ingredients, cooked, and served pizzas and pasta within the restaurant. Operated cash
register. Cleaned restaurant at night after closing.

Personal

Am of presentable appearance. 5' 9", 163 lbs., dishwater blond hair, hazel eyes. Enjoy (1)
golfing after work and on weekends, (2) time spent with friends, and (3) dating. Marriage
in imminent future.

The physical appearance of your résumé is probably more important than that of any other document you will ever produce. If you do not have access to a high-quality typewriter or computer printer, you should have the résumé prepared professionally. Have it duplicated on résumé paper (24-pound stock), not ordinary typing paper. The duplicated copies of the résumé should be free of smudges and shadows. Don't try to make your résumé stand out by gimmicks, such as unusual typefaces, colored inks, or extra large headings. The résumé should mark you as a professional in every way.

`WRITING ASSIGNMENT` Résumé

Use the guiding questions that follow to help you design your own résumé.

Step one   Begin by assessing your qualifications:

What is my educational background?
  schools attended
  fields of study
  grade point average
  special training or certification

What work experience have I had?
  previous employers
  job titles
  duties/responsibilities

What honors or awards have I received?
  leadership awards
  academic awards
  service awards
  membership in academic or professional organizations
  other indications of merit

What are some of my hobbies or special interests?
  recreational activities
  volunteer work
  membership in social organizations

What people would be good references for me?

Step two   Assess your prospective employers:

What kind of work would I like to have?

Which of my qualifications would be most appealing to my employer?

How can I highlight these qualifications in my résumé?

Step three   Prepare a preliminary draft of your résumé, and show it to your Discovery Group. Use their comments to prepare a final draft for your teacher.

Correspondence

Business communications often take the form of a letter. We write letters to inquire about products or services, to respond to complaints or claims, to explain company policies, and for a thousand other reasons. Whatever career you plan on pursuing, whatever job goal you might have, the skill of writing good business letters is one that will never become outdated. Bank presidents, teachers, auto mechanics, electricians, salespeople, nurses, electricians, lawyers — whatever the occupation, whatever the training, our lives involve reading and writing business letters.

The importance of being able to write clear, appropriate letters has steadily increased as our country has moved from an industrial-based to a service-based economy. Although it is still possible for a person with limited communication skills to get an entry-level position, the road to advancement is literally paved with paper. Any managerial or decision-making position requires the ability to communicate effectively through the written word.

Because of the importance of writing ability to job performance, more and more employers are requiring that applicants submit writing samples or take writing tests in order to qualify for jobs. The rising popularity of the personal computer has made business correspondence even more important to industries throughout the world. Just before the age of personal computers, it seemed as though the telephone was replacing some business correspondence — but even then written documentation of business conversations, negotiations, and agreements was still essential. Now electronic mail (see "Byte-Size Bulletin," chapter 4) and fax machines have made possible the rapid transmission of written information. An understanding of the purpose and audience for business letters is even more essential now to your success in the business community than it might have been in the past.

There are at least three reasons for using letters as your means of communication within the business community:

A letter provides a permanent record of a transaction. This permanence is useful for future reference and, in some cases, for legal purposes.

A letter can be sent simultaneously to multiple parties. Doing this is generally easier than trying to contact several people by phone or arranging for a conference call.

A letter is generally superior for conveying complex information. Anyone who has tried to take down names, dates, prices, stock numbers, and so on over the telephone knows that this can be a time-consuming and tedious process, with a high risk of error.

Formatting a Business Letter   Format is an important feature of business letters. When writers use the term **format**, they are referring to the way a piece of writing appears on the page. The appearance of a business letter is an important part of the message.

Because everyone in the business world is very conscious of time, you need to make sure that your document is visually appealing and that the information is easy to read and understand. The following are the most crucial elements of the letter's format:

Margins

Leave at least an inch margin around your letter to create a "picture frame" effect.

Paragraph length

Keep paragraphs short, usually no more than three or four sentences.

Lists

Use lists, either numbered or bulleted, to organize important information.

Use of white space

Single-space the body of your letter, but double-space between paragraphs and the other elements of the letter (e.g., inside address, salutation, closing).

On the following pages, you will find examples of various formats for business letters, but all of them attempt to make the letter easy to read and visually appealing.

Personal computers have allowed writers much freedom when it comes to format. Today, writers can decide whether to italicize a word or put it in boldface. They can determine the size and face of their type. Just a short time ago, these features were considered only by the professional typesetter. But in this age of desktop publishing, writers themselves can decide on these features.

EXERCISE 5.10 **Letter Format**

Read the letter on the facing page. Evaluate the effectiveness of its format. Is there sufficient white space? Are margins adequate? Are paragraphs too long? too short? What is the effect of the quotations? of the postscript?

Accelerated-Education University
89762 Catalina Drive
Desert Hills, Arizona 32401
602/773-9483
Fax: 602/773-0973
Telex: 806043

"WITHOUT A DEGREE, YOU CAN NEVER HOPE TO REACH YOUR FULLEST PROFESSIONAL POTENTIAL."

Thus said a nationally known business leader at a recent televised conference. In fact, those persons with college degrees earn an average of 40% more than those who have never availed themselves of higher education.

At Accelerated-Education University, we take into consideration all of your personal background and education, either formal or informal, and calculate all of your accomplishments toward college-level, transferable hours so that you may complete your degree at our institution, or you may transfer the credits into any other college of your choice — and we do it all at a fraction of the cost (not to mention the work) of attending even the least expensive institution of higher learning. And if you choose to complete your education at AEU, you will be able to walk out with diploma in hand in just a few short weeks. Are you worried about time? Don't even think of it — we at AEU know how busy you are and, therefore, all of your study and schoolwork is done at your convenience.

Upon leaving our institution, you will have earned an Arizona State authorized bachelor's, master's, or doctorate degree* without the necessity of attending boring classes and listening to dull lectures:

> *"As an executive with a hectic schedule, I found it impossible to attend regular college classes. AEU offered me a way to circumvent the normal requirements of traditional colleges. I have been favorably impressed with how easy it is to obtain college credit, and I am happy to say that today I can proudly point to the diploma on my wall and call myself "doctor" at dinner parties. My degree has certainly given me a prestige I could have received no other way."*

> *Leland Johnson, Ph.D.*
> *Consolidated Industries*

> *"With my busy schedule, both professionally and socially, I thought it would be impossible for me to further my education. How wrong I was! The professional, caring staff of AEU taught me how easy it is to become an educated person in our society and how beneficial a diploma would be in raising my salary. The Accelerated-Education program allowed me to get my degree at my convenience, and I will ever be grateful to those who assisted me."*

> *Hester P. Robertson*
> *Personnel Manager*
> *Watusi, Ltd.*

As you can see from testimonials such as these from our graduates, the benefits of enrolling now are tremendous. In just weeks you, too, can proudly display your diploma, printed in 8 carat gold, above your desk.

If you could benefit from a degree but have just not known how to obtain one, look no further. AEU is your means of achieving all your career ambitions. Call now for a personal evaluation of your personal and professional achievements — or return the postage paid card today for our free catalog and informational brochure.

Sincerely,

Knox Hardcastle

Knox Hardcastle, Ph.D.
Dean

P.S. For an in-depth evaluation of the college hours for which you now qualify, call today the AEU hotline at 1-800-YOU-GRAD. Our counselors are available around the clock to assist you.

Accelerated-Education University is authorized to confer degrees by the Superintendent of Correspondence Instruction, EUIO, Office of Licensed Business and Trade Schools.

In some companies, all letters are prepared using a uniform format. In most places, however, you will choose a format that is suitable to your own situation. The format of a letter also includes the arrangement of the basic elements of the business letter. These elements include:

The **heading** (the writer's address if not included on the letterhead and the date)

The **inside address** (the address of the person receiving the letter)

The **salutation** (where the writer formally greets the reader)

The **body** (which conveys the information)

The **complimentary close** (where the writer "signs off")

The **signature** (where the writer verifies and takes responsibility for the information by signing the letter)

EXERCISE 5.11 **Elements of a Business Letter**

Compare the various letters included in this chapter. What typical elements of the business letter do they contain? How are these elements arranged on the page? What variations do you observe?

Writing Good-News and Bad-News Letters   Letters are usually classified as "good news" or "bad news" based on the probable reaction of the reader. Good news might be extending a job offer to an applicant or recognizing outstanding service to an organization. If the reader is likely to respond positively to your letter, you can begin immediately with the good news and follow with detailed information. Note how the writer of the following letter immediately begins with the good news and stresses the rewards that are coming to the reader.

Buford Farms, Inc.

Route 6, Box 237 / Dukeville, AR   84042

August 9, 1993

Mrs. Darlene Donald
338 Union Street
Butlersville, MN 78219

Dear Mrs. Donald:

Congratulations! Your slogan, "So fresh, it almost oinks," was selected as the Grand Prize winner in our contest. Buford Sausage is known for the freshness of its product, and we feel you captured this quality perfectly in your clever slogan.

As Grand Prize winners, you and one guest of your choice will spend three days and two nights at Hog Wallow Amusement Park. I am sure you will find this to be an unforgettable experience. You will also receive 300 pounds of delicious Buford Sausage.

Please contact Loretta Buford in our Customer Services Department (1-800-4BU-FORD) to make arrangements for your trip and to receive your sausages.

Sincerely,

Billy Bob Buford

Billy Bob Buford
Vice-President of Sales and Marketing

Although you expect good news to be received eagerly by your reader, you should still make clear the extent of the benefits being offered. If you are offering a job to someone, you should sell her or him on the advantages of working for your company. If you are recognizing someone who has given 20 years of service to an organization, you should sincerely praise that loyalty. If your letter seems to be written perfunctorily, you can strip away the significance of the award.

BYTE-SIZE BULLETIN: FORM LETTERS AND MAILING LISTS

When you frequently send a letter that contains the same information, you may need to develop a form letter. By using a word processor, you can make a form letter seem less impersonal. Most word processing software allows you to create a primary file containing the standard information of the letter, leaving codes for the personalized items, such as the lines in the inside address and the salutation, to be inserted when you merge a secondary file containing this information. The process of inserting the names and addresses into the letter is referred to as mail **merging**.

Using mail merge has several advantages over a customized letter:

You save time. Preparing individual letters is time-consuming. With mail merge you only type the name and address of the reader the first time you prepare the mailing list.

You save money. You're only out the costs of the paper and of bulk mailing one letter. If your reader responds positively, you've made a great return on your investment, and if negatively, you haven't lost much.

Because of the magnitude of correspondence some organizations have to send out, form letters are to some degree indispensable. However, there are dangers in form letters which you should keep in mind:

Because the same information is being disseminated to many addresses, your reader may tend to ignore your message the same way you ignore junk mail.

Many organizations do not personalize any information in their form letters, and the letters are therefore so general that the message is not pertinent to the readers.

Because it is much easier to send out form letters than individual letters, some organizations use them much too often, thereby making their audience callous to any communication coming from their offices.

As you can see from these warnings, almost all the dangers in form letters and mass mailings are due to the audience's negative reaction to impersonal communication. To alleviate the audience's perception of being addressed by a machine, some companies overcompensate by pulling certain lines from the secondary files and using them nauseatingly often in the letter's body. You probably have received a letter similar to this:

Mrs. Bisbody, don't you want to have your house at **3916 Iris Lane** be the envy of all your neighbors in **Albany, New York**? That is why we are offering to you, **Mrs. Bisbody**, our special garden package at the all-time low price of $19.95. Your home at **3916 Iris Lane** will be the garden spot of **Albany**.

The writer has simply taken out lines from the address file and merged them into the paragraph. And, apparently to call the reader's attention to how sincere he is, the author has even boldfaced the merged lines.

When used discreetly, the merging of secondary file lines into the body of the letter can be effective, but beware of overkill. Many people are repulsed by the false sense of familiarity created by such tactics. The best way to impress your readers, as always, is to demonstrate that you're aware of their needs and can offer a solution to their problems. And there are better ways to demonstrate this awareness than by repeating their names throughout a letter.

EXERCISE 5.12 **Evaluating Good-News Letters**

Read the following good-news letters, and discuss with your Discovery Group how successful the writers have been in achieving their intentions.

Letter 1: Induction into an Honorary Society

Ego Unlimited
3759 Hallowed Hills
Academe Hollow, WI 98770

September 30, 1993

Mr. Paul Landers
2874 Parkwood Estates
Washbank, WI 98264

It gives me great honor to announce your election as a new member of Ego Unlimited. You have shown great promise as a scholar and as a leader. Your scholastic record indicates your potential, and your leadership ability has been demonstrated repeatedly. I am sure that you will prove to be a valuable member of our select group.

Paul, Ego Unlimited stands for the best in scholastic endeavor. Your G.P.A. indicates that you soar far above your peers in areas of academic pursuits. Your admittance into our honorary society is, of course, contingent upon your continual drive toward educational excellence.

We are also confident that your qualities of leadership will continue to be manifest. As a leader of scholars, you must stand forth as a sterling beacon of pure light amongst the blighted darkness of ignorance (such as that so aptly exemplified by our President at the last Council meeting). As we at Ego Unlimited continue our assaults upon the depths of obdurate simpletonianism and, yes, upon even what might be called obtuse stupidity in the common people, we are enlisting your aid. Together, we fight ever onward as leaders of the light of the mind.

Paul, if you will accept the challenge, if you will join arms with our band, we glorious few who excel in the echelons of intellectual prowess, join us at 7:00 p.m., October 17, at Hallowed Hills. You will be inducted into Ego Unlimited, and you will become a soldier of the intellect in our crusade.

I. M. Vain

I. M. Vain, Ph.D., LL.D., MTV, etc.

Activity

1. Does the writer make clear the benefits of belonging to the organization? What appeal is being made?

2. How do you react to the language in this letter (e.g., "blighted darkness," "obdurate simpletonianism")? Is it possible that the language could have the opposite effect from what the writer intended?

Letter 2: Selection of the Woman of the Year

 Snipesville Chamber of Commerce

Snipesville, Iowa 89765

September 30, 1993

Susan Hapstead
2984 Meadowlark Circle
Snipesville, IA 89765

Dear Mrs. Hapstead:

As you may know, Snipesville has long had a Man of the Year award to recognize the outstanding person in our community. This year, John Dunleavy, President of Consolidated Industries and well-known civic leader, received the Man of the Year Award at our annual Chamber of Commerce banquet.

Last year certain people in the community pushed for an award to recognize the achievement of Snipesville women. We are all, of course, aware of the "little woman" behind the man, and we certainly feel it is time to recognize the achievement of women in our community. We all know the important role that women play in taking care of children, keeping house, and serving in ladies' auxiliary organizations.

I am sure you will be flattered to know, Susie, that our men picked you to receive the first "Woman of the Year" award. Your husband, Albert, has been extraordinarily successful in his realty business. Your son Bobby has been a standout on the Snipesville Snipers basketball team. And your daughter Trish does a great job cheering the boys on from the sidelines. We know much of their success can be attributed to a great mom and homemaker. And who could forget that cherry pie you brought to the Snipesville Charity Picnic and Rummage Sale last spring? You are a credit to your kind.

Please drop by the Snipesville Chamber of Commerce office and pick up your plaque at your convenience. My girl Betty will have it for you.

Sincerely,

Archibald Bunker

Archibald Bunker
Chairman

Activity

1. Does the writer make clear the importance of the award? What appeal is being made?

2. What offensive phrases do you detect in this letter?

The bad-news letter is generally more difficult to write. Bad news is usually conveyed in general terms, but you must be sure the reader understands the decision that has been made. When possible, begin the bad-news letter with a positive introduction (sometimes referred to as a **buffer**). Even if you are writing a collection letter or replying to a complaint, it is important to keep the tone of the bad-news letter as courteous as possible. Arousing your reader's hostility seldom advances your cause. Treating your employees and customers with respect not only is a sign of civility but also is just good business sense. If you vent your frustration on a supplier because of a late shipment, you may find that person less than sympathetic when you need a rush order. It is generally good advice not to "burn bridges behind you."

Read the following letter and notice how the writer has defused a potentially bad-news situation.

DenChew-Fix
where all your smiles come true
4519 Toothmark Drive
San Dentate, CA 29806

January 21, 1994

Allan Diddleman
2348 W. 37th Street
Vermouth, CA 97112

Dear Mr. Diddleman:

I was glad to read in your letter that you have been using DenChew-Fix denture adhesive for over 28 years. We are proud to have many loyal customers like yourself.

I forwarded your suggestion — to offer DenChew-Fix in various tropical flavors — to our Product Development Department. Although they feel that there might be some interest in flavored denture adhesives, they don't believe that a sufficient market exists at this time to make mass production feasible.

We value our customers' comments and suggestions, and encourage you to write to us again in the future.

Cordially yours,

Noreen Thomas

Noreen Tomas
Customer Representative

When we are having a conversation with our friends, we listen to *how* they are speaking as well as to what they are saying. If they speak quickly, we know that they are excited or angry. If they pause frequently, they may be indicating that the subject is painful for them to discuss. Similarly, we can infer a *tone* from written communications. When we read, we discern the writer's tone from the words that have been selected and the way they have been arranged. How would you describe the tone of the following statement?

> The Commander desires that the call last 20 minutes. Enjoy your visit, and if refreshments are offered, you may accept as you desire. When it is time to leave, make your excuses and depart. One might say, "Thank you, Col. and Mrs. _____, for your hospitality; we have enjoyed the visit and we must be leaving." You may be asked by the Commanding Officer not to hurry off, but to stay. Your reply at this time is "Thank you, but we must be going." Then go without lingering.

Most people would find this letter to be very impersonal. Although the occasion of the letter is a social visit, the intention is clearly to complete the obligatory visit with as little inconvenience to the commander as possible. The letter does not overtly say "I am doing this only because it is required," but that message is conveyed through the tone of the letter.

In revising your work, be sure that the tone of your writing matches your intentions. Particularly if you are writing in response to a sensitive situation, you may want to have someone who is not personally involved to read your letter for tone. An outside reader can frequently find problems with tone that aren't apparent to the writer. Frequently, you will need to change only a word that is too harsh or a phrase that makes you appear indecisive. But these small changes can make a tremendous difference in the reader's reaction.

EXERCISE 5.13 **Evaluating Buffer Statements**

Discuss the following buffer statements with your Discovery Group. Which would be most effective? Why?

1. You should not be disappointed by your last-place finish in the annual Bike-a-Thon. No one really expected you to finish the race at all.

2. We had over 750 applicants for the three travel scholarships that we offer to the International Trade Conference. Although we are unable to offer you a scholarship, we hope that you will be able to attend the conference. I have enclosed a complimentary ticket to the President's Reception to be held after the opening session on Thursday.

3. We received your application for County Engineer on November 30. Did you not know that the deadline was November 1? Besides, we couldn't make head-nor-tails of your résumé. Next time you submit an application somewhere, try to be halfway organized with your materials.

4. I am responding to the complaint you filed with us on October 19. We are, indeed, grateful that you have paid your bills regularly over the past 11 years. Unfortunately, we cannot dismiss the late charges for the bill in question because of your excellent payment record.

5. When I viewed your painting, "Phony Spumoni," I was immediately struck with your fresh new vision of the subject. I laughed; I cried; I searched my soul. I felt a hundred emotions welling up inside of me. In fact, I think you are on the verge of an artistic breakthrough of monumental proportions. You are crafting a vision of human experience that will live on, as Rembrandt and Picasso have lived on. But what are we to do? So many wonderful artists, and so little room in our gallery.

WRITING ASSIGNMENT **Addressing a Customer's Complaint**

Imagine that you are involved in one of the following bad-news situations. Try to address the customer's complaint as realistically as possible. You may need to invent some details in order to provide an explanation. You can even offer compensation if you feel it is justified, but be prepared to defend your actions to your supervisor.

1. The 800 Disaster
   You work for a long-distance telephone company. Recently, an equipment failure caused all of your toll-free 800 lines to go down for an entire day. You have received an angry letter from a television shopping channel that claims it lost $200,000 in business due to the loss of its 800 service. How will you respond?

2. A Melted Container
   You work for a major supplier of household plastic goods, such as bowls and storage containers. Your label promises that all of your merchandise is "dishwasher safe." You receive a letter from a customer stating that one of the containers you manufacture melted in the dishwasher. The container itself has been thrown away. Your company refund policy stipulates that the customer must provide evidence that the product was damaged. The customer is asking for a refund of $2.19, the original price of the container. How will you respond?

3. Fumes in the Neighborhood
   You work for a small company that recycles car batteries. An accident at your plant released some fumes into the neighborhood. Although the fumes caused some people's eyes to sting, public-health officials found no evidence of any long-term health hazard. One of the residents has written an angry letter asking for $10,000 in compensation and threatening legal action. How will you respond?

4. The 2-4-1 Special
   You have taken over the management of a restaurant. The former manager heavily advertised "2-4-1" on Tuesday; that is, two people could eat for the price of one. You have decided to discontinue this policy, which proved very unprofitable. An angry customer has written to you, demanding that you honor the "2-4-1" policy. How will you respond?

5. Smokeout Confusion
    You are the leader of the local chapter of the American Cancer Society. Each year you hold a fundraising drive in April called the "Smokeout." Another charity, called the American Cancer Fund, has decided to hold a "Smokeout" drive in March. You know that the public will be confused, and you question the motives of the other agency, which has refused to open its books to a consumer watchdog group. How will you respond?

THE CRITICAL MOMENT

Whenever you write a résumé or a letter, you are trying to present yourself in the best light possible. Some people believe that all writing should be plain, simple, and direct. Others think that writers should use their ability to win the best possible reception for what they have to say. Which of the following practices do you think are justifiable? Which are not?

1. Donna Plummer lost her job in 1983 when the company she worked for was bought out by a larger corporation. She spent over a year looking for a new job. Instead of leaving a gap on her résumé, she lists her work for this year as "Consultant." (Technically, this is true. She often consulted with associates who were still working for the company, but she was not paid for this work.)

2. Buddy Chuggers worked as a student assistant for Professor Rudyard, who had a federal grant to study the effectiveness of natural pesticides. Buddy's job was mainly copying and making deliveries, but he lists the job on his résumé as "Technical Assistant on $265,000 Rudyard Grant."

3. Daphne Beauchamp worked several summers hawking peanuts and popcorn at the home games of the Pascagoula Pigeons. She lists this on her résumé as "Retail Sales Experience."

4. Morton Fipse, the manager of Zippy Cleaners, plans to fire Chip Dockers. He is required by company policy to write a formal letter explaining the reasons for his decision. The real reason is that Chip has a bad attitude. Mr. Fipse doesn't know if he can fire someone for simply having a bad attitude. Also, he knows that such a letter might make it difficult for Chip to get another job, and he doesn't want to ruin Chip's life. He decides to say that Chip is being laid off because work is slow at the cleaners. In fact, work is a bit slow at the time that Mr. Fipse is writing the letter although he expects it to pick up again in the fall, and he probably will have to hire someone to replace Chip at that time.

CHAPTER 6

Writing to Analyze

You may think of good writing as simply conveying a message in as few words as possible. And there is much to commend a simple and direct approach to communication. However, many times your readers are expecting more from you than just passing along information. Suppose you found the following message stuck on your desk with one of those yellow stick-on notes.

MT&S needs written estimate on expansion project. Call Steve with details. Must reply by noon.

This message clearly expects a lot of you as the reader. The writer assumes that you know about the "expansion project" with MT&S. He assumes that you know Steve, what Steve's connection is to the project, and where he can be reached. And even if you know all of this, you still may be puzzled by the message. Does MT&S really need a "written" estimate, or can the figures be given over the phone to Steve? Who must reply "by noon"—you or Steve? As this message suggests, a short message is not simple if it leaves out important details or fails to provide a context for the information.

Much of the writing that people are asked to do goes beyond simply conveying information. If Congress passes new legislation about child care, many people will want to know how it will affect them personally. They will be less interested in reading the actual legislation than in knowing the "big picture." Will working parents receive additional tax benefits? Will daycare facilities be more closely regulated? Will companies be required to provide daycare services? To answer these questions, you will have to analyze the basic information carefully and then draw some conclusions based on sound reasoning.

REASONING

Imagine yourself locked in a room by a couple of escaped convicts. You immediately begin to consider your options. What are the possible avenues of escape? Pick the lock? Break down the door? Escape through the ceiling? If you decide the ceiling is the best route, you are confronted with another set of difficulties. How can you get through the ceiling tiles? How will you climb up to the ceiling? (On television, the hero probably would find a ladder that happened to be left behind by a work crew. In real life, you'll probably just have to wait for someone to unlock the door and let you out.) Whenever we are confronted with a problem, our minds automatically go to work, sorting out options and testing tentative solutions. The ability to gather information, assess its usefulness, and then come to a conclusion is based on the use of reason.

A basic tool of reason is the ability to draw inferences from information. For instance, in trying to determine our plan of escape from the locked room, we might observe that the ceiling tiles are suspended on a thin metal grid. Knowing that the metal grid would be unlikely to hold our weight, we would look for another way out. The ability to draw inferences is crucial to making informed decisions.

Drawing Inferences

An **inference** is a logical conclusion that can be drawn from basic facts or information. We all make inferences every day. We notice that it's cloudy outside and decide to carry an umbrella. We hear on the radio that a major highway is under construction, and we take a different route to work. We read that crime is on the increase in our neighborhood and make a mental note to install deadbolt locks on the doors. One benefit of ready access to information is that it allows us to make informed decisions—to draw sound inferences—that can make our lives better.

Because we make inferences so readily, we may be inclined to think of them as mere guesses or "hunches." However, a guess does not necessarily rely on logic. If the forecast doesn't call for rain, but we carry an umbrella because we have a "feeling" it might rain, we have not made an inference at all. Good inferences are based on reliable evidence.

Obviously, if we are misinformed, we will make poor inferences. Suppose I see my next-door neighbor taking his umbrella to the car, and I decide to take mine along as well. Later I find out my neighbor was returning a borrowed umbrella. My inference ("My neighbor is carrying an umbrella; it's probably going to rain.") turns out to be mistaken. Inferences are seldom perfect. Most of us have carried our umbrellas around needlessly on days that were supposed to rain according to the weather forecast. Still, it is important to remember that an inference is an informed judgment, not merely a guess.

EXERCISE 6.1 **Drawing Inferences**

Read the following facts and inferences. Which inferences are supported by the facts? Which inferences are unsupported or mistaken?

1. Fact: In 1961 Roger Maris hit 61 home runs, more than any other major league player has ever hit in a single season.
    Inference: Roger Maris was the greatest batter of all time.

2. Fact: From 1979 to 1984 the price of crude oil rose from $17.72 per barrel to $28.63. During this same period the price of gasoline at the pump rose from $.85 to $1.12 per gallon.
    Inference: Increased crude oil prices were passed along to the consumer.

3. Fact: Ford sold more pickup trucks than Chevrolet in 1989.
    Inference: Ford makes better trucks than Chevrolet.

4. Fact: In 1937 the *Hindenburg*, a German airship, exploded into flames, killing 35 people aboard.
    Inference: Commercial flight in airships has been abandoned because airships are inherently dangerous.

5. Fact: The Fourteenth Amendment to the *Constitution* prohibits discrimination on the basis of sex.
    Inference: Private clubs that have historically excluded women can be forced to admit female members.

6. Fact: High-speed "bullet" trains have been successful in Europe and Japan.
    Inference: Bullet trains are the answer to America's mass transit problems.

Making Inferences about People   Careful reading is really a process of drawing inferences. Suppose you are reading a biography of Amelia Earhart, a famous aviator. As you read, you encounter numerous facts:

> She began flying at age 25.

> She was the first woman to make a solo flight across the Atlantic.

> She died mysteriously in 1937 while attempting a solo flight around the world.

Your understanding of Amelia Earhart, however, is more than a collection of facts. As you read, you want to know what kind of person she was. Did she see herself as a trend-setter? Did she like being the center of public attention? Was she a risk-taker? Why did she capture the popular imagination? To answer these questions, you will have to make inferences from your reading.

EXERCISE 6.2 **Inferences about People**

When we say we "know" someone in more than a superficial way, we usually mean that we know how the person would respond in various circumstances. Ask these 10 questions of one of your classmates, and then try to draw some inferences about the kind of person he or she is.

1. Would you parachute from an airplane if given an opportunity?

2. How do you react when you see an insect in your home?

3. What kind of activity puts you to sleep?

4. What kinds of things do you like to make?

5. What is your favorite comic strip?

6. Name one of your favorite movies.

7. You see a car stalled along the road. What is your first thought?

8. You make a trip to a department store to buy a specific item, but when you arrive, the clerk tells you that it is out of stock. What is your response?

9. If you could live anywhere you wanted, where would it be?

10. What characteristics do you look for in a good friend?

Write a one-page description of the person you interview based on these inferences. Include a thesis statement that summarizes what you have learned about this person. For instance, you might write that "Jerome likes to try new things, likes to be with people, and likes to get his own way." You would support the fact that he likes to try new things by noting in your paper how eager he was to go skydiving or to help a stranded motorist.

Constructing a view of a person from reading a biography is much the same as getting to know people in real life. As you learn more about them, you begin to see patterns of behavior and begin to understand what motivates them. Read the following excerpts from *Narrative of the Life of Frederick Douglass, An American Slave*.

Hope of Freedom

From my earliest recollection, I date the entertainment of a deep conviction that slavery would not always be able to hold me within its foul embrace; and in the darkest hours of my slavery, this live word of faith and spirit of hope departed not from me, but remained like ministering angels to cheer me through the gloom. (56)

Learning to Read

The plan which I adopted, and the one by which I was most successful, was that of making friends of all the little white boys whom I met in the street. As many of these as I could, I converted into teachers. With their kindly aid, obtained at different times and in different places, I finally succeeded in learning to read.

When I was sent on errands, I always took my book with me, and by doing one part of my errand quickly, I found time to get a lesson before my return. I used to carry my bread with me, enough of which was always in the house, and to which I was always welcome; for I was much better off in this regard than many of the poor white children in our neighborhood. This bread I used to bestow upon the hungry little urchins, who, in return, would give me the more valuable bread of knowledge. (65)

Fight with Apprentices

My fellow-apprentices [in a Baltimore shipyard] very soon began to feel it degrading to them to work with me. They began to put on airs, and talk about the "niggers" taking the country, saying we all ought to be killed; and, being encouraged by the journeymen, they commenced making my condition as hard as they could, by hectoring me around, and sometimes striking me. I . . . struck back again, regardless of consequences; and while I kept them from combining, I succeeded very well; for I could whip the whole of them, taking them separately. They, however, at length combined, and came upon me, armed with sticks, stones, and heavy handspikes. One came in front with a half brick. There was one at each side of me, and one behind me. While I was attending to those in front, and on either side, the one behind ran up with the handspike, and struck me a heavy blow upon the head. It stunned me. I fell, and with this they all ran upon me, and fell to beating me with their fists. I let them lay on for a while, gathering strength. In an instant, I gave a sudden surge, and rose to my hands and knees. Just as I did that, one of their number gave me, with his heavy boot, a powerful kick in the left eye. My eyeball seemed to have burst. When they saw my eye closed, and badly swollen, they left me. With this I seized the handspike, and for a time pursued them. (129–30)

The first excerpt reveals that Douglass felt a sense of destiny in his attempt to escape from slavery. He was a profoundly religious man and drew great strength from his sense of divine mission. The second excerpt reveals his cleverness and determination. Instead of wallowing in self-pity, Douglass acted upon his desire to escape from slavery by learning to read and write. He recognized that white slave-owners maintained their control over slaves by keeping them ignorant. His ingenious scheme for learning from white children allowed him to overcome the limitations of illiteracy. Finally, Douglass was a man of great physical strength and courage. He decided after being viciously beaten by a cruel master that death was preferable to indignity. This resolve is clearly displayed in his resistance of the bigotry of the young apprentices.

Making Inferences about Situations   Because we are, by nature, rational or thinking creatures, we naturally look for a purpose in the things that go on around us. If you notice a steady stream of cars stopping at your neighbor's house, you naturally begin to wonder why. If you further notice that the guests stay for only a few minutes before returning to their cars, your suspicions may be aroused further. You begin to think of possible reasons for so many people coming and going. Of course, it's important not to jump to conclusions too quickly. You may call the police to break up a drug ring only to find that the visitors are dropping in to see a newborn baby.

EXERCISE 6.3 **Inferences about Situations**

Meet with your Discovery Groups to discuss the following events. What are the facts in each case? What inferences can be drawn?

1. Reckless Driver
    You are driving down a country road late at night. A car in front of you is swerving all over the road. You see the car go off the road and into a ditch. You pull over to see what has happened. The driver of the car is conscious, but his eyes are bloodshot and his speech is slurred. You see several crushed beer cans on the floorboard of the car. What has happened?

2. Missing Newspaper
    Each day when you come home from work, you look forward to reading the evening paper. Lately, you have been finding the paper all over the yard — under the hedge, in the flower bed, along the street. Also, the time when the paper is being delivered has been erratic. Sometimes it is there when you first get home; other times it doesn't arrive until after dark. Today you come home, and there is no paper. You check the yard several times during the course of the evening, but it is bedtime now and the paper still has not arrived. What has happened?

3. Rejected Lover
    You are a volunteer worker at a local recreation center. Each day when you come to work, you lock your purse up in the bottom file drawer in the office. Lately, you have been having difficulty with one of the young men at the recreation center. He follows you everywhere and clearly wants to be more than just a friend. You make clear that you are not interested in having a romantic relationship. He gets angry, calls you some names, and promises to make you sorry. That night when you get ready to leave, you discover that your purse is missing. What has happened?

We make inferences about people in order to understand their motives and to explain their behavior. We make inferences about situations to determine their causes, to assess their effects, and to determine a course of action.

Classifying

As we have seen already, reasoning through a problem requires gathering information that will help us to understand the situation. Information is more useful to us when it is logically organized than when it is randomly presented. **Classification** is the process of sorting information into logical categories.

Suppose you were writing a book about different kinds of games. You might begin by listing common games:

checkers	chess
poker	backgammon
Sorry™	hearts
gin rummy	spades
bridge	Monopoly™
Scrabble™	Uno™

In classifying these games, we look for categories that include two or more of the games we have listed. For instance, we might categorize the games this way:

Board games	Card games
checkers	hearts
chess	spades
backgammon	gin rummy
Sorry™	bridge
Scrabble™	poker
Monopoly™	Uno™

However, there are many other ways we could categorize the games: by their degree of difficulty, by the ages that usually play the game, by the amount of chance versus skill involved, and so on. The method of classification depends on the purpose we have for using the information.

EXERCISE 6.4 Classifying

1. For each group that follows, put the items in appropriate categories. Then think of a second way to classify the items in each group.

    Group 1

    George Washington

    Franklin D. Roosevelt

    Dwight Eisenhower

George Patton

Ulysses S. Grant

Robert E. Lee

Colin Powell

Stonewall Jackson

Abraham Lincoln

Group 2

triangle

sphere

circle

square

rectangle

cube

pyramid

cylinder

trapezoid

2. Make a list for one of the following subjects and then sort the information on your list into suitable categories.

cars

flowers

TV shows

music

sports

places you would like to visit

your favorite foods

Whenever we classify, we need an underlying concept or principle that explains the way we have divided the topic. For instance, if we divide games into board games and card games, the organizing principle is the material used to play the game. If our organizing principle is not clear or consistent, we may wind up with overlapping categories. The following haphazard classification resulted from the writer failing to understand the organizing principle:

Reasons for dropping out of college

Good reasons:

getting sick

lack of money

family problems

Common reasons:

couldn't get a loan

not doing well in courses

working too much

illness

emotional difficulties

don't like teachers

Unusual reasons:

couldn't find the school

poisoned in cafeteria

kidnapped by Mafia

Clearly, "good" reasons could also be "common" reasons. It is not surprising, then, to find financial reasons ("lack of money" and "couldn't get a loan") under both categories. Similarly, "emotional problems" and "family problems" clearly overlap. Even the "unusual reasons" category overlaps the other two. "Poisoned in cafeteria" overlaps the "illness" and "getting sick" items in the preceding categories. Here is the same classification with a clear organizing principle:

Reasons for dropping out of college

Personal reasons:

poor health

lack of money

lack of time

emotional problems

Academic reasons:

poor academic performance

dissatisfied with teachers or school

suspended for disciplinary reasons

By using the source of the problem as the organizing principle ("personal" vs. "academic"), the writer eliminates the overlapping categories in the earlier example. The act of classifying information not only helps you organize your ideas, but also often helps you recognize "gaps" in your information. In addition, classifying can help you see relationships among the different categories you have identified.

Making Comparisons

Another way of sorting information when we are reasoning our way through a problem is to make a **comparison**. Actually, we *compare* similarities and *contrast* differences. We could make a comparison of two brands of diet cola, or we could contrast basketball as it was played in the 1950s with the way it is played now. Frequently, we both compare and contrast as we write, noting similar features and recognizing important differences. We might compare a Toyota Celica to a Lamborghini because they are both sports cars, but we certainly would find a considerable contrast in the prices.

In making a comparison, we usually have to limit the number of features that we can compare. In comparing two restaurants, we might consider such factors as quality of the food, variety of the menu, service, atmosphere, and price. We probably would not include specific information about the names of the waiters or the color of the carpet unless it significantly affected our overall opinion of the restaurant. (A yellow shag carpet in an elegant restaurant probably would deserve some comment.)

EXERCISE 6.5 **Making a Comparison**

Meet with your Discovery Group to discuss the factors you would compare for *one* of the following items. Be prepared to report your findings to the class.

a hospital

an amusement park

a laundromat

a cemetery

a child's toy

a pet

Comparisons may be organized in two different ways: whole to whole or part to part. The whole-to-whole comparison provides a complete description of one category before moving on to the next. A whole-to-whole comparison of the Beatles to the Rolling Stones might look like this:

Beatles

Dominant rock group from 1956 to 1964

Early albums focused on romantic love

Late albums more concerned with social issues and psychedelic movement

Each member had a strong following

Most of the songs written by Paul McCartney and John Lennon

Had four members

Rolling Stones

Leading rock group from 1964 to 1970

Early albums fostered "bad boy" image

Late albums demonstrated frustration with society

Mick Jagger the best-known member

Most of the songs written by Mick Jagger and Keith Richards

Had five members

A part-to-part comparison considers only one aspect of each category at a time. A part-to-part comparison of various cancers might look like this:

Understanding Cancer

Frequency

More than 50,000 cases annually: lung, colorectal, breast, prostate, kidney/bladder, uterine/cervical/ovarian

Fewer than 50,000 cases annually: oral, skin (excluding nonmelanoma), leukemia

Chances of survival

Five-year survival rate above 50%: colorectal, breast, prostate, kidney/bladder, uterine and cervical, oral, skin

Five-year survival rate below 50%: lung, ovarian, leukemia

The whole-to-whole form of comparison is probably more commonly used because it allows for full development of one idea before moving on to the next. However, the part-to-part comparison has the advantage of identifying crucial factors and making contrasts clearer. The method you choose will depend on the nature of your subject and the needs of your audience.

EXERCISE 6.6 **Part-to-Part Comparison**

How would you make a part-to-part comparison of the Beatles and the Rolling Stones given the preceding information? What are the essential points of comparison?

EXERCISE 6.7 **Different Methods of Comparison**

Read the summaries of the three fairy tales below. Make a list of similarities and differences you find in the tales. Write two brief outlines of the stories, one using a whole-to-whole comparison and one using the part-to-part method. After you finish, discuss in your Discovery Group the advantages of the different methods of comparison.

Cinderella is one of the most popular fairy tales of all time. In this story, the villain is a wicked stepmother who spoils her vain daughters while treating Cinderella cruelly. Cinderella is rescued by a fairy godmother who helps her finish her chores and provides splendid clothes and a fine carriage to take her to the ball. Cinderella's escape is temporary, however. When the clock strikes midnight, her clothes turn to rags and her carriage to a pumpkin. Her deliverance is complete only when a messenger from the prince discovers that her foot alone will fit the glass slipper left at the palace on the previous night. Cinderella thus escapes her stepmother by marrying the prince.

In *Sleeping Beauty* the antagonist is an evil fairy. At her christening a princess is given love, beauty, wisdom, and other wonderful things by the good fairies. But an evil fairy, who had not been invited to the feast, curses the princess, saying that she will prick her finger on a spindle and die when she turns sixteen. One of the good fairies comforts the king and queen, saying that the princess will not die but sleep for a hundred years until awakened by a handsome prince. In spite of the king's decree that all spindles be burned, the princess is pricked by a spindle on her sixteenth birthday. After a hundred-year sleep, she is awakened by the kiss of a prince, who takes her away to marry her.

In *Snow White* the young princess is the victim of her evil stepmother. The wicked queen looks each day in a magic mirror which proclaims her "fairest of them all" until the youthful princess surpasses her in beauty. Fearing the queen, Snow White runs off to the forest where she is befriended by the seven dwarfs. However, the queen finds her hiding place and, disguised as a peddler, gives her a poisoned apple. She falls into a death-like trance until awakened at last by the kiss of Prince Charming.

Determining Causes

In reasoning through a problem, we need to do more than collect and organize information. As well as knowing *what* happened, we frequently want to know *why* something happened. Whenever we ask why something happened, we are concerned with causes. When laboratory scientists look for a cure for a disease, they must first begin by trying to understand what causes the disease to occur. When a manager learns that her company's advertising has been unsuccessful, she wants to know what went wrong and what can be done to prevent future failures. Sometimes we ask why just because we have a desire to know. For centuries people have been devastated by plagues of locusts swarming over the land, devouring everything in sight. Yet no one knew what became of the locusts in the years between these outbreaks. Finally, a Russian biologist named Boris Uvarov discovered that the locusts are actually ordinary grasshoppers. When forced into crowded conditions, these grasshoppers grow larger and change color, transforming themselves into swarms of locusts. As well as seeking to understand causes in order to better our world, we study causes in order to satisfy our natural curiosity.

EXERCISE 6.8 **Determining Causes**

In your Discovery Group, discuss the following incidents and try to identify the breakthrough that came from understanding an underlying cause.

1. In 1928 Alexander Fleming observed a green mold under a microscope. The unusual quality of this mold was that it inhibited the growth of many harmful bacteria. What had Fleming discovered?

2. In 1854 John Snow studied water from a public water pump that drew water from a well just a few feet from a sewer pump. He examined the pump handle for signs of organisms. What did he discover?

3. In July of 1885 Louis Pasteur was asked to administer, in increasingly potent doses, a virus originally taken from the spinal cord of a rabbit that had died of rabies to a nine-year-old boy bitten by a mad dog. After the sequence of 13 doses, the boy was cured. What had Pasteur proved?

4. In 1813 Joseph Niepce became interested in lithography, an art form that consisted of placing greased designs on stone. Later, he began trying to produce these designs automatically, using silver chloride exposed to sunlight. In his attempts to work with light-dark patterns that imitated nature, he succeeded in producing what?

Sometimes it is easy to jump to conclusions about why something happens without sufficient evidence. Sometimes we are blinded by our own prejudices or previous experiences. Sometimes we are led astray by false reports or erroneous evidence. For instance, many people believe that flying on a commercial jet is dangerous. This may be partly due to the fear that many people have of flying. Certainly the publicity given to airplane crashes also contributes to this fear. However, flying is statistically safer than bus or rail transportation, and much safer than driving your own automobile. It's important not to let feelings overshadow our judgment when analyzing causes. Here are four common mistakes people make in analyzing causes:

1. *We fail to recognize multiple causes.* We all have a natural tendency to oversimplify the causes for complex events. "Kids aren't doing well in school because they spend all of their time playing video games." "All accidents are caused by human stupidity," and so on. Most events have more than a single cause.

2. *We believe that because one event follows another, the first must have caused the second (i.e., the "post hoc" fallacy).* Primitive superstitions were often caused by coincidental events. The hooting of an owl was thought to foretell someone's

death. The conjunction of certain stars in the sky was a sign of good fortune. The appearance of a black cat was an evil omen. Such superstitions are still prevalent today. People often wear certain clothes for good luck, or believe that they must follow a certain routine if they are to succeed in some enterprise.

3. *We fail to look beyond the immediate cause.* It is possible to focus on the immediate cause of a problem and ignore more significant causes. "Pistol Pete" Maravich, a flamboyant professional basketball player in the 1970s, died of a heart attack on January 5, 1988, while playing basketball with some friends. Although one could argue that the stress of the game "caused" Maravich's heart attack, the real cause was a congenital heart defect that had gone undetected.

4. *We don't recognize the necessary cause of an event.* A necessary cause is one that must be present in order to produce the result. The word "cause" suggests that a result is inevitable. We might erroneously say that someone's love for cheesecake "caused" that person to be overweight. However, causes do not always lead inevitably to results. Not everyone who loves cheesecake will necessarily be overweight. The necessary cause of being overweight is taking in more calories than the body consumes.

EXERCISE 6.9 **Mistakes in Analyzing Causes**

In your Discovery Group read the following problems aloud and see if you agree with the causes that have been suggested. If you believe the wrong cause has been identified, try to explain the weakness in the reasoning.

1. It is only natural for powerful nations to conquer weaker nations. This is the reason we have wars.

2. Every time Lindy wears his blue socks, we win our softball game.

3. Shana watches too many daytime soap operas. That's why her own life is in such a mess.

4. Your brother got a job as a stockbroker, and he ended up committing suicide. If you get a job as a stockbroker, you will do the same thing.

5. Montalban will be a great president because he gives wonderful speeches.

6. I always sit in the third seat in the row closest to the door. That way I know I'll do well on my test.

7. The only reason Jones is playing professional football is that he got a lucky break. His high school coach knew a professional scout who got him a tryout with the team.

WRITING CASE STUDIES

One frequently encountered form of writing that requires all the analytical skills you have practiced is the case study. Usually the person writing a case study begins by making extensive observations about the subject of the study. For instance, if you want to know what the patterns of social interaction are among gorillas, you may pack your duffel bag and go live among them, as did Dian Fossey. You don't know exactly what you're going to find out, but you take extensive notes about what you see. How do gorillas sit? How do they move about? What features distinguish the different members of the troop? You would record your own reactions, such as "Once within the thick bamboo, I felt a small bit of the magic of the wilderness when fresh elephant droppings were sighted, as well as signs of gorilla" (*Gorillas* 22). In addition to subjective impressions, you would document objective findings: "One favored gorilla food item harbored by the *Hagenia* is a narrowleaf fern (*Pleopeltis excavatus*), which hangs down individually suspended from thick moss pads on the tree's nearly horizontal lower limbs" (*Gorillas* 23). Researchers sometimes refer to such notes as "thick" description.

Having collected extensive notes, you are ready to begin the analysis. You draw inferences from the animals' behavior. If the gorillas always bare their teeth before an aggressive act, then you assume that baring the teeth is a sign of displeasure. You begin to classify the various activities of the gorilla. Perhaps as you look over your list of observations, you see that they naturally fall into the categories of "food gathering," "relationships," and "play." And you begin to discover causes for certain behaviors. If you discover that when one of the gorillas leaves, the others always follow, you may infer that one of the gorillas is the designated leader of the troop.

Case studies are often focused on human behavior. When a group of people are brought together, who emerges as the leader? How does the leader exert authority? How do others express dissent? What other roles emerge in the group? Is there a rebel? an encourager? an organizer? By watching the activity of the group carefully, you can learn a great deal about the way groups function and how people relate to one another in groups.

EXERCISE 6.10   **Planning a Case Study**

Meet with your Discovery Group to plan a case study you can pursue as a team. Here are some possible topics to consider:

- the behavior patterns of people in a work setting — a grocery store, an insurance office, a factory, a fire station

- a particular place on campus — dormitory, student center, library, gymnasium

- the interactions of a particular group — a class, a fraternal organization, a church, a club

- the behavior of people in a recreational setting — a baseball game, a bowling alley, a nightclub, a professional wrestling match

- a particular kind of television show — news, daytime soaps, family comedies, detective and police dramas

After selecting a topic, begin to plan your strategy for the case study. What sites will you visit? When will you go? Will you go as a group, individually, or perhaps in pairs?

Organizing the Case Study

The particular elements that go into your case study will vary depending on your subject, your approach, and the nature of your findings. However, most case studies have these elements:

1. *Background:* Why did you choose this subject to study? What did you hope to learn?

2. *Method:* How did you go about studying your subject? When did you make your observations? What was your relationship to the people being studied?

3. *Observations:* What did you observe? What patterns emerged?

4. *Conclusions:* What did you learn from the study? How might what you learned apply to other situations? What else would you like to know that you didn't find out?

EXERCISE 6.11 Notes for a Case Study

Read the following "thick description" of an event and answer the questions that follow.

> At approximately 4:00 p.m. the family left the house at 4055 East Fourth Street to   1
> walk to a nearby park. Eloise, a 61-year-old grandmother, and Margaret, her 36-year-old
> daughter-in-law, were walking side-by-side. A few steps in front of them was Alicia, the
> 5-year-old granddaughter of Eloise. About 30 feet behind them were Mark, Eloise's 34-year-
> old son, and Donnie, her 7-year-old grandson. All of the family members were walking on
> the left side of the street, facing traffic.
>
> As the group began walking up a steep hill in the 3900 block of East Fourth Street,
> they heard a loud roar from an automobile engine. Mark said later, "You hear cars racing
> around in this neighborhood quite a bit. I really didn't think anything about it." As the
> vehicle sped up Fourth Street, Margaret turned around to see what was making so much
> noise. By this time, the vehicle had almost reached the group. All of a sudden the vehicle
> swerved toward Mark and Donnie. "I could feel the wind from the vehicle as it passed,"
> said Mark. "It was close, very close."
>
> "I don't think the van missed Mark by more than a few inches," said Margaret.
>
> The van continued up Fourth Street and then turned right at the next intersection,
> Covington Avenue.
>
> Margaret and Mark grabbed their children, and all five members of the family moved   5
> onto the lawn of the resident at 3901 East Fourth Street. The family debated whether to
> proceed on to the park. When the resident, a middle-aged woman, emerged from the home,
> they explained what had just occurred, and the woman offered to take them home in her
> car. The family declined.

A couple of minutes later, the group heard the van again. This time it was coming from the opposite direction. Margaret urged Mark to try to get near enough to get the van's license plate number. As Mark approached the street, one wheel of the van came up over the curb and into the yard. Mark turned and ran back toward the house. The van re-entered the street and sped back down the hill.

At approximately 4:20 p.m., the family returned home, and Mark called 911 to report the reckless driver. He reported that a "tan-colored van" had nearly run over him in the 3900 block of East Fourth Street. The operator acknowledged the information and hung up.

Mark's and Margaret's descriptions of the van and driver differed. Mark recalled a man with "long brown hair" but no beard. The van was an "old work van, probably a Ford Econoline." Margaret said the man looked "scroungy, with long gray hair and a scraggly beard." The van was a "dingy white" and was smashed on the passenger side. She recalled that the man had "wild eyes" as though he were high on drugs. Mark said only that he looked "angry."

A few minutes later the family warned an elderly couple walking on Fourth Street about the reckless driver. The man said that he knew the van and where the driver lived. Mark walked to the home, only two blocks away, and positively identified the van. On returning, he called 911 again with the new information and demanded that a police officer be sent to investigate. "Does someone have to get killed," he shouted, "before you do anything?"

At approximately 5:10 a police officer arrived at the home. He said that he could not arrest the driver because he had not actually seen the incident occur. Mark could make a citizen's arrest, but the officer did not think it would accomplish anything. "You and I will go down and fill out a lot of papers, and he'll claim that someone else who looks a lot like him took the van, and he'll be back home watching TV before you and I are done filling out the papers." The officer also warned of possible retaliation by the driver.

Mark did not file a citizen's arrest. Eloise sent a letter to the editor of the local paper, complaining about the failure of law enforcement to protect citizens. The letter was printed a few days later.

Activity

1. How adequate are these notes?

2. What do you think is the general subject to which these particular observations belong?

3. Can you draw any conclusions from these notes?

WRITING ASSIGNMENT Preparing a Case Study

The case study is designed as a cooperative effort, requiring the participation of each member of your group. Although it would be impossible to have each member do exactly the same amount of work, your goal should be to apportion both research and writing tasks as equitably as you can.

Try to use your group's meeting times wisely. You need to try to accomplish something every time you get together. Think in terms of immediate objectives as well as your overall goals. For instance, you might assign someone in your group to bring copies of the Equal

Opportunity Act for everyone in your group (not just ask someone to "get some information about employment opportunities"). If you have been given an assignment by the group, be sure to have it ready when it is due. If meetings are scheduled outside of class, make every effort to attend and be on time.

The following steps will guide your group in preparing a case study.

Step one   Elect someone to serve as chairperson of your group. This person will need to be strong enough to keep the group on track, yet not so dictatorial that he or she is unwilling to listen to others. In other words, the chairperson needs to be a balance between Hitler and Gandhi. In principle, all decisions made by the group should be unanimous; however, if the group is divided, the chairperson may need to make the final decision.

A secretary will also be needed — someone with clear handwriting and the ability to identify the main points of a discussion. The secretary should write the minutes of each meeting and read them at subsequent meetings. One of the secretary's first duties is to prepare a directory for the group with names, addresses, and phone numbers. This should be duplicated, and each member given a copy.

Step two   At your initial meeting, the group will need to decide on the subject of their study. (You may be assigned an area to investigate, or you may want to use the suggestions in exercise 6.10). Then discuss the purpose and scope of the group's project, with the ultimate goal of formulating a comprehensive research question that will be the goal of the group's investigation. For example, a group studying classroom attendance policies at your school might make this their research question:

> Should our school have a uniform classroom attendance policy? If so, what should this policy be?

Your group may, of course, revise the research question as you go along, but each member should be clear at all times what the purpose and scope of the project is.

Step three   Each member of the group will do some library research. At your second meeting, each member should bring copies of printed information that is relevant to the group's research. The group may want to divide up the research in some way to cut down on duplication. For instance, one group member might bring a copy of the attendance policy in the current college catalog, another might bring copies of attendance policies in course syllabi, another might bring an article about attendance policies printed in an educational journal, and so on.

The group will also want to assign group members to do interviews, field research, surveys, and the like. For instance, in discussing a uniform attendance policy, each member might be assigned to talk to a professor or an administrator in order to get a cross section of current attitudes and opinions on this issue.

Step four   The group may already have defined some research areas, but by the third group meeting will want to make formal assignments for the written report. Divide up the report in any way that seems appropriate. Here are some possible divisions:

According to the source of information

This is appropriate when the source material coincides neatly with the natural divisions of the report. For instance, a paper about the hiring practices of various businesses around town might be divided in such a way that each group member is responsible for describing at length the practices of a particular business. (One member would be assigned to write a summary/conclusion.) However, such a close relationship between the sources of information and the logical divisions of the report is probably the exception rather than the norm. Usually each section will be based on several different sources of information.

According to the type of information

This is probably the most frequent method of division. Each group member discusses one aspect of the research question. For instance, in discussing the quality of health care on campus, one member might discuss financial aspects, another would look at the health problems of students, yet another would report on how health care is administered, and so on.

According to a "problem analysis"

The problem analysis discussed in chapter 4 can be an effective means of dividing your topic:

Problem analysis

   I. What is the nature of the problem? (definition)
  II. What is the background of the problem? (history)
 III. What are the requirements for a successful solution? (criteria)
  IV. What are some possible solutions? (options)
   V. What is the best solution? (decision)
  VI. How can this solution be put into effect? (implementation)

Step five   It's important to divide the paper in such a way that each member writes a section. The entire group then reviews and edits each section. The goal is to make each section fit smoothly into the final report. You must tie together the sections with more than a paper clip.

Step six   You will need to make arrangements to have the final report typed. The group may agree to split the expenses of having the report typed professionally, or two or three members may volunteer to type the final draft on a word processor. If one member takes on the entire burden of typing the final report, the group ought to find some way to compensate this altruistic (and perhaps masochistic) typist.

The final report should contain the following sections:

Cover page. Include the names of all of your group members.

Outline. Each section should be followed by the name of the group member who wrote that section.

Abstract. This is a brief overview of the paper's contents.

Body of the report
Be sure the title is on the first page.
Separate the sections of the report with subheadings; in parentheses after the subheading put the name of the person who authored that section.
Follow the guidelines for citations in chapter 8.

Works Cited
Follow the correct manuscript style (see chapter 8).
List only sources actually used in the paper.

One of the joys of using a word processor is the ease and speed with which documents can be printed. After you have finished writing, you simply send a command to print, and the word processor does the rest. Anyone who has wrestled with a typewriter late at night—hitting the wrong keys, realizing too late that you have typed the same line twice or skipped a line, trying to make corrections with whiteout—will quickly appreciate the convenience of making all corrections on screen before printing. And if you realize after printing that you need to add a paragraph or move text around, you easily make those changes without retyping the entire document.

Printers for word processors fall into several different categories. They range in price from an economy model that can be purchased for around a hundred dollars to a top-of-the-line laser printer that may cost several thousand.

- **Dot matrix printers** are the most common printers for drafts of papers that do not have to be "letter quality" (the quality of letters you would see on a manuscript produced by a typewriter with a good ribbon). Dot matrix printers produce letters by pressing a series of pins over a ribbon and onto the paper. How many pins there are and how many times they run over the ribbon to produce the letter determine the quality of type. Usually you may select among three qualities of print: near letter quality (NLQ), standard quality, or draft quality. To make your choice, you may either issue a command to the word processor or set the quality control on the printer itself.

- A **daisy wheel printer** resembles a typewriter keyboard in that the uppercase letters, lowercase letters, and numbers are molded into a metal or plastic wheel that spins. When the wheel spins to the correct letter, the letter strikes the ribbon, which imprints the letter onto the paper. As you might imagine, all of this spinning is a time-consuming process. Therefore, it usually takes quite a while to print with a daisy wheel.

- An **inkjet printer** squirts a minute amount of ink onto the computer paper, thereby speeding up the printing process considerably. Instead of using pins or a wheel to imprint letters through a ribbon, the printer directly applies the ink to the paper. The popularity of inkjet printers is increasing, and, primarily because of its speed, the inkjet printer is rapidly replacing the daisy wheel type.

- The highest quality of type is produced by a **laser printer.** This printer uses a laser beam to apply powdered ink in the shape of letters to a metal drum. This drum rotates and presses the ink onto the paper. The impression created by a laser printer is sharp, clear, and easily read, and is especially desirable for professional documents such as résumés, application letters, and business proposals.

Today's word processors offer a variety of type styles and point sizes (a character's style and size make up its **font,** a term you'll hear often in conjunction with printers). When picking a font, make sure that the size is not too small or large for the reader and that the style is appropriate for your audience and purpose. For instance, you probably would alienate many of your readers if your business proposal were printed this way:

Use an appropriate font for your audience and purpose.

Remember that your goal is to draw attention to your ideas, not your typeface.

WRITING CRITICAL ESSAYS

We read literature for various reasons. Some literature helps us to escape from our own world. Some literature helps us to understand what it is like to see the world from a different perspective. Some literature helps us to understand our own experiences, almost as if the writer knew us and were putting our stories into words. As you read literature, you will understand more about the power of language and about the human experience.

Writing about a literary work, such as a poem or short story, requires the same kind of careful attention you used in analyzing people and situations. As you read, you will make inferences about the meaning of certain words or the importance of certain actions. Of course, you can never be entirely sure that your interpretation of a particular literary work is exactly what the author had in mind. You might wish sometimes that you could ask the author to explain the meaning of the work. However, even some authors claim not to know exactly what their works mean. They insist that the individual reader's interpretation of the work is just as important as what they might have intended to say. However, you can make a good case for your interpretation only when you make your main points clear and use the literary text to support your own ideas about it.

Analyzing a Poem

Most of us probably have asked at one time or the other, what is the purpose of a poem? Poetry often seems difficult to understand, almost as though the poet were intentionally trying to hide the meaning of the poem.

But poetry can also stir something deep within us. I can remember distinctly the first time I heard the words:

> Eleanor Rigby picks up the rice in the church
> Where a wedding has been.
> Lives in a dream.

The song echoed my own feelings of loneliness and alienation. We've all had similar experiences of lyrics that have lingered in our mind or snatches of poetry that seemed to capture our feelings beyond our own power to express them.

Although every literary artist is working with subtle shades of meaning, this tendency is most pronounced in poetry. As you read a poem, you must be sensitive to not only *what* is said but *how* it is said as well.

Observe how the words Dorothy Parker uses in the following poem provide a clue to its meaning.

One Perfect Rose

A single flow'r he sent me, since we met.   1
    All tenderly his messenger he chose;
Deep-hearted, pure, with scented dew still wet—
    One perfect rose.

I knew the language of the floweret;   5
    "My fragile leaves," it said, "his heart enclose."
Love long has taken for his amulet
    One perfect rose.

Why is it no one ever sent me yet
    One perfect limousine, do you suppose?   10
Ah no, it's always just my luck to get
    One perfect rose.

At first, Parker seems to be writing a sentimental love poem. She uses elegant expressions, such as "floweret" and "with scented dew still wet." But in the final stanza, her intention is clear. The rose is a poor substitute for material satisfaction—the "limousine." And from the lofty expression of the first two stanzas, she sinks to the ordinary "just my luck" to make her sarcasm clear. The change in style reinforces Parker's mockery of romantic traditions.

As "One Perfect Rose" indicates, the reader of poetry must pay close attention to the style of the poem in order to fully understand its meaning. In the following poem by Emily Dickinson, we will examine the way the sound, diction, and structure of the poem help to determine its meaning.

[A Narrow Fellow in the Grass]

A narrow Fellow in the Grass   1
Occasionally rides—
You may have met Him—did you not
His notice sudden is—

The Grass divides as with a Comb —   5
A spotted shaft is seen —
And then it closes at your feet
And opens further on —

He likes a Boggy Acre
A Floor too cool for Corn —   10
Yet when a Boy, and Barefoot —
I more than once at Noon

Have passed, I thought, a Whip lash
Unbraiding in the Sun
When stooping to secure it   15
It wrinkled, and was gone —

Several of Nature's People
I know, and they know me —
I feel for them a transport
Of cordiality —   20

But never met this Fellow
Attended, or alone
Without a tighter breathing
And Zero at the Bone —

Begin your interpretation of a poem by making observations: the use of sound and rhythm, interesting word choices, the overall structure of the poem. In the following section, these elements of poetry are illustrated with sample observations from "A Narrow Fellow in the Grass."

Sound   A good poem pleases the ear as well as the eye. It often is helpful to read the poem aloud in order to appreciate the poet's use of sound.

1. Rhythm

    The poem has a definite rhythm. There are usually three beats to each line (a FLOOR too COOL for CORN), but sometimes four (the GRASS diVIDES as WITH a COMB).

2. Rhyme

    There are rhymes in the last two stanzas ("me" and "cordiality"; "alone" and "bone"). The rhymes connect the second and fourth lines of these stanzas.

3. Consonance

    Consonance is sometimes called "half rhyme." Look for consonance at the end of verses. The final consonants must be the same but the preceding vowels different in order to have consonance. For instance, Dickinson uses consonance in the fourth stanza:

> Have passed, I thought, a Whip lash
> Unbraiding in the *Sun*
> When stooping to secure it
> It wrinkled, and was *gone* —

The words *Sun* and *gone* both end with the same consonant, but the preceding vowels are different.

4. Alliteration

    We have all heard beginning consonants repeated for effect (the "Dynamic Duo," the "Sound of Silence"). Dickinson uses alliteration in lines such as "too cool for Corn" and "Boy and Barefoot."

5. Assonance

    Assonance is not quite as noticeable as alliteration, but it works much the same way. The poet repeats vowel sounds instead of consonants to create assonance. The short "i" sound is repeated in this verse by Dickinson: "His notice sudden is —"

Diction   Diction refers to the poet's word choices. Dickinson is particularly notable for interesting, and sometimes startling, diction such as the following:

narrow Fellow

rides (Why not "slithers"?)

The Grass divides as with a Comb —

spotted shaft

Boggy Acre

Floor too cool for Corn

a Boy and Barefoot —

Whip lash / Unbraiding in the Sun

stooping to secure it

wrinkled

Nature's People

transport / Of cordiality

Zero at the Bone

You may find it helpful to characterize the poet's diction as (1) formal or informal, (2) concrete or abstract, (3) literal or figurative.

Formal or informal   Formal language usually contains longer and less commonly used words. Informal language is the language of ordinary, conversational speech. Generally, Dickinson has used informal language. Few of her words would not be recognized by most readers. (The use of "transport / Of cordiality" to mean something like an "emotional attachment" is perhaps an exception.)

Concrete or abstract   Words that refer to things you can experience with your senses are concrete—a dining room chair, the newspaper, an afternoon nap. References to ideas and concepts are usually abstractions—the pursuit of happiness, industrial productivity, equal opportunity. Dickinson is not easy to categorize in this regard. She uses many concrete references (e.g., grass, floor, corn, boy, sun), but her abstractions are frequent as well. For instance, "narrow Fellow" is more abstract than "snake"; "Nature's People" is more abstract than "animals"; and "Zero at the Bone" is more abstract than "paralyzing fear." Dickinson often seems to be intentionally ambiguous. Her purpose, however, is not to hide her meaning but to involve the reader in the poem. She insists that the reader actively engage in the reading in order to fully understand the poem.

Literal or figurative   Literal language is straightforward and transparent. "His car was badly in need of repair" is an example of literal language. Figurative language, on the other hand, requires the reader to look beyond the ordinary meaning of words. "His car was a dog" is not to be taken literally. In order to understand this sentence, the reader must understand that *dog* stands for something of poor quality.

In Dickinson's poem "A Narrow Fellow in the Grass," the idea of the grass dividing "as with a Comb" is an example of figurative language. This particular figure is called a **simile**. The writer introduces a simile with the words *like* or *as* to indicate that the comparison being made is not literal. In this poem, the parting of the grass is something like the parting of hair with a comb.

In some cases, a writer makes a direct comparison without using *like* or *as*. Such direct comparisons are called **metaphors**. If you say that you are *as* hungry "as a wolf," you have used a simile. If you say that you *are* a "hungry wolf," you have used a metaphor. The metaphor is, in some ways, a more daring device because the reader must recognize the comparison without any overt clues.

When Dickinson writes about the "narrow Fellow" in the grass, she is using a metaphor. In fact, the "narrow Fellow" or the "spotted shaft" is never identified as a snake. The reader must make this interpretation from the context of the poem.

Two other common types of figurative language are metonymy and synecdoche, which are often confused. When a writer uses **metonymy** (pronounced muh-TAHN-uh-me), a term closely related to the actual subject is substituted for it (e.g., "gray hair" for age or wisdom, "sword" for military power). In a **synecdoche** (pronounced si-NEK-duh-key), a part of something represents the whole or, less

LANGUAGE NOTE: THE LANGUAGE OF POETRY

Poetry before the nineteenth century tended to depend a great deal on technique. Poetic lines frequently had a precise **meter**, as regular as the "beat" in a song. Take, for example, these lines from Sonnet 23 by William Shakespeare:

> Oh, learn to read what silent love hath writ:
> To hear with eyes belongs to love's fine wit.

If you read these lines aloud, you will hear a definite pattern of five beats to the line. This is referred to as **pentameter** ("penta" = five). You may also notice that each accented syllable is preceded by an unaccented one. This is referred to as an **iamb**. Thus, Shakespeare's iambic pentameter verse follows this pattern:

> di-dah di-dah di-dah di-dah di-dah

Note also that the final words in each line rhyme (writ-wit), forming a **couplet**. There is also a good deal of wit and wordplay (e.g., "to hear with eyes"). Shakespeare exemplifies the conscious craft that went into much poetry before the nineteenth century.

Poetry before 1800 was also frequently characterized by a preoccupation with courtly society and with classical mythology. Both of these elements are seen in the following lines from Alexander Pope's *Rape of the Lock*. In the poem, a wealthy baron attempts to cut a locket of hair from the beautiful, but vain, Belinda. In this passage, the victorious baron exults in the power of the scissors to cut off Belinda's beautiful hair.

> Steel could the labor of the Gods destroy,
> And strike to dust the imperial towers of Troy;
> Steel could the works of mortal pride confound,
> And hew triumphal arches to the ground.
> What wondering then, fair nymph! thy hairs should feel,
> The conquering force of unresisted Steel?

Although modern poetry is too diverse to make useful generalizations, many contemporary poets tend to write in "ordinary language" and to write about everyday experiences. This poem by William Carlos Williams illustrates the simplicity and apparent artlessness of much modern poetry:

> *Exercise No. 2*
>
> The metal smokestack   1
> of my neighbor's chimney
> greets me among the new leaves
>
> it is a small house
> adjacent to my bigger one   5
> I have come in 3 years

> to know much of her
> an old lady as I am an old man
> we greet each other
>
> across the hedge   10
> my wife gives her flowers
> we have never visited each other

There are no mythological themes or noble characters here. The poet simply considers the isolation of neighbors in an urban environment. The language is familiar and simple, but the last lines convey forcefully the sense of loss that comes from a relationship that never goes further than an occasional greeting "across the hedge."

Not all modern poets are so concerned with the inner life as Williams. Many actively protest poverty, racial inequality, and other injustices. Some even retain an interest in the classical themes we mentioned earlier, although seldom in the manner of Shakespeare or Pope.

If you find poetry interesting, you may want to browse a bookstore for selections that interest you, attend a reading by a poet in your area, or even try your hand at writing your own poetry.

commonly, the whole represents the part. For instance, the captain calls for all "hands" on deck. The "hands" represent the sailors. Similarly, a rancher will speak of selling so many "head" of cattle even though, clearly, whole cows are being sold.

Another common form of figurative language is **personification**, or giving human characteristics to animals, ideas, emotions, or inanimate objects. When Dickinson speaks of animals as "Nature's People," she is personifying them. Objects are often personified by the actions attributed to them. For instance, if a poet writes that fenceposts "stood at attention," these objects are being personified.

Structure   Most poems are divided into stanzas, usually indicated by an extra space inserted between lines. In analyzing the structure of a poem, you will want to consider the way stanzas are developed and the relationship among the stanzas. "A Narrow Fellow in the Grass" has five stanzas, two with four verses and one with eight verses. The first two stanzas are closely connected. Dickinson begins with the idea that most of us have had an encounter with the "narrow Fellow" and then describes such an encounter. In the next stanza, we are told that although snakes may prefer cool and wet places, we may encounter them in the noonday sun. And again, such an encounter is described. The final two stanzas form the third unit. We are told of the way that most animals inspire feelings of affection, but that the snake is usually an instrument of terror.

Interpretation   Generally, it is best to assess carefully the sound, diction, and structure of a poem, as we have done here, before beginning to analyze its meaning. As you read the poem carefully, you will begin to ask questions that are central to the meaning of the poem:

Who is the "narrow Fellow"? Why isn't it identified as a snake?

Is it significant that the encounter occurs at "Noon"?

What is the meaning of a "Whip lash / Unbraiding"?

Why does the appearance of a snake inspire such terror?

At this point, you must speculate on what the poem means. You might, for instance, argue that Dickinson feels we have been uncharitable to the snake who is, after all, a "fellow" creature, another one of "Nature's People." Alternatively, you might want to argue that the ambiguous "narrow Fellow" makes the snake seem all the more sinister, just as the idea of "liquidating" a person can seem more chilling than the more commonplace reference to someone being "killed" or "murdered."

Legend has it that Eve was tempted at noon in the Garden of Eden. Thus, Dickinson's reference to "Noon" might lead to an inference that the "narrow Fellow" is not merely a snake, but the embodiment of evil.

The fourth stanza is particularly difficult. Does the "Whip lash / Unbraiding" refer to the snake striking? uncoiling? or perhaps the rippling bands on the snake's back? And what is the meaning of "secure" in line 15? To secure the snake could mean to capture it, or it could mean to hold it in place. In either case, the Boy is unable to secure it, and the snake escapes.

After you have thoroughly analyzed the poem, you should come to some general sense of what you feel the poem is about. Try to express that idea in a sentence before you begin drafting your paper. Here is a sample draft of a critical essay on "A Narrow Fellow in the Grass":

Death Comes in Time:

Emily Dickinson's "A Narrow Fellow in the Grass"

Time places a spell on all of us. Day after day passes. We turn the calendar ₁ pages. We celebrate another birthday. Yet, we are still surprised to see how quickly the years have passed. "How did I get to be this old?" we ask, as though we had been asleep. In "A Narrow Fellow in the Grass," Emily Dickinson shows us both sides of time: the seduction of time passing unnoticed and the shock of seeing ourselves as suddenly older.

The frightening aspect of time is introduced in the first stanza of the poem. Few images produce more terror than that of a snake in motion, the "narrow Fellow" of the poem. In line 3 we are told, "You may have met him," as we have all met time. The shaft caused by the snake closes and "then opens further on" (8). Time is fleeting: We see a moment and then it passes and something else happens a minute later. The previous moment is erased, but there is also hope of the one "further on."

In the third stanza, the persona of the poem explicitly raises the theme of passing years by thinking back to when he was a "Boy and Barefoot." The phrase suggests not only the innocence of youth but also the awareness of lost youth. The boy was oblivious to the passing of time or the dangers of the snake; the adult looks back and sees more clearly what time means.

The ultimate assault on time comes in lines 13–16. Just as children may think they can pluck a star out of the sky by reaching out their hands for it, the young boy bravely attempts to secure time in the form of the snake. The appearance of the snake in this stanza is even more abstract. The "narrow Fellow" has become "a Whip lash / Unbraiding in the Sun," a mere wrinkle in the grass. The attempt to "secure" time is sheer folly.

In the last two stanzas, Dickinson explores the final event in human time — death. The "narrow Fellow" to this point has represented only the rapid passing of time, but in contrasting the snake to "Nature's People," Dickinson raises the specter of the Biblical serpent in the Garden of Eden. The snake was the tempter of Adam and Eve. And the penalty for their disobedience was death. The snake is no longer something to be "secured" in a child's fantasy; it is the object of raw terror, the suffocation and panic conveyed by Dickinson's phrase "tighter breathing / And Zero at the Bone" (23–24).

For most of us, the passing of time is seen as natural. We occasionally worry about growing older, but we treat time itself as a neutral fact of existence. In "A Narrow Fellow in the Grass," Dickinson makes Time the incarnation of evil, the snake in the grass, the sentence of death on us all.

EXERCISE 6.12 **Responding to a Critical Essay**

Analyze the essay on Dickinson's "A Narrow Fellow in the Grass," using the following questions to guide your discussion.

1.   Did you think this poem was about the passing of time when you first read it?

2.   Where is the thesis sentence in the essay? Does the writer maintain this thesis throughout the essay?

3.   What kinds of information does the writer use to support the thesis? Has the writer distorted the meaning of the poem in any way?

4.   Do you think the thesis is adequately supported? Why or why not?

WRITING ASSIGNMENT Analyzing a Poem

Step one Browse through the poems that follow these instructions, and select one that you find interesting. The poem you choose may appeal to you because you've had a similar experience or because the poet has given you some new insight, or you may choose one simply because you like the sound of the language. Don't be intimidated by an older poem or one that seems strange to you—often these are the poems that are most satisfying to study.

Step two Once you have decided on your approach to the poem, write a discovery draft. Include as many specific references to the poem as possible. If you think the poem uses many "s" sounds to create an evil and sinister mood, quote the lines where the "s" sounds are repeated. If you think the poet's diction is formal, provide examples of formal words used in the poem. The more evidence you bring from the text, the more convincing your argument will be for a particular interpretation.

Step three After finishing your draft, ask yourself these questions:

1. What is the main point I am making about this poem?

2. What evidence have I brought from the poem (quotations of lines and phrases, analysis of structure) to support that point?

3. What changes should I make in my next draft to clarify my main point and to strengthen the evidence for it?

Step four When you have a draft that clearly expresses your interpretation of the poem, share it with your Discovery Group. Have your group answer these questions:

1. What is the writer's main point? Did the writer cause you to think about this poem in a new way?

2. What evidence is used to support that writer's interpretation of the poem? What other evidence might be added?

3. What changes should the writer make at this point?

Step five Revise the paper and submit the final draft. Include with your final paper the initial notes you made about the poem, the preliminary thesis, your rough drafts, your self-evaluation, your peer reviews, and a short statement of the way your paper changed through successive revisions.

Poems for the Critical Essay

"*Out, Out —* "

The buzz-saw snarled and rattled in the yard   1
And made dust and dropped stove-length sticks of wood,
Sweet-scented stuff when the breeze drew across it.
And from there those that lifted eyes could count
Five mountain ranges one behind the other   5
Under the sunset far into Vermont.
And the saw snarled and rattled, snarled and rattled,
As it ran light, or had to bear a load.
And nothing happened: day was all but done.
Call it a day, I wish they might have said   10
To please the boy by giving him the half hour
That a boy counts so much when saved from work.
His sister stood beside them in her apron
To tell them "Supper." At the word, the saw,
As if to prove saws knew what supper meant,   15
Leaped out at the boy's hand, or seemed to leap —
He must have given the hand. However it was,
Neither refused the meeting. But the hand!
The boy's first outcry was a rueful laugh,
As he swung toward them holding up the hand   20
Half in appeal, but half as if to keep
The life from spilling. Then the boy saw all —
Since he was old enough to know, big boy
Doing a man's work, though a child at heart —
He saw all spoiled. "Don't let him cut my hand off —   25
The doctor, when he comes. Don't let him, sister!"
So. But the hand was gone already.
The doctor put him in the dark of ether.
He lay and puffed his lips out with his breath.
And then — the watcher at his pulse took fright.   30
No one believed. They listened at his heart.
Little — less — nothing! — and that ended it.
No more to build on there. And they, since they
Were not the one dead, turned to their affairs.

ROBERT FROST

A Poison Tree

I was angry with my friend: 1
I told my wrath, my wrath did end.
I was angry with my foe:
I told it not, my wrath did grow.

And I waterd it in fears,   5
Night & morning with my tears:
And I sunned it with smiles,
And with soft deceitful wiles.

And it grew both day and night,
Till it bore an apple bright.   10
And my foe beheld it shine,
And he knew that it was mine.

And into my garden stole,
When the night had veild the pole;
In the morning glad I see,   15
My foe outstretched beneath the tree.

WILLIAM BLAKE

A Noiseless Patient Spider

A noiseless patient spider,   1
I mark'd where on a little promontory it stood isolated,
Mark'd how to explore the vacant vast surrounding,
It launch'd forth filament, filament, filament, out of itself,
Ever unreeling them, ever tirelessly speeding them.   5

And you O my soul where you stand,
Surrounded, detached, in measureless oceans of space,
Ceaselessly musing, venturing, throwing, seeking the spheres to
    connect them,
Till the bridge you will need be form'd, till the ductile anchor
    hold,
Till the gossamer thread you fling catch somewhere, O my soul. 10

WALT WHITMAN

Sonnet 29

When, in disgrace with Fortune and men's eyes,   1
I all alone beweep my outcast state,
And trouble deaf heaven with my bootless cries,
And look upon myself and curse my fate,
Wishing me like to one more rich in hope,   5
Featured like him, like him with friends possessed,
Desiring this man's art, and that man's scope,
With what I most enjoy contented least;
Yet in these thoughts myself almost despising,
Haply I think on thee, and then my state,   10
Like to the lark at break of day arising
From sullen earth, sings hymns at heaven's gate;
    For thy sweet love rememb'red such wealth brings
    That then I scorn to change my state with kings.

WILLIAM SHAKESPEARE

I Heard a Fly Buzz — When I Died

I heard a Fly buzz — when I died —   1
The Stillness in the Room
Was like the Stillness in the Air —
Between the Heaves of Storm —

The Eyes around — had wrung them dry —   5
And Breaths were gathering firm
For that last Onset — when the King
Be witnessed — in the Room —

I willed my Keepsakes — Signed away
What portion of me be   10
Assignable — and then it was
There interposed a Fly —

With Blue — uncertain stumbling Buzz —
Between the light — and me —
And then the Windows failed — and then   15
I could not see to see —

EMILY DICKINSON

Incident

He came back and shot. He shot him. When he came   1
back, he shot, and he fell, stumbling, past the
shadow wood, down, shot, dying, dead, to full halt.

At the bottom, bleeding, shot dead. He died then, there
after the fall, and the speeding bullet, tore his face   5
and blood sprayed fine over the killer and the grey light.

Pictures of the dead man, are everywhere. And his spirit
sucks up the light. But he died in darkness darker than
his soul and everything tumbled blindly with him dying

down the stairs.   10

We have no word

on the killer, except he came back, from somewhere
to do what he did. And shot only once into his victim's
stare, and left him quickly when the blood ran out. We know

the killer was skillful, quick, and silent, and that the victim   15
probably knew him. Other than that, aside from the caked
        sourness
of the dead man's expression, and the cool surprise in the fixture

of his hands and fingers, we know nothing.

    IMAMU AMIRI BARAKA

Ozymandias

I met a traveller from an antique land,   1
Who said — "Two vast and trunkless legs of stone
Stand in the desert. . . . Near them, on the sand,
Half sunk a shattered visage lies, whose frown,
And wrinkled lip, and sneer of cold command,   5
Tell that its sculptor well those passions read
Which yet survive, stamped on these lifeless things,
The hand that mocked them, and the heart that fed;
And on the pedestal, these words appear:
My name is Ozymandias, King of Kings,   10
Look on my Works, ye Mighty, and despair!
Nothing beside remains. Round the decay
Of that colossal Wreck, boundless and bare
The lone and level sands stretch far away."

    PERCY BYSSHE SHELLEY

Mirror

I am silver and exact. I have no preconceptions.   1
Whatever I see I swallow immediately
Just as it is, unmisted by love or dislike.
I am not cruel, only truthful —
The eye of a little god, four-cornered.   5
Most of the time I meditate on the opposite wall.
It is pink, with speckles. I have looked at it so long
I think it is a part of my heart. But it flickers.
Faces and darkness separate us over and over.

Now I am a lake. A woman bends over me,   10
Searching my reaches for what she really is.
Then she turns to those liars, the candles or the moon.
I see her back, and reflect it faithfully.
She rewards me with tears and an agitation of hands.
I am important to her. She comes and goes.   15
Each morning it is her face that replaces the darkness.
In me she has drowned a young girl, and in me an old woman
Rises toward her day after day, like a terrible fish.

    SYLVIA PLATH

'The world is too much with us; late and soon'

The world is too much with us; late and soon,   1
Getting and spending, we lay waste our powers:
Little we see in Nature that is ours;
We have given our hearts away, a sordid boon!
This Sea that bares her bosom to the moon;   5
The winds that will be howling at all hours,
And are up-gathered now like sleeping flowers;
For this, for everything, we are out of tune;
It moves us not. –Great God! I'd rather be
A Pagan suckled in a creed outworn;   10
So might I, standing on this pleasant lea,
Have glimpses that would make me less forlorn;
Have sight of Proteus rising from the sea;
Or hear old Triton blow his wreathèd horn.

    WILLIAM WORDSWORTH

Traveling through the Dark

Traveling through the dark I found a deer   1
dead on the edge of the Wilson River road.
It is usually best to roll them into the canyon:
that road is narrow; to swerve might make more dead.

By glow of the tail-light I stumbled back of the car   5
and stood by the heap, a doe, a recent killing;
she had stiffened already, almost cold.
I dragged her off; she was large in the belly.

My fingers touching her side brought me the reason —
her side was warm; her fawn lay there waiting,   10
alive, still, never to be born.
Beside that mountain road I hesitated.

The car aimed ahead its lowered parking lights;
under the hood purred the steady engine.
I stood in the glare of the warm exhaust turning red;   15
around our group I could hear the wilderness listen.

I thought hard for us all — my only swerving — ,
then pushed her over the edge into the river.

WILLIAM STAFFORD

Analyzing a Short Story

Everyone enjoys a good story. In stories we find amusement, excitement, trag-edy, wisdom, and foolishness. Sometimes we recognize people and actions that are familiar to us, and sometimes we are able to enter into worlds completely different from our own. The good storyteller is able to offer us in a few pages a richly rewarding experience that well repays the time we have taken to read it.

Elements of the Short Story   Every short story shares certain common elements. Most stories have an element of **conflict.** One of our impulses in reading the story is to find out how the conflict will be resolved. How will the spendthrift repay the money he has squandered? How will the young girl react to her lover's betrayal? Another important element of the story is the development of the **characters.** After reading a story, the characters may seem as genuine to us as people we have known in real life. We often speak of the **plot** of the story as simply *what happens* — the restless cowboy falls in love, gives up his gun and saddle, and settles down to be a farmer. However, the plot of the story often may rearrange the normal chronological order of events. The author may begin the story in the middle, flash back to earlier events, and then move the story on to its conclusion. Another way the author can affect the

way we read the story is by using a particular **point of view.** The author may tell the entire story in the first person. The "I" of the story may be a major character or a casual observer on the fringes of the action. The author who writes in first person is generally "limited" to telling about what the narrator of the story could logically be expected to know. This is an example of the first-person point of view:

> I had known the captain long enough to see behind his oily manners and forced smiles. He was vicious in a petty way, forbidding the crew to sing while at their tasks or upbraiding a man publicly for a loose button.

On the other hand, the writer may tell the story in the third person. In the third person, the author is free to reveal the inner workings of a character's mind:

> He had come to this place for one purpose only. In fact, his whole life had been directed to this single end. He had studied revenge the way a child might practice piano, and he was prepared now for the ultimate recital. He felt elation, near ecstasy, as he screwed the silencer onto the end of his pistol.

One other useful term in discussing the short story is the concept of **theme.** Although every short story presents unique characters and situations, many stories share common themes. There are lots of stories about coming of age, about chasing after an illusion, about finding love and losing love. Usually, the theme of a good story is not easily reduced to a simple truism (e.g., "Don't neglect your friends."), but speaks to the complex conditions and choices presented in life. In other words, if you look to the short-story writer to "solve" life's problems, you will be disappointed. The short story provides insight into the human condition without reducing it to a fairy tale.

In analyzing a short story, you will use many of the reasoning skills discussed in this chapter. You will need to draw inferences from your reading; to classify the story according to its plot, characters, theme, and other characteristics; and to make comparisons about such things as the motives of the characters and the options available to them. In the following story by Max Apple, notice how the author contrasts two attitudes toward life.

Selling Out

by Max Apple

When he was thirty, my father, a careful man, bought a "piece   1
of the Rock," a twenty-thousand-dollar chunk to be exact. At thirty-
eight, in good health and during the Korean War, he doubled it. At
forty-six with a slightly elevated BP (155/94) they let him buy fifteen
thousand additional with a ten-percent premium hike. At fifty he beat
the actuarial tables. We thought it was only an upset stomach. He
dropped two Alka Seltzers in a half glass of water and died before
they melted. After funeral expenses I was left with $53,000, which
the Prudential man wanted me to leave in on a million-dollar policy
on myself.

"I'll take the fifty-three," I said.

My father's cousin, H.B., a broker, said, "For safety's sake let's
put it in a fund. There you're protected. Who knows what can happen
with an individual stock? And far be it from me to take upon myself
the responsibility of a discretionary account for my orphaned cousin.
However, if you'd like . . ."

"Buy the fund," I said.

The commissions came out to a little over three thousand; that   5
left between forty-nine and fifty thousand. It was in 1965.

I put it all out of mind, worked in a bookstore, and went to
community college at night. The fund reinvested the dividends and
capital gains. In the hot market of early 1968 I had on one particular
day, April 7, $187,000 in the fund. The next April 7 it was down to
$81,000. I always check on April 7 because it's the day Dad died.
Every Christmas when I get a calendar from H.B.'s office, right after
I fold out its clever cardboard leg, I circle April 7 and try to buy the
Journal for the eighth. I called H.B. in 1969 to tell him I was down
$106,000 in one year.

"It's the goddamn war," he said. "It's killing the street. And the
back-room mess is worse every day. Be glad you're in a fund. The
Dow has been underwater for two years. I've got customers calling
me saying, 'H.B., I'm dead, should I sell?' Another year like this
and I'll be dead too. You can only take so many losses and that's it.
Be glad you're in the fund . . . however if you'd like . . ."

"I'll stay in the fund," I said.

In October 1971 I was thirty, not in love, and remembered the
fund. A doctor told me I had high blood pressure, ought to lose
weight and get more exercise. I had "stroke potential," he said. I
thought about it and decided to strike.

I quit the bookstore, shaved my beard, bought a blue gabardine   10
suit, and started reading the *Journal* every day. I also read *Barrons*
and the *Dow Theory Forecast.* I answered a Merrill Lynch ad and
received a free Standard and Poor's list of all listed stocks in a little
gray paperback that looked like a mouse next to my dictionary.

After a month and a half I realized it was futile for me to study
the market and made my move anyway. I had planned to wait until
April 7, but I was impatient.

In December, my shoes wet with slush, I slid into H.B.'s office
wearing my blue suit.

"Please sell the fund," I said.

"What do you mean, sell the fund?"

"Sell it — write out a sell order. How long will the sale take?"   15

"A minute. It will take a minute, but why sell? Your fund beats
the Dow every year. The market is weak."

"How's the back-room mess?"

"Better," he said. "If Nixon takes care of the inflation. You
watch us move. Your fund is worth — Mary, add up these figures
please." She came through the open door at his side from where I
heard the noise of computers, adding machines, and girl talk. You
could smell coffee. In seconds she was back with a slip of white
paper for H.B. I noticed her ass when she bent to hand it to him. He
looked only at the amount.

"About eighty-seven thousand dollars on today's market."

"Sell it," I said.   20

"Just like that?"

"Just like that. Are there any commissions?"

"No, you paid them all when you bought in."

"Do I have that money as credit with you right now?"

"As soon as the sale goes through, if you want it."   25

"Sell it."

"You're sure?"

"I'm sure."

"Mary, sell twelve thousand, four hundred and thirty and a
fraction shares of Diversified Fund Ltd." He looked as if large numbers made him sad.

It was 9:07. At 9:11 Mary came back with a confirmation of   30
sale, $87,211.18.

"You can bet one of the fund managers will call me about that
sale. It's unusual for them to lose a big chunk all at once. Most people,
you know, take it as monthly income. They have faith in the future
of the economy."

"I'm going out in the lobby to watch the tape," I said, "and I'm going to start trading against that eighty-seven thousand."

"Trading what? Talk to me a little. How many cousins do I have? You could blow it in an afternoon, everything." Now there were tears in his eyes. I did not doubt his sincerity.

"I might," I said, walking into the lobby where the prices streamed under the ceiling in electric orange. He followed me from his office, and Mary, when I looked back, was peeking from out the back room, leaning way over on one leg.

I sat down in the front row on a padded theater chair. It was like   35
watching a dull French movie. I had a pad and pencil and knew some of the ticker symbols from studying the Standard and Poor's booklet. The first one I recognized was Sony Superscope. I have nothing against the Japs. The selling price at 9:15 was 18. I wanted to buy in round numbers but 5,000 shares came to $90,000.

"Buy forty-five hundred Sony Superscope at eighteen."

On the seat next to me H.B. said, "He's lost his mind." He said it as if I wasn't there.

"Listen," I said, "if you don't want the commissions there are plenty of other brokers." I didn't even look at him but kept my eyes on the board. He added up the price of 4,500 shares to be sure I had enough to cover, then he told Mary to buy. Then things were dull for maybe forty-five minutes. Sony was not a hot number at that hour. I watched my purchase go across. It took about a tenth of a second, about as long as it had taken my father's upset stomach to become cardiac arrest.

I smoked some filter-tip Kools that one of the other brokers gave me. H.B. went back to his office. I was almost sorry that I had put everything into the first buy. It made waiting dull. Watching for Sony, I practiced my recognition of the other symbols. I knew only about one in ten. I started checking some in the Standard and Poor's book, but I had only checked Kaiser Aluminum (KL) and US Industries (USI) before I saw Sony Superscope go across at 18¾. H.B. came out and slapped me on the back.

"You knew something, eh? So why couldn't you tell a cousin?   40
Did I ever do anything that wasn't in your best interest?" He slapped me across the shoulders. At 11 Sony hit 19¾ and though I wanted to wait for even numbers, I was bored with SOS and sold. I recognized U.S. Steel and Pabst Brewing and bought a thousand of each. There was enough left to pick up 500 of an unlisted chicken raising conglomerate that the man on the seat behind me had been watching all morning. At noon I was holding the steel,

the beer, and the chickens.

"Mary," I said when I noticed her long thighs in a miniskirt under the flashing orange figures, "would you run out and get me a strawberry malt and some french fries from Mr. Quick?" She hesitated. "We don't usually . . ." Then she must have caught a high sign from someone in the office behind me. "Glad to," she said as I gave her a dollar. She smelled like an Easter egg.

At the noon break I noticed things in the office surrounding me. The chairs were American Seating (AmS), the desks Shaw Walker (ShW), the toilet paper Scott (Sc). On H.B.'s desk was a Ronson pencil sharpener (Rn), a Sheaffer pen (ShP), and, of course, the back room was full of IBM (IBM) and Xerox (X).

I asked Mary if I could see the label at the back of her blouse as she handed me the french fries. She did not quite blush, waited for a sign, got none, bent toward me as I rose to read Koret of California (KC) above her second vertebra.

"Thank you," I said as she slinked toward the computers, glancing back to me the shared secret of size eight.

I surmised that her underwear was nylon (DuPo). Through the tinted safety glass (LOF) of H.B.'s outer office I noticed two consecutive Mercury Montereys (FM). 45

That afternoon I traded all of the above. A quarter point I figured for commissions, a half point might be a small profit, but I would have the pleasure of watching the accrual of my father's life move across the big board. Measured in tenths of a second, my father and I controlled about two seconds of the American economy. By 2 p.m. H.B. was constantly at my side. One entire girl in the back room was assigned solely to my transactions. She sweated through her Ban Roll-On (BrM) 51½/62. My only loser was the chicken conglomerate, down ¼. By 2:30 I had come back to the $187,000 of April 7, 1968. I put it all into Occidental Petroleum at 2:35 for two reasons: It was volume leader of the day, and the President, Armand Hammer (like the baking soda), was a friend of V. I. Lenin during the revolution. I sold it at 2:58, making an extra $41,000.

When the orange lights stopped circling the room, H.B. hugged me. "I'm crazy, not you," he said. "It will be a week before the back room can straighten out what you did today. You're a rich man now . . . you were before."

"That's capitalism," I said. "Mary," I called to the back room. She arose from her computer, stepped over a small hill of puts and calls. I held my arm out from my body at the elbow. She fit like destiny and moved in.

Making Observations about a Short Story   In chapter 1 we used the "5 W's and an H" to organize our observations about an event. This method also works well as a way of organizing observations about a short story. Here is a sample list of observations on "Selling Out":

Who?

narrator

narrator's father

"Prudential man"

H.B., father's cousin, the broker

doctor

Nixon

Mary

Armand Hammer

Lenin

What?

father's investment in life insurance

son's investment in "the fund"

studying the market

selling the fund

trading on impulse

making a fortune

leaving with Mary

Where?

bookstore

community college

broker's office

back room

lobby

What?

ages

dollar amounts

health — blood pressure, "stroke potential"

family relationships

business magazines — the *Journal, Barrons, Dow Theory Forecast*

dates

"padded theater chair"

"electric orange" stock board

stocks

ticker symbols

When?

Korean War

April 7 — day his father died

bought the fund in '65

hot market of 1968 — fund worth $187,000

1969 — fund lost $106,000

October 1971 — quit job

December — decided to sell fund

buying and selling at various times through the day

Why?

fear of death

need for love

irrationality

impatience

boredom

capitalism

How?

invest cautiously — listen to advice, invest in insurance or mutual fund

take risks — speculate in stocks, buy and sell on impulse

Having made these observations, we begin to see a pattern emerging. Clearly, the author is making a contrast between two styles of life, between prudent investment (even the name "Prudential" suggests this) and wild speculation. But there are other themes running through this story as well. What is the narrator's attitude toward communism and capitalism? In what way are individuals controlled by huge corporations and conglomerates? Why is Mary treated as a kind of trophy for financial victory?

Another way to analyze this story is by listing key passages. As with poetry, the short-story author often uses language in interesting and unusual ways. A list of key passages in "Selling Out" might be something like this:

> We thought it was only an upset stomach. He dropped two Alka Seltzers in a half glass of water and died before they melted.

> Every Christmas when I get a calendar from H.B.'s office, right after I fold out its clever cardboard leg, I circle April 7 and try to buy the *Journal* for the eighth.

> I answered a Merrill Lynch ad and received a free Standard and Poor's list of all listed stocks in a little gray paperback that looked like a mouse next to my dictionary.

> "Trading what? Talk to me a little. How many cousins do I have? You could blow everything in an afternoon, everything."

> I sat down in the front row on a padded leather chair. It was like watching a dull French movie.

> I watched my purchase go across. It took about a tenth of a second, about as long as it had taken my father's upset stomach to become cardiac arrest.

> . . . I would have the pleasure of watching the accrual of my father's life move across the big board.

> "Mary," I said when I noticed her long thighs in a miniskirt under the flashing orange figures, "would you run out and get me a strawberry malt and some french fries from Mr. Quick?"

> I held my arm out from my body at the elbow. She fit like destiny and moved in.

Of course, your list of "key" passages might be different. In fact, a case might be made for the importance of every sentence since a short-story writer has to pack a good deal of meaning into every line. After compiling a list of key passages, you will begin the process of drawing inferences. Let's look closely at the first sentence on the list:

> We thought it was only an upset stomach. He dropped two Alka Seltzers in a half glass of water and died before they melted.

What does this tell us about the father? about the son? One student drew the following inferences.

> The death came suddenly, without warning. Maybe this put a sense of terror or dread into the son. He knew life was unpredictable, could be over at any moment. This may have led to his "live for the day" attitude. The father is never

described. He doesn't seem like a person, just an account. The writer doesn't talk about the funeral, just the funeral expenses. Maybe the father was just the "breadwinner," maybe he never really got to know his children. The father's death is always associated with his money. When the son recalls his father's death later, it's always to check on his account. The money has become in some way his surrogate father.

EXERCISE 6.13   **Drawing Inferences from a Short Story**

Select one of the key passages (either from the preceding list or from your own reading of "Selling Out") and freewrite a paragraph, drawing inferences from the passage.

Writing a Discovery Draft   Having brainstormed about the passage, we are now ready to write a discovery draft. We want to explore the son's relationship to his father, and we think these are points that we'll want to consider:

Main idea: Although the son thinks he is different from his father, he still believes that money is "the measure of the man."

His father, the "careful man"

The son, reckless and impulsive

Both believe money is the ticket to happiness

Discovery Draft

One of the key ideas in "Selling Out" is in the title. The idea of "selling out" was a key phrase in the 70s. "Selling out" meant being more concerned about money than human values. Business was the bad guy that could justify any kind of evil in the name of profit.

The father in the story represents the older generation that lived through the Depression and struggled to make ends meet. He is described as "a careful man." His generation was conservative with their money. They were afraid that another depression could come, and they would lose it all. The father puts all of his savings in a life insurance policy with Prudential. But at 50 his life is over, and the author seems to imply that he has little to show for it except for his insurance policy.

The son is a different breed. He works at a bookstore and is going to community college at night. Education seems to be important to him. Another hint about him comes after he learns about his own high blood pressure. He quits his job at the bookstore and shaves his beard. The beard probably represents the hippie, anti-establishment lifestyle. Shaving the beard is a symbol that he is joining the materialistic set. This seems confirmed when we learn that he has bought "a blue gabardine suit," the businessman's uniform.

Although the son seems to be joining the business world, he doesn't do things the same way as his father. Instead of accumulating money slowly through work, he risks everything on a few speculations in the stock market. And there are hints about his socialist leanings, when he invests in Occidental Petroleum, in part, because "the President, Armand Hammer (like the baking soda), was a friend of V. I. Lenin during the revolution."

Although the father was cautious and the son more carefree with his money,   5 both of them believed that money was the ultimate power. The father invests because he wants security. The son invests because he was "thirty, not in love" and because he had "stroke potential." He doesn't just want to die with money in the bank. He wants to use his money to buy the things he wants in life. The fairy tale comes true when he makes a killing in stocks and walks off with Mary, the sexy secretary. Perhaps the author is even suggesting that Marxism and capitalism are not so far apart. Although these two systems believe different things about who should control money, both of them believe that economics holds the key to personal happiness.

The short story which follows this assignment, "The Lottery Ticket," was written by Anton Chekhov (1860–1904), a Russian dramatist and short-story writer who often wrote about the sadness experienced in the lives of ordinary people. In reading this story (or in reading others suggested by your instructor), follow the general pattern of moving from observation to interpretation.

WRITING ASSIGNMENT Analyzing a Short Story

Step one   Read "The Lottery Ticket" twice. The first time read quickly to get an overall impression. The second time read more carefully, noting key passages and items of interest.

Step two   After your second reading, make a list of observations. You may want to use the 5 W's and an H, or another of the techniques described in chapter 1.

Step three   After you have finished making notes, write a discovery draft exploring essential ideas in the story. After you have finished, ask yourself these questions:

1.   What is the main point I am making about this short story?

2.   What evidence have I brought from the story (quotations, summaries, references to key passages) to support that point?

3.   What changes should I make in my next draft to clarify my main point and to strengthen the evidence for it?

Step four   Continue drafting and revising. When you have a satisfactory draft, share it with your Discovery Group. Have your group answer these questions:

1.   What is the writer's main point? Did the writer cause you to think about this story in a new way?

2.   What evidence is used to support that point (quotations, summaries, references to key passages)? Is the evidence slanted or distorted in any way?

3.   What changes should the writer make at this point?

Step five   Revise the paper and submit. Include with your draft all the preliminary drafts and notes you made and a short statement of the way your paper changed through successive revisions.

The Lottery Ticket

by Anton Chekhov

Ivan Dmitritch, a middle-class man who lived with his family on an income of twelve 1
hundred a year and was very well satisfied with his lot, sat down on the sofa after supper and began reading the newspaper.

"I forgot to look at the newspaper today," his wife said to him as she cleared the table. "Look and see whether the list of drawings is there."

"Yes, it is," said Ivan Dmitritch; "but hasn't your ticket lapsed?"

"No; I took the interest on Tuesday."

"What is the number?"   5

"Series 9,499, number 26."

"All right . . . we will look . . . 9,499 and 26."

Ivan Dmitritch had no faith in lottery luck, and would not, as a rule, have consented to look at the lists of winning numbers, but now, as he had nothing else to do and as the newspaper was before his eyes, he passed his finger downwards along the column of numbers. And immediately, as though in mockery of his scepticism, no further than the second line from the top, his eye was caught by the figure 9,499! Unable to believe his eyes, he hurriedly dropped the paper on his knees without looking to see the number of the ticket, and, just as though some one had given him a douche of cold water, he felt an agreeable chill in the pit of the stomach; tingling and terrible and sweet!

"Masha, 9,499 is there!" he said in a hollow voice.

His wife looked at his astonished and panic-stricken face, and realized that he was not 10
joking.

"9,499?" she asked, turning pale and dropping the folded tablecloth on the table.

"Yes, yes . . . it really is there!"

"And the number of the ticket?"

"Oh, yes! There's the number of the ticket too. But stay . . . wait! No, I say! Anyway, the number of our series is there! Anyway, you understand. . . ."

Looking at his wife, Ivan Dmitritch gave a broad, senseless smile, like a baby when a 15
bright object is shown it. His wife smiled too; it was as pleasant to her as to him that he only mentioned the series, and did not try to find out the number of the winning ticket. To torment and tantalize oneself with hopes of possible fortune is so sweet, so thrilling!

"It is our series," said Ivan Dmitritch, after a long silence. "So there is a probability that we have won. It's only a probability, but there it is!"

"Well, now look!"

"Wait a little. We have plenty of time to be disappointed. It's on the second line from the top, so the prize is seventy-five thousand. That's not money, but power, capital! And in a minute I shall look at the list, and there — 26! Eh? I say, what if we really have won?"

The husband and wife began laughing and staring at one another in silence. The possibility of winning bewildered them; they could not have said, could not have dreamed, what they both needed that seventy-five thousand for, what they would buy, where they would go. They thought only of the figures 9,499 and 75,000 and pictured them in their imagination, while somehow they could not think of the happiness itself which was so possible.

Ivan Dmitritch, holding the paper in his hand, walked several times from corner to   20
corner, and only when he had recovered from the first impression began dreaming a little.

"And if we have won," he said — "why, it will be a new life, it will be a transformation! The ticket is yours, but if it were mine I should, first of all, of course, spend twenty-five thousand on real property in the shape of an estate; ten thousand on immediate expenses, new furnishing . . . travelling . . . paying debts, and so on. . . . The other forty thousand I would put in the bank and get interest on it."

"Yes, an estate, that would be nice," said his wife, sitting down and dropping her hands in her lap.

"Somewhere in the Tula or Oryol provinces. . . . In the first place we shouldn't need a summer villa, and besides, it would always bring in an income."

And pictures came crowding on his imagination, each more gracious and poetical than the last. And in all these pictures he saw himself well-fed, serene, healthy, felt warm, even hot! Here, after eating a summer soup, cold as ice, he lay on his back on the burning sand close to a stream or in the garden under a lime tree. . . . It is hot. . . . His little boy and girl are crawling about near him, digging in the sand or catching ladybirds in the grass. He dozes sweetly, thinking of nothing, and feeling all over that he need not go to the office today, tomorrow, or the day after. Or, tired of lying still, he goes to the hayfield, or to the forest for mushrooms, or watches the peasants catching fish with a net. When the sun sets he takes a towel and soap and saunters to the bathing-shed, where he undresses at his leisure, slowly rubs his bare chest with his hands, and goes into the water. And in the water, near the opaque soapy circles, little fish flit to and fro and green water-weeds nod their heads. After bathing there is tea with cream and milk rolls. . . . In the evening a walk or *vint* with the neighbors.

"Yes, it would be nice to buy an estate," said his wife, also dreaming, and from her   25
face it was evident that she was enchanted by her thoughts.

Ivan Dmitritch pictured to himself autumn with its rains, its cold evenings, and its St. Martin's summer. At that season he would have to take longer walks about the garden and beside the river, so as to get thoroughly chilled, and then drink a big glass of vodka and eat a salted mushroom or a soused cucumber, and then — drink another. . . . The children would come running from the kitchen-garden, bringing a carrot and a radish smelling of fresh earth. . . . And then, he would lie stretched full length on the sofa, and in leisurely fashion turn over the pages of some illustrated magazine, or, covering his face with it and unbuttoning his waistcoat, give himself up to slumber.

The St. Martin's summer is followed by cloudy, gloomy weather. It rains day and night, the bare trees weep, the wind is damp and cold. The dogs, the horse, the fowls — all are wet, depressed, downcast. There is nowhere to walk; one can't go out for days together; one has to pace up and down the room, looking despondently at the grey window. It is dreary!

Ivan Dmitritch stopped and looked at his wife.

"I should go abroad, you know, Masha," he said.

And he began thinking how nice it would be in late autumn to go abroad somewhere   30
to the South of France . . . to Italy . . . to India!

"I should certainly go abroad too," he wife said. "But look at the number of the ticket!"

"Wait, wait! . . ."

He walked about the room and went on thinking. It occurred to him: what if his wife really did go abroad? It is pleasant to travel alone, or in the society of light, careless women who live in the present, and not such as think and talk all the journey about nothing but their children, sigh, and tremble with dismay over every farthing. Ivan Dmitritch imagined his wife in the train with a multitude of parcels, baskets, and bags; she would be sighing over something, complaining that the train made her head ache, that she had spent so much money. . . . At the stations he would continually be having to run for boiling water, bread and butter. . . . She wouldn't have dinner because of its being too dear. . . .

"She would begrudge me every farthing," he thought, with a glance at his wife. "The lottery ticket is hers, not mine! Besides, what is the use of her going abroad? What does she want there? She would shut herself up in the hotel, and not let me out of her sight . . . I know!"

And for the first time in his life his mind dwelt on the fact that his wife had grown   35
elderly and plain, and that she was saturated through and through with the smell of cooking, while he was still young, fresh, and healthy, and might well have got married again.

"Of course, all that is silly nonsense," he thought; "but . . . why should she go abroad? What would she make of it? And yet she would go, of course. . . . I can fancy. . . . In reality it is all one to her, whether it is Naples or Klin. She would only be in my way. I should be dependent upon her. I can fancy how, like a regular woman, she will lock the money up as soon as she gets it. . . . She will look after her relations and grudge me every farthing."

Ivan Dmitritch thought of her relations. All those wretched brothers and sisters and aunts and uncles would come crawling about as soon as they heard of the winning ticket, would begin whining like beggars, and fawning upon them with oily, hypocritical smiles. Wretched, detestable people! If they were given anything, they would ask for more; while if they were refused, they would swear at them, slander them, and wish them every kind of misfortune.

Ivan Dmitritch remembered his own relations, and their faces, at which he had looked impartially in the past, struck him now as repulsive and hateful.

"They are such reptiles!" he thought.

And his wife's face, too, struck him as repulsive and hateful. Anger surged up in his   40
heart against her, and he thought malignantly:

"She knows nothing about money, and so she is stingy. If she won it she would give me a hundred roubles, and put the rest away under lock and key."

And he looked at his wife, not with a smile now, but with hatred. She glanced at him too, and also with hatred and anger. She had her own daydreams, her own plans, her own reflections; she understood perfectly well what her husband's dreams were. She knew who would be the first to try to grab her winnings.

"It's very nice making daydreams at other people's expense!" is what her eyes expressed. "No, don't you dare!"

Her husband understood her look; hatred began stirring again in his breast, and in order to annoy his wife he glanced quickly, to spite her at the fourth page on the newspaper and read out triumphantly:

"Series 9,499, number 46! Not 26!"   45

Hatred and hope both disappeared at once, and it began immediately to seem to Ivan Dmitritch and his wife that their rooms were dark and small and low-pitched, that the supper they had been eating was not doing them good, but lying heavy on their stomachs, that the evenings were long and wearisome. . . .

"What the devil's the meaning of it?" said Ivan Dmitritch, beginning to be ill-humored. "Wherever one steps there are bits of paper under one's feet, crumbs, husks. The rooms are never swept! One is simply forced to go out. Damnation take my soul entirely! I shall go and hang myself on the first aspen-tree!"

THE CRITICAL MOMENT

Even everyday conversation can be hard to understand if we lack a context for what is being said. For instance, if someone came up and told you to "run a check on Barnes," you might not be sure what you were being asked to do. However, if you worked in a bank, you might immediately understand that you were being asked to run a credit check on a customer named Barnes.

Understanding poetic language presents even greater difficulties for most readers. How would you interpret these lines by Sylvia Plath?

> The hills step off into whiteness
> People or stars
> Regard me sadly, I disappoint them.

In some cases, we get clues from the context of the poem. These lines are taken from a poem titled, "Sheep in Fog." We might interpret the "whiteness" of the first line, then, to be the fog settling on the hills.

But even when the literal meaning becomes clear, we still must consider the symbolic or metaphorical meaning of the poem. Does "whiteness" suggest "peace" or "oblivion" or "despair" in this poem?

Not all poetry is as difficult to understand as Plath's, but reading any poem raises certain issues about how we read and interpret poetic language. Consider these issues as you think about the nature of poetic language.

1. Is the meaning of a poem open to various interpretations, or is there one right meaning?

2. Can a poem mean anything a reader wants it to mean?

3. Does analyzing the meaning of a poem help us to appreciate it more?

4. Are poets intentionally vague, or are there other possible reasons why some poetry is hard to understand?

5. What would be lost if we made a prose statement out of a poem?

Writing to Persuade

Listen to the heartbeat of America.

You got the right one, baby. Uh-huh.

Just do it.

Unless you've been living on a deserted island for the past few years, you probably recognize all of these slogans and the products they represent. Companies spend millions of dollars on advertising every year in order to create public demand for their products. They frequently associate their products with famous athletes, glamorous models, and Hollywood celebrities. Because of the deceptive and manipulative practices of so many advertisers, you may have wondered if *persuasion* is just another name for taking advantage of people. Is persuasion always unethical?

Although persuasion can be unethical, it need not be so. A doctor may try to persuade us to change our diet in order to improve our health. Public safety experts encourage us to install smoke alarms in our houses. Recently, many celebrities have joined in a campaign to encourage us to read more books. All of these are worthwhile causes that deserve our attention. Clearly, persuasive appeals can be to our benefit.

In an ideal world perhaps there would be no shysters or con artists appealing to our emotions and our vanities for their own personal gain. All products would perform as advertised, and all services would be fairly priced and cheerfully performed. However, because our world is far from ideal, caveat emptor — Let the buyer beware! — is still the best advice. Instead of relying on others to make our decisions for us, we need to examine persuasive appeals carefully to protect ourselves from unscrupulous salespeople.

The need to examine persuasive appeals is true in the world of ideas as well as in the world of commerce. The history of science is full of half-baked ideas and bogus claims. Physicians of the eighteenth century believed that bleeding patients would rid them of fevers. Some nineteenth-century psychologists claimed that personality was connected to the size and shape of the skull. In our own time, people have sought relief from arthritis in copper bracelets and a cure for cancer in apricot pits. Similarly, ideas in philosophy, history, politics, art, and psychology need to be weighed and evaluated carefully. Ideas are to our minds what food is to our bodies, and we need to be careful about "swallowing" everything we hear.

In this chapter, we discuss the way persuasive appeals are made. We consider what constitutes a legitimate claim and how seemingly good arguments can be deceitful. We also consider how you can construct your own arguments to persuade others.

A MODEL OF ARGUMENT

At the root of any argument is a claim.* The **claim** is what you are attempting to prove. A claim may be a simple statement: "Easy credit has encouraged many Americans to buy luxury items that they cannot afford." Or the claim may be a command: "Buy savings bonds." In either case, the claim must be supported by **evidence**. One weakness of most advertising is a lack of evidence. When you hear a claim such as "Buy a Schnitzelwagen 380x. It's the RIGHT choice," you should immediately ask, "Why is it the right choice?" What evidence does the manufacturer offer to show that it is a quality vehicle? that it offers superior features to the competition? that it is fairly priced?

Types of Evidence

Evidence may take many forms. A product description is a form of evidence: "The Schnitzelwagen 380x is powered by a 5.0-liter turbocharged V6 engine." If these are desirable features in the car you wish to purchase, then this description may convince you to buy a Schnitzelwagen. Test results can also be a form of evidence: "The Schnitzelwagen 380x has an EPA mileage rating of 12 mpg." If you can live with low gas mileage, you may be undeterred by these figures. If not, you'll look for another car. In either case, you are better able to make an informed judgment.

Some qualities of a product cannot be described objectively. The attractiveness of a car is often a matter of personal taste. Some people like shiny red sports cars, whereas others prefer sedate gray sedans. We sometimes seek out expert opinion on matters that cannot be reduced to a numerical rating. A test driver reporting on the performance of a car might write the following evaluation:

---

*This model of argument was formulated by the British philosopher Stephen Toulmin and is frequently referred to as the Toulmin model.

The Schnitzelwagen handled like a cement truck during our test ride. To say that acceleration was sluggish is an understatement; it was completely torpid. However, there were some thrills on the ride. The suspension was so loose that rounding a gentle bend at 25 mph put you in danger of swerving out of control. We were especially appreciative of the seat belts on the 380x since the brakes were clearly designed to throw the driver through the windshield. Despite these small drawbacks, I am seriously considering buying a 380x . . . for my ex-wife.

As well as understanding a product better through detailed descriptions, test results, and expert opinions, we may want to consider how the product was built, with what other models it is classed, and how it performed in comparison with those models. In other words, we may want to *analyze* the product, using those measures we discussed in chapter 6. We might argue that a car is superior because it takes advantage of new technology (cause–effect), because it offers more features than similarly priced models (classification), or because it outperforms the competition (comparison). All of these methods of analysis provide evidence for the car's superiority.

Although we have discussed persuasion primarily in relation to products, these same forms of evidence are used in establishing historical trends or evaluating artistic performances. In either case, the writer must use specific evidence drawn from the performance itself to support the claim.

EXERCISE 7.1 **Use of Evidence in a Movie Review**

In reviewing *Dances with Wolves,* what forms of evidence do these two movie critics use?

Riding to Redemption Ridge

by Richard Schickel, *Time*

John J. Dunbar (Kevin Costner) is an almost too perfect example of the new American male, that improbable beau ideal who has been created out of recent feminist fantasies and the failure of certain old-fashioned masculine dreams.

Dunbar drops out of his executive position in a large, hierarchical organization engaged in morally questionable work in order to get closer to nature—his own and Mother's. Once settled in the wilderness, he proves to be a sensitive and caring ecologist, tenderly nursing the land and its creatures. When, eventually, he encounters members of a culture that is alien to him, he is open to their ways, making no effort to impose his on them. Quite the opposite; he becomes an earnest convert to their life-style. When he finds a wife, he is exemplary in his gentle attentiveness and supportiveness as she struggles to find and assert a "personhood" that was confused by events in her early history.

What a guy! What an anachronism! For Dunbar is not a 1990s yuppie who suddenly decides to take his Sierra Club membership seriously. He is a lieutenant in the U.S. Cavalry, circa 1864. Given command of a small fort deep in Sioux country, he finds that its garrison has mysteriously disappeared. That provides him the freedom for self-discovery and for developing peaceable relationships with the Indians, as well as a romance with Stands with a Fist, a white woman who was taken captive by Indians as a child (hauntingly played by Mary McDonnell).

Dances with Wolves — it is the name the Sioux give Dunbar — is a movie that is very easy to make fun of, and not merely because of Dunbar's risible ahistoricism. It would be nice, for instance, to meet some white man, other than Dunbar, who is not a brutish lout. And it would not harm the film if there were one or two bad-natured Sioux visible in it. (The Pawnee, who obviously need a p.r. consultant, are portrayed as the scourge of the prairies.) It is, as well, all too easy to see why Costner — or any actor — would want to direct himself in the role: all that time alone on the screen, looking swell and acting noble, in a movie that runs three self-indulgent hours.

But *Dances with Wolves* is also a movie to take seriously. If the essence of the western   5
is riders on a ridgeline, surveying virgin countryside and reveling in their freedom to ride to a horizon unvexed by civilization, then it really does not make any difference if they are wearing feathers or Stetsons. The point has always been to remind us that open land shaped American history and character, and to make us ponder the cost of fencing off our former spaciousness and degrading the peoples who lived within it.

As a director, Costner is alive to the sweep of the country and the expansive spirit of the western-movie tradition. The good guys and the bad guys have exchanged their traditional roles in his film, but their contentions are staged with style and energy. In this reversal there is, just possibly, redemption, not only of historical crimes but also of a movie genre lately fallen into decrepitude. It is possible, surprisingly, to imagine John Ford happy in the great multiplex in the sky.

New Age Daydreams

by Pauline Kael, *The New Yorker*

A friend of mine broke up with his woman friend after they went to see *Field of*   1
Dreams: she liked it. As soon as I got home from *Dances with Wolves,* I ran to the phone and warned him not to go to it with his new woman friend. Set during the Civil War, this new big Indians-versus-Cavalry epic is about how the white men drove the Native Americans from their land. But Kevin Costner, who directed *Dances with Wolves* and stars in it, is not a man who lets himself be ripped apart by the violent cruelty of what happened. He's no extremist: it's a middle-of-the-road epic. Lieutenant Dunbar (Costner), a Union officer, sees that the Sioux have a superior culture — they're held up as models for the rest of us — and he changes sides. Costner must have heard Joseph Campbell on PBS advising people to "follow your bliss." This is a nature-boy movie, a kid's daydream of being an Indian. When Dunbar has become a Sioux named Dances with Wolves, he writes in his journal that he knows for the first time who he really is. Costner has feathers in his hair and feathers in his head.

Once our hero has become an Indian, we don't have to feel torn or divided. We can see that the white men are foulmouthed, dirty louts. The movie — Costner's debut as a director — is childishly naive. When Lieutenant Dunbar is alone with his pet wolf, he's like Robinson Crusoe on Mars. When he tries to get to know the Sioux, and he and they are feeling each other out, it's like a sci-fi film that has the hero trying to communicate with an alien race. But in this movie it's the white men who are the aliens: the smelly brutes are even killing each other, in the war between the North and the South. Luckily, we Indians are part of a harmonious community. Dances with Wolves has never seen people "so dedicated to their families." And he loves their humor.

At the beginning, there's a bizarre Civil War battle sequence with the wounded Lieutenant Dunbar riding on horseback between rows of Union and Confederate soldiers, his arms outstretched, welcoming bullets in a Christlike embrace, and throughout the movie he is brutalized, seems dead, but rises again. (Does getting beaten give Costner a self-righteous feeling? Even when it's as unconvincingly staged as it is here?) There's nothing really campy or shamelessly flamboyant after the opening. There isn't even anything with narrative power or bite to it. This Western is like a New Age social-studies lesson. It isn't really revisionist; it's the old stuff toned down and sensitized.

Costner and his friend Michael Blake, who worked up the material with him in mind and then wrote the novel and the screenplay, are full of good will. They're trying to show the last years of the Sioux as an independent nation from the Sioux point of view. And it's that sympathy for the Indians that (I think) the audience is responding to. But Costner and Blake are moviemaking novices. Instead of helping us understand the Sioux, they simply make the Sioux like genial versions of us. The film provides the groovy wisdom of the Sioux on the subjects of peace and togetherness: you never fight among yourselves — you negotiate. Each of the Indian characters is given a trait or two; they all come across as simpleminded, but so does the hero. Even the villains are endearingly dumb, the way they are in stories children write.

There's nothing affected about Costner's acting or directing. You hear his laid-back, surfer accent; you see his deliberate goofy faints and falls, and all the closeups of his handsomeness. This epic was made by a bland megalomaniac. (The Indians should have named him Plays with Camera.) You look at that untroubled face and know he can make everything lightweight. How is he as a director? Well, he has moments of competence. And the movie has an authentic vastness. The wide-screen cinematography, by Dean Semler, features the ridges, horizons, and golden sunsets of South Dakota; it's pictorial rather than emotionally expressive, but it's spacious and open at times, and there are fine images of buffalo pounding by.

Mostly, the action is sluggish and the scenes are poorly shaped. Crowds of moviegoers love the movie, though — maybe partly because the issues have been made so simple. As soon as you see the Indians, amused, watch the hero frolicking with his wolf, you know that the white men will kill it. Maybe, also, crowds love this epic because it's so innocent: Costner shows us his bare ass like a kid at camp feeling one with the great outdoors. He's the boyish man of the hour: the Sioux onscreen revere him, because he's heroic and modest, too. TV interviewers acclaim him for the same qualities. He's the Orson Welles that everybody wants — Orson Welles with no belly.

5

Warrants

A clearly worded claim and sound evidence provide the basis for an argument. However, most arguments require other elements as well. Suppose you were presented with the following argument:

Neebox are the finest athletic shoes you can buy. Whether you enjoy running, tennis, basketball, baseball, soccer, or golf, you'll find Neebox has a shoe that exceeds your expectations. The secret of Neebox's outstanding performance is a space-age material called *solerflexus*. And all Neebox shoes are made with soler-flexus. Neebox — the right shoe for you.

If we diagramed the argument presented in this advertisement, it would appear as follows:

Evidence ————————————→ **Claim**

Neebox are made with solerflexus.   Therefore, Neebox are the finest
                                           athletic shoes.

But what is "solerflexus"? we might ask. And why does it make Neebox better shoes? In other words, we want to know how the evidence supports the claim. The statement that connects the evidence to the claim is the **warrant.** Suppose the preceding advertisement included this information:

In laboratory tests, solerflexus showed greater resiliency and durability than any material previously used in athletic shoes. Solerflexus will absorb more shock, give you a springier step, increase your jumping power, and last longer than any conventional material.

This information explains the reason that solerflexus makes Neebox superior to other brands of athletic shoes. Our model of argument can now be expanded to include these three elements:

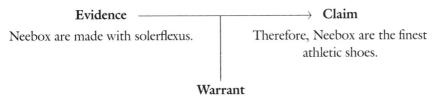

Evidence ————————————→ **Claim**

Neebox are made with solerflexus.   Therefore, Neebox are the finest
                                           athletic shoes.

Warrant

. . . because solerflexus has greater resiliency and durability than conventional materials.

In actuality, all arguments have warrants, whether stated or unstated. If you shout, "Get out of the house! There's a fire!" you probably will not have to specify, "Because remaining in the house during a fire may result in death or serious injury." However, unless your warrant is obvious, you should state it overtly rather than rely on the reader to supply it for you.

EXERCISE 7.2 **Warrants in a Movie Review**

In a movie review, the warrants are usually the implied standards of good screenwriting, acting, directing, and cinematography. For instance, Schickel condemns Costner's "ahistoricism." In other words, he believes that a good movie should portray a historic figure realistically, even if that means violating modern sensibilities. Schickel suggests that *Dances with Wolves* would be a better movie if the lieutenant were less concerned about ecology and more hostile to Indians. Of course, if you don't believe that movies should be historically accurate, then the evidence Schickel presents is unconvincing.

What other warrants are implied in the reviews by Schickel and Kael? Discuss with your Discovery Group the warrants you have found and whether or not you agree with them.

EXERCISE 7.3   Models of Argument

Complete the following diagrams by providing the necessary information.

1. An argument about illegal drugs

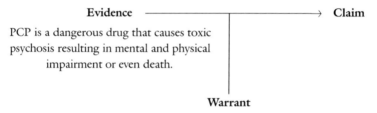

Evidence ——————————————→ **Claim**

PCP is a dangerous drug that causes toxic
psychosis resulting in mental and physical
impairment or even death.

Warrant

By making drugs illegal, we can discourage their use.

2. An argument about flame-retardant clothing

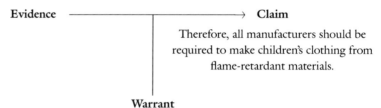

Evidence ——————————————→ **Claim**

Therefore, all manufacturers should be
required to make children's clothing from
flame-retardant materials.

Warrant

By regulating the manufacturers, we can
prevent further needless injury and death
to children.

3. An argument about protecting wilderness lands

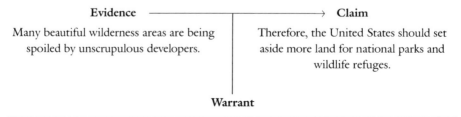

Evidence ——————————————→ **Claim**

Many beautiful wilderness areas are being
spoiled by unscrupulous developers.

Therefore, the United States should set
aside more land for national parks and
wildlife refuges.

Warrant

Reservations

Even when evidence, warrant, and claim are all in place, some arguments still have weaknesses. See if you can spot the weaknesses in this argument:

> With four games remaining, the Midtown Mosquitoes seem a sure bet to win the Central League this year. They demolished their first five opponents by the combined score of 86-3. The secret to the Mosquitoes' success is big Hector Martinez, who has pitched over 22 scoreless innings and is batting .468 with 8 homeruns, 2 triples, and 11 doubles.

The claim in this argument is clear: The Mosquitoes should win the Central League championship. The evidence is compelling as well. They have overwhelmed their first five opponents, and they have a potential all-star in Hector Martinez. The warrant is unstated, but the writer clearly believes that the ease with which the Mosquitoes have won their first five games indicates the team's ability to conquer their remaining opponents.

Still, we might wonder if the Mosquitoes have benefited from an easy schedule in the early part of the season. Perhaps they will face the most difficult teams in the final four games. Another weakness in this argument is suggested, almost ironically, by the prominence of Hector Martinez. What happens if Martinez is injured or misses part of the season for some other reason? More than one team has fallen apart in the absence of their best player. Having thought this argument over we are now ready to state some **reservations** about the claim. We might think of reservations as the loopholes in a contract, those minor points that have a way of undoing the whole agreement. Frequently, we express reservations through the use of "unless" statements. The claim will hold *unless* other factors intervene.

Evidence	Claim
With the help of Hector Martinez's outstanding hitting and pitching, the Mosquitoes are 5–0.	Therefore, the Mosquitoes will win the Central League.

Warrant

The outstanding hitting and pitching that allowed the Mosquitoes to dominate their opponents in the first five games indicate their ability to win the remaining games.

Reservations

. . . unless the first five opponents
were weak teams.
. . . unless the team loses Hector
Martinez.

LANGUAGE NOTE: QUALIFICATION

As we have stressed in this chapter, you must state the claim of your argument clearly. If you word your claim vaguely or ambiguously, your reader will be confused and probably frustrated as well. However, you should not confuse a clear claim with an absolute one. You cannot argue every point with absolute certainty. For instance, if you think that people are less careful with their money than they were 20 years ago, you might be tempted to state your claim this way:

> CLAIM: No one knows the value of a dollar anymore.

However, a blanket statement like this is easy to challenge. If I know of a single person that is careful with money — perhaps an elderly person living on a limited budget or a student working her way through school — I've disproved your argument. Unless we are convinced that our argument holds for every case, we'll probably want to state our claim in less than absolute terms:

> CLAIM: Few people know the value of a dollar anymore.

Whenever we are holding a claim with limited evidence or with some reservations, it is best to state our conclusions somewhat tentatively. We often do this by using **qualifiers,** words that indicate the degree of confidence we have in our claim. For example:

> The bond market *probably* will decline.

> Indoor soccer has proved to be *marginally* successful.

> Home sales are *likely* to fall in the second quarter of the year.

Although you may feel a qualifier weakens your claim, it frequently has just the opposite effect on your reader. It shows that you recognize the possibility of exceptions and that you are not dogmatically committed to your position. For this reason, many people believe that the use of a qualifier is the sign of a well-educated person who understands that many results are contingent upon circumstances and cannot be predicted with absolute certainty.

Obviously, some claims are stronger than others. If our evidence is shaky or our warrant seems doubtful or we uncover a whole string of reservations, we may want to *qualify* our claim. Qualifiers such as "usually," "commonly," or "in some cases" indicate the degree of confidence we are expressing in our claim. For this reason, most claims are qualified to some degree.

Arguing for Specific Audiences

The purpose of presenting evidence and establishing a warrant is to secure your audience's belief in your claim. But what if your audience refuses to accept your evidence? In a famous play by Molière, a wealthy aristocrat named Orgon has been duped by Tartuffe, a religious hypocrite. As well as stealing his estate, Tartuffe attempts to seduce Orgon's wife. Despite his family's pleas, Orgon remains convinced of Tartuffe's goodness. In the climactic scene, Orgon hides beneath a table while Tartuffe nearly rapes his wife. Only by catching him in the act is Orgon finally convinced of Tartuffe's hypocrisy. As Molière demonstrated so well in *Tartuffe*, the amount of evidence necessary to produce conviction varies from individual to individual. In designing your own arguments, you will need to consider carefully the amount of evidence necessary to convince your audience.

One way to increase the force of your evidence is by establishing the reliability of your sources. If you produce facts or statistics to verify your claim, you must indicate where they were obtained. If you use expert opinion as evidence for your claim, you will need to explain why your source is qualified to render judgment on this matter. If you argue that the Battle of Gettysburg was the turning point in the Civil War, you are more likely to be believed if you quote an eminent historian instead of your Uncle Ebenezer.

Similarly, warrants sometimes need to be substantiated. Imagine that a friend of yours tries to persuade you to invest $500 in a penny stock called Adventure Unlimited, which you are told specializes in "leisure technology." He tells you that the stock doubled in value in the past three months and that in a few more months your $500 will become $1,000.

The warrant for your friend's claim is that the future price of the stock can be predicted from its past performance. Unfortunately, nothing could be further from the truth, especially in penny stocks. Many penny stocks are pure scams. Adventure Unlimited may have no assets at all. The value of the stock has increased because gullible investors have been persuaded to put money into a "dummy" corporation. The early investors will sell out quickly and make an enormous profit. The latecomers will be left holding worthless shares. The $500 you invest will be worth nothing.

On the other hand, suppose you are asked to invest $500 in a company that makes spare parts for aircraft. You do a little homework and find that the cost of the stock plummeted when the company was slapped with a major lawsuit. However, the suit has been settled, and the company remains very profitable. Your friend tells you that because the price of stock in the company is low and the company's profits are high, now would be an excellent time to buy. This warrant is generally true, and your friend's argument is reasonable (although no investment is a "sure thing").

WEAKNESSES IN ARGUMENTS

The model of argument provides a useful way of discussing the reasons that arguments fail. Think of your argument like a car—let's say a Model A Ford. In order for the Model A to work, the wheels, the engine, the steering, and the other

FIGURE 7.1: Breakdowns in Argument

parts have to be working together. A nail in the tire can bring the whole car to a halt. Similarly, if any element of your argument is weak, it weakens the whole. Just as different parts of the Model A are liable to break down in particular ways—tires go flat, engines get out of tune—each element in the model of argument is subject to particular problems (see figure 7.1).

Problems with Evidence

One of the most frequent problems in arguments is simply a **lack of evidence.** We may debate the merits of the U.S. space program or the dangers of global warming all day, but if we are not well informed, we cannot come to valid conclusions. When we hear an appeal, no matter how sincerely or earnestly it is communicated, we need to look for the evidence that supports the claim.

Lack of evidence is fairly easy to detect; other problems with evidence can be more subtle. Sometimes evidence is **falsified** or **distorted** in order to make a point. Although reporters generally pride themselves on their objectivity, there have been occasional lapses. In one of the best-known cases, Janet Cooke received a Pulitzer Prize for a report about drug addiction that appeared in the *Washington Post.* Although Cooke claimed to have reported on real people, subsequent investigation revealed that the stories were deliberate falsifications.

Distortion is sometimes less deliberate than falsification, but no less dangerous in its results. In telling a story, we are all tempted to "add a few details" for effect. We say "he must have been going a hundred miles an hour" when we know that the real speed was more like 70 or 80 mph. Sometimes we distort information in order to impress people ("We jumped off this cliff that was about a hundred feet high!"). Sometimes we distort information because we really don't remember ("I think I read somewhere that about 90 percent of the population doesn't like coconut.").

And sometimes we distort information in order to make our own position look stronger. Imagine that you have received poor service at a restaurant. You ask to speak to the manager, and you want to make a strong case against the waiter. In the following dialogue, the customer's inner thoughts have been placed in brackets.

MANAGER: I understand you are unhappy with the service.

CUSTOMER: It was so bad that I'll never come here again.
[*Of course, I could change my mind if you run another special.*]

MANAGER: What was wrong?

CUSTOMER: Well, first of all, the waiter completely ignored us when we tried to order.
[*The restaurant was crowded. I suppose he might have had trouble getting to us as quickly as he liked.*]

MANAGER: What else?

CUSTOMER: Then he got our order totally fouled up.
[*Actually, he brought the right food, but he did get our drinks switched.*]

MANAGER: How did he treat you?

CUSTOMER: He was very rude. He even cursed us as we were leaving.
[*Well, he wasn't friendly. Of course, he was so busy, he really didn't have time for small talk. And I'm not sure if he cursed us or not, but he was mumbling to himself as we were leaving.*]

Probably most of us have been guilty of this kind of distortion. However, such distortion can do a tremendous amount of damage. A day later, we may have forgotten the whole affair, but the waiter may suffer repercussions for months.

Another subtle form of distorting evidence is through a **slanted** report. What inference would you draw from the following facts?

Item A: The suspect was seen prying open a back window of the darkened house at 414 Montgomery Avenue.

Item B: A short while later the suspect was seen carrying a heavy object out of the house.

Item C: The suspect was arrested with many valuable tools belonging to the owner of 414 Montgomery Avenue.

Problems with Warrants and Claims

Given these three items of information, many of us would assume that the suspect had stolen the tools. However, if we learned that the suspect was the son of the owner of 414 Montgomery Avenue, we might look on this information differently. If we learned, additionally, that the "suspect's" car had broken down a few blocks away and that he had left his keys in the car, what seemed like a criminal act turns out to be quite innocent.

As the preceding case illustrates, it is important to hear all sides of a story before drawing a conclusion. We should never deliberately omit information in order to make our case appear stronger. One of the reasons a free press is so valued in this country is because we believe that a well-informed citizenry is best able to make decisions affecting the future of us all. By omitting unfavorable evidence, we unfairly prejudice decisions. Furthermore, when our opponents reveal the suppressed evidence, we are likely to be publicly discredited.

As well as being weakened by problems with evidence, arguments are weakened by warrants that are **unacceptable** or **irrelevant.** For instance, we might argue that we could immediately put an end to all automobile accidents by making it unlawful to drive a car. Clearly, the warrant for such a claim would be unacceptable to most people. Few people would be willing to sacrifice their personal freedom to drive in order to prevent automobile accidents.

Irrelevant warrants are sometimes difficult to detect. Sometimes we are buried under an avalanche of facts without ever realizing that they are not relevant to the claim the writer is making. For instance, a leading educational theorist has argued that children are not learning to read because they are bored with the books they have to read in school. See if you can find the weakness in the warrant for the author's claim:

> The books from which children learn to read constitute an insult to their intelligence. Children come to school with a well-developed vocabulary of, on the average, about 4,000 words, some of them quite difficult ones. Even the least verbal of first-graders has mastered over 2,000 words. And then they are taught from primers containing a vocabulary of not more than 150 different words, out of which it is impossible to construct a meaningful story. . . . Children respond to this paucity of interesting material by becoming utterly disgusted with these texts.

While it is true that children come to school with a large speaking vocabulary, that does not mean they are able to recognize these words in print. It is unlikely that children would become interested in books containing hundreds of words they could not recognize. In fact, many children apparently enjoy simple and repetitive texts—think of the popularity of Dr. Seuss books over the years. Thus, it would appear that the speaking vocabulary of children may be largely irrelevant to the number of different words that should be contained in their first readers.

Finally, even if we have evidence that is genuine and a warrant that is relevant, we must be careful of **overstating** our claim. If we have found evidence that shows rodents are responsible for destroying food supplies and spreading disease, we can make a strong argument for efforts to eradicate these pests. We should be careful, however, of claiming that we are "on the verge of a human catastrophe unrivaled since the outbreak of the bubonic plague." Many readers may distrust even a legitimate claim if it is presented so sensationally. In general, we should make a claim that is supported by the evidence we have collected rather than making a sweeping generalization that can be easily disproved.

EXERCISE 7.4 **Weaknesses in Argument**

Identify weaknesses in the following arguments.

1. It is time for a change in this country. We have had enough of the status quo. What is needed is a fresh new vision of what government can be about. By electing Homer T. Fogle, you can be a part of bringing needed change to this country.

2. The U.S. Census Bureau estimates that by the year 2030 over 20 percent of the U.S. population will be 65 years of age or older. This will precipitate the greatest social crisis ever known to humankind.

3. Some people have wondered why credit card companies have continued to charge high rates of interest, typically from 17 to 20 percent, when the prime lending rate is at its lowest point in decades. What many people do not consider is that credit card companies employ thousands of people in our country. And these are good jobs with good benefits and good working conditions. Furthermore, the credit industry does not produce pollution or use up valuable natural resources. It is important that we consider the big picture when we begin to evaluate credit card companies.

4. You think amusement parks are safe! Well, think again! I'll bet about 90 percent of the people who go to amusement parks come away feeling sick at their stomach. And I know they have accidents at these parks. You just don't hear about them because they pay the newspapers to keep them hushed up. I had a friend who heard from a friend that at HappyWorld Amusement Park the roller coaster came off the track and a whole bunch of people were hurt. I'm telling you, anytime you go to one of those amusement parks, you're taking your life in your hands.

ARGUMENTS ABOUT DEFINITIONS

At first, it might seem impossible to argue about definitions — after all, a thing *is* what it *is*. But, in fact, arguments about what something *is* go on all the time. When times are bad for business, some people call it a "depression"; some call it a "recession"; and some call it an "economic slowdown." Clearly, an "economic slowdown" sounds less serious than a depression. Technically, a recession is defined as a decline in the gross national product that lasts for two consecutive quarters. But as one comedian noted, when you lose your job it's merely a recession; when I lose *my* job, it's a depression.

In some cases, the definition of a word or concept may not be controversial. You can assume that the reader will accept the dictionary definition or some other standard usage of the word. But in some cases, what we choose to call something and how we define it are at the basis of the argument. Note the difficulties faced by author Karen Lindsey in trying to define the word *family:*

> In writing this book [*Friends as Family*], I've had to make choices about terminology. This is always sticky, since words inevitably attempt to pin down human experience, and human experience always exists in countless variations. What do we call the family as we know it? The nuclear family is only a recent phenomenon, springing out of the older extended family. "Family of origin" is inaccurate if it attempts to include grandparents, aunts, uncles, and cousins whom we may not even meet until we are five, ten, or thirty, but who are still part of that concept called family. "Biological family" comes closest, and I have chosen to use it, but not without trepidation, since both marriage and adoption are integral parts of it.

In her book, Lindsey argues that the idea of family ought to be extended to include friends who share our lives in deep and personal ways. In order to make her argument, she must first convince her readers that the concept of family should not be limited to "biological family."

Methods of Definition

In general we argue definitions by looking at the ways words have been used historically, by the ways they are used currently, or by suggesting new meanings for words. One of the sources for the historical meaning of words is the *Oxford English Dictionary*. The *OED*, as it is frequently called, contains not only definitions but also sample uses of the word from past writers. For instance, if we wanted to argue that the idea of "culture" in the modern sense — an appreciation for art, history, music, etc. — sprang from the old idea of "cultivation," or tilling the soil, it might be useful to quote some historical uses of the word. The *OED* gives the earliest meaning of *cultivation* as "the action or practice of cultivating the soil; tillage, husbandry." However, by the seventeenth century the word was commonly used to mean "the cultivating or development (of the mind, faculties, manners, etc.); improvement or refinement by education and training." By 1873 the English poet and essayist Matthew Arnold could write, "Culture [is] acquainting ourselves with the best that has been known and said in the world."

More often, we are interested in contemporary uses of words. For instance, the word *rhetoric* has meant historically the study of effective speech and writing. However, in recent times it is usually used in the sense of "empty rhetoric," high-sounding talk that avoids the real issues. Frequently, we will appeal to the way people use words rather than to their traditional definitions in arguing for a particular meaning of a word.

EXERCISE 7.5 **Definitions in Context**

Read these passages that appeared in contemporary periodicals. What definition is implied for the boldfaced words?

1. Here's the idea: You take hazardous waste — sewage sludge, PCBs, old chemical weapons, almost anything — and stuff it into what amounts to an enormous pressure cooker, possibly one drilled deep beneath the earth's surface. And presto! Instead of toxic crud, you've got carbon dioxide, water, and maybe some salts and ammonia. The process, called **supercritical oxidation,** can break down any organic compound. You filter out possible dangerous heavy metals from the waste stream, and what's left is harmless. (*The Birmingham News*, 3 Sept. 1991)

2. On November 2, 1981, thousands of computers around the nation got very sick. Machines tied to the "Internet" network at universities, companies, and the military were all struck by a "**worm**" — a program that burrows from system to system, leaving copies of itself in each infected machine. The programmer apparently had innocuous intentions but botched the job: he unwittingly ordered his brainchild to deluge computers on the network with commands, slowing each to a standstill. (*Newsweek*, 29 July 1991)

3. There are some short-term costs that will be incurred. But better to compensate the losers, through special adjustments as a part of the FTA [Free Trade Agreement] negotiations, than to destroy the larger overall benefits. This is not a **zero-sum game.** The FTA will be a new engine of growth that will enrich both sides and enable them to meet the global competition from regional blocs now forming in Asia and Europe. (*U.S. News & World Report*, 8 July 1991)

Sometimes we give new meanings to old words or coin new words to express a particular idea. Until recent years, the word *bashing* referred primarily to physically striking something, as in, "The vandal bashed in the headlights of the Oldsmobile." But in the eighties the idea of bashing was extended to include the idea of insulting or belittling people. The word frequently was attached to particular individuals or groups that were under attack, e.g., "male bashing," "Arab bashing," or "Barry Manilow bashing." By coining these new words, writers and speakers were able to bring attention to the demeaning words and actions directed toward certain individuals or groups of people.

In the following example, Philip Lopate, a poet and critic, uses a new word, *foundation-think*, to express the philosophy held by many sources that fund charitable organizations.

Every day, worthwhile organizations struggling to stay alive find that their proposals have been turned down for some smooth-sounding reason that has nothing to do with the program's worth. If the program has already been in operation, many foundations don't want to fund it because they can't take credit for starting it. If the program conversely is brand new, they don't want to take the chance. Or the foundation has already funded something in that locale. Or they are no longer interested in supporting "services," they want to support basic change. They have a million rationalizations for all their moves which change from one year to the next. . . . When you look more closely at the system of rationales which may be called "*foundation-think*," very little of it stands up.

Extended Definitions

Clearly, arguments about definitions become more important as terms and concepts become more complicated. It is hard to imagine a case in which one would want to argue the definition of *cabbage*. On the other hand, defining a word like *hero* or *socialist* nearly always provokes some discussion. Such words generally require an **extended definition** rather than a simple sentence. The writer must bring to bear examples and other illustrations intended to demonstrate the precise meaning of the word being considered.

EXERCISE 7.6 **The Extended Definition**

The following essay by Aristides (pseudonym for Joseph Epstein) is an extended definition of the word *vulgar*. After reading the essay, discuss the questions that follow with your Discovery Group.

What Is Vulgar?

What's vulgar? Some people might say that the contraction of the words *what* and *is*   1
itself is vulgar. On the other hand, I remember being called a stuffed shirt by a reviewer of a book of mine because I used almost no contractions. I have forgotten the reviewer's name but I have remembered the criticism. Not being of that category of writers who never forget a compliment, I also remember being called a racist by another reviewer for observing that failure to insist on table manners in children was to risk dining with [A]paches. The larger criticisms I forget, but, oddly, these goofy little criticisms stick in the teeth like sesame seeds. Yet that last trope — is it, too, vulgar? Ought I really to be picking my teeth in public, even metaphorically?

What, to return to the question in uncontractioned form, is vulgar? Illustrations, obviously, are wanted. Consider a relative of mine, long deceased, my father's Uncle Jake and hence my granduncle. I don't wish to brag about bloodlines, but my Uncle Jake was a bootlegger during Prohibition who afterward went into the scrap-iron — that is to say, the junk — business. Think of the archetypal sensitive Jewish intellectual faces: of Spinoza, of Freud, of Einstein, of Oppenheimer. In my uncle's face you would not have found the least trace of any of them. He was completely bald, weighed in at around two hundred fifty pounds, and had a complexion of clear vermilion. I loved him, yet even as a child I knew there was about him something a bit — how shall I put it? — outsized, and I refer not merely to his personal tonnage. When he visited our home he generally greeted me by pressing a ten- or twenty-dollar bill into my hand — an amount of money quite impossible, of course, for a boy of nine or ten, when what was wanted was a quarter or fifty-cent piece. A widower, he would usually bring a lady-friend along; here his tastes ran to Hungarian women in their fifties with operatic bosoms. These women wore large diamond rings, possibly the same rings, which my uncle passed from woman to woman. A big spender and a high roller, my uncle was an immigrant version of the sport, a kind of Diamond Chaim Brodsky.

But to see Uncle Jake in action you had to see him at table. He drank whiskey with his meal, the bottle before him on the table along with another of seltzer water, both of which he supplied himself. He ate and drank like a character out of Rabelais. My mother served him his soup course, not in a regular bowl, but in a vessel more on the order of a tureen. He would eat hot soup and drink whiskey and sweat — my Uncle Jake did not, decidedly, do anything so delicate as perspire — and sometimes it seemed that the sweat rolled from his face right into his soup dish, so that, toward the end, he may well have been engaged in an act of liquid auto-cannibalism, consuming his own body fluids with whiskey chaser. . . .

. . . . .

The *Oxford English Dictionary*, which provides more than two pages on the word, is rather better at telling us what vulgar was than what it is. Its definitions run from "1. The common or usual language of a country; the vernacular. *Obs*." to "13. Having a common and offensively mean character; coarsely commonplace; lacking in refinement or good taste; uncultured, ill-bred." Historically, the word vulgar was used in fairly neutral description up to the last quarter of the seventeenth century to mean and describe the common people. Vulgar was common but not yet contemned. I noted such a neutral usage as late as a William Hazlitt essay of 1818, "On the Ignorance of the Learned," in which Hazlitt writes: "The vulgar are in the right when they judge for themselves; they are wrong when they trust to their blind guides." Yet, according to the OED, in 1797 the *Monthly Magazine* remarked: "So the word *vulgar* now implied something base and groveling in actions."

From the early nineteenth century on, then, vulgar has been purely pejorative, a key   5 term in the lexicon of insult and invective. Its currency as a term of abuse rose with the rise of the middle class; its spread was tied to the spread of capitalism and democracy. Until the rise of the middle class, until the spread of capitalism and democracy, people perhaps hadn't the occasion or the need to call one another vulgar. The rise of the middle class, the spread of capitalism and democracy, opened all sorts of social doors; social classes commingled as never before; plutocracy made possible almost daily strides from stratum to stratum. Still, some people had to be placed outside the pale, some doors had to be locked — and the cry of vulgarity, properly intoned, became a most effective Close Sesame. . . .

It would be helpful in drawing a definitional bead on the word vulgar if one could determine its antonym. But I am not sure that it has an antonym. Refined? I think not. Sophisticated? Not really. Elegant? Nope. Charming? Close, but I can think of charming vulgarians — M. Rabelais, please come forth and take a bow. Besides, charm is nearly as difficult to define as vulgarity. Perhaps the only safe thing to be said about charm is that if you think you have it, you can be fairly certain that you don't. . . .

Coming at things from a different angle, I imagine myself in session with a psychologist, playing the word association game. "Vulgar," he says, "quick, name ten items you associate with the word vulgar." "Okay," I say, "here goes:

1. Publicity

2. The Oscar awards

3. The Aspen Institute for Humanistic Studies

4. Talk shows

5. Pulitzer Prizes

6. Barbara Walters

7. Interviews with writers

8. Lauren Bacall

9. Dialogue, as an ideal

10. Psychology."

This would not, I suspect, be everyone's list. Looking it over, I see that, of the ten items, several are linked with one another. But let me inquire into what made me choose the items I did.

Ladies first. Barbara Walters seems to me vulgar because for a great many years now she has been paid to ask all the vulgar questions, and she seems to do it with such cheerfulness, such competence, such amiable insincerity. "What did you think when you first heard your husband had been killed?" she will ask, just the right hush in her voice. "What went on in your mind when you learned that you had cancer, now for the third time?" The questions that people with imagination do not need to ask, the questions that people with good hearts know they have no right to ask, these questions and others Barbara Walters can be depended upon to ask. "Tell me, Holy Father, have you never regretted not having children of your own?"

Lauren Bacall has only recently graduated to vulgarity, or at least she has only in the past few years revealed herself vulgar. Hers is a double vulgarity: the vulgarity of false candor — the woman who, presumably, tells it straight — and the vulgarity provided by someone who has decided to cash in her chips. In her autobiography, Miss Bacall has supposedly told all her secrets; when interviewed on television — by, for example, Barbara Walters — the tack she takes is that of the ringwise babe over whose eyes no one, kiddo, is going to pull the cashmere. Yet turn the channel or page, and there is Miss Bacall in a commercial or advertisement doing her best to pull the cashmere over ours. Vulgar stuff. Give her, I say, the hook.

Talk shows are vulgar for the same reason that Pulitzer Prizes and the Aspen Institute 10
for Humanistic Studies are vulgar. All three fail to live up to their pretensions, which are extravagant: talk shows to being serious, Pulitzer Prizes to rewarding true merit, the Aspen Institute to promoting "dialogue" (see item 9), "the bridging of cultures," "the interdisciplinary approach," and nearly every other phony shibboleth that has cropped up in American intellectual life over the past three decades.

Publicity is vulgar because those who seek it — and even those who are sought by it — tend almost without exception to be divested of their dignity. You have to sell yourself, the sales manuals used to advise, in order to sell your product. With publicity, though, one is selling only oneself, which is different. Which is a bit vulgar, really.

The Oscar awards ceremony is the single item on my list least in need of explanation, for it seems vulgar prima facie. It is the air of self-congratulation — of, a step beyond, self-adulation — that is so splendidly vulgar about the Oscar awards ceremony. Self-congratulation, even on good grounds, is best concealed; on no grounds whatever, it is embarrassing. But then, for vulgarity, there's no business like show business.

Unless it be literary business. The only thing worse than false modesty is no modesty at all, and no modesty at all is what interviews with writers generally bring out. "That most vulgar of all crowds, the literary," wrote Keats presciently — that is, before the incontestable evidence came in with the advent and subsequent popularity of what is by now that staple of the book review and little magazine and talk show, the interview with the great author. What these interviews generally come down to is an invitation to writers to pontificate upon things for which it is either unseemly for them to speak (the quality of their own work) or upon which they are unfit to judge (the state of the cosmos). Roughly a decade ago I watched Isaac Bashevis Singer, when asked on a television talk show what he thought of the Vietnam War, answer, "I am a writer, and that doesn't mean I have to have an opinion on everything. I'd rather discuss literature." Still, how tempting it is, with an interviewer chirping away at your feet, handing you your own horn and your own drum, to blow it and beat it. As someone who has been interviewed a time or two, I can attest that never have I shifted spiritual gears so quickly from self-importance to self-loathing as during and after an interview. What I felt was, well, vulgar.

Psychology seems to me vulgar because it is too often overbearing in its confidence. Instead of saying, "I don't know," it readily says, "unresolved Oedipus complex" or "manic-depressive syndrome" or "identity crisis." As with other intellectual discoveries before (Marxism) and since (structuralism), psychology acts as if it is holding all the theoretical keys, but then in practice reveals that it doesn't even know where the doors are. As an old *Punch* cartoon once put it, "It's worse than wicked, my dear, it's vulgar."

Reviewing my list and attempting to account for the reasons why I have chosen the   15 items on it, I feel I have a firmer sense of what I think vulgar. Exhibitionism, obviousness, pretentiousness, self-congratulation, self-importance, hypocrisy, overconfidence — these seem to me qualities at the heart of vulgarity in our day. It does, though, leave out common sense, a quality which, like clarity, one might have thought one could never have in overabundance. (On the philosophy table in my local bookstore, a book appeared with the title *Clarity Is Not Enough;* I could never pass it without thinking, "Ah, but it's a start.") Yet too great reliance on common sense can narrow the mind, make meager the imagination. Strict common sense abhors mystery, seldom allows for the attraction of tradition, is intolerant of questions that haven't any answers. The problem that common sense presents is knowing the limits of common sense. The too commonsensical man or woman grows angry at anything that falls outside his or her common sense, and this anger seems to me vulgar.

Vulgarity is not necessarily stupid but it is always insensitive. Its insensitivity invariably extends to itself: the vulgar person seldom knows that he is vulgar, as in the old joke about the young woman whose fiancé reports to her that his parents found her vulgar, and who, enraged, responds, "What's this vulgar crap?" Such obvious vulgarity can be comical, like a nouveau riche man bringing opera glasses to a porno film, or the Chicago politician who, while escorting the then ruling British monarch through City Hall, supposedly introduced him to the assembled aldermen by saying, "King, meet the boys." But such things are contretemps merely, not vulgarity of the insidious kind.

In our age vulgarity does not consist in failing to recognize the fish knife or to know the wine list but in the inability to make distinctions. Not long ago I heard a lecture by a Harvard philosophy professor on a Howard Hawks movie, and thought, as one high reference after another was made in connection with this low subject, "Oh, Santayana, 'tis better you are not alive to see this." A vulgar performance, clearly, yet few people in the audience of professors and graduate students seemed to take notice.

A great many people did notice, however, when, in an act of singular moral vulgarity, a publisher, an editor, and a novelist recently sponsored a convicted murderer for parole, and the man, not long after being paroled, murdered again. The reason for these men speaking out on behalf of the convict's parole, they said, was his ability as a writer; his work appeared in the editor's journal; he was to have a book published by the publisher's firm; the novelist had encouraged him from the outset. Distinctions — crucial distinctions — were not made: first, that the man was not a very good writer, but a crudely Marxist one, filled with hatreds and half-truths; second, and more important, that, having killed before, he might kill again — might just be a pathological killer. Not to have made these distinctions is vulgarity at its most vile. But to adopt a distinction new to our day, the publisher, the editor, and the novelist took responsibility for what they had done — responsibility but no real blame.

Can an entire culture grow vulgar? Matthew Arnold feared such might happen in "the mechanical and material civilisation" of the England of his day. Vladimir Nabokov felt it already had happened in the Soviet Union, a country, as he described it, "of moral imbeciles, of smiling slaves and poker-faced bullies," without, as in the old days, "a Gogol, a Tolstoy, a Chekhov in quest of that simplicity of truth [who] easily distinguished the vulgar side of things as well as the trashy systems of pseudo-thought." Moral imbeciles, smiling slaves, poker-faced bullies — the curl of a sneer in those Nabokovian phrases is a sharp reminder of the force that the charge of "vulgar" can have as an insult — as well as a reminder of how deep and pervasive vulgarity can become.

But American vulgarity, if I may put it so, is rather more refined. It is also more 20 piecemeal than pervasive, and more insidious. Creeping vulgarity is how I think of it, the way Taft Republicans used to think of creeping socialism. The television commercial by a once-serious actor for a cheap wine, an increased interest in gossip and trivia that is placed under the rubric Style in our most important newspapers: so the vulgar creeps along, while everywhere the third- and fourth-rate — in art, in literature, in intellectual life — is considered good enough, or at any rate, highly interesting.

Yet being refined — or at least sophisticated — American vulgarity is vulnerable to the charge of being called vulgar. "As long as war is regarded as wicked," said Oscar Wilde, "it will always have its fascination. When it is looked upon as vulgar, it will cease to be popular." There may be something to this, if not for war then at least for designer jeans, French literary criticism, and other fashions. The one thing the vulgar of our day do not like to be called is vulgar. So crook your little finger, purse your lips, distend your nostrils slightly as you lift your nose in the air the better to look down it, and repeat after me: *Vulgar! Vulgar! Vulgar!* The word might save us all.

Activity

1. How is *vulgar* defined in this essay?

2. Do you agree with this definition?

3. Would you consider someone like Uncle Jake to be vulgar? Do you think television commentators like Barbara Walters are vulgar?

4. As a group, list 10 things you consider to be vulgar.

WRITING ASSIGNMENT **An Extended Definition**

Step one   Write an extended definition for one of the terms that follows (or select a word of your own choosing after consulting with your instructor).

vulgar	aggressive	middle class
liberal	alcoholic	noble
bigot	rich	wimp
date (as in a social engagement)	handicapped	ecology
	rape	passion
fanatic	intellectual	justice

Step two   Make a list of situations where you have heard this word used. You also might want to consult the *OED* for some historical uses of this word.

Step three   Write a discovery draft in which you explore various examples of the use of this word. Include your own sense of how the word is properly defined.

Step four   Meet with your Discovery Group. Have each member of the group try to define your word in a different way. Respond to their definitions, either defending your own point of view or incorporating these new definitions into your own.

Step five   Continue drafting until you are satisfied with your work. Edit the final paper carefully.

ARGUMENTS ABOUT CAUSES

All of us frequently ask the question "Why?" Why did the electricity go off? Why did the Red Sox lose? Why did the student fail chemistry? Whenever we ask "Why?" we are searching for causes. We need to understand what caused something in order to control it. If the electricity went off because of a storm, we simply will wait for the power to come back on. If it went off because of faulty wiring, we will need to have the wiring repaired.

We can try to determine what caused something in a variety of ways. We may begin by considering all the possible causes. We might read up on what has historically caused such events to occur or conduct an investigation to determine possible causes. Suppose our question is "Why do people enjoy automobile races?" Let's begin with a list of possible reasons:

People are fascinated by speed. It's exhilarating to watch cars spinning around a track at 200 mph.

Nobody knows who is going to win a car race. I think people enjoy the suspense. A driver can lead for 99 laps and have an engine conk out at the last minute.

It's a good excuse to goof off and drink beer all afternoon.

A car race is a spectacle from start to finish. The lap cars, the checkered flag, the roar of the engines, the furious activity of the pit crews—it's all one great show.

Let's be honest—people go to see the wrecks.

Car racing is the ultimate sport of skill and nerve. You don't have to be six feet tall or weigh 300 pounds to race a car. Racing requires planning, strategy, physical endurance, and the ability to take risks.

Automobile racing is part of the American dream. What kid hasn't wanted to punch it all the way to the floor and see how fast he could go? Since we can't drive 200 mph, we pay money to watch others do it for us.

Automobile racing is an important testing ground for new innovations. Many advances in technology, from rear view mirrors to fuel injection, were used on a race track long before they were introduced on factory cars.

In many cases, we'll recognize **multiple causes** for an individual event. You might think people attend automobile races because they enjoy the speed of the cars, the skill of the drivers, and the spectacle of the race. However, you may want to challenge some of the ideas people have about race fans—that they are all beer-guzzling rednecks or that they are all titillated by death and destruction. In order to establish real causes, you probably would want to sample the opinion of people who attend automobile races. The comments of these people would become the evidence to support (or contradict) your own thoughts about why people attend automobile races.

EXERCISE 7.7   Analyzing Causes

Choose one of the questions below and work with your Discovery Group to develop a list of possible reasons.

Why do teenagers get pregnant?

Why do people use drugs?

Why are we interested in outer space?

Why do people watch soap operas?

Why do people want to be rich?

Why do people lie?

Why do people play games?

Why do people starve themselves?

Why do children play make-believe?

Why do people work?

Why do people like professional wrestling?

Why do people buy books?

Why do people go to concerts?

Why do people watch television?

WRITING ASSIGNMENT **An Argument about Causes**

We frequently write about causes when we want to understand why something went wrong or we want to improve our current way of doing something. Sometimes we explore causes simply because of curiosity. In either case, we will want to be sure that we understand all the underlying causes for an event and that we present sound evidence to back our claims.

Step one   Ask your own "why" question, or use one from the list in exercise 7.7, and develop a list of possible reasons.

Step two   Collect information, using interviews, surveys, or published information to establish the causes for this event.

Step three   Write a discovery draft, exploring the different causes for this event.

Step four   Read your draft to the Discovery Group and have them answer these questions:

1.   What information did the writer gather that surprised or interested you in some way?

2.   How believable do these causes seem?

3.   Where is more evidence needed? What kind of evidence is required?

4.   What is the logic behind the order of the causes given; for instance, does the writer proceed from less important to more important causes? Should the order be changed?

5.   Has the writer neglected any obvious causes?

6.   What would you change about this paper?

Step five   Continue drafting and revising based on your group's comments. Submit your final draft with all of your preliminary drafts and notes. Also include a short statement of how your understanding of your subject progressed as you conducted your research and how you used the comments of your group to improve your writing.

ARGUMENTS ABOUT VALUES

Perhaps you've heard the old adage "Never discuss religion or politics with your friends." Many people shy away from discussing controversial subjects because they don't believe such subjects can be discussed rationally. No one wants to start an argument that creates anger and hostility instead of understanding. However, it is important to be able to discuss our values calmly and rationally. Whether we are discussing corporal punishment or capital punishment, we need to begin by presenting our case clearly and consistently.

Of course, not all value judgments are controversial. In our society, we would find general agreement that child abuse is wrong, that judges should not take bribes, that cocaine is a dangerous drug. We can find agreement on these issues because we share common values—children should be treated with love and respect, judges should be impartial, physical and mental health should be encouraged. In writing about specific issues, we need to appeal to these common values.

If we think of our value judgments as claims and our common values as warrants, we see that arguments about values clearly conform to the model of argument described earlier.

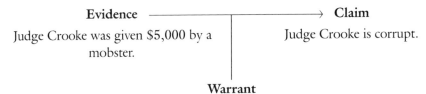

Evidence ————————————→ Claim

Judge Crooke was given $5,000 by a mobster.   Judge Crooke is corrupt.

Warrant

Judges who accept money from mobsters will hand down corrupt verdicts.

EXERCISE 7.8 **Arguments about Values**

Complete the model of argument for these value judgments:

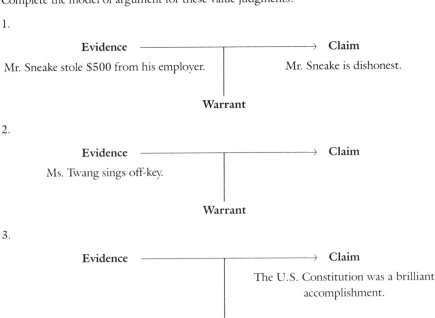

1.

Evidence ————————————→ Claim

Mr. Sneake stole $500 from his employer.   Mr. Sneake is dishonest.

Warrant

2.

Evidence ————————————→ Claim

Ms. Twang sings off-key.

Warrant

3.

Evidence ————————————→ Claim

The U.S. Constitution was a brilliant accomplishment.

Warrant

4.

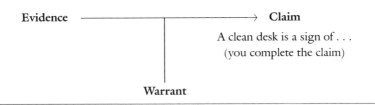

Evidence ————————————————→ Claim

A clean desk is a sign of . . .
(you complete the claim)

Warrant

Whenever we make a statement that contains a value judgment like "New Mexico is a wonderful state," we generally base our judgment on a set of criteria we have developed for "wonderful states." Of course, we may simply be parroting what others have said about New Mexico. If so, we are merely offering uninformed opinion. But if we have some knowledge of New Mexico (and other states), we should be able to support our opinion by explaining how New Mexico meets the criteria we have developed for wonderful states. Suppose we use the following criteria:

A wonderful state has . . .

. . . a varied landscape. (1)

. . . many recreational opportunities. (2)

. . . a strong cultural heritage. (3)

. . . a clean environment. (4)

To demonstrate that New Mexico fits the criteria for a wonderful state, we might give the following evidence:

1. Varied landscape. From the spectacular Sangre de Cristo mountains to the shifting dunes of White Sands National Monument, New Mexico offers a variety of scenic wonders.

2. Recreational opportunities. Anglers will enjoy fishing along the Chama River. Skiers will enjoy the challenge of the slopes at Angel Fire, Red River, or one of the other ski areas. Explorers will test their strength along the trails of the Pecos Wilderness. Equestrians will cheer on the horses at Ruidoso Downs. Spelunkers will seek out Carlsbad Caverns National Park. And the scientific minded will want to see Los Alamos Scientific Museum and the Atomic Museum in Albuquerque.

3. Cultural heritage. In Santa Fe you can discover the Spanish heritage that goes back to 1609. In Taos you will find treasures of Native American art and craft. Reminders of the Old West are everywhere — Fort Sumner and the grave of Billy the Kid, the Kit Carson memorial, and long forgotten ghost towns. And an even more distant past echoes through the ruins of Bandelier National

Monument, Aztec Ruins National Monument, and the Gila Cliff Dwellings National Monument.

4.   Clean environment. New Mexico is still largely an unspoiled state. You will enjoy the clean air and pure waters.

Establishing a set of criteria helps to make clear the basis for our value judgment. Of course, someone else might define a wonderful state differently. They might insist that it have a city with a cosmopolitan flair like Los Angeles or New York. Or they might insist that it have a beautiful seacoast. And given such criteria, New Mexico might not be judged so highly. But whatever criteria we choose to use, we show that our judgments are not arbitrary or capricious, but carefully considered.

EXERCISE 7.9 **Developing a Set of Criteria**

Select one of the following subjects and work with your Discovery Group to develop a set of criteria.

a classic car

an obnoxious salesperson

a well-run department store

a terrible restaurant

a good book

a delicious chef's salad (or some other food item)

a beautiful cemetery

a bad television show

a good dog

a funny cartoon

a miserable vacation

WRITING ASSIGNMENT **An Evaluation**

Writing a convincing evaluation is one of the most challenging writing assignments and also one of the most satisfying. Because values are deeply embedded in all of us, we tend to react emotionally to evaluative arguments. In writing on the issues below, you will need not only to collect evidence but also to be sensitive to the feelings and attitudes of those who hold opinions different from your own.

Step one   Select one of the subjects below and freewrite on it for five minutes.

1.   We often hear quoted that phrase from the Declaration of Independence that declares our right to "life, liberty, and the pursuit of happiness." Are these rights absolute, or are

they earned in some way? For instance, we deprive some citizens of the right to liberty when they violate certain laws of society. Could it also be argued that we deprive people of life by providing inadequate health care? Do we deprive people of the pursuit of happiness when they receive an inferior education? What are our rights? Where do they come from? On what grounds should those rights be suspended?

2. Imagine that advances in genetic engineering made it possible to choose various features of your children—intelligence, hair color, complexion, creativity, and so on. Would you take advantage of this advanced technology? Why or why not?

3. What if certain food supplements recommended in a popular book on dieting could lead to illness or even death for some people? Should the book be withdrawn from circulation? What if a book describing methods of suicide leads to increased teenage suicide? Should its publication be halted? What if a book advocating violence and anarchy leads to an upsurge in youth gangs? Should such a book be banned? What if thousands of children respond to a book by a religious leader telling them to leave their parents and live on a commune with no contact with the outside world? Should such a book be repressed? Would you describe such attempts to restrict the flow of information as censorship? What is censorship? Is it ever justified?

4. The parents of an eleventh-grader have decided to move to a new city. The father and mother have both received attractive offers for jobs that will mean more money and prestige. In addition, they will be closer to their relatives. Their eleventh-grade child refuses to leave, insisting on the right to stay in her own school and keep her existing friends. Should the parents have the right to make the child move?

5. A wealthy investor has bought a highly successful chain of clothing stores. He takes the profits from the clothing stores and reinvests them in another business. Ultimately, so much money is drained from the clothing-store chain that it goes bankrupt. Employees are laid off, and creditors are paid only a small portion of what is owed them. The profits that have gone into the other business, however, cannot be touched, and the investor retains all of this money. Although there is a public outcry, the owner defends himself, saying it is his right to decide where his money is invested. Had the government stopped him from reinvesting his profits in another business, it would amount to state control of private enterprise, that is to say, socialism. Would you defend the owner's right to reinvest profits in another business? Should creditors have a right to pursue money invested in the other business (even if doing so might ruin that business and destroy the life savings of other investors in that business)? Is government responsible for making businesses operate in a fair way, or should market forces be allowed to run their course?

Step two Write down your basic position. For instance, if you are writing about the right of Americans to life, liberty, and the pursuit of happiness, your position might be that these are ideals to be sought, not rights which can be unconditionally guaranteed. Next, write down two or more implications of your position. Choose specific situations where the position you have taken would make a difference. For instance, you might note that those serving in the armed forces are categorically deprived of certain liberties for the good of the country. Your position on the right to liberty would be consistent with current military codes of conduct. Now write a discovery draft that explains your position and shows its logical implications.

Step three   Imagine an opponent that probably would disagree with the stance you have taken in your writing. Ask your Discovery Group to respond to your paper as that opponent. For instance, if you defend the right of the government to control business, your group should read the paper as though they were business tycoons who thought they should be free to do whatever they pleased with their own money.

Step four   Rewrite your paper, trying to answer the specific objections raised by your group in step three. Submit your final draft with all of your preliminary drafts and notes.

BYTE-SIZE BULLETIN: COLLABORATIVE WRITING

Most real-world documents are produced by teams working together to collect, organize, and synthesize materials. A software designer may have an idea for a new computer game called Dueling Dojos. She writes a brief description of the game, how long it would take to develop, and so on. A supervisor reads the proposal, raises some questions, and sends it back to the designer. The designer answers the questions to the supervisor's satisfaction, and the supervisor sends it to a marketing department to see if the people there think it would be successful. The marketing department thinks it's a super game with great potential sales. However, some aspects of the game seem very similar to an existing game called Battling Bongos, so the supervisor has the legal department look into possible patent infringement. The legal department thinks the two games have enough differences to avoid a suit by the developers of Battling Bongos. The supervisor has a technical writer prepare a report that includes the description of the game, the marketing report, the legal department report, along with the production schedule and estimated costs. The supervisor then presents this report to the division manager for final approval. Clearly, the development of a proposal for Dueling Dojos requires the writing of a number of people, some of whom have never even met.

Computers can make this kind of collaboration work even better. By using a word processor, the software designer was able to revise the original proposal quickly and efficiently in response to the supervisor's suggestions. The marketing department solicited the opinions of field representatives from all over the United States. They sent their responses back to the main office by hooking their personal computers up to a telephone line with a computer modem. The legal department was able to search patents quickly through an electronic database. As well as preparing the final report on a computer, the technical writer used a spell checker and a style checker to search for spelling and stylistic errors. Because all the computers at the main office are networked (each computer can retrieve documents from other computers in other offices), none of these reports may have ever been on paper until the final version was printed out.

If you have access to a computer, explore the opportunities for collaborative work that are available to you. You may participate in computer "discussion groups" over a network that help you develop ideas for your writing or that respond to drafts you have written. Or you may find it useful to exchange disks containing parts of a report that you are writing collaboratively with a group. Computers can frequently reduce the labor involved in developing a document so that you can focus on the important ideas you are trying to communicate.

THE CRITICAL MOMENT

Although it is clearly wrong to falsify or distort evidence, is it wrong to ignore evidence that weakens your own position? For instance, if you are arguing that college athletics strengthens the character of young men and women, should you mention only the positive aspects of participation in athletics — teamwork, perseverance, and the like — or should you also mention possible negative effects? Here are some questions to help you think through this issue:

1.   When someone explains an issue to you, do you want to get the whole story or only what the writer is willing to tell you?

2.   How do you respond to an argument in which the writer has ignored what seems to be an obvious shortcoming or weakness?

3.   What happens to a writer's credibility if you learn that he or she has suppressed important information?

CHAPTER 8

Writing to Investigate

DISCOVERING YOUR TOPIC

The best topics, like tomatoes, are home grown. You probably will enjoy research more if you pick your own topic. Because you will invest a considerable amount of time into your research project, you should be deeply interested in the topic you have chosen. What are the subjects that interest you? What questions puzzle you? Luther Burbank, the pioneering horticulturist, once crawled through an entire potato field on his knees, looking for a seed pod that was crucial to one of his experiments. His research was clearly driven by an intense desire to know. If you are intensely interested in your area of research, you also will be driven to know more.

In order to conduct your research, you need more than a topic: You need a research question. Suppose you are fascinated with professional wrestling. You might list these as potential research topics:

The growth of professional wrestling

The history of professional wrestling

Professional wrestling: The athletes and the fans

Hulk Hogan: The man and the myth

Although these topics may suggest some interesting lines of development, none of them raise specific questions. If you begin with a general topic, you are likely to wind up with nothing more than a weak summary. Your research will be more interesting if you state the goal of your research more precisely. In other words, you must take on the role of an investigator, not merely a reporter. Here are some investigative questions:

Is professional wrestling dangerous? Are the faked blows sometimes mistimed so that they result in real injuries? Do some athletes lose their temper and become overly aggressive?

How do athletes train for professional wrestling? Are some wrestlers really better, or is it all a matter of "hype"? How do amateur wrestlers feel about the pro circuit?

Is professional wrestling a degrading sport? Who are the "good guys" and the "bad guys" in the sport? How do the costumes reinforce the images?

Who are the fans of professional wrestling? Do they take it seriously? How do they behave during a match? How does watching professional wrestling affect children? Do fans tend to act out the aggressive activity they see in the sport?

As you investigate your topic further, the direction of your report will become more clearly defined, but you must begin with questions that are worth pursuing.

EXERCISE 8.1 Topics for Investigation

In your Discovery Group, discuss which of these questions might be interesting to investigate. Which questions seem to have obvious conclusions? How could these questions be reworded to make them more interesting?

1. Are political elections "bought" in America?
2. Are children in America sometimes abused?
3. Does legalized gambling lead to more organized crime?
4. Is the bald eagle an endangered species?
5. How should you respond when somebody on the street asks you for money?
6. Is Japan a major economic power in the world?
7. Why is an airplane crash front-page news and the AIDS epidemic relegated to the back pages?
8. What kind of care is provided for children whose parents have been taken to jail?
9. Do many Americans enjoy collecting things?
10. What happens when a man goes out of state and refuses to pay alimony to his ex-wife?
11. Should vicious dogs be used to protect buildings, construction sites, and so on?
12. Is a steady diet of junk food bad for you?

EXERCISE 8.2 Questions for Research

Write five questions that you think would yield interesting research. If you can't think of any questions, browse current periodicals in the library. Meet with your Discovery Group to discuss which questions they feel would be most worthwhile for you to pursue.

COLLECTING INFORMATION: LIBRARY RESEARCH

Once you have decided on an interesting question, you are ready to begin your research. But before going to the library to see what others have said about your topic, consider what you already know and what you need to know. In other words, conduct a knowledge inventory, as we discussed in chapter 4.

Suppose you have become interested in a local referendum to legalize dog racing in your county. You listed these questions to investigate:

What benefits would come from dog racing?

What would be the drawbacks? Would crime increase?

Would some people bet the money for "baby's new shoes" on the dogs?

Would the dogs be treated humanely?

Now you conduct a knowledge inventory to see what you already know about the subject. Here's what you come up with:

Greyhounds are usually (always?) used for racing.

The dogs chase a fake rabbit.

Many people currently drive to other tracks to bet.

A percentage of the take would benefit schools and community services.

There have been reports of mistreated animals.

Operations will be supervised by a state commission.

The owner will reportedly profit greatly from the track.

As you write what you know, you will raise some additional questions to investigate. You may find it helpful to consider these systematically, using a method like the 5 W's and an H discussed in chapter 1. Begin to think about where the information could be obtained to answer the questions you raise:

5 W's and an H	Sources
WHO?	
Who will be the *owners*?	Interviews with the owners.
Are they trustworthy?	Interviews with other business leaders.
Are they good managers?	Public records.

WHAT?

What are the *results* of dog racing? increased revenue? increased crime? increased tourism?

Interviews with experts on dog racing.

Published studies of dog racing.

Interviews with proponents and opponents of dog racing.

What are *public attitudes* toward dog racing?

Surveys.

WHERE?

Where is the new track to be *located?*

Interviews with developers, Realtors, area residents.

WHEN?

When will the issue be brought to a *vote?*

Interviews with voting officials, developers.

If passed, when will *construction* begin?

When would *racing* begin?

WHY?

Why should dog racing be *allowed/prohibited?*

Interviews with civic leaders, church leaders, citizens.

HOW?

How will *profits* be spent?

Interviews with developers, other track owners. Reports of earnings from other tracks.

How will the *dogs* be treated?

Interviews with veterinarians, animal welfare groups.

Locating Library Resources

Often you will begin your research in the library. You may want to look at back issues of the local newspapers to see what advocates and opponents of dog racing are saying. Perhaps you can find books or articles that discuss the sport. In some cases, all the information on a topic may come from print sources. If you are interested, for instance, in the Dead Sea Scrolls or the Bayeux Tapestry, you will

CALVIN and HOBBES © 1989 Watterson. Universal Press Syndicate

rely primarily on published materials about these artifacts (unless you have access to a specialist in this area). Even if you are planning to do some original research, you will want to know what others have said about your subject so that you can ask informed questions of your sources.

Library resources are usually divided into four main categories. *Reference materials,* such as indexes, encyclopedias, and biographical dictionaries, provide quick access to general information. *Books* provide detailed information on particular topics. *Periodicals,* such as magazines, journals, and newspapers, provide current information on a multitude of subjects. Many libraries serve as repositories of *government documents* published by state and federal governments. In addition to these four main categories of information, there are maps, recordings, rare books, manuscripts, and many other items of interest in a library's holdings.

Reference Materials   The reference collection of a library is usually housed in a separate room from the main collection. Reference materials provide easy access to specific items of information. Unlike most books, they are not designed to be read from start to finish. The entries are often alphabetized or carefully indexed so that you can quickly find the particular item of information you seek.

Reference books are often good places to begin your search because they contain general information. The reference librarian will be of great help to you in beginning your search and may be able to guide you to specific bibliographies that will help you locate sources on your topic.

The reference book you select will depend on the kind of information you need:

Information needed	Source
1. Need background information on an unfamiliar subject or specific factual information on your subject?	Consult an **encyclopedia** (such as the *Encyclopaedia Britannica* or the *Encyclopedia Americana*).

2. Need information about words and their meanings? — Consult a **general dictionary** (such as the *American Heritage Dictionary* or *Webster's Ninth New Collegiate Dictionary*).

3. Need information about unusual words or word histories? — Consult an **unabridged dictionary** (such as the *Oxford English Dictionary* or *Webster's Third New International Dictionary Unabridged*).

4. Need help finding information in magazines, newspapers, or other periodical publications? — Consult an **index** (such as the *Readers' Guide to Periodical Literature* or the *New York Times Index*).

5. Need more detailed information about the content of articles in magazines or professional journals? — Consult an **abstract** (such as *Sociological Abstracts* or *Chemical Abstracts*).

6. Need information about important people? — Consult a **biographical dictionary** (such as the *Dictionary of American Biography* or *Who's Who in America*).

7. Need lists of biographical or historical information or statistical information about the United States? — Consult an **almanac** (such as the *World Almanac* or the *Statistical Abstract of the United States*).

EXERCISE 8.3 **Finding Information in Reference Sources**

Where would you look first to find the answers to the following questions?

1. What was Houdini's real name?

2. What motion picture won the Academy Award in 1942?

3. Who led the movement for free public education in America?

4. What is a panjandrum?

5. Who was the first woman telegrapher?

6. What was the meaning of "nice" in 1600?

7. What were some of the most common remarks made by reviewers of the novel *Gone With the Wind* when it was first released?

8. What military campaigns were led by Alexander the Great?

9. What percent of the U.S. population lived in poverty during 1990?

10. What Broadway show sold the most tickets during the 1980s?

11. Who was the commissioner of major league baseball when Pete Rose was banned from participation?

12. What mutual fund outperformed all others from 1985 to 1990?

13. What colors are in Denmark's flag?

14. What is the highest recorded price ever paid for a painting?

15. What is the address of the National Crop Insurance Association?

Books   In searching for the books you will use in your research, you probably will use either a card catalog or a computerized index. (See "Byte-Size Bulletin: Using Computer Databases" for information on a computer search.) In the card catalog, books are generally listed by author, title, and subject. In most cases, you will begin your research with a subject in mind unless you have already obtained a bibliography providing specific authors and titles.

Most subjects can be identified in various ways. If you've ever used the Yellow Pages, you know that finding the right subject entry can be tricky. If you want your car repaired, you don't look under "Car Repair," but under "Automobile Repairing & Service." However, if you want your car washed, you look under "Car Washes," not "Automobile Washing." Subject searches in the card catalog can present similar difficulties. If you are looking for books about eighteenth-century Scottish poets, do you look under "literature" or "poetry"? Do you look under "Scotland" or "Great Britain"? Is there a separate category for the eighteenth century, or are all the Scottish poets lumped together? (Incidentally, the correct answer is "Scottish poetry, 18th century.")

One way to resolve this problem is simply to keep looking under different subject headings until you find the right one. Sometimes you will find a card directing you to the right subject heading. For instance, if you look under "Substance Abuse," you may be told to "See: Drug Abuse, Alcoholism." It also may be helpful to consult the *Library of Congress Subject Headings*. The LCSH, which is usually kept on a stand near the card catalog, lists thousands of possible subject headings. If you look up an official subject heading, it will appear in bold print. If your subject heading is not an official one, the LCSH will suggest other subject headings to try. The LCSH also suggests related areas that might help in your search.

EXERCISE 8.4 **Library of Congress Subject Headings**

Which of these are official subject headings in the LCSH? What subject headings should be used for those that are not official?

family planning	defense information
pornography in mass media	motion pictures
child behavior	pathological gambling
death penalty	

BYTE-SYZE BULLETIN: USING COMPUTER DATABASES

Traditionally, the student doing library research goes to the card catalog or periodical index, locates the copy of the book or magazine, and begins taking notes. However, computerized on-line reference services are changing this conception of library research. Writers are now even able to access library sources from the convenience of their own homes by means of personal computers and modems.

Your library may have CD-ROM databases such as InfoTrac, which can help you find the sources you need. You simply type in a descriptor (usually a Library of Congress subject heading). To narrow your search, you may use more than one descriptor; for example, your first descriptor might be "computers" and your second, "games."

Narrowing your topic by using specific search words is very important when using commercial database services such as DIALOG, which offers access to over 200 individual databases, or BRS, which offers close to 70. In using these services, you are billed according to the individual database charge (and these charges vary greatly) and according to the amount of time you spend on-line. It is, therefore, to your advantage to know as specifically as possible what you are looking for before dialing into these services. The database you're accessing may give you bibliographic information about the source, it may give an abstract of the information found in the source, or it may reprint the entire source so that all you have to do is tear the paper from the printer and read it.

One of the many advantages in using computerized databases is speed. An on-line search can save you days of research on extensive projects, and the cost of the search may be worth the time you save. Convenience is another advantage. You need not wander from floor to floor in the library — in fact, if you have a personal computer and modem at home, you might not need to go to the library at all. And, third, in using a computerized database, you are assured of the most current information. Printed books and periodicals are difficult to revise and reprint, but databases such as *Grolier's Electronic Encyclopedia* or *Academic American Encyclopedia* are updated about every three months. By using these services, you know that you are getting the most recent information available.

Computerized on-line reference services are predicted to grow rapidly during the next few years. And it's easy to see why: On-line research services provide ready access to the latest information needed for investigating topics and making decisions.

Once you have found the correct subject heading in the LCSH, use the card catalog to find the books your library has on the subject. If you find many books on your subject, be selective about the ones you choose to look up. The title of the book will be your first clue. Titles frequently reveal not only the subject of the book, but something about the author's treatment of it as well. If you are researching an endangered species, you probably will be more interested in *Black Rhinoceros: A Vanishing Species* than in *The Big Black Rhino: A Bedtime Story*. Also, pay attention to the number of pages and the year of publication. On some topics, a book that is way out of date or has a sketchy treatment of the topic may be useless to you.

Be sure to write down carefully the *call number* of the books you select — a missing letter or an inverted digit will cost you dearly in time and frustration. Consult the location chart in your library to find where books with the call numbers you have selected are shelved.

Don't be surprised if you can't find all the books on your list. Some of them may be checked out, lost, or stolen. Others may have been reshelved incorrectly by library patrons. If you cannot find a particular book that would be useful in your research, speak to the librarian at the circulation desk, who may be able to recall the book from another library patron. Or the book may be obtainable on inter-library loan. Both of these procedures, however, will take some time.

Before checking out the books you have located, take a minute to look them over. You may find that a book you have selected has been written for an expert audience, and you are a novice on the subject. Or the book may be so simple that it provides you with no new information. You may even decide to use a copying machine for the few pages that interest you rather than checking out the book itself. (However, be sure you have recorded the complete bibliographic information for documents that you copy.) Remember that lugging a stack of books home is only the beginning. The real work consists of reading these books critically and taking notes that will help you in writing your paper.

Periodicals   The most up-to-date research in any field appears in periodicals — newspapers, magazines, newsletters, quarterlies, reviews, journals, and other periodical publications. However, finding this information can be challenging, as indexing services are always a step behind the actual publication of the articles. If you are writing on the emerging popularity of pre-Columbian art, browse through current art magazines as well as consulting the *Art Index*.

Nearly every subject field has a special index or abstracting service that catalogs the major journals in the field. The following list is only representative of the many specialized indexes available to the researcher:

Art Index

Biological and Agricultural Index

Business Periodicals Index

Cumulated Index Medicus

Education Index

Engineering Index

Environmental Abstracts

General Science Index

Humanities Index

Modern Language Association International Bibliography

Public Affairs Information Service Bulletin

Social Science Index

Wall Street Journal Index

Women's Studies Abstracts

For the most useful abstracts and indexes in the fields you are researching, consult E. P. Sheehy's *Guide to Reference Books* or William A. Katz's *Introduction to Reference Work*. There may also be published guides to reference works in the specific field you are investigating. Ask your librarian about their availability.

EXERCISE 8.5 **Using Indexes and Abstracts**

Select one of the following topics and find the indexes and abstracts that would be useful in researching the topic.

music of the sixties

effects of pollution on shellfish

designs for electric cars

Indian pottery

telecommunication satellites

James Macpherson's "Ossian" poems

education of the hearing impaired

Indexes provide information about published articles in a condensed format. You may need to consult a list of abbreviations to know, for instance, that *AFIMS* is the *American Film Institute Monograph Series*.

Government Documents   To locate government documents, you usually will need to go to a separate section of the library. In this section, you will find documents published by local, state, and federal agencies and publications of some international organizations, such as the United Nations.

Publications of the U.S. government are considered to be in a class by themselves. (The U.S. Government Printing Office is the largest publisher in the world.)

As well as providing the reports of federal agencies, government documents often provide important information on consumer affairs. Locate government documents using the *Monthly Catalog of U.S. Government Publications,* a comprehensive index of all government documents. You might also consult the *Index to U.S. Government Publications,* which indexes 180 of the most used government periodicals.

How Much Information Is Enough?

Library research can be a time-consuming procedure, and it is easy to spend so much time in the library that you have little time to prepare your report. At some point you will need to stop your library research and begin drafting your paper. Although it may be tempting to keep looking up one other article or one more book, don't use library research as a delaying tactic to keep from writing your paper. In fact, you should begin writing sections of your paper early in the research process and then add information as your research progresses.

How many sources you need will depend on the nature of your topic, whether or not you will be doing field research as well as library research, the length of your report, the kind of sources that are available, and many other factors. In some cases, your instructor may specify a minimum number of sources, but you may need more than the required minimum in order to answer your research question adequately.

If you don't find sufficient resources on your topic, you may be defining your search too narrowly. If you are interested in greyhound racing, for instance, you may want to look at *horse racing* as well in order to know which sport is more popular and which is more expensive. Because many people attend greyhound races in order to bet, you might need some general information on *gambling.* You might even want to look at *state lotteries* to compare the income available from another state-sanctioned form of gambling. One of the reasons for doing a research report is to bring together information from several related fields in order to answer your research question.

However, you may find yourself overloaded with materials instead of scrambling for an adequate number of sources. In this case, re-evaluate your research question. Sometimes you will need to limit your subject. That is, you might begin with the question "Are animals mistreated when used in athletic events?" which would include all kinds of animals, from polo ponies to jumping frogs. You might then decide to limit your subject to a more specific question, "Are the greyhounds being used for racing mistreated by their owners?" Another option is to focus your question more narrowly. Instead of considering all forms of mistreatment, you could ask, "Are drugs being used to improve the athletic performance of animals?" You might draw examples from many different sports — horse racing, mule diving, frog jumping, dog racing, goat roping — but you would be interested in only one aspect of animal abuse.

EXERCISE 8.6 **Limiting Research Questions**

How could these research questions be limited by narrowing the subject or focusing the question?

1. What social issues are discussed in the plays of Henrik Ibsen?
2. What are some currently popular forms of music?
3. What can be done about household accidents?
4. What are some different ways of financing a major purchase?
5. Does skill or chance determine the outcome of most games?
6. Are some sports violent by nature, or could more rules make them safer?
7. Can international agreements be effectively enforced?
8. Why do people collect things?
9. What makes a person admirable?
10. What are the differences between broadcast and print journalism?
11. How has birth control affected our ideas about dating, marriage, and children?
12. Can insects be controlled without the use of pesticides?
13. How are female vocalists in the nineties different from those in the seventies?
14. What is the importance of clothing in today's society?

Evaluating Your Sources

In chapter 2 we considered your need to establish credibility as a writer. You can demand credibility from the writers whose ideas you use in researching your paper, and you will expect them to be knowledgeable about the subject. You will expect them to present the evidence and reasoning that led to their opinions, and to be honest and fair.

You can tell much about the author's credibility from reading the book or article. Does the author possess the relevant facts? Is the source of the author's information identified? Does the tone of the article suggest that the author is treating the subject objectively?

You can also tell a great deal about the credibility of your source based on the publisher. Supermarket tabloids, like the *Globe* and *National Enquirer,* are notorious for exaggerated and distorted reports. Personal memoirs, private letters, and publications of small, special-interest groups are more likely to contain errors than the works published by large, reputable publishers. Publishers generally pride themselves on accuracy and integrity in reporting, and they have established elaborate review procedures to make sure their reporting is honest and fair. However, no publication is perfect, and the frequency with which retractions are printed in major publications should make us wary of accepting any fact without reservation. Generally, if you come across information that seems extraordinary or "unbelievable," attempt to verify it in other sources. In her research on the spread of the Black Death through Europe during the Middle Ages, Barbara Tuchman found varying reports of the number who had died from the plague in Avignon, France. One observer placed the death toll at 120,000 people. However, Tuchman disregarded this report when she learned that the city probably had fewer than 50,000 residents.

Virtually every magazine and newspaper publishes opinion and analysis as well as factual reporting. If a writer expresses opinions that differ from your own, do not immediately label the writer or the publication as "biased." Read such an article carefully, and note what you feel are the errors in the writer's evidence or reasoning. You may find it helpful, in fact, to quote this writer's opinion in your paper and then to refute it, systematically, based on your own research. If you are writing about gun control, your case will be strongest if you examine the positions of both the National Council to Control Handguns and the National Rifle Association. If you are writing about obscene lyrics in popular music, you might want to read articles in *Christianity Today* and *Rolling Stone*. You can find helpful information in many articles that appear in special-interest publications.

Reading for Background Information

If you are tackling a topic that is relatively unfamiliar to you, it may be useful to take a knowledge inventory (see chapter 4) as a way of getting started. Also, do some background reading that will help you understand the major trends, ideas, and issues in this field of research. Reference works are helpful for obtaining general information about people, places, historical periods, and specialized terms. Newspapers, magazines, and journals will acquaint you with the latest developments in the field. You may also want to look at books written for a generalist audience that provide an overview of the field.

Taking Bibliographic Notes

In courtroom dramas, you probably have heard the defense attorney object, "That's hearsay evidence, Your Honor, and inadmissible." The law does not consider evidence from third or fourth parties to be reliable since information passed along from one source to another is frequently altered or distorted.

In writing an academic report, you must follow certain rules in order to make your evidence "admissible." First, clearly identify your sources. Although in conversation you might declare, "I read somewhere that only one percent of those arrested for committing a crime actually serve any jail time," such a statement would never hold up in an academic report. You must know the exact source of the information — who did the research, what law enforcement agencies were included in the study, and where the results of the study were published. Although including detailed publication information may seem unnecessary, it is one way of keeping misinformation from proliferating.

Your readers will expect you to present your bibliographic information in a particular format. Biologists, psychologists, journalists, and other groups have developed different formats for organizing this information, and the format you use on a particular paper needs to follow the standards of the group (or professor) for whom you are writing. Notice the differences in capitalization, punctuation, and placement of publication facts in these different styles:

Modern Language Association

> Kuhn, Thomas. *The Structure of a Scientific Revolution*. 2nd ed. Chicago: U of Chicago P, 1970.

Chicago Manual of Style

> Kuhn, Thomas. *The Structure of a Scientific Revolution*. 2d ed. Chicago: University of Chicago Press, 1970.

Council of Biological Editors

> Kuhn, T. 1970. The structure of a scientific revolution. 2nd ed. Chicago: Univ. of Chicago Press.

American Psychological Association

> Kuhn, T. (1970). *The structure of a scientific revolution* (2nd ed.). Chicago: University of Chicago Press.

As you can see, the differences between these styles can sometimes be slight, but your ability to follow a prescribed format indicates your concern for meticulous and accurate research.

Handbooks for each of the preceding styles can be obtained in bookstores or on loan from your library. The examples in this chapter conform to the Modern Language Association (MLA) style.

Many researchers find it convenient to take bibliographic notes on three-by-five-inch index cards. By taking one note per card, you can easily alphabetize all of your sources when you complete your research. You may also want to make a note on your bibliography card about the scope or usefulness of this source. Figures 8.1 and 8.2 show two bibliography cards, one for a book and one for a journal article, respectively.

One of the most frequent problems encountered by students in their research is the tendency to omit important information from bibliographic references. If you are careful to make complete bibliography cards as you go, you won't find yourself

PS
351
.D5
1967

#9

Thomas H. Dickinson
Playwrights of the New American
Theater.
Freeport, NY/Books for Librarians
Press, Inc.

1925   331 pages

Will be useful for first 25 years of this century.
Particularly helpful for historical perspective on
Eugene O'Neill.

FIGURE 8.1: Bibliography Card for a Book

#12

Hirotsugu Yamauchi
"Developmental Study of Moral Judgments
by Japanese Children."

Psychological Reports. Vol. 68, No. 3, Part 2, June 1991
pp. 1131-1136.

Could have implications for section on comparative
training in ethics in American and Japanese
children.

FIGURE 8.2: Bibliography Card for a Journal
Article

going back to the library or hunting through stacks of duplicated materials for the information you need.

EXERCISE 8.7 Format for Bibliographic Entries

The following bibliographic entries are the kinds most often used by students in their research. After observing each model, organize the listed information that follows into the correct format for the MLA style.

1. Book with one author

Model

Schlesinger, Arthur Meier. *The Cycles of American History*. Boston: Houghton, 1986.

Publication Information

Place of publication: Bloomington, Indiana
Date of publication: 1984
Publisher: Indiana University Press
Title of book: *Women as Mythmakers: Poetry and Visual Art by Twentieth-Century Women*
Author: Estella Lauter

2. Anthology (the collected works of several authors)

Model

Erdrich, Louise. "The Lady in the Pink Mustang." *Harper's Anthology of 20th Century Native American Poetry*. Ed. Duane Niatum. San Francisco: Harper, 1988. 338–40.

Publication information

Title of anthology: *Confirmation: An Anthology of African American Women*
Page numbers of story: 59–69
Title of story: "Madame Bai and the Taking of Stone Mountain"
Author of story: Toni Cade Bambara
Editors of anthology: Amiri Baraka and Amin Baraka
Publisher: Quill
Place of publication: New York, New York
Date of publication: 1983

3. Book with multiple authors

Model

Bernstein, Carl, and Bob Woodward. *All the President's Men*. New York: Simon, 1974.

Publication information

Title of book: *Brain, Mind, and Behavior*
Authors: Floyd E. Bloom, Arlyne Lazerson, and Laura Hofstadter
Date of publication: 1985
Publisher: W. H. Freeman
Place of publication: New York, New York

4.   Encyclopedia article

Model   Highsmith, Robert M. "Conservation." *Encyclopedia Americana*. 1987 ed.

Publication information

Title of encyclopedia: *Collier's Encyclopedia*
Author: Beatriz Pastor
Title of article: "Latin American Literature"
Date of edition: 1990

5.   Weekly or monthly periodical

Model   Turque, Bill. "The War for the West." *Newsweek* 30 Sept. 1991: 18–32.

Publication information

Name of periodical: *Time*
Anonymous author
Date of publication: August 18, 1967
Page numbers of article: 24–25
Name of article: "Corruption in Asia"

6.   Journal with continuous pagination

Model   Fisher, Wesley A., and Leonid Khotin. "Soviet Family Research." *Journal of Marriage and Family* 39 (1977): 365–74.

Publication information

Date of publication: 1984
Page numbers of article: 50–57
Name of journal: *Art Journal*
Name of article: "A Public Voice: Fifteen Years of Chicano Posters"
Author: Shifra M. Goldman
Volume number: 44

7.   Newspaper

Model   Scott, David Clark. "Mexico's Press Guards Its Freedom." *Christian Science Monitor* 26 Sept. 1991: 12–13.

Publication information

Date of publication: September 4, 1991
Author: Beverly T. Watkins
Name of newspaper: *Chronicle of Higher Education*
Name of article: "The Electronic Classroom"
Page numbers of article: A26–A28

Making a Preliminary Outline

Making a preliminary outline helps you begin to think about how your paper may take shape. Based on your background knowledge and your review of available sources, you probably have some notion of what the major divisions of the paper will be. The preliminary outline is generally sketchy, and, as the name suggests, it is subject to revision as your research progresses. In fact, the process of outlining and notetaking should be going on simultaneously during the development of your research paper. You will use the headings from your outline to identify the notes you are taking. As you become more informed about your subject, you will add new headings and revise the old ones.

The preliminary outline usually consists of the research question followed by the major points and a few subheadings. This is an example of a preliminary outline for a research project on the hazards of eating shellfish:

Shellfish Hazards

Research question: What hazards are posed by eating shellfish?

I. The shellfish industry
   A. Producers
   B. Consumers
II. Illnesses related to shellfish consumption
   A. Number of people affected
      1. Illnesses
      2. Fatalities
   B. Causes
      1. Related to pollution of shellfish beds
      2. Related to food preparation
      3. Other causes
III. Possible solutions
   A. Government
      1. Controlling pollution
      2. Regulating production
   B. Personal
      1. Changes in diet
      2. Changes in obtaining and cooking

Although preparing a preliminary outline is helpful in planning your research, don't let it control your outlook on the subject. You might decide to focus on the risks posed by poachers who fish on condemned shellfish beds — or to examine the political struggles between lobbyists for the fishing industry and consumer protection groups. Keep your mind open to different approaches to your subject.

Taking Information Notes

Taking good notes is one of the most crucial stages in the development of your research paper. You have already practiced summarizing and paraphrasing in chapter 4. And in chapter 5 you learned to use quotations effectively in an informative report. In working with a more complex research project, you will use all of these skills. You will **summarize** when you are interested in the main ideas of a book or an article. You will **paraphrase** when you are interested in detailed information, but not in the exact words the author has used. Finally, you will use **quotations** when you need the author's precise wording in order to establish the authority behind the statement, to maintain the accuracy of the legal or technical language, or to preserve the beauty or wit of the original statement.

Another kind of note that you will use frequently is the **factual note**. If, for instance, you were discussing Martin Luther King's "I Have a Dream" speech, you might have factual notes on the date and location of the speech, the occasion that prompted the speech, and the number of people in attendance. In taking factual notes, you must get names and numbers correct. If you accidentally wrote down "Jefferson Memorial" instead of "Lincoln Memorial" for King's speech, you would have lost the symbolic significance of his having spoken at the memorial of the "Great Emancipator."

Also, be sure to provide sufficient context for the facts you put in your notes. Scientific research is usually conducted under controlled conditions. If you change the conditions, you invalidate the research. Suppose, for instance, you came across an article called "Desirability Ratings of 110 Personality-Trait Words" by Stephen Bochner and Theresa Van Zyl. After reading the article, you made the note that appears in figure 8.3. This note could be very misleading. Bochner and Zyl used 110 personality-trait words to be evaluated by the subjects. They intentionally omitted words that were "obscene, extreme, or highly emotive." Words like "pinhead" and "geek" do not appear on the list. The subjects for the study were 171 students at the University of New South Wales. Thus, the results do not reflect people in general, but young, well-educated Australians. The factual note should spell out the conditions of the research in order to place the information in context, as shown in figure 8.4.

In most research projects, the majority of the notes will be paraphrases and factual notes. Summary notes are helpful for providing background information, but they don't contain the specific evidence needed to establish your claim. Quotations should be used sparingly because too many quotations will interrupt the flow of your paper. Don't write down quotations in order to avoid the effort it takes to paraphrase your materials. Paraphrasing forces you to think through what the author is saying as you read.

Many researchers take notes on four-by-six-inch notecards. In taking notes, clearly identify the source of the information and the page number on which it appears in the source. If you number your bibliography cards, you can cross-reference your notecards, using this number. That is, if you have a bibliography card for Bochner and Zyl that is indexed as #3, all the information notes that you take from this article will also have a #3 in the upper right corner.

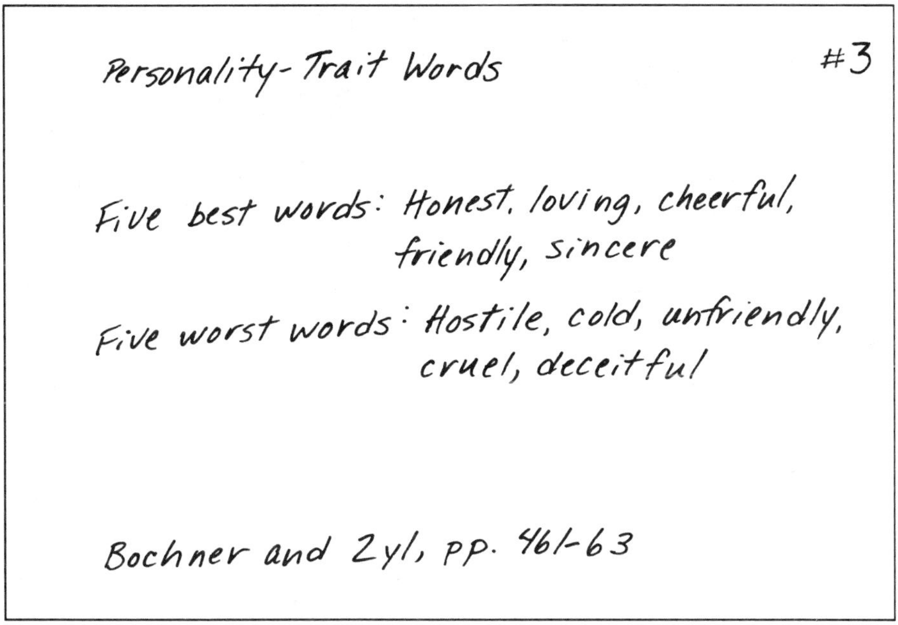

Personality-Trait Words   #3

Five best words: Honest, loving, cheerful,
friendly, sincere

Five worst words: Hostile, cold, unfriendly,
cruel, deceitful

Bochner and Zyl, pp. 461-63

FIGURE 8.3: A Misleading Note

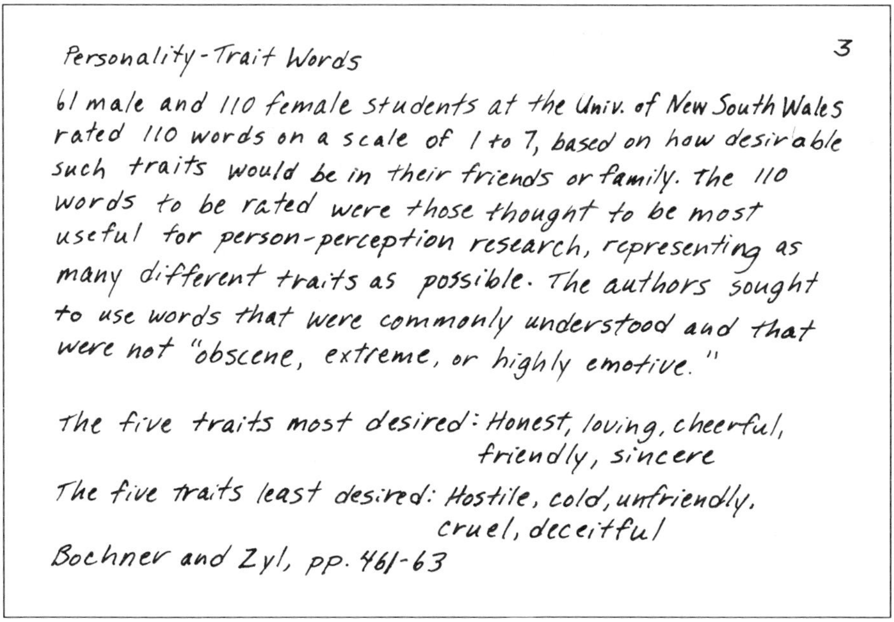

Personality-Trait Words   3

61 male and 110 female students at the Univ. of New South Wales
rated 110 words on a scale of 1 to 7, based on how desirable
such traits would be in their friends or family. The 110
words to be rated were those thought to be most
useful for person-perception research, representing as
many different traits as possible. The authors sought
to use words that were commonly understood and that
were not "obscene, extreme, or highly emotive."

The five traits most desired: Honest, loving, cheerful,
friendly, sincere
The five traits least desired: Hostile, cold, unfriendly,
cruel, deceitful
Bochner and Zyl, pp. 461-63

FIGURE 8.4: A Clear Note

LANGUAGE NOTE: PUNCTUATING QUOTATIONS

The technicalities of punctuating quotations can become confusing for the researcher. The following guidelines should help as you use quotations within your paper.

> If you are simply quoting what the author of your source has written, enclose the author's words in double quotation marks. If the quotation comes at the end of a sentence, and if the sentence ends in a period, the ending double quotation marks come after the period. For example:

> > Sophocles wrote, "The crown of happiness is to be wise."

Similarly, commas go inside a terminal quotation mark.

> > Sophocles wrote, "The crown of happiness is to be wise," but my crown of happiness would be 14k gold.

If the terminal punctuation mark is a question mark or an exclamation point, consider who is asking the question or making the exclamation. If *you* are asking the question or making the exclamation, the punctuation goes outside the quotation marks. However, if the question or exclamation comes from *your source*, the punctuation mark must go inside the double quotation marks.

> > *Tom Sawyer* begins with Aunt Polly screaming, "TOM!"
> > (Exclamation point is for the quotation.)

> > Was it Antigone who said, "When my strength fails, I shall try no longer"?
> > (Question mark is for the sentence, not the quotation.)

Remember, if you are using a documentation style that calls for internal parenthetical citations, the citation is not being quoted, but it is part of the sentence. Therefore, place the ending double quotation marks around the last word of the quotation, include the citation information within parentheses, and then end your sentence with the terminal punctuation mark.

> > One visitor to El Salvador wrote, "Terror is the given of the place" (Didion 14).

> If one quotation is enclosed inside of another, use single quotation marks (usually the apostrophe on your keyboard) for the interior quotation.

> > The pastor stopped and then said quietly, "The *Proverbs* teach us that 'pride goeth before destruction.'"

> If you are using a source that has used another source and you want to quote this secondary source, it is usually advisable to find this source and to quote directly from it; in fact, your instructor may require that you do this. If it is impossible to locate this secondary source (and if your primary source has done field research, it usually will be), then note that the original was "quoted in" another source.

In a hearing before the U.S. Committee on Foreign Relations, Robert White, former American ambassador to El Salvador, gave compelling evidence that "D'Aubuisson and his group are responsible for the murder of Archbishop Romero" (qtd. in Didion 101–02).

Occasionally, you might need to delete a few words from a quotation, either because they are unnecessary or because you need to make the sentence fit more smoothly into your own writing. You do this by using ellipsis points, three periods with spaces before and after them. Note how omitted information has been indicated in the following examples.

Original   In the United States, as fast as the Euro-American invaders forcefully displaced the native inhabitants from their own sorts of traditional commons, the land was opened to new settlers. (Gary Snyder, *The Practice of the Wild*)

Quoted with an omission

In *The Practice of the Wild* Gary Snyder observes, "In the United States, as fast as the Euro-American invaders forcefully displaced the native inhabitants from . . . traditional commons, the land was opened to new settlers" (33).

Be careful not to delete words that would cause the meaning of the quotation to be distorted.

Original   The human dilemmas, in such situations, are of an extraordinary kind: for patients are here faced with disease as a seduction, something remote from, and far more equivocal than, the traditional theme of illness as suffering or affliction. (Oliver Sacks, *The Man Who Mistook His Wife for a Hat*)

Distorted quotation   In *The Man Who Mistook His Wife for a Hat* Oliver Sacks contends, "The human dilemmas, in such situations, are of an extraordinary kind: for patients are here faced with . . . the traditional theme of illness as suffering or affliction" (91).

In this case, the writer has reversed the meaning of Oliver Sack's quotation. Sacks argues that illness can be tempting for some people rather than an affliction to be avoided. The ellipsis has negated that original meaning.

In general you will omit only small amounts of material when you use the ellipsis points. If your omission extends past the end of the sentence, put a period right after the word where the ellipsis begins and then add the three periods with spaces between them. You may also insert words into a quotation by putting them in brackets (not parentheses). Notice how the following quotation has been altered through the use of brackets and ellipsis points.

Original   Computer-generated environments that create the illusion of three-dimensional worlds are giving scientists the ability to work surrounded by images of molecules and other objects that they once had to use an electron microscope to study.

"You can take a stroll on an insect's eye or take a tour of an integrated circuit," says Thomas A. Furness, director of the Human Interface Technology Laboratory at the University of Washington. His laboratory hopes to bring "virtual realities," as the computer-created worlds are often called, into broad public and scientific use. (David L. Wheeler, "Computer-Created World of 'Virtual Reality' Opening New Vistas to Scientists")

Altered quotation   One of the most recent uses of computer technology is in producing what is called "virtual reality":

> Computer-generated environments that create the illusion of three-dimensional worlds are giving scientists the ability to work surrounded by images of molecules and other objects that they once had to use an electron microscope to study.
>
> "You can take a stroll on an insect's eye or take a tour of an integrated circuit," says Thomas A. Furness, [whose] Human Interface Technology Laboratory. . . . hopes to bring "virtual realities," as the computer-created worlds are often called, into broad public and scientific use. (Wheeler A6)

If your source material has made a technical error, such as a misspelling, you may indicate that the error is the original author's and not yours by inserting the word *sic* in brackets within the quotation directly after the error.

> An editorial writer for our local paper commented that "Mayor Fenderbuss is now to [sic] old to handle the demands of the job."

EXERCISE 8.8 **Taking Notes**

Read the following article. What information would you use for factual notes? What information should be summarized, paraphrased, or quoted? Make sample notecards for each of the four kinds of notes.

Spare the Prod, Spoil the Child

by Dyan Machan

Does learning how to cope with pressure at an early age necessarily put you on the track to being a better manager or scientist?

Educators at the privately funded Johns Hopkins Center for Talented Youth think so. Their thesis is that the best students often go unchallenged in the classroom, can't move at their own pace and are ultimately frustrated and turned off by the educational process. Their solution: Push kids as hard as you can, as early as you can.

Underchallenging the best and brightest, they argue, will shortchange this country of future leaders. Lighting fires under the talented is at least as important as providing remedial programs for the less gifted, and probably more so. Along with recently publicized falling test scores among high school students, William Durden, the Johns Hopkins Center director, cites two other grim facts: Japan has passed the U.S. in the number of patents per year, and, according to the International Association for the Evaluation of Educational Achievement, top U.S. students rank at the bottom in math and science among developed nations.

On the other side are those who say programs for the gifted are elitist and needlessly stressful to impressionable young minds. And to save money, Connecticut, New York and California are cutting back on these programs. John Katzman, founder of Princeton Review, a firm that prepares kids to take aptitude tests, says some gifted programs are great. But he warns parents: "It's not worth making your kids crazy about."

The Hopkins program is one of the largest and oldest of more than 35 centers nation-   5
wide that offer gifted kids from ages 11 to 17 a chance to take advanced courses during summer and after school. How do you define "gifted"? Even the 11-year-olds in the program must have at least 930 out of a possible 1,600 combined math and verbal score on the Scholastic Aptitude Test. The national average is 896 for college-bound seniors.

"Stress is not a dirty word," says Durden. "Stress and competition are important for educational advancement. The American school system has gone out of its way to eliminate every form of academic competition. Some schools shy away from using standardized tests for their brightest students for fear the comparison may harm the students' self-esteem."

How tough is the Johns Hopkins program? A FORBES reporter visited a program run by the Johns Hopkins Center on the Skidmore College campus — one of six colleges where CTY offers classes. This summer over 500 students attended the Skidmore three-week summer sessions, where they took high school- and college-level courses in subjects like math, history and writing.

At Skidmore, the first thing one notices is that boys and girls are about evenly divided, with a heavy representation of Asian teenagers but few blacks or Hispanics. Second, these kids, apart from their intelligence, are otherwise normal. So normal that many seem a bit embarrassed to be there; they are often unwilling to tell their friends back home they attend "nerd camp." Matthew Keeler, 15, a sophomore at Ridgefield High School, in Ridgefield, Conn., says his friends just wouldn't understand the appeal of spending five hours a day in classroom lectures and at least two more hours each evening studying under strict supervision.

Keeler, who concedes his parents bribed him with a new leather jacket to take the Scholastic Aptitude Test at 13 instead of the normal 17, has attended the courses for the last three summers. Despite his slight embarrassment at being there, he's unquestionably happy he is: "Here you can have an intelligent conversation."

Stress? It's there. Take Jennifer Nam, a quiet, rule-abiding 15-year-old. The school's   10
rule is that students' lights are out at 10:15 p.m., but Nam, a sophomore at Watchung Hills Regional High School in New Jersey, breaks the rule. Enrolled in European history, Nam, whose parents came from Korea, says, "I was so lost. Everyone knew what's going on but me." To keep up, she sometimes got up at 5:30 a.m. and stayed up to 11:30 p.m. So how does the overworked, overwhelmed Nam feel about the demanding program? "I love it."

She's not alone in having to stay on her toes. Here 11-to-17-year-olds take a full year of high school chemistry, for instance, in 15 days.

Yes, there's plenty of stress. In some classes, competition means self-esteem is actively bashed. In a writing course, for example, eight students and a teacher form a semicircle around a 14-year-old who looks as if she's ready to cry. Her classmates have each read her essay, and each gets a crack at ripping it apart. The final blow comes from the teacher, Philip Boshoff: "Your observations are insightful, but your writing sounds stupid." The 14-year-old bites her lip, looks down but doesn't cry.

Boshoff explains why he was so tough on the girl: These students are so accustomed to getting A's and pats on the back for everything they turn in that they no longer feel challenged in regular schools. "They generally thank me for the constructive criticism they never had," Boshoff says.

Connie Chuang, 15, a sophomore at Dwight Englewood, in Englewood, N.J., says she wishes she could study math all day long. What she hated was having to break for the activities like volleyball or choir. Says Chuang, "Math is awesome."

What many of the students seem to dread most is going back to their regular high   15
schools, where they'll probably be intellectually undernourished. Says Keeler: "That's like giving a weight lifter 10-pound weights to work out."

These kids are saying something important: Spare the prod, spoil the child.

COLLECTING INFORMATION: FIELD RESEARCH

Field research is the broad label given to research done outside the library. Some research questions require obtaining information not available through library resources. If you want to know about "youth gangs," in general, you will be able to locate library resources on this topic. If you want to know if gangs exist in your community, how prevalent they are, and if they pose a threat to the community, you probably will need to talk with police officers, social workers, and even gang members to understand better the local situation. In doing field research, you frequently will "break new ground;" that is, you will compile information not available from any other source.

Field research can be a time-consuming process. Be realistic about what you can do in the time allowed for your research project. It takes time to set up interviews, to conduct surveys, or to make observations related to your research. It also takes time to assess the results of the study and to put the results into a form that is useful to the reader. However, the time you spend on field research will be some of the most interesting and enjoyable work you do in college. Frequently, such research can lead to changes on your campus or in your community. Student projects of this kind have led to better lighting on campus, improved access for disabled students, and many other practical results.

Observations

Making observations is second-nature to most of us. If you are a vendor at a baseball park, you are observing what people eat (hot dogs in the early innings, peanuts and candy later), where buyers sit (the high rollers are in the box seats; you'll be lucky to sell a coke in the outfield), and so on. Your observations allow you to make strategic decisions (don't bring out hot dogs in late innings).

In most cases, it will be useful to write down your observations in a log that gives the date, your observations, and any other relevant information (for instance, the game was rained out, or it went into extra innings). Record the information as soon as possible. In fact, if you can record your observations as you watch, this is ideal. The longer you wait, the harder it will be to remember all the details. Your log book will be your source of evidence when you begin to make your final report.

Be as objective as possible in making your observations. You might actually want to count the number of hot dogs you sold instead of relying on your general impression. Make your descriptions as detailed as possible. Saying that one of your customers "looked like a big spender" is too vague. Saying that one of your customers "wore a satin team jacket and paid with a $50 bill" is more precise.

After completing your observations, organize the notes from your log book into a report. You will be making inferences from the observations to support your conclusions. Most of your conclusions probably will be qualified. Seldom is human behavior as predictable as the outcome of a chemistry experiment. You will also want to make your reservations clear (ice cold cokes are a great seller in the summertime *unless it rains*).

EXERCISE 8.9   **Making Observations and Inferences**

These observations about student behavior during an exam have been organized in tabular form. Meet with your Discovery Group to discuss the inferences that could be made from this table.

Test-Taking Behavior and Exam Performance

	A	B	C	D	E
Marcos	5	5	7	2	71
Dunleavy	6	2	0	0	58
Yo	2	4	6	0	92
McBride	1	3	0	0	99
Latta	3	1	4	1	84

A = row where the student sat; 1 = front, 6 = back
B = order in which exams were turned in
C = number of erasures or markouts on the exam
D = number of exam questions not answered
E = grade on exam

Surveys

Frequently, you will want information that can't be derived from observations. Surveys can help you find out about people's attitudes, beliefs, concerns, patterns of behavior, and reactions to current events and may provide many other insights not obtainable directly through observations. Keep in mind, however, that surveys reveal what people think, not necessarily what is really happening. If you ask people how many hours per week they work, they may overestimate or underestimate the actual time they are on the job.

Surveys must be prepared carefully in order to get the information desired. The precise wording of a question can radically alter the response of those being surveyed. For instance, compare these two questions:

Do you believe our city's streets are adequately maintained?

Have you ever had a problem while driving on our city's streets?

The first question asks the respondent to make a judgment about the adequacy of street maintenance. The second question is so ambiguously worded that almost any driver would respond "yes." Although the researcher may wish to imply in the second question that the "problem" has to do with the condition of the streets, that is by no means the necessary interpretation. The "problem" could just as easily have been a traffic light malfunction or a reckless driver. The second question, therefore, lacks *reliability*. A question is reliable only when it is understood by various readers in the same way.

As well as reviewing questions for reliability, the researcher must make sure that questions have *validity*, that is, that they measure what the researcher wants to know. Suppose you were trying to discover whether religion played an important role in your friends' lives, and you asked them these questions:

Do you own a Bible?

Do you attend church regularly?

Do you look to God for guidance in your life?

Which of these questions best indicates the role of religion in your friends' lives? The first question has little validity. The mere fact that someone owns a Bible does not indicate that he or she is religious. Church attendance is a better indicator, but it is possible to attend church for reasons unrelated to a person's religious convictions. There are also those who do not attend church and yet feel that religion plays an important role in their lives. (Notice also that "Bible" and "church" imply Christian beliefs as opposed to a more general notion of religion.) The third question probably is the best indicator of the role religion plays in your friends' lives and therefore is the most valid of the three questions.

Survey questions can be either objectively scored or open ended. The following are examples of questions that can be objectively scored:

1. How long have you worked for Plymouth Petroleum? ____ years

2. Are you currently looking for work elsewhere? ____ yes ____ no

3. What is your job category? (check one)
   ____ management   ____ technical   ____ clerical   ____ other

4. Which of these factors are the most important for you in selecting employment? Rank from 1 (highest) to 5 (lowest).
   ____ job satisfaction
   ____ salary
   ____ employee benefits
   ____ relationship with boss and co-workers
   ____ working environment (location, facilities, etc.)

Objectively scored items are preferable when you are considering large numbers of people and when you can predict the general categories of response most people will make. Open-ended questions are more appropriate for investigating causes and ideas that are not predictable:

> Why do you think most people choose to leave Plymouth Petroleum?

> What changes would you like to make in your working conditions?

In some cases, you may be able to sort the answers on open-ended responses into categories. In other cases, you may choose to select from various open-ended replies the ones that seem most practical or useful for your purposes. Working with open-ended replies can be time-consuming, but they can also provide important information not obtainable through predetermined categories.

Here are some general guidelines for preparing an effective survey:

1. Before designing your survey, write down what you are hoping to learn.

2. Make your questions as simple and direct as possible.

3. Don't ask questions that require information unavailable to your respondents.

4. Indicate clearly how responses are to be entered (checking a box, filling in a blank, etc.).

5. Make sure that the survey can be filled out in a reasonable amount of time.

6. Test your survey on a sample group.

7. Before conducting the survey, plan the way your results will be tabulated and used.

EXERCISE 8.10   Evaluating a Survey

The owner of a local movie theater was interested in finding out what factors made people select one theater to attend over another. Read the following survey and meet in your

Discovery Groups to evaluate it. Are the questions reliable? valid? Should other questions have been asked? Could any questions be eliminated? Are objective and open-ended questions used appropriately?

Theater Survey

Name _____

Telephone Number _____

Place of employment _____

Date _____

Number of times you go to a motion picture theater in a year _____

Please take a few minutes either before or after the movie to fill out this brief questionnaire. Place it in the marked box by the door as you leave.

Circle the number responding to the following scale:

1 — Completely agree
2 — Somewhat agree
3 — Don't know, don't care, or does not apply
4 — Somewhat disagree
5 — Completely disagree

THEATER SURVEY   2

1. I like romance movies.
                      1   2   3   4   5

2. I like adventure stories.
                      1   2   3   4   5

3. The atmosphere of a movie theater is important to me.
                      1   2   3   4   5

4. The temperature of a movie theater is important to me.
                      1   2   3   4   5

5. The location of a movie theater is important to me.
                      1   2   3   4   5

6. The admission price to a movie theater is important to me.
                      1   2   3   4   5

7. Please circle your response to the following question:
   I came to this theater today (or tonight) because:
   a. I like the refreshments at the snack bar.
   b. I like the type of movie being shown.

c. I like the actors in this movie.

d. This theater is close to my house.

e. Going to movies is my favorite form of entertainment.

Please answer the following questions with short answers. You may complete your answers on the reverse side of this sheet.

1. What makes you choose one movie theater instead of another?

2. What do you like about this theater?

3. What do you dislike about this theater?

4. What do you like about other theaters in town?

5. What do you dislike about other theaters in town?

6. What suggestions would you make for improving this theater?

Interviews

One of the best sources of information on your research question may be people in your community. Most of us have a network of friends and associates who can help us in our research. If you are researching a medical question, you might see what information your doctor can provide. Realtors, merchants, teachers, civic leaders, media personalities, and other people you may know are all useful sources of information and opinion. These individuals may, in turn, be able to lead you to other resource people.

In some cases, you may have to rely on directories or information services to lead you to an appropriate source. Most people are willing to help a student researcher, and they may even be flattered that someone is interested in their area of expertise. However, if you are seeking information of a sensitive nature, you may have a harder time getting the information you need. One student who was trying to find out the cost of a diploma (in order to compare the actual cost of the diploma with the university's diploma fee) received little cooperation from either the university administration or the company specializing in graduation supplies. After several tries, she ultimately did learn a range of prices that could be charged for diplomas, and a customer-service representative for the company hinted that her university's diplomas were probably on the lower end of that range. Although this information was not as precise as the student researcher would have liked, she was able to indicate that the actual cost of the diploma was only a fraction of the university's required diploma fee. When investigating sensitive topics, you must be persistent in order to get answers to your questions.

Before conducting an interview, become as well informed about your subject as possible. With a background knowledge of the subject, you won't waste time obtaining general information from your resource person and can move on to more complex issues. For instance, it would be unnecessary to ask a doctor what immunizations are required by the state — this information could be obtained quickly by calling the county health department. You might want to ask your doctor, however, if the risk of some vaccinations is greater than the risk of contracting the disease.

You must always conduct interviews professionally. Call for an appointment, and be sure that you have clear directions to the place where you will meet your resource person. Come equipped with a sturdy notebook or clipboard, extra pens and pencils, and your interview questions. If you plan to tape the interview, be sure to ask permission. Before you arrive, make sure the tape recorder is in good working order, and record the date and time of the interview, the person being interviewed, and any other useful information on the tape. Make it a goal to arrive early for the interview so that you will have some extra time if you are delayed in traffic or have difficulty finding a parking place.

Conducting a good interview is definitely an art. In general, good interview questions ask for more than a "yes" or "no" answer. The questions you ask should be in the resource person's area of expertise. Have a series of questions prepared to guide your discussion, but don't expect the interview to follow the prescribed format exactly. Some of your questions may be answered in the course of conversation before you ask them; others may become irrelevant. Be sure to ask follow-up questions for clarification. Such questions reveal that you are listening carefully and that you value your resource person's ideas.

EXERCISE 8.11   Evaluating Interview Questions

A student wrote the following questions in preparation for interviewing his family physician about the role of the general practitioner in modern medicine. Which questions seem appropriate? Which do not? Should the order of the questions be changed in any way?

1. Is the general practitioner being replaced by pediatricians, internists, and a variety of other specialists?

2. Has the emphasis on specialization undermined the authority of the general practitioner in any way?

3. Have you ever misdiagnosed a patient? Were the consequences serious?

4. What kinds of personal skills are needed by a general practitioner?

5. How long have you been working as a general practitioner?

6. Do you drink? How much?

7. How do you keep abreast of new advances in medicine?

8. General practitioners usually make less money than specialists. Does that mean that general practitioners are less competent than specialists?

9. I had a friend named Alice Struthers who was a former patient of yours. She claims that you were insensitive to women patients. I would like to hear your side of this.

10. Many general practitioners work in clinics. What are the advantages of private practice versus a clinic?

After completing your interview, draft a brief summary of the interview as quickly as possible. If your notes get "cold," you may have difficulty remembering what was said and you are more likely to make mistakes. If you have doubts about a quotation or about the facts you have collected, confirm the information you recorded with a follow-up phone call.

Conducting an interview can be one of the most exciting steps in completing a research project. You will find that most people are eager to share their knowledge with others and are flattered that you are interesting in learning from them. Don't be afraid to ask hard questions or to repeat a question that you feel wasn't adequately answered. In general, though, you will find that you learn the most by simply being enthusiastic about the subject under discussion.

EXERCISE 8.12 **Preparing Interview Questions**

Prepare a survey or a set of interview questions on a topic you wish to investigate. Make copies for your Discovery Group and ask them to suggest ways to improve the survey or interview questions.

If you have never done field research before, you may be surprised to learn that the information you gather by conducting an interview or attending a lecture must be documented in the same way you would library research. You also should be aware of the way you document a concert, a film, a television program, or a recording. Depending on the nature of your research, you may use many sources that are not traditional written documents.

EXERCISE 8.13 **Documenting Field Research**

Below are some models in the MLA style of materials you might want to document. After observing the models, organize the listed information into the correct format for the MLA style.

1. Interview

Model	Anderson, Maria. Personal interview. 18 Feb. 1991.
Information	Type of interview: Personal
	Name of interviewee: Robert Smithson
	Date of interview: May 3, 1990

2.   Letter

Model	Walters, Barbara. Letter to the author. 27 Oct. 1988.
Information	Author of letter: Susan Hernandez Type of letter: Personal Date on letter: Sept. 10, 1991

3.   Performance

Model	*Les Misérables*. By Alain Boublil and Claude-Michel Schönberg. Music by Claude-Michel Schönberg. Lyrics by Herbert Kretzmer. Dir. John Caird and Trevor Nunn. Casa Mañana Theatre, Fort Worth. 25 July 1991. Based on Victor Hugo's *Les Misérables*.
Information	Theater: John F. Kennedy Center for the Performing Arts Composer: Leonard Bernstein Title of work: *Mass* Date of performance: Sept. 8, 1971 City of performance: Washington, D. C.

4.   Film

Model	*Mary Poppins*. Dir. Robert Stevenson. With Julie Andrews, Dick Van Dyke, David Tomlinson, and Glynis Johns. Walt Disney Studios, 1964.
Information	Actors: Liza Minnelli, Michael York, Helmut Griem, and Joel Grey Director: Bob Fosse Distributor: ABC Pictures/Allied Artists Year of release: 1972 Title: *Cabaret*

5.   Television program

Model	*Sesame Street*. PBS. KERA, Dallas. 15 Oct. 1991.
Information	Broadcast date: Feb. 9, 1964 Name of program: *The Ed Sullivan Show* Network: CBS Local station and city: WNAC, Boston

6.   Recording

Model	*Rhapsody in Blue*. Audiotape. Cond. Eugene Ormandy. Philadelphia Orch. Columbia, YT 35496, 1978.
Information	Name of song: "Mexico" Year of release: 1975 Performer: James Taylor Title of album: *Gorilla* Catalog number: BS 2866 Manufacturer: Warner Brothers Records

WRITING ASSIGNMENT Observation Report

Choose a location or an event that will allow you to make a log of your own observations. After logging your observations, prepare a report that summarizes your conclusions. Here are some possible sites for your observations:

> concert
>
> municipal court
>
> city council meeting
>
> student government meeting
>
> juvenile detention center
>
> museum
>
> shopping mall
>
> recital
>
> tourist attraction
>
> county jail
>
> clippings and posters on faculty offices
>
> high school dramatic or athletic event

ORGANIZING YOUR INFORMATION

If you have done a thorough job of collecting information — notes on books and articles, interview reports, survey data, etc. — you may be overwhelmed by the task of weaving all of these diverse threads into a coherent pattern. All the books and articles you have read were written for purposes and audiences different from your own. You must order and develop the information you have collected for your readers.

Stating Your Claim

In beginning a research project, you must formulate a research question. After completing your research, you should be able to state an answer to that question. Your answer to the research question will become the claim that is the basis of your research report. This claim is sometimes referred to as a *thesis,* a *controlling idea,* or a *proposition.* Whatever it is called, it is essential that you make clear to the reader the conclusion you have drawn from your investigation. The following examples illustrate how research questions become the basis of the claims made in the research report.

Question	What has been the effect of advances in medical technology for the hearing impaired?
Claim	New advances in microelectronics and microsurgery offer hope for thousands of patients now suffering from hearing loss and deafness.
Question	Did James Macpherson write the "Ossian" poems?
Claim	Although Macpherson claimed the poems were written by an ancient Gaelic poet, the consensus of scholars is that Macpherson fabricated these poems.
Question	What effect have advances in telecommunications had on political affairs?
Claim	The ability to transmit news and information rapidly contributed to the destabilization of the Soviet Union and the Eastern Bloc nations.
Question	Why did Bob Dylan achieve legendary success as a singer and songwriter in the sixties?
Claim	Dylan's success can be attributed to his poetic ability, his identification with the counterculture, and his recognizable style.

The claim that you make in your research report frequently will represent a judgment on your part, but it will be an informed judgment based on research. Don't be alarmed if some of the information you collect does not support the claim you are making. On many questions, informed sources can, and do, disagree. When you find information that contradicts your claim, you should not simply disregard it. Rather, attempt to explain why the author is mistaken, misinformed, arguing from false premises, or otherwise in error. Recognizing opposing views and answering their objections squarely will make your own claim stronger.

EXERCISE 8.14 **Evaluating Claims**

What is wrong with these claims?

1. Although it cannot be proven, there can be little doubt that our destinies are guided by the stars.

2. I think people who commit terrible crimes deserve whatever they get.

3. It is difficult to know whether the presence of a standing army is an incentive for a nation to plot a war of aggression.

4. The economic factors that affect many people's lives are sometimes reduced to something called "cost of living," which, in turn, affects the fixed income of people through COLAs, but these do not take into account the other factors that are important to

people's lives such as mobility, aesthetics, and security, which cannot be given a monetary value, but which are, nonetheless, very important to people's happiness.

5.   Is the "traditional family" still the ideal for American society? Who knows?

Arranging Your Information

Having accumulated many notes on your subject, you may find it overwhelming to place all of these materials in order. If you have worked on an outline for your paper while collecting more information, your work may be easier at this point. If you have placed your notes on notecards, you can simply make stacks for each of the major points in your outline. Then arrange the cards within those stacks in the order you wish to present the information. In general, the arrangement of your material will reflect these general patterns:

According to your information
   Begin with background information of a general nature and move to more complex and sophisticated ideas.

According to your readers' needs
   Address the readers' major concerns near the beginning of the paper. Your introduction may need to create interest for the readers or assure them that you will treat the subject fairly.

According to patterns of logical thought
   Many investigative reports follow the problem-analysis format discussed in chapter 4. Sometimes reports move from examining discernible effects (e.g., tornado damage) to finding probable causes (e.g., failure of an early warning system). Some reports look first at causes (e.g., warning labels on cigarettes) and then consider their effects (e.g., discouraging smoking). Look for the logical patterns that should guide the development of your report.

Of course, you may find that the pattern of your information, your readers' needs, and logical thought are all at work in your paper. The reader usually needs to be acquainted with background information before moving to more complex ideas, and most readers appreciate seeing a logical line of development as the paper progresses. However, if there is a conflict among these three patterns, the readers' concerns should always be considered first. For instance, you may need to demonstrate the importance of your subject before moving into an explanation of terms and concepts.

Drafting Your Report

Writing a first draft of a research report can seldom be completed in one sitting. In fact, many writers find it helpful to draft sections of the report as they are collecting research materials. When you have completed your background research, you might want to draft that section of the paper. When you have completed your field research, write up the results while the information is fresh on your mind. By the time you complete your research, you may need only to write an introduction and add your own analysis and conclusions.

Drafting is best done at full speed. Don't stop to worry if a sentence doesn't sound quite right. There will be time later for revising and editing. If you need additional information or can't find a note, leave a reminder to go back later and fill in the missing information. Material to be inserted later is frequently set off by brackets in this manner:

[Information on 1968 Democratic Convention goes here]

If you stop to hunt for the missing information, you may lose the flow of your thought.

SUPPORTING YOUR POSITION

While drafting your paper, you will need to incorporate the notes obtained from your reading. The information you take from your notes should fit smoothly into the flow of your argument. Imagine encountering this as the first paragraph in a report:

> According to James Gleick, "The patterns that people like Robert May and James Yorke discovered in the early 1970s, with their complex boundaries between orderly and chaotic behavior, had unsuspected regularities that could only be described in terms of the relation of large scales to small" (114). The pioneering mathematical work of Mandelbrot helped to substantiate that "a fractal is a way of seeing infinity" (98).

Clearly, such an introduction would be impenetrable for the average reader. You need to provide a context — background and explanatory information — that would make this information more approachable for a general audience. Here is the paragraph rewritten to provide such a context:

> Traditionally, mathematics has been concerned with describing stable conditions. Think back to your high school algebra. When asked to solve $2x = 6$, you learned that x must equal 3, not 5, or 7, or some other number. Recently, however, many scientists have begun to investigate the possibilities of studying randomness, irregularities, erratic fluctuations — in a word, chaos. One of the first proponents

of this new science of chaos was Edward Lorenz, a meteorologist studying one of the most unpredictable elements in nature — the weather. Lorenz's work was picked up by James Yorke, a physicist who gave the name "chaos" to these studies of "deterministic disorder" (Gleick 69). Robert May, a biologist, used Lorenz's ideas to explain why fish populations move through predictable cycles even though some fluctuations in population are completely chaotic. The mathematical basis for much of the research on chaos was supplied by Benoit Mandelbrot. Mandelbrot gave the name "fractal geometry" to his study of "irregular patterns in natural processes" and "infinitely complex shapes" (103). Although fractal geometry may sound like mathematical mumbo jumbo, Mandelbrot's calculations lie behind many practical concerns — from predicting cotton prices to understanding the arrangement of arteries in the human body.

Although this paragraph still treats complex material, the reader is supplied some context for the information. If you find that you are simply stringing together one notecard after another as you write, like so many beads on a necklace, you probably have not provided a sufficient context for your reader.

Citing Your Sources

As you include information taken from your notes, you will need to identify properly the source of your information. The process of providing bibliographic information within the text of your paper is called **citation**. You will cite not only direct quotations, but also the facts you have gathered and the ideas you have paraphrased. In the past, many handbooks recommended elaborate numbering systems for citing sources. Most style guides now recommend parenthetical notes that briefly indicate the source and the page number. For full bibliographic information, the reader turns to the list of "Works Cited" at the end of the paper.

The current MLA documentation style is an "internal parenthetical citation" style because the citation appears within the paper itself. You use the author's last name to indicate the source followed by a page number to indicate where this particular quotation, summary, or paraphrase can be found.

John Searle has argued that computers do not "understand" stories in the way that humans do (Penrose 18–21).

Note that within the parentheses, you do not place any punctuation between the word used for cross-referencing and the page number. However, if you are citing two works by the same author, you would place within the parentheses the author's last name *followed by a comma,* an abbreviated form of the title, and the page number of the reference.

One scholar once called literary criticism "a mystery-religion without a gospel" (Frye, *Anatomy of Criticism* 14). The same scholar later applied the methods of literary criticism to the gospel (Frye, *Great Code* 129–35).

If the source is obvious from the context, such as when the author's last name appears within the sentence itself, the page number is all that you need within the parentheses.

In the *Anatomy of Criticism,* Northrop Frye called literary criticism "a mystery-religion without a gospel" (14).

You may be wondering, "Should every note I use in my paper be followed with a bibliographic citation?" In all probability, most of your notes will require a citation. In citing your sources, you are acknowledging an intellectual debt to the original author. That debt might be to the work of a statistician, a reporter, a commentator, or a researcher. Whenever you include information that can clearly be identified with a particular source, you should cite it. Some information does fall into the area of "common" knowledge. It would be unnecessary to cite any particular source in order to establish that Abraham Lincoln was the sixteenth president of the United States or that a kilometer is approximately .621 mile long. You will, of course, be exercising your judgment as to what constitutes common knowledge. However, you should *always* cite:

quotations

expressions of opinion

facts not readily available from a standard reference work

facts that are controversial or contrary to popular beliefs

theoretical or philosophical ideas

anecdotes and other illustrative materials

If you find that your paragraphs are laden with citations, the answer is not to eliminate the citations, but to provide more contextual information that introduces, explains, interprets, or even refutes your source materials.

EXERCISE 8.15   Using Source Materials to Establish a Claim

Below are eight notes on the subject of household accidents. Write a paragraph in which you claim that household accidents are a serious health hazard. Use the source materials to help establish your claim. Be sure to provide an adequate context for the source materials that you use in this paragraph.

United States. Dept. of Labor. Bureau of Labor Statistics. *Occupational Injuries and Illnesses in the United States by Industry, 1985*. Washington: GPO, 1987.

The following statistics appear for 1985 for workers within the home: 16.1% were injured in incidents involving household cooking equipment; 9.0% were injured in incidents involving household refrigerators and freezers; 12.1% were injured in incidents involving household laundry equipment; 11.5% were injured in incidents involving electric housewares and fans; 8.9% were injured in incidents involving household vacuum cleaners; and 17.6% were injured in incidents involving other household appliances (11–12).

United States. Dept. of Housing and Urban Development. *People & Fires.* Washington: GPO, 1977.

According to Patricia Roberts Harris, secretary of Housing and Urban Development, "Every year over 6,000 people die as a result of fire in the home, while many others are injured or disfigured. Every year fire also causes millions of dollars in property losses" (2).

Silverman, Harold M. *The Consumer's Guide to Poison Protection.* New York: Avon, 1984.

"Most poisonings occur inside the victim's own home or in the home of a friend or relative (80.5%). Only 6.6% occur outdoors. The exact locations of 8.5% of the poisonings are unknown; 4.4% of the cases are classified as having occurred in a location other than those already mentioned" (3).

Van Goethem, Larry. "The Dangers in Your Garage." *Reader's Digest* Aug. 1988: 141–44.

"Imagine that your home contained a small factory with high explosives, dangerous industrial tools and potentially lethal energy sources. Sound farfetched? Not really, because this 'factory' is your garage. The National Safety Council (NSC) says that each year household accidents kill about 20,000 Americans and injure another three million" (141).

Van Goethem, Larry. "The Dangers in Your Garage." *Reader's Digest* Aug. 1988: 141–44.

According to David Coswell, NSC program manager in home safety, "The [garages] often contain a wider variety of hazards [than factories]. And homeowners, unlike people on the job, seldom understand or carry out proper safety precautions" (142).

Baker, Susan P., Brian O'Neill, and Ronald S. Karpf. *The Injury Fact Book.* Lexington, MA: Lexington Books, 1984.

"Falls are the most common cause of nonfatal injury in the United States and the second leading cause of both spinal cord and brain injury, accounting for about one-fifth of these injuries. Each year 1 person in 20 receives emergency room treatment because of a fall. . . . In addition to producing substantial morbidity and disability, falls are a major cause of injury death, surpassed only by motor vehicles and firearms. Among unintentional injury deaths, only those from motor vehicles exceed falls. In addition, in an unknown number of deaths a fall initiates or contributes to the sequence of events leading to death but is not mentioned on the death certificate. As a result, the total number of deaths related to falls may be far greater than that attributed to falls on death certificates. . . . The place where injury occurred is specified for about two-thirds of all fatal falls. In the majority of cases where the place of injury is specified, the injury occurs at home. This proportion is highest among young children and lowest at ages 15–19" (113–14).

Baker, Susan P., Brian O'Neill, and Ronald S. Karpf. *The Injury Fact Book*. Lexington, MA: Lexington Books, 1984.

According to *The Injury Fact Book*, "Burns and fires are surpassed only by motor vehicle crashes, falls, and drownings as a cause of unintentional injury death" (139). This fact takes on even greater weight when one realizes that "deaths associated with post-crash fires are counted among deaths from motor vehicle and airplane crashes" (139). Baker, O'Neill, and Karpf write that three-fourths of all deaths from fires and burns are caused by housefires (139).

Long, Kim, and Terry Reim. *Kicking the Bucket*. New York: William Morrow, 1985.

Long and Morrow state that the fourth leading cause of death in this nation among all age groups is accidents and that about one-third of all accidents occur in the home (56).

Avoiding Plagiarism

In 1988 Senator Joseph Biden was one of the leading contenders for the Democratic presidential nomination. However, Biden's candidacy was derailed when it was learned that he had "borrowed" parts of his campaign speeches from a British politician, Neil Kinnock. Had Biden given credit to Kinnock for the words he borrowed, the race for the Democratic nomination might have come out differently. As it was, Biden was considered intellectually dishonest, and his campaign collapsed.

As Biden's case indicates, you must be careful about citing the sources you use. Place any direct quotations in quotation marks. Make sure that all of your paraphrases are significantly different from the original; do not simply substitute a word here and there. For every source you use, properly cite it in the text and give complete bibliographic information in the "Works Cited" at the end of your paper.

EXERCISE 8.16 **Recognizing Plagiarism**

The following paragraph is taken from Thomas Paine's *Common Sense*. Which of the student sentences below would be considered plagiarism?

Original paragraph

Society in every state is a blessing, but government even in its best state is but a necessary evil; in its worst state an intolerable one; for when we suffer, or are exposed to the same miseries *by a government,* which we might expect in a country *without govern-ment,* our calamity is heightened by reflecting that we furnish the means by which we suffer. Government, like dress, is the badge of lost innocence; the palaces of kings are built on the ruins of the bowers of paradise. For were the impulses of conscience clear, uniform, and irresistibly obeyed, man would need no other lawgiver; but that not being the case, he finds it necessary to surrender up a part of his property to furnish means for the protection of the rest; and this he is induced to do by the same prudence which in every other case advises him out of two evils to choose the least. *Wherefore,* security being the true design and end of government, it unanswerably follows, that whatever *form* thereof appears most likely to ensure it to us, with the least expence and greatest benefit, is preferable to all others.

Student sentences

1. Thomas Paine, in *Common Sense*, proclaims that government even in its best state is but a necessary evil.

2. According to Thomas Paine, suffering which is imposed on us by our own actions is the hardest kind of misfortune to bear.

3. The author of *Common Sense* believes that security is the true design and also the end of government (Paine 13).

4. Paine suggests that the institution of government is a result of man's imperfection (13).

5. Paine indicates that mankind would not need government if the bowers of paradise were not ruined (13).

6. Paine believes that if man were perfect and if "the impulses of conscience" were "clear, uniform, and irresistibly obeyed," governments would be unnecessary (13).

Preparing the Final Manuscript

Your research project has required considerable labor on your part to produce. You should take care to make the final manuscript reflect the care that went into writing your report. Generally, a report has some or all of these elements:

title page

brief abstract or summary of the report's contents

outline or table of contents

the body of the report

works cited

appended materials (e.g., survey forms, survey results, tables, pictures, tran-scriptions of interviews, etc.)

More information about these elements is provided in chapter 9.

Here are some suggestions for improving the appearance of your final manuscript:

Type or print your report on good-quality 8½-by-11-inch paper.

Use a type font and size that is easy to read. *Avoid fancy script typefaces* and fonts smaller than 10 points.

Use a dark ribbon with black ink. Few things are more frustrating to a reader than having to contend with print that is difficult to read.

Double-space your entire text (including quotations and "Works Cited").

The first line in each paragraph should be indented five spaces.

Quotations longer than four lines should be indented as a block, 10 spaces from the left margin.

Place your name and the page number in the upper right corner of every page after the first.

Be sure that your title appears on the first page even if you have a title page.

Staple or paper-clip your paper in the upper left corner. Do not place your paper in a binder unless your instructor recommends doing so.

Make a copy of your paper before submitting it to your instructor.

Be sure to proofread your paper carefully. Careless typographical errors, misspellings, missing words or citations, and other routine errors can mar an otherwise outstanding report. If you detect errors in time, you will want to retype or reprint the page on which they occur. However, if you cannot retype the page, make the correction neatly with black ink.

A SAMPLE INVESTIGATIVE REPORT

Although every research project has its own unique demands, this is the way that one student prepared her investigative report.

Discovering a Topic

At the beginning of the Monday morning class period, Camtu Philmon's instructor passed around a list of 27 topics of current interest, ranging from recent developments in intercollegiate sports to the changes taking place in Eastern Europe and the former Soviet Union. After looking over the list, students were to decide on two or three top choices and discuss these with the other students in their group.

Camtu wrote down "sexual harassment," "whale protection," and "computer technology" on her paper. She really wanted to write about computers, but she thought it might be too boring. However, her Discovery Group suggested that if she really wanted to write about computers, she should at least explore that option. Camtu knew she would have to focus on one aspect of computers since the report was to be a maximum of eight pages. She also knew that she couldn't waste time researching different subjects since the final draft of the document was due in three weeks. After meeting with her group, Camtu made a list of some possible research questions on computer technology:

What are "super" computers?

How did computers get started?

How do computers work?

What do people do with their home computers?

How do some people work at their own homes using a computer?

What are the advantages and disadvantages of doing artwork on a computer?

Can prolonged computer use be hazardous to one's health?

How are computers affecting video production?

How is a computer network set up?

How do computer viruses work?

Camtu discarded some questions simply because she wasn't interested in the topic. For instance, she thought the questions about how computers got started and how they worked were less interesting than the ways people are currently using them. She was really interested in computer art and video, but she felt that it might take her longer to understand the technical aspects of these topics than she had been allowed for this report. She finally decided that researching the way people use computers to work at home would be both interesting and manageable. In thinking about her research question, she realized that it was not entirely clear whether she was writing about people with their own businesses or those who worked for someone else but were allowed to do their work at home. She rewrote the research question to clear up this ambiguity:

Research question

How are computers allowing some people to work at home that traditionally would have worked in an office?

Having written the research question gave Camtu a sense of direction as she began investigating the topic.

Collecting Information

Camtu had taken an introductory course on computers, so she knew a little about computer technology. However, she had limited knowledge about the business applications of computers. She decided to conduct a knowledge inventory to see what she did know about her research question, although most of her inventory consisted of questions.

Modems send data (reports, letters, accounts, virtually anything written) over a telephone line.

What is a modem? how does it work? — most readers may not know about this.

How many people work at home on a computer? Are they paid the same way as if they worked in an office?

What are the advantages/disadvantages of working at home?

Need some descriptions of people who are actually doing it.

What do companies think about employees working outside the office? Aren't they worried that their employees will "goof off"?

Is working at home on a computer just a fad? Is it pretty much a yuppie kind of thing (like cellular telephones in BMWs)? Or could it really revolutionize the whole concept of "offices" and the urban structure? (Imagine downtown office buildings vacant as everybody works on personal computers at home!)

After completing her knowledge inventory, Camtu had a better idea of what she would need to learn in order to answer her research question.

Camtu had recently read an article about people who worked at home on computers and sent their work to a main office using modems. She wasn't sure, however, what subject heading this would fall under. One of her group members suggested that she try looking under "telecommunications." Camtu made plans to start her research that night after she got off from her afternoon job. She wanted to conduct interviews and possibly send out questionnaires, so she decided to ask people at work if they knew anything about using modems or telecommunications in the workplace.

After her morning classes, Camtu reported for work at the large downtown bank where she was employed as a part-time proof machine operator. During her break she asked her fellow employees and supervisor if they had any experience with telecommunications. Travis said that he used a terminal connected to a modem to call up credit reports and also to check on credit limits on VISA and MasterCard. Maria told Camtu that she used telecommunications to send daily reports to the correspondent bank concerning demand deposit accounts; savings accounts; certificates of deposit; and newly opened, deleted, and altered accounts. While talking with Maria and Travis, Camtu found out that at least 15 of the customers who had opened accounts within the past seven months were telecommuting to other areas of the country, and she realized that these customers might be interested in filling out a questionnaire.

When Camtu arrived at the library that evening, she went right to work. Deciding that current information about the subject would be the most valuable, she did not consult the card catalog. Instead, she went straight to the library's computerized index, InfoTrac. InfoTrac stores information about hundreds of magazine articles on a compact disc. By typing in her subject on the computer screen, Camtu was getting the same results as searching through dozens of hard-copy indexes such as the *Readers' Guide to Periodical Literature*. On her library's InfoTrac, Camtu had the opportunity to choose among three indexes: the *National Newspaper Index,* the *General Periodicals Index,* and the *Government Documents Index*.

Camtu began with the *National Newspaper Index* and keyed in "telecommunications" as her search word. As she was browsing through the subheadings of this topic, Camtu realized that she would need to be more specific. One of the subheadings was "telecommuting," which sounded exactly like the topic she had in mind.

After keying in "telecommuting," Camtu noted that there were 11 subtopics, including such subjects as "equipment and supplies," "forecasts," "government policy," "public opinion," and "social aspects." Because Camtu was primarily interested in how this trend was developing, personal experiences with the subject, and the technology used, she chose "growth," "personal narratives," and "technological innovations" as her three subtopics. After printing out the information from the *National Newspaper Index,* Camtu went to the *General Periodicals Index,* using the general topic of "telecommuting" and the subtopics of "case studies," "evaluation," "research," "statistics," and "surveys." Camtu did not find any documents listed under "telecommuting" in government documents.

Looking over her printout from InfoTrac, Camtu decided that she had enough information to complete her project without requesting material from the interlibrary loan system. She ultimately decided to use two journal articles, "Sandy's Working at Home Today," published in the June 1, 1987, issue of *Industry Week* and "How Corporate America Takes Its Work Home: Part I," published in the July 1989 issue of *Modern Office Technology*. She also decided to use three articles found in her search of the *National Newspaper Index*. These sources, along with her interviews with Travis and Maria, she included in the list of "Works Cited" at the end of her paper.

As Camtu read, she took notes on each article. The questions she had written earlier helped her identify the ideas in the articles that were most relevant to her report.

Organizing the Information

After conducting her field and library research, Camtu decided that telecommunications was indeed changing the workplace today in important, fundamental ways, and she believed that the changes in the next few years would be even more dramatic. She decided that these beliefs would form the claim of her essay.

Camtu also decided that she would need to present both sides of her subject; therefore, she planned to include both the advantages and disadvantages of telecommuting. In fact, her thesis would neither be a glowing tribute to the technology that made telecommuting possible nor a doomsday account of a society ruled by computers. She would try to establish that new technology was making some fundamental changes in the ways that people worked.

Based on this general organizational pattern, she drafted a preliminary outline:

I. The rise of telecommuting
  A. Scenario of current urban lifestyle
  B. Examples of places where telecommuting is most popular
  C. Statistics regarding growth of telecommuting

II. Benefits to workers and companies
  A. More time for other activities
  B. Ability to set own hours
  C. Savings on transportation to and from workplace and savings on work clothing

III. Detriments to workers and companies
  A. Family interruptions
  B. Must be self-motivated worker
  C. Sense of isolation from other workers
  D. Lack of inspiration due to lack of interaction with other human beings

IV. The future of telecommuting
  A. Review of equipment needed for telecommunications
  B. Other changes in workplace
  C. Mobility of society today
  D. Location is becoming less and less important
  E. Personal application of telecommunication "revolution"

Supporting a Position

Camtu found many sources in the library to support her position that changes in telecommunications technology were revolutionizing the workplace. Almost all the pertinent information she found in the library was contained in periodicals. Although there were some books in the stacks and reference areas, much of the material was outdated. To learn about the ways local residents were using telecommunications, she distributed questionnaires to 15 bank customers whom she had identified as telecommuters. The responses to these questionnaires provided information that she could not have obtained in any other way. She also included information she had gathered from her interviews with Travis and Maria in her report.

As you read over Camtu's final draft on the following pages, note how she quotes, summarizes, and paraphrases her sources. Also pay attention to the tone of the report and the techniques she uses to engage her readers' interest.

Camtu Philmon   1

Professor Jackson

English 1301

23 November 1990

Yuppies in the Country: 2

An Examination of the Benefits and Detriments of Telecommuting

Like your job but want to get away from the hassles of big city living? Tired of

the smog-filled, danger-laden 7:30 a.m. freeway traffic, the continual inconsequential

telephone interruptions, and the gossip around the water cooler, but want to keep your

$250,000 annual salary and strong benefits package? Look no further; high technol-   3

ogy has just come up with the solution where you may have your proverbial cake and

eat it too. You, like the Feld family of Minnesota, can become "techno-peasants,"

living life in the pure country air while enjoying the benefits of computer linkups,

VCRs, and other accoutrements of city life (Reynolds 14).   4

With recent innovations in telephone systems, personal computers, and fax trans-

mission, workers in our information-based society are experiencing the freedom of

living anywhere they wish and are still maintaining careers in large urban centers. In

cities such as Santa Fe, New Mexico; Telluride, Colorado; and Park City, Utah; more   5

and more residents are "telecommuters," a term coined by Dr. Jack Nilles, Director

of Information Technology at the Center for Futures Research at the University of

Southern California (Kuzela 34). The freedom to choose one's preferred geographical

location is certainly one of the main attractions in telecommuting. If the sparkling

waves of Waikiki Beach beckon or if sun glistening off the snow-mantled Rocky

Mountains invokes your presence, your work will not stop your going. Simply pack

up the computer and modem or fax machine and you are on your way.

1. Most instructors prefer a heading with your name, the instructor's name, the class, and the date in the upper left-hand corner of the first page. Double-space your heading unless you are instructed to do otherwise. Your instructor may request a formal title page (see chapter 9 for an example).

2. The title of your report should be interesting as well as informative. College reports often have subtitles. The main title arouses the reader's curiosity; the subtitle is more descriptive of the report's contents. Center the title on the page with additional space above and below it.

3. Note the two rhetorical questions, the first one short and the second fairly long, with which Camtu begins her paper. Using such "hooks" as rhetorical questions, anecdotes, or scenarios in your introduction will entice the reader to remain with you. Also note how the cliché in the reply to these questions is turned to the writer's advantage and how she directly addresses her audience throughout this introduction without a monotonous repetition of second-person pronouns.

4. In many documentation styles, including that of the Modern Language Association, parenthetical citations at the conclusion of quoted, paraphrased, or summarized material allow the reader to cross-reference the complete bibliographic information at the end of the paper. Careful readers will want to be able to verify the sources of information you have used in your writing. Usually, the author's last name and the page number of the material are included in the citation.

5. By citing specific cities in which telecommuters live, Camtu makes her writing more interesting and conveys the general idea that telecommuters have the freedom to locate in scenic and remote places. Readers wanting to know more about telecommuting might decide to read Kuzela's article that is referred to in the citation at the end of the sentence. (Note that the citation is part of the sentence and that the terminal punctuation mark—in this case, a period—comes after the closing parenthesis.)

C. Philmon

2

Telecommuting is growing by an annual rate of 8%, and it has been estimated
that, by 1993, 34.8 million people will do their work at home ("How" 58). Many of
these workers have annual salaries that exceed $250,000, and they are changing the
lifestyles in the communities in which they have recently relocated (Clifford A36).
For many telecommuters, their new lifestyles are realizations of lifelong dreams. Although there are both benefits and detriments for telecommuters, telecommuting has
fundamentally altered the urban experience.

On the positive side, telecommuting can allow more time with family, especially
with children. Sandy Hale, a Pacific Bell manager, has been telecommuting since her
second baby was born and considers telecommuting in many ways to be "the ideal
answer" for her work/family dilemma (Kuzela 35). With the use of home-based personal computers, employees may stay home one or two days of the week and simply
transmit their work to the office via modem, or they may stay home the entire work-
week and confer with fellow workers in teleconferences over either the telephone or a
modem. Not only do parents save money on child care, but they and their children
also seem to enjoy a more rewarding personal relationship than can be afforded to
many traditional workers. As Maria Hernandez, bookkeeper at Hilford National Bank
and mother of two preschoolers, indicates, "Mothers in traditional working environments are continually having to prioritize responsibilities. Too often it is the children
who lose out."

. . . .

As we have seen, both benefits and detriments characterize the trend in telecommunications. Workers can spend more time with their families; they can save money

6

7

8

9

10

11

6. The article "How Corporate America Takes Its Work Home: Part I" was published anonymously in *Modern Office Technology*. Therefore, an abbreviated, unique form of the title, "How," identifies the source in the internal parenthetical citation.

7. Specific figures, such as $250,000, generally require a citation. Kuzela's article appeared in a newspaper; the "A" stands for the first section of the paper, and the "36" indicates the page number within the section.

8. After attempting to convince her audience that telecommuting is a growing trend in the workplace, Camtu, with the beginning of this paragraph, begins to examine the positive and negative sides of her subject. Sometimes the writer of a research paper presents both sides and then goes on to advocate a particular position. This research paper is more informative than persuasive and allows the reader to form his or her own conclusion.

9. The two specific examples of Sandy Hale and Maria Hernandez in the paragraph ground Camtu's statements in real situations concerning real people.

10. Since this quotation is from a personal interview with Maria Hernandez, no citation is included other than the interviewee's name in the initial clause of the sentence. Notice how Camtu nicely integrates both primary sources, such as interviews and surveys, along with secondary sources, which she found in the library, into her own text.

11. The introductory clause in this paragraph indicates that Camtu is summarizing her paper in preparation for the conclusion.

C. Philmon

3

in commuting, meals, and clothing. They can be their own bosses, be more produc-   **12**
tive, and work at their own peak times (Olmos 2). In addition, employers can benefit
by increased morale and productivity. But to be successful, telecommuters must be
continually self-disciplined, extraordinarily motivated, and relatively independent in
their work. And even these exemplary workers many times need the stimulation that
comes from face-to-face interaction with colleagues.

If you really want to escape from downtown urban environments and if you are   **13**
experiencing restrictions in your career due to your being tied to a limited geographical location, telecommuting may well be a viable solution for you. Although Don
Bachman of Montana may be exaggerating the benefits when he says, "Buy a fax and
live in paradise" (Clifford A1), the advantages of joining the ranks of those who work
over modems and fax machines are alluring. Whatever you may believe about the
advantages or disadvantages of telecommuting, it is clear that this trend will have
continuing important psychological and sociological implications. And just how dramatic these implications may be for all of us remains to be seen.

12. After the first sentence of the paragraph (the topic sentence), Camtu devotes two sentences to the benefits and two to the detriments, thereby indicating that she has presented a balanced view of the subject.

13. In the concluding paragraph Camtu again addresses her reader directly, just as she did in her report's introduction. She emphasizes her impartial perspective by stating that her source may be exaggerating in promising paradise, reiterates the growing importance of the trend, and anticipates future developments.

C. Philmon

8

Works Cited **14**

Clifford, Frank. "City Office, Home on the Range." *Los Angeles Times* 29 Oct. 1989: **15**
A1+.

Hernandez, Maria. Personal interview. 2 Nov. 1990.

"How Corporate America Takes Its Work Home: Part I." *Modern Office Technology*
July 1989: 49+.

Kuzela, Lad. "Sandy's Working at Home Today." *Industry Week* 1 June 1987: 34–35.

Magill, Travis. Personal interview. 2 Nov. 1990.

Olmos, David. "New Technology Opens Door for More Workers to Stay at Home."
Los Angeles Times 6 Oct. 1988: sec. 4: 2.

Reynolds, Cynthia Furlong. "Goodbye City, Hello Country Life." *Christian Science
Monitor* 11 Jan. 1989: 14.

14. If your bibliography contains only sources that you have actually quoted, paraphrased, or summarized, use the title "Works Cited." If, on the other hand, your bibliography consists of sources you've just examined as well as those that you have used in the paper, call your bibliography "Works Consulted." Sometimes, in very long papers, you may have both a Works Cited page and a Works Consulted page; however, in shorter papers these pages are usually combined under "Works Consulted." Center the title at the top margin of the page.

15. Notice that Camtu uses a variety of sources (newspaper, magazine, and journal articles and personal interviews) in her paper. Your instructor usually will suggest the number and types of sources you are expected to use; if no suggestion is made, try for a variety (note that, since she is examining a recent trend, Camtu includes no books as sources).

Appendix A:

Survey Form for Telecommuters

I am conducting a research project concerning telecommuting for a college course. Since you are involved in telecommuting, or are a telecommuter yourself, would you please take a few moments to fill out the following questionnaire. Any responses and comments you make will be appreciated and will add to the completeness of my research on this project. If you would like a final copy of my research report, just let me know on this form. Otherwise, your name and address are optional. Thanks.

Name _____

P.O. Box or Street Address _____

City, State, and ZIP Code _____

I would like to receive a final copy of the research report (please circle your response): Yes   No

Answer the following questions by circling the number indicating your response, using the following scale:

1 – Strongly agree

2 – Moderately agree

3 – Undecided or not applicable

4 – Moderately disagree

5 – Strongly disagree

Telecommuter Survey

2

1. I believe that telecommuting is changing today's workplace in important ways.

           1   2   3   4   5

2. I believe that the impact of telecommuting will increase throughout the coming decade.

           1   2   3   4   5

3. I am satisfied with my decision to telecommute.

           1   2   3   4   5

4. Telecommuting offers more benefits to the worker than the traditional workplace environment does.

           1   2   3   4   5

5. As a telecommuter I miss the collegiality with other workers and many times feel a lack of inspiration or motivation in my work.

           1   2   3   4   5

6. I believe that the benefits I receive from telecommuting outweigh the detriments.

           1   2   3   4   5

Please answer the following questions with short answers. You may complete your answers on the reverse side of this sheet.

1. What do you believe are the primary advantages of telecommuting?

Telecommuter Survey

3

2. What do you believe are the primary disadvantages of telecommuting?

3. What motivated you to become a telecommuter?

4. If a friend were thinking about becoming a telecommuter, what advice would you give to that person?

EXERCISE 8.17 **Evaluating an Investigative Report**

Did Camtu organize her report well? Did she convey information about the benefits and drawbacks of telecommuting adequately for an eight-page document? What did she do well? What could have been improved? What other comments do you have about Camtu's report?

WRITING ASSIGNMENT **Investigative Report**

Step one   Review the research questions you developed in exercise 8.2. Select what you feel is the most promising line of research and submit it to your teacher for approval.

Step two   Write a brief plan for conducting your research.

1.   What sources of information will you use? Be as specific as possible.
Library resources:

Field research:

2.   Where will you obtain this information?

3.   Write a brief time chart that projects when you will complete various phases of your report. Write down the days you plan to spend in library research, in conducting interviews, or in other research activities.

Step three   Gather the information for your report. Be sure to keep accurate bibliographic information on all the library sources you use. Remember to write a report of any interviews you conduct as soon as possible after the interview (before your notes get "cold").

Step four   As you complete various phases of your research, write those sections of your report. Write a complete rough draft of your report in time to get a response from your Discovery Group.

Step five   Make copies of your rough draft and submit them to your Discovery Group for review. Collect written responses to these questions:

1.   Write one sentence that sums up the author's basic purpose in writing this paper.

2.   Assess the evidence the author has used to support the thesis. Is it accurate? thorough? convincing? What else might the writer include to strengthen the thesis?

3.   Does any information seem irrelevant? Are there places where the report could be cut without harming its effectiveness?

4.   Is the report well organized? Does the writer proceed systematically through the subject? Are there any gaps or breaks in the continuity of the report?

5.   What might the author do to improve this paper in the next draft?

Step six   Keep revising the paper until it is ready to submit. Be sure to review the paper for readability, correctness, and style (see chapters 9–11). Include all the materials requested by your instructor with your final draft. Remember that exercising care in the preparation of your manuscript will enhance both the appearance and the credibility of your report.

THE CRITICAL MOMENT

In this chapter we have stressed the importance of information in order to make sound judgments on issues of importance. Recognizing this principle, company executives often exclaim, "Information is power!" For example, a manager can make a better argument for a budget increase if she or he can show that the division is making substantial profits for the company.

Because it is important for citizens to be well informed, our Congress passed a Freedom of Information Act that guarantees access to public information. For instance, the federal government was forced to release photos showing the debris that was recovered from the space shuttle *Challenger* when a reporter filed under the Freedom of Information Act.

Of course, many people are concerned about how much access other people have to personal information about them. Few people, for instance, would want their income tax returns or credit history to become public information.

Think through your answers to the following questions about access to information in our society.

1. Which of the following items of information should the media be able to obtain? Why?
   a. Records of the ways in which campaign funds were spent by a politician
   b. The criminal record of a man arrested for driving while intoxicated
   c. The records of a psychiatrist treating a man accused of strangling a woman to death
   d. Military documents during time of war
   e. Government information that is marked as "classified"
   f. Alimony payments being made by a bank vice-president

2. Should the media interview people who have just experienced a tragic loss?

3. Should courtroom trials be shown on television?

4. Should teachers have the right to review their students' prior academic records? Should students have the right to review their professors' teaching evaluations?

5. When should information be considered private?

PART III

Editing

CHAPTER 9

Editing for Readability

Editing is frequently considered the least rewarding part of the writing process. By the time you begin editing, you may feel you have already finished the most crucial phases of your work — you have decided on your purpose, found a focus for your writing, and considered the needs of your audience. What remains is simply "tidying up," putting on the final polish.

Good writers know, however, that editing can make a tremendous difference in the reception a reader gives to their ideas. Careless errors can jeopardize your credibility. In some cases, your whole message may be ignored because of a failure to edit carefully. I know of several employers who routinely dismiss applicants who have spelling errors on their résumés. They reason that if an applicant doesn't take the time to check over spelling, he or she probably won't be careful in other tasks required on the job. On the other hand, clear and well-crafted sentences often indicate a person who strives for excellence, even in small details.

In a sense, we can compare good editing to the polish on a car. If a car looks like it just came back from racing the Baja, splattered with mud and grime, few will look beyond this surface appearance to see the quality of the vehicle. If, however, a car has been meticulously waxed and shined, the observer quickly notices the beauty of the design and the luster of the paint. A good wax job is no substitute for a well-built car, but unless the surface shines, few will look much farther. Similarly, good editing cannot rescue writing that is thoughtless or poorly arranged, but it does show good writing to its best advantage.

In the following chapters, we will consider three kinds of editing that can help ensure that your work gets the best possible reception from your readers. In chapter 9, we look at making the document "readable," that is, writing in such a way that we enable the reader to progress through the document with a minimum of confusion and misunderstanding. In chapter 10, we will consider the conventions of correct usage so that we can keep the reader's attention on what we have to say rather than on how we are saying it. Finally, in chapter 11 we will look at matters of style. Although any adjustment in language can be considered "stylistic," we will consider the ways that we can make our writing graceful as well as functional in this last chapter.

WRITING TO BE READ

The best measure of readability is always the response of a real reader. If a reader halts at an unfamiliar word or has to reread a section to understand the basic idea, you can directly observe the difficulties that document presents for that reader. However, you may not always have the luxury of testing your writing on enough readers to know how it will be generally received. You will then have to rely on your own judgment about your readers' general competence with language and their familiarity with your subject. In this section, we consider elements that help to determine readability: simplicity, brevity, directness, emphasis, and coherence.

Simplicity

Compare the following sentences:

The pathological condition of inflamed and constricted bronchi brought on by exposure to allergens may contribute to reduced cardiovascular performance.

Patients with asthma often have difficulty in running, climbing stairs, and other strenuous forms of exercise.

The first sentence is not "wrong," but the medical terminology may make it difficult for many people to read. The writing is clearly intended for an expert audience. The second sentence is easier to understand although it may be less precise. Especially when writing about subjects on which we have expert knowledge, we need to use ordinary language when writing for general audiences.

EXERCISE 9.1 **Revising for Simplicity**

Rewrite the following sentences for a general audience. Use the dictionary to find definitions of words that are unfamiliar to you.

1. His vituperative remarks could be heard all over the corporate edifice.

2. The celerity of our computers for the processing of informational data is prodigious to the human rationality.

3. The inconstancy of remuneration for our hourly employees has led to significantly higher rates of employee resignation.

4. As she steadily imbibed the effervescent intoxicant, she began to exhibit signs of vertigo.

5. The aerobic capabilities of the pneumonic organs were precluded from optimum performance standards due to the intractability of the disabling traits of his infirmity.

In recent years, many studies have indicated that basic reading and writing skills are on the decline in America. Declining scores on the verbal portion of college entrance tests have been a particular cause for concern. According to the Business Council for Effective Literacy, a national information clearinghouse, 27 million Americans over age 17 lack competencies necessary to function in society. Another 45 million Americans are considered marginal in their abilities. In a 1988 study by the National Assessment of Educational Progress, 53% percent of the students could not give an adequate response to an informative writing task; 64% could not give an adequate response to a persuasive writing task.

These concerns about reading and writing ability have generated a controversy about the textbooks used in elementary and secondary schools. Some school systems and some textbook publishers have insisted that textbooks conform to readability formulas for the age level of the students for whom a textbook is targeted. Thus, a fourth-grade book is written using short sentences and simple vocabulary. Critics have complained that such policies result in the "dumbing down" of textbooks. Instead of requiring the most out of children, they cater to the average student's abilities. As students are challenged less, these critics reason, their verbal performance will decline even more, resulting in a downward spiral of less being demanded and less being achieved.

Other educational leaders have countered that to write books without concern for reading level is to doom some students to failure. If the reading material is too challenging, students will become frustrated and quit trying. These educators believe that in writing textbooks authors should take into account the abilities of students who will use them. To do otherwise, they feel, would be neither a humane nor a democratic course of action.

The implications of this debate affect all writers. In this chapter, we encourage you to use a simple, direct style and to consider the needs of your reader. However, we feel strongly that readability cannot be determined simply by a formula. As well as the difficulty of the material, a writer must consider the reader's interest in the subject, the organization of the material, and many other factors. Ideally, any written document depends on a successful relationship between writer and reader. The writer needs to understand the needs of the reader and to present information clearly and coherently. The writer will, thus, neither "dumb down" the writing and pander to the "lowest common denominator" nor mystify the reader with jargon and buzzwords that are outside the reader's understanding. The reader needs to attend carefully to what is being said and to accept the challenges of new ideas and new vocabulary. Mutual understanding requires the best efforts of both writer and reader.

The desire to write in a simple, direct manner should not necessarily lead us to avoid "big words." First, if our readers are familiar with a technical term, it will be more confusing to them if we avoid using it:

Tonya had decided to enter the profession of those who are propelled aboard rockets into outer space.

Tonya had decided to be an astronaut.

Because *astronaut* is a commonly understood term, there is little reason to avoid using it. Second, we should not avoid difficult terminology if our purpose in writing is to introduce our readers to new ideas and concepts. Particularly if a term is of central importance to understanding the subject, it is important to introduce the reader to its meaning. Notice how the writer in the following paragraph carefully leads up to the definition of a difficult word.

> We frequently hear comparisons between computers and the human brain. A clever student is told, "You have a mind like a supercomputer." On the other hand, the central processing unit of a computer is often referred to as the "brains" of the machine. However, many people are unaware that studies of the similarities and differences between the functioning of computers and the human brain have achieved the status of a science. In 1948 Norbert Weiner coined the word *cybernetics* to describe the comparative study of complex electronic computers and the human nervous system. Although cybernetics may sound like something out of a science fiction movie, the study of cybernetics has tremendous implications for the way we will live in the twenty-first century.

As this example indicates, simplicity is a matter not only of using readily understood words but also of introducing new words in such a way that they do not confuse or intimidate the reader.

Brevity

Another indication of readability has to do with the length of sentences. The average sentence length of writing intended for adult readers is about 20 words per sentence. As sentences become longer, they often require us to read closely in order to understand how different parts of the sentence are related. Writers in the nineteenth century frequently placed great demands on their readers, as this passage indicates:

> Meanwhile there was the snow and the low arch of dun vapour — there was the stifling oppression of that gentlewoman's world, where everything was done for her and none asked for her aid — where the sense of connection with a manifold pregnant existence had to be kept up painfully as an inward vision, instead of coming from without in claims that would have shaped her energies. — "What shall I do?" "Whatever you please my dear:" that had been her brief history since she had left off learning morning lessons and practicing silly rhythms on the hated piano.

This sentence from George Eliot's *Middlemarch* is 97 words long. It contains 4 independent clauses, 6 dependent clauses, and 12 phrases. Eliot crafted this sentence carefully, and the length of the sentence may actually contribute to the sense of emotional distress that she is describing. However, it would clearly be a mistake to express public safety information in a sentence like this:

> After extensive testing of underground aquifers in Calhoun County, laboratory results obtained through standard testing procedures presented conclusive results, now subject to independent verification, that although the heavy concentrations of mineral salts are, in themselves, no particular hazard to local residents, the spot concentrations of As_2O_3, probably due to agricultural runoff infiltrating underground reservoirs, are in excess of Environmental Protection Agency standards, rendering current underground sources unreliable.

This 66-word sentence contains a vital fact: The underground water supply has been contaminated with arsenic. Such information should not be buried in a myriad of details about testing procedures.

In general, consider sentence length in terms of the complexity of the information you are conveying. If you want to express a simple idea, 20 words may be too long. Conversely, if you are expressing a complex idea, a lengthy sentence may be easier to understand than several simple sentences in isolation.

EXERCISE 9.2 Revising for Brevity

Rewrite the following sentences, breaking up sentences that are too long, combining sentences that are too short, and deleting any information that seems unnecessary. If you believe a sentence should stand as written, justify your decision.

1. Due to the fact that the conference participants represent a somewhat diverse group of institutional structures, positions within those institutions, and levels of experience in those positions, it might be appropriate at this time to have a division of the meeting into several interest groups since these smaller groups would allow for more individual participation and group interaction, and the smaller groups would also allow topics to be discussed that relate only to the needs and concerns of a small group of the conference membership.

2. Although the plot of Anne Tyler's *Dinner at the Homesick Restaurant* is ingenuous, and sometimes rather bizarre, the novel depends less on the intricacies of its plot structure than on its superb characterizations: the well-meaning, but clumsy Cody; the favored child, Ezra; the woman who loves too much, Jenny; the irresponsible father; and the domineering mother; but in the climactic scene at the Homesick Restaurant, character and situation all come together in a wonderfully miserable and delightfully madcap ill-fated dinner.

3. Last night I saw *A Midsummer Night's Dream*. It was playing at the Spotlight Theater. The play was enjoyable. The lighting was effective. The sets were attractive. The acting was superb. Shakespeare obviously is a masterful writer.

4. Even though basketball is technically a "noncontact" sport, such a description can only suffice for the uninitiated, for in reality the brutal pounding endured by the players of this sport, especially those who do battle under the rim, certainly rivals the physical contact in sports such as football and hockey; however, basketball players do not have the protective equipment worn by football and hockey players, nor do the penalties assessed for personal fouls really deter physical contact because some contact is legitimate, some contact is never seen by the referees because of the fast-paced nature of the game, and, of course, in no other sport is the intentional foul as predictable as it is in the waning minutes of a basketball game.

5. This computer is sophisticated. It has a 486 Intel® microprocessor. Internally, there is a 120MB hard drive. In addition, there is a 3 and 1/2 inch floppy disk drive, and there is a 5 and 1/4 inch floppy disk drive. There is also 4MB of RAM within the computer system. The VGA monitor makes anything on the screen look good.

Directness

As well as the length of a sentence, the way a sentence is structured affects its readability. Sentences in English usually follow this pattern:

subject   +   verb   +   object
We   +   celebrate   +   our freedom.

Of course, other patterns are possible. We could say:

Our freedom we celebrate.

Such inversions of normal sentence order are sometimes used for literary effect or on ceremonial occasions. For instance, marriage vows frequently include the statement: "With this ring I thee wed." Such language is perfectly appropriate for this formal occasion. On the other hand, saying "With this phone I thee call" sounds ludicrous.

As well as sentence order, the placement of modifiers affects the readability of a sentence. We normally place adjectives before the nouns they modify and place adverbs before or after the verbs they modify. If we place modifiers in the wrong position or if we separate them from the words they modify, the result is often a confusing or awkward sentence:

The man muscular and his partner petite skated on the ice clad in colorful costumes gracefully.

By rearranging the modifiers, we make the sentence much easier to read:

Clad in colorful costumes, the muscular man and his petite partner skated gracefully on the ice.

Emphasis

By varying word order and the placement of modifiers, we can also direct the reader's attention to the most important ideas we wish to communicate. Compare these two sentences:

The principal, who sometimes lost her temper, was a kind and generous woman.

The principal, who was a kind and generous woman, sometimes lost her temper.

In the first sentence, the writer has emphasized the principal's kindness and generosity by placing this information in the main clause. In the second sentence, the main clause emphasizes the principal's occasional problems with her temper.

Placing information at the beginning of a sentence also is a way of emphasizing its importance. Compare these two sentences:

A land flowing with milk and honey was promised to Abraham.

Abraham was promised a land flowing with milk and honey.

The first sentence emphasizes the quality of the land. The second sentence emphasizes the importance of Abraham as the one who received the promise.

We also can create emphasis by using modifiers to focus attention on a particular idea. Sometimes we may try to modify every noun and verb in a sentence in order to produce more descriptive or picturesque writing, but the result is often a lack of focus. When we selectively describe the words we wish to emphasize, the purpose of the sentence becomes clear. Compare these two sentences:

Modifiers selected carefully

Place the loosened clamp over the free end of the hose. Push the hose onto the metal collar, and then slide the clamp forward past the flange and tighten.

Modifiers used too abundantly

With your fingers place the loosened serrated metal adjustable clamp over the unattached end of the standard high-temperature automobile radiator hose. Vigorously push the aforementioned hose forward onto the anodized aluminum collar of the radiator, and when this action has been completed, slide the loosened serrated metal adjustable clamp past the position of the small flange near the terminal position of the collar and gradually turn the worm screw of the adjustable clamp until the clamp has been sufficiently tightened.

Although the second sentence is more precise than the first, it is a good example of information "overkill." The profuse description tends to mask the essential actions necessary for installing the hose. If a description of the radiator, the hoses, or the clamps is necessary, the writer should provide it in a section prior to the explanation of how to install the hose.

Writers can achieve emphasis within a paragraph by varying sentence length. In the following example taken from her book *Practicing History*, notice the way Barbara Tuchman uses a short sentence to provide a dramatic conclusion:

> Research is endlessly seductive; writing is hard work. One has to sit down on that chair and think and transform thought into readable, conservative, interesting sentences that both make sense and make the reader turn the page. It is laborious, slow, often painful, sometimes agony. It means rearrangement, revision, adding, cutting, rewriting. But it brings a sense of excitement, almost of rapture; a moment on Olympus. *In short, it is an act of creation.*

Of course, writers may also create emphasis through a long sentence. Observe the way Tom Wolfe, in his book *The Right Stuff*, creates the sense of pandemonium aboard an aircraft carrier in this incredibly long sentence:

> This was a skillet!–a frying pan!–a short-order grill!–not gray but black, smeared with skid marks from one end to the other and glistening with pools of hydraulic fluid and the occasional jet-fuel slick, all of it still hot, sticky, greasy, runny, virulent from God knows what traumas — still ablaze! — consumed in deto-nations, explosions, flames, combustion, roars, shrieks, whines, blasts, horrible shudders, fracturing impacts, as little men in screaming red and yellow and purple and green shirts with black Mickey Mouse helmets over their ears skittered about on the surface as if for their very lives (you've said it now!), hooking fighter planes onto the catapult shuttles so that they can explode their afterburners and be slung off the deck in a red-mad fury with a *kaboom!* that pounds through the entire deck — a procedure that seems absolutely controlled, orderly, sublime, however, compared to what he is about to watch as aircraft return to the ship for what is known in the engineering stoicisms of the military as "recovery and arrest."

Such a long sentence is clearly exceptional, but it does achieve Wolfe's purpose of conveying a sense of the frenetic activity aboard a carrier.

EXERCISE 9.3 Emphasis within a Sentence

Read the following sentences and discuss with your Discovery Group what ideas are being emphasized in each one.

1. Louisiana, which has lost about a million acres in the past hundred years, is witnessing the gradual disappearance of its coastal marshes.

2. Louisiana, which is witnessing the gradual disappearance of its coastal marshes, has lost about a million acres in the past hundred years.

3. The legacy of Alaska is its vast, unspoiled wilderness.

4. Its vast, unspoiled wilderness is the legacy of Alaska.

Then compare the following paragraphs and discuss with your Discovery Group how the emphasis is changed.

5. Marie Curie was one of the pioneers in the study of radioactive particles, along with Antoine Henri Becquerel, Pierre Curie, Ernest Rutherford, and William Röntgen. Curie received a Nobel Prize for physics in 1903 along with Becquerel and her husband, Pierre Curie, for her pioneering work in radioactivity. The earliest experiments with radioactivity had been conducted with uranium. Marie Curie was one of a handful of scientists who began a search for other minerals with radioactive properties. She soon discovered that thorium possessed similar properties (G. C. Schmidt was working on this simultaneously in Germany). Curie also knew that pitchblende was highly radioactive. She was ultimately able to isolate pure radium from this ore with the help of the chemist Andre Debierne. This achievement led to another Nobel Prize, this time in chemistry. In 1906 Marie Curie was appointed to fill the position left vacant after her husband's tragic death. She was the first woman to be a professor at the Sorbonne. Curie's later years were devoted to medical research with radioactive substances and to the accumulation of radium for research purposes.

6. Near the beginning of the twentieth century, the study of radioactive particles was pioneered by scientists like Antoine Henri Bacquerel and the Curies in France, William Röntgen in Germany, and Ernest Rutherford in England. In 1903 the Nobel Prize for physics was awarded to Antoine Henri Becquerel, Pierre Curie, and Marie Curie for their pioneering work in radioactivity. The earliest experiments with radioactivity had been conducted with uranium. A small group of physical scientists, including Marie Curie, were eager to see if the radioactive properties exhibited by uranium were found in other elements. In Germany G. C. Schmidt discovered that thorium was also radioactive (Marie Curie was working on this simultaneously in Paris). Since pitchblende was highly radioactive, the Curies hoped to find new radioactive elements in this ore. With the help of the chemist Andre Debierne, Marie Curie was able to extract pure radium from pitchblende. After her husband's tragic death in 1906, Marie Curie was appointed to fill his position, making her the first woman professor at the Sorbonne. Medical research with radioactive substances and the accumulation of radium for research purposes were the principal achievements of Curie's later years.

Coherence

Most of us can recall moments when we've been incoherent—perhaps we were frightened or awakened in the middle of the night. Our ideas were confused and disconnected. No one could make out exactly what we were trying to say.

Obviously, in most communication situations we strive for coherence. We want our sentences and paragraphs to be clearly connected and for one idea to lead naturally into the next. One way we create this sense of connectedness is by repeating key words and ideas.

> *Violent crime* is tearing apart our neighborhoods. *Violent crime* is causing our people to live in fear and suspicion. *Violent crime* has robbed us of our dignity and raped us of our self-respect.

The repetition of exact words can be very effective in creating a sense of connection, but obviously such repetition can become wearisome. In some cases, we may choose related words to provide a sense of continuity:

> *Violent crime* is tearing apart our neighborhoods. This *violence* is causing our people to live in fear and suspicion. We have been *robbed* of our dignity and *raped* of our self-respect.

Although the exact words *violent crime* are not repeated in each sentence, the connection to *violence* in the second sentence is clear, and even the words *robbed* and *raped* in the third sentence carry on this theme.

Substituting one word for another cannot be done indiscriminately. In some cases, the use of synonyms can create confusion for the reader:

> I was disturbed when I received the message from the *physician*. I called my *doctor* and made an appointment to discuss the test results. When the *cardiologist* entered the room, I could tell the prognosis was grim. On returning home, I explained to my wife the plan of treatment I had been given by the *health-care professional*.

Although it is sometimes tempting to substitute synonyms for the sake of variety, we must be careful not to confuse the reader. Generally, if we are making a second reference to the same person, we should either repeat the noun or use a pronoun:

> I was disturbed when I received the message from the *cardiologist*. I called him and made an appointment to discuss the test results. When *he* walked into the room, I could tell that *his* prognosis was grim. On returning home, I explained to my wife the plan of treatment I had been given.

One of the most frequent problems with coherence is the result of omitting an important thought. Often the writer assumes more than the reader is likely to know

Many word processors allow writers to eliminate keying in all the letters of words or phrases that they use repetitively by incorporating a feature known as "macros." Macros allow writers to program a series of keystrokes that can be recalled by the touch of one key in the same way you might program your telephone to dial a friend's house by pressing only one key. Any series of words you often use may be "macroed" to save you time. If you're working on long documents, such as a business proposal, you could macro the boilerplate (paragraphs that would appear in any proposal distributed by your company) and bring up entire sections of the paper with a single touch of a key.

Good writing is, of course, fresh and, at least to some degree, original. You probably would, therefore, never want to macro large sections of a paper to be used repeatedly for the documents you produce for your classes. However, you might wish to macro headings such as your name, the class, the instructor's name, and perhaps even the date (a code would command the word processing program to insert the current date, as indicated by the operating system, into the heading).

You might also wish to use macros to make your format consistent. For example, if you want your third heading within the paper to be centered, bold, underlined, Courier typeface, and 14 points, you might delegate these features to a single keystroke instead of issuing this series of directions manually.

Words or phrases consistently used with a specific audience, such as the complimentary closing always employed with a certain customer, may be macroed to save the effort of keying in the same information time and again. Some word processing programs, such as WordPerfect, feature a programming language for complex uses within their macro function, but for most writing tasks, the basic macro commands are all you will need.

or has mentally supplied a connection that isn't actually in the paper. Read the paragraph below and consider where information has been omitted:

> *Boyz N the Hood* begins with a violent shooting. The next day Kiesha asked Ricky what happened. Ricky told her that someone got "smoked" in a drive-by shooting. The rest of the movie tells the story of Tré, who goes to live with his father in south central L.A.

As you read this paragraph, you probably find yourself asking several questions. What is the significance of the shooting to the rest of the movie? Who are Kiesha and Ricky? What is their connection to the shooting? Who is Tré? What is his connection to Kiesha and Ricky?

One of the secrets to successful editing is being able to put yourself in the reader's place. What information would a reader probably need to connect the ideas in the sentences below?

Herschel Walker rushed for 2,411 yards during the 1985 season of the New Jersey Generals. However, he has never enjoyed great success in the National Football League.

Awakenings is a sad, haunting movie about a doctor's attempt to reach a group of psychotic patients through drug therapy. *Awakenings* has little in common with *Dead Poets' Society* and *Good Morning, Vietnam*.

Aspirin is still an effective pain medication. Acetaminophen is used for children as well as adults. Ibuprofren, the newest analgesic to be widely promoted, is often recommended for those with sensitive stomachs.

Here are the same sentences with the necessary information added:

Herschel Walker rushed for 2,411 yards during the 1985 season of the New Jersey Generals, a team in the short-lived United States Football League. However, he has never enjoyed great success in the National Football League.

Awakenings is a sad, haunting movie about a doctor's attempt to reach a group of psychotic patients through drug therapy. Robin Williams's portrayal of the introverted doctor in *Awakenings* has little in common with the exuberant professor he played in *Dead Poets' Society* or the zany DJ in *Good Morning, Vietnam*.

Aspirin is still an effective pain medication. However, aspirin has been linked to development of Reye's syndrome in children. Because acetaminophen does not present this threat, it is used for children as well as adults. Both aspirin and acetaminophen are acids and can cause stomach discomfort. For this reason, ibuprofren, the newest analgesic to be widely promoted, is often recommended for those with sensitive stomachs.

As well as connecting ideas through the repetition of key words and phrases, we often use verbal "signposts" to indicate the direction of our thoughts or the connection between ideas. Here are some of the signposts commonly used to signal the development of an idea:

Indications of order

First, second, third, etc.

Next

Also

Finally

Indications of cause or effect

Because

Since (when meaning "because")

For this reason

Consequently

Therefore

As a result

Indications of time

Before

Then

Subsequently

After

Since (when meaning "after")

Indications of similarity

Similarly

Identically

In the same way, fashion, manner, etc.

Indications of contrast

However

On the other hand

Yet

Nevertheless

Instead

Rather

Indications of amplification

Furthermore

Additionally

Moreover

For example

For instance

Actually

Indications of the writer's reaction

Fortunately

Mercifully

Oddly enough

Surprisingly

Regrettably

Using these signposts can be extremely helpful in guiding the reader through a complicated idea. Although the following passage was written for a "specialist" audience of computer users, even a reader who doesn't understand the technical language can see the way that the author has used signposts to organize the information.

> *Fortunately*, computer-based facsimile (CBF) integrates the speed of fax transmission with the convenience of the personal computer. Documents produced on the computer are *first* converted into Huffman code, which is the code used by traditional fax machines. Pixels are *then* converted, or "modulated," to digital information and sent in an analog form (*for example*, in a series of tones or sounds). *At the receiving end*, the analog signal is *subsequently* converted, or "demodulated," into digitized information (a series of 1s and 0s). Optical Character Recognition (OCR), Direct Inward Dialing (DID), or Dual-Tone Multi-Frequency Encoding (DTMF) are *finally* used to deliver documents sent to fax servers to appropriate users. *However*, a PC-to-fax expansion board may be installed into any standalone personal computer, further increasing the speed and convenience of computer-based facsimile.

EXERCISE 9.4 **Revising for Coherence**

Revise the following paragraphs to make them more coherent.

1. The impact of his confession devastated her. Was he presuming too much on their friendship? Roberta was startled that he would admit to such an action. What was the penalty for kidnapping? He had been a good friend. She didn't want to hurt him. Lawyers were expensive, and could they be trusted? Where was the child now, she wondered? How could she know what action to take? Surely Alicia would know what to do. Would the restaurant be closed yet?

2. The competition was stiffer this year. Many companies were producing high-tech equipment now. Vendors were aggressive in marketing. Demand for the suppliers' products was high. Suppliers had raised their prices by an average of 21%. Workers were attracted to lucrative jobs in service industries. They wanted a career ladder built into the company infrastructure. The Rogers Corporation was finding it difficult to fulfill contractual obligations.

3. The term "politically correct" has become a buzzword. Why should people be asked to monitor their speech? Why did some people take offense where none was meant? When people first used "Ms." instead of "Mrs.," that had seemed radical. Or what about "chairperson" instead of "chairman?" Some feel it is progressive. It will usher in a new

age of understanding. Some feel it is regressive. After all, wasn't McCarthyism about producing political correctness? People have different feelings about this concept. It is an important concept. We need to understand its implications in greater detail.

WRITING EFFECTIVE INTRODUCTIONS

The purpose of the introduction is to place information in a useful context and to provide a clear sense of purpose. In chapter 2, we considered how the thesis of a paper prepares the reader for the information that will follow. However, introductions also are often used to convince the reader that the document at hand is, indeed, worth reading. Of course, some readers are so motivated that this function of the introduction is limited:

> The C-19 "Feather-Fall" parachute is designed for convenience, comfort, and durability. The exclusive "wind tuck" feature allows for maximum maneuverability without loss of stability in adverse wind conditions. The following instructions should be read CAREFULLY AND COMPLETELY before any attempt to flight-test the parachute.

The writer of this introduction assumes that the reader has some interest in the subject. The description of the parachute's design features is brief and direct. The tone of the final sentence is brusque. The writer's subtext seems to be "Read this if you know what's good for you!" Because the reader needs the information as a matter of personal safety, the writer can virtually demand that the instructions be read carefully.

Most introductions cannot assume a highly motivated reader. Whether you are introducing a new idea, a new product, or a new philosophical position, you will want to convince the reader that your subject is important and deserves attention. You can secure this attention in various ways, as the following examples indicate.

Vivid description

> In a display at the Hiroshima Peace Museum, among half-melted lumps of metal and glass, blasted bits of brick and stone and swatches of burned clothing, sits the charred remnant of a wrist watch. The minute and hour hands have been burned away, but their shadows remain, imprinted forever by the brilliant flash of the first nuclear weapon ever exploded over a city. (Lydia Dotto)

In the midst of the action

> The Mercedes taxi sped along the country highway. For the tenth time since we left Paris that morning, I looked at the piece of paper in my hand. (Christopher Scanlon)

The two of us — my mother and I — walked south on Fifth Street one morning to the corner of Q Street and turned right. Half of the block was occupied by the Lincoln School. It was a three-story wooden building, with two wings that gave it the shape of a double-T connected by a certain hall. It was a new building, painted yellow, with a shingled roof that was not like the red tile of the school in Mazatlán. I noticed other differences, none of them very reassuring. (Ernesto Galarza)

Personal anecdote

One summer, along about 1904, my father rented a camp on a lake in Maine and took us all there for the month of August. (E. B. White)

I remember, to start with, that day in Sacramento, in a California now nearly thirty years past, when I first entered a classroom — able to understand about fifty stray English words. (Richard Rodriguez)

Long ago — in Germany, near the end of the war — two corpsmen came into the field and lifted me into a litter. They were so careful and gentle that for their sake I gave a little groan, though I felt no pain. They strapped the litter to some metal bars above the back seat of their jeep. One of them sat beside me while the other drove. It was dark. Lying on my back, I could see nothing of the jeep. I floated slowly through the sweet air of a spring night, the head of the corpsman, with the cross outlined against the circle of white on the back of his helmet, bobbing and drifting along with me. On a hillside I saw a bonfire and heard some unfamiliar plaintive song. (James McConkey)

Startling statement

Turtles are a kind of bird with the governor turned low. (Edward Hoagland)

I do not believe in Belief. (E. M. Forster)

No young man believes he shall ever die. (William Hazlitt)

Surprise

An icy flower
The shade struggles near dry hills
Autumn sunset

Haiku such as this, obscure and enigmatic, were once in vogue. It is gauche, of course, to ask poets what such poems mean. In this case, it would also be pointless, for the poem was written by my computer. (Robert Schadewald)

Quotation

O death, where is thy sting? O grave, where is thy victory? Where, indeed. Many a badly stung survivor, faced with the aftermath of some relative's funeral, has ruefully concluded that the victory has been won hands down by a funeral establishment—in disastrously unequal battle. (Jessica Mitford)

"We fear," remarked an Eskimo shaman responding to a religious question from the explorer Knud Rasmussen some fifty years ago. "We fear the cold and the things we do not understand. But most of all we fear the doings of the heedless ones among ourselves." (Loren Eiseley)

Interesting event

The grapevine had it that thirty-four men, putting up $10,000 each, would convene in Benny Binion's Horseshoe Casino in Las Vegas to settle the world poker championship and thereby make the winner temporarily rich. (Larry L. King)

These examples certainly do not exhaust the possibilities for effective introductions. The important thing is that your introduction causes the reader to want to read on, to see what you have to say, to hear you out.

Incidentally, some commonly used introductions are particularly uninviting to the reader:

In this paper I will discuss . . .
(Were you forced to write this paper?)

The subject of my paper is . . .
(Won't I know what the subject is after I begin reading about it?)

Few people are aware of the ancient art of origami . . .
(Maybe that's because few people care.)

The federal deficit (or "government regulations" or "rising medical costs") is probably one of the biggest problems in the world today.
(There are lots of problems in the world. What does this have to do with me?)

Have you ever wondered what industrial chemists do?
(I never have. Why should I now?)

Think carefully about the opening statement in your paper. Will it capture the reader's interest, provoke further reading, suggest a new idea? If the reader stops after the first sentence, nothing else you write will really matter.

EXERCISE 9.5 Evaluating Opening Statements

The following opening statements were written by college students. Which of them do you think are successful? What, if any, are common elements in the successful introductions?

What, if any, are common elements in the less successful openings? Would some of these introductions be successful with one audience and not another? Discuss your responses with your Discovery Group.

1. Television has a great influence on children.

2. Mama dropped off my little sister and me in front of the school doors. I took Nicki's frail hand in mine and told her not to worry.

3. The chilling ring of the telephone woke me.

4. Contrary to popular belief, not all movies are made strictly with comedy in mind.

5. Today's media cover a variety of subjects because of the widespread interests of the audience.

6. He was a handsome man with snowy hair that was combed to one side. He had big, brown eyes that overflowed with joy when he talked to you.

7. Campus parking could be greatly improved.

8. These days in our world, people's opinions and preferences get in the way of other people's.

9. "Turn that trash off right this minute, young lady!" my mom hollered from the other room.

10. Science progresses further each day, and in the field of genetics, the advances are mind boggling.

11. One of the biggest issues surrounding society today is whether or not the press has the right to exploit celebrities or make up nonsense stories.

12. As I walked off the cracked-up, patched together runway, I saw hundreds of faces staring at me. I was probably the only white face they had ever seen.

WRITING EFFECTIVE CONCLUSIONS

A conclusion can sometimes be the most difficult part of the paper to write. You may feel that you've said all that you want to say but know that you can't just "drop" the reader without some kind of conclusion. However, a summary of your main ideas may seem unnecessary and tedious, especially in a short paper. Professional writers often speak of providing a sense of "closure"—the idea that readers sense that everything has been completed that the writer set out to do without having to see a literal "The End" after the last paragraph.

The conclusion in writing serves a similar purpose to the final scene in a movie or dramatic performance. Without seeing the credits starting to roll or the curtain closing, the viewer knows that the performance has concluded. On those occasions where the performance leaves us "hanging" at the end, wanting to know the outcome for certain events, we often feel cheated or denied. Your conclusion should leave your reader feeling that the job has been done.

Of course, one way to signal the completion of your task is by using a signpost at the end of your paper. If you write "finally," "in conclusion," "to sum up," or the like, even the least perceptive reader will know that the end is nigh. However, the best conclusions often require no signposts because the reader recognizes intuitively that the end has come.

Although every letter, essay, story, or report may suggest a different conclusion that is particularly "right" for that writing task, we want to demonstrate conclusions used by some of our favorite writers. These conclusions will indicate the variety of ways authors provide that sense of closure.

In his "Letter from a Birmingham Jail," Martin Luther King argues that Americans, black and white, must fight against racial discrimination through nonviolent protest. He concludes the letter with an appeal for a better world, one free of the current atmosphere of hate and prejudice:

> I hope this letter finds you strong in the faith. I also hope that circumstances will soon make it possible for me to meet each of you, not as an integrationist or a civil-rights leader but as a fellow clergyman and a Christian brother. Let us all hope that the dark clouds of racial prejudice will soon pass away and the deep fog of misunderstanding will be lifted from our fear-drenched communities, and in some not too distant tomorrow the radiant stars of love and brotherhood will shine over our great nation with all their scintillating beauty.
>
> Yours for the cause of Peace and Brotherhood,
>
> *Martin Luther King, Jr.*

As King's letter indicates, persuasive appeals often conclude with a final appeal, much like a lawyer making a summation in a court trial or, in King's case, like a preacher making a final plea to his parishioners.

Sometimes a writer concludes with a visual image that sums up the main idea of the essay. In "Marrakech," George Orwell describes the complete apathy of colonial powers toward the plight of Africans and Asians. He also explains the fear of these imperialists that the natives would someday turn on their white conquerors. He concludes with a striking image of a regiment of Senegalese soldiers marching under the orders of their white European officers:

> It was curious, really. Every white man there has this thought stowed somewhere or other in his mind. I had it, so had the other onlookers, so had the officers on their sweating chargers and the white NCOs marching in the ranks. It was a kind of secret which we all knew and were too clever to tell; only the Negroes didn't know it. And really it was almost like watching a flock of cattle to see the long column, a mile or two miles of armed men, flowing peacefully up the road, while the great white birds drifted over them in the opposite direction, glittering like scraps of paper.

Some authors end with a representative anecdote, a story that somehow sums up the truth they have been presenting. In "On Going Home," Joan Didion tries to explain the gulf separating those belonging to the pre–World War II generation with their strong sense of extended family and traditional morality and those born into the affluence of the sixties and seventies. She sums up her comparison with a brief vignette on her daughter's birthday:

> It is time for the baby's birthday party: a white cake, strawberry-marshmallow ice cream, a bottle of champagne saved from another party. In the evening, after she has gone to sleep, I kneel beside the crib and touch her face, where it is pressed against the slats, with mine. She is an open and trusting child, unprepared for and unaccustomed to the ambushes of family life, and perhaps it is just as well that I can offer her little of that life. I would like to give her more. I would like to promise her that she will grow up with a sense of her cousins and of rivers and of her great-grandmother's teacups, would like to pledge her a picnic on a river with fried chicken and her hair uncombed, would like to give her *home* for her birthday, but we live differently now and I can promise her nothing like that. I give her a xylophone and a sundress from Madeira, and promise to tell her a funny story.

In many cases, the best course is to end simply and directly. A report might simply conclude with a recommendation in this manner:

Recommendation

    The Vernher Laboratory should immediately comply with all municipal fire code regulations, including recharging or replacing fire extinguishers, placing emergency lights at all exits, and installing fire alarms in all rooms.

Such a conclusion leaves the reader with a clear sense of what should be done with the information that has been given. Informative papers typically end by interpreting the significance of the data that have been provided, by making suggestions for action, or by recommending future studies to be undertaken.

ORGANIZING LONGER PAPERS

In longer papers, you might want to provide additional devices to help the reader, such as a title page, an abstract, a table of contents, and subheadings within your paper to indicate the organization and development of your ideas.

The *title page* lets the reader see at a glance the subject of a report and its source. Here is a sample title page for a lengthy report:

IDENTITY AND AUTHORITY
IN THE JOURNALS OF AMERICAN WOMEN PIONEERS

by
Amaranta Arcelia Rojo Garcia

Submitted to
Professor Eileen Sanders
English 3365

May 5, 1993

The *abstract* is a brief summary of the paper's contents in which the author's conclusions or recommendations are clearly stated. The abstract must be brief and concise so that busy readers can tell quickly whether the information being conveyed is relevant to their own concerns. Notice how the following abstract quickly conveys the overall purpose and scope of the paper:

Schemers and Scoundrels in American Literature

Abstract

Charlatans of various kinds have long assumed an important role in American literature, from the "King" and "Duke" in *Huckleberry Finn* to L. Frank Baum's *Wizard of Oz*. Through a study of various literary portrayals of the charlatan, two different types emerge. The "schemer" is an idealist who is really a co-conspirator with a public that also wishes for a better world. The "scoundrel" is a cynic who believes that his fortune can be increased only by reducing the fortunes of others.

The *table of contents* is another formal device for preparing the reader to see the overall organization of a paper. In longer works, the table of contents allows readers to locate the particular information they need.

American Naval Disasters

Another formal way to indicate divisions in the body of your paper is through the use of *subheadings*, which are often tied to the table of contents or to a detailed outline of your paper. Subheadings are usually placed at the left margin and either underlined or italicized in order to set them off from the rest of the text.

Remember the *Maine!*

The sinking of a ship has frequently been the catalyst for the outbreak of war. Because ships are floating "outposts" of military power, they are especially vulnerable to attack. However, in the case of the USS *Maine*, there was never conclusive evidence that the ship was attacked by Spanish forces. The *Maine* had been sent to Havana . . .

Most short papers do not require such formal methods of orienting the reader as abstracts and subheadings. In fact, such devices can seem disruptive in an informal essay. However, every paper should have a clear sense of purpose and be logically arranged and developed.

VISUAL DISPLAYS OF INFORMATION

Another way to help the reader is by providing visual displays — lists, tables, charts, diagrams, drawings, and so on. Notice in the following example how changing to a more visually oriented format makes the information much easier to understand:

Without a list

Changing Oil on Your Vehicle

Every three months or 3,000 miles, you should change your vehicle's oil and oil filter. By doing this, you will prohibit the buildup of sludge inside your engine, flush out tiny bits of grime and dirt which eat away at precision metal parts, and enable the engine to perform more efficiently by cutting down on friction. All you need to change your oil are a car stand or ramp, a wrench to loosen the drain plug, an oil pan for collecting the used oil, an oil filter wrench, an oil filter, and about four to six quarts of oil (depending on the size of your engine).

With a list

Changing Oil on Your Vehicle

Every three months or 3,000 miles, you should change your vehicle's oil and oil filter. By doing this, you will:

* prohibit the buildup of sludge (muck which accumulates inside an engine),
* flush out tiny bits of grime and dirt which eat away at precision metal parts, and
* enable the engine to perform more efficiently by cutting down on friction.

To change your oil, you will need the following supplies and equipment:

* CAR STAND or RAMP
* WRENCH to loosen the drain plug
* OIL PAN for collecting the used oil

- OIL FILTER WRENCH
- OIL FILTER
- 4–6 quarts of OIL

Preparing a List

We encounter lists in many different places — directories, menus, announcements, and instructions. Lists can usually be categorized as *random* or *ordered*. A random list has no particular arrangement — for instance, a catalog might request buyers to list their color preferences for sweaters with a list of options:

01 - forest green

02 - burgundy

03 - navy blue

04 - light brown

The numbers are simply a convenience for those completing the order form and do not represent any particular order.

Many lists are organized for particular purposes, however. In a directory of names, we expect the entries to be listed alphabetically with last names first. In giving directions, we expect the steps to be presented in the order that they will be performed. Many patterns are governed by convention. On a menu, for instance, entrees are frequently grouped into breakfast, lunch, and dinner choices. Appetizers appear before entrees, and so on. In general, attempt to make the information as accessible to the reader as possible.

Lists are indicated with various typographical features. They are usually set off from the body text, indented, and placed in columns. If the information is presented in a random list, each item is usually preceded by a dash or bullet or some other symbol:

Halloween Supplies

–fake blood
–chain saw
–rope

Condominium Amenities

- view of the ocean
- hot tub and sauna
- room service
- kitchenette

Premium Checking Plan

* no service charge
* 6% interest
* detailed account summaries
* $2,000 minimum balance

When appropriate, clearly indicate the order of items on a list. Here are some examples of ordered lists:

Affixing Your Renewal Sticker

1. Make sure the license plate is clean and dry.
2. Peel the protective backing off the sticker.
3. Affix the sticker in the lower right corner of the license plate.

The English Literary Heritage Tour

Day One: London. Fleet Street. Globe Theatre. St. Paul's.
Day Two: Canterbury Cathedral. Dover.
Day Three: Stratford-upon-Avon. Shakespeare landmarks.
Day Four: Lake District.
Day Five: Oxford. Bodleian Library.

Candidates for Treasurer

Baker, Alicia
Caan, Edward
Flyte, Tony
Richards, Neville
Vetch, Leopold

Preparing Graphics

Because we live in a visually oriented society, no discussion of enhancing your readability would be complete without a discussion of visual aids and their use in clarifying information for your readers. Although there are many ways writers use visuals, we will concentrate on five: the pie chart, the line graph, the multiple bar graph, the segmented bar graph, and the combined line/bar graph.

Pie Charts   Let's suppose you are doing a paper on aging in American society and want to show visually that the percentage of older Americans is increasing. If you are analyzing the increase year by year, the pie chart would be a good choice of graphic. In the pie chart, you present percentages as if they were slices of a pie. The entire pie equals 100% of the data (in this case, of the U.S. population). The slices

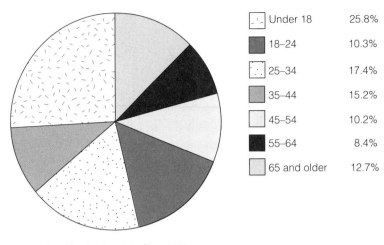

Age Distribution in U.S. —1990

FIGURE 9.1: Pie Chart

indicate the percentage of Americans falling within the designated age brackets. You may use a different pie chart for each year you are analyzing.

As you can see from the pie chart in figure 9.1, it's difficult to distinguish the variance between the 55–64, 45–54, and 18–24 age brackets. If it were important for your reader to see these distinctions, it would be better to use a line graph or a bar graph. The pie chart loses its effectiveness if the differences among the slices are less than 5%. And if you have more than eight variables, the pie chart (or most other charts or graphs, for that matter) can become confusing. But if fewer than eight things are being compared and if the disparity between the sizes is relatively large, the pie chart can enhance your paper and, because of its visual appeal, can add interest to the document.

Line Graphs   To show trends in your subject, you might choose to use a line graph. Line graphs allow readers to see increases and decreases over time. Because of their use in scientific documents, line graphs look more formal than pie charts, but they have the advantage of allowing the reader to distinguish numerical values more precisely. In the line graph in figure 9.2, note that the projected increase in percentage of Americans 65 and older and the projected decrease in the under-18 population are highlighted.

Multiple Bar Graphs   Multiple bar graphs can be effective if used wisely. Don't try to compare over three variables; if you do, the bars become an indecipherable mountain range, and the reader becomes lost in the valleys and peaks. The multiple bar graph is effective if the variables on the horizontal axis are being examined individ-

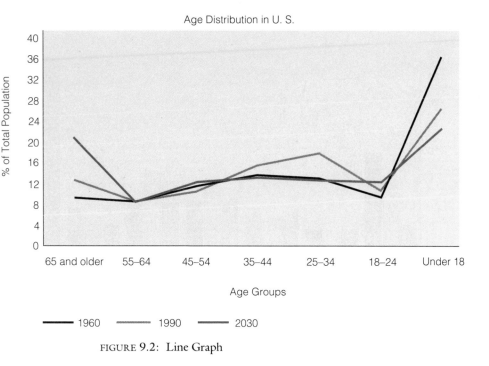

FIGURE 9.2: Line Graph

ually (change within a single age bracket) as well as collectively (comparison of changes among age brackets), as shown in figure 9.3. Because of its inherent visual appeal and the ease with which readers can distinguish between items, the multiple bar graph combines some of the best features of the pie chart and the line graph.

Segmented Bar Graphs   Segmented bar graphs, like multiple bar graphs, allow readers to analyze variables found on the horizontal axis easily. However, the vertical axis sometimes causes problems. Notice that in the segmented bar graph in figure 9.4 the reader must calculate percentages for each age bracket after the foundation level of the year 1960. The difficulty in visually distinguishing percentages over the foundation level detracts from the effectiveness of segmented bar graphs. But these graphs can be visually appealing, and the reader can distinguish general trends with little difficulty.

Combined Line/Bar Graphs   To help the reader overcome some of the problems in interpreting the segmented bar graph, you might choose to use a combined line/ bar graph. As you can see in figure 9.5, the reader has the foundation of the first year, 1960, graphed as a bar, and all the other years are plotted above or below that foundation as lines showing increases and decreases. Some readers find the combined line/bar graph easier to read than a segmented bar graph.

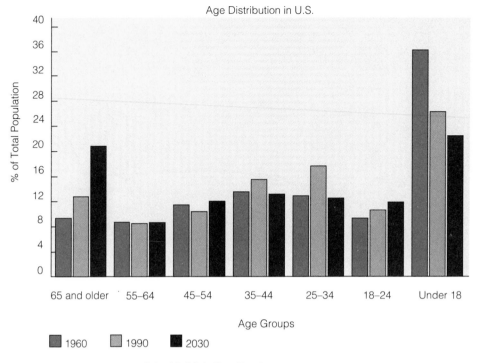

FIGURE 9.3: Multiple Bar Graph

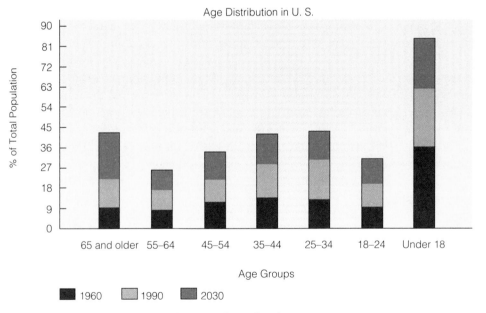

FIGURE 9.4: Segmented Bar Graph

Age Distribution on U. S.

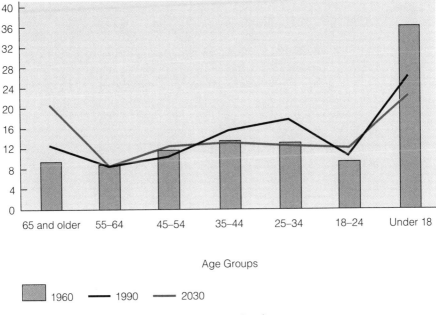

FIGURE 9.5: Combined Line/Bar Graph

You may wish to examine other types of visuals as you explore the best ways to enhance your readability. Photographs are useful in presenting exactly how your subject appears, and multiple photographs of the same subject help readers see differences in angles and in appearances over time (think of the photos, used to show weight loss, of the obese person eight months ago and the same person, slim and healthy looking, today). Pictographs, which show percentages with multiple pictures of the subject, can be interesting and effective. The last time I ate at the International House of Pancakes, the place mat was a pictograph illustrating the fact that if IHOP stacked up all the pancakes it serves in one day the stack would be as tall as the Sears Building in Chicago; however, the place mat, being used for a persuasive as well as an informative purpose, did not show the customer that the pancakes would not be nearly as wide as the Sears Building. This use of graphics illustrates that they can be used for persuasion as well as for information and can enhance the readability and interest of both types of documents.

THE CRITICAL MOMENT

In this chapter we have considered some basic principles of readability. However, we did not consider the case of readers who do not speak English. When we are considering the "readability" of a document, we might also consider if it should be translated into languages other than English. Most of us have grown accustomed to seeing instructions for appliances and other manufactured goods written in several languages. In an international market, manufacturers have to consider that their products might be used by people with many different language backgrounds.

In some cases, the use of multiple-language documents can become controversial. In recent years, groups like U.S. English have campaigned to make English the only official language of the United States. The advocates of the "English-only" movement warn that political strife can result when a country is divided into various language groups. As a case in point, they cite the current hostility between French-speaking and English-speaking provinces in Canada. They believe that government documents written in languages other than English and bilingual educational programs in schools will only perpetuate the use of minority languages.

Those opposed to the English-only movement note that millions of immigrants have entered the United States over the years, and although they were never required to learn the language, they and their children eventually did adopt English as their first language. They believe that refusing to provide information in the native languages of U.S. citizens would cut non-English speakers off from essential services and disenfranchise them of basic rights. In addition to causing human suffering, refusing to provide warnings in other languages can be expensive. For instance, employees who are not given basic safety information in a language they can understand might have costly accidents. Also, children who cannot begin studying math, history, and science until they master the English language are likely to be hopelessly behind their classmates. This lack of educational materials in their native languages can lead to students dropping out of school and leading less productive lives than they might have otherwise.

How would you respond to these questions about the English-only movement?

1. Is a single official language necessary for national unity?

2. Are some languages superior to other languages?

3. Does losing one's native language also mean losing a part of one's heritage?

4. Should students whose first language is English be required to learn a second language?

5. Can an employer threaten to fire an employee if he or she does not learn English?

6. Should election ballots be written in all the languages spoken within that voting district?

7. Do bilingual educational programs hinder students from learning English?

CHAPTER 10

Editing for Correctness

Many people find following standard rules of grammar and punctuation to be an unnecessary bother. They may think of these rules as the etiquette of language — like trying to remember which fork to use first at a formal banquet. Others may find thinking too much about how they speak or write to be a kind of prissiness — like being overly concerned about your personal appearance. They may even think that people who pay too much attention to language are not genuine or sincere.

It is true that some grammar rules do not seem necessary for basic communication. If I hear someone say, "I don't have no food," I know perfectly well what the person means. And if I refused someone food on the basis of poor grammar, I would, indeed, be worthy of contempt.

On the other hand, we all must recognize that language depends on a system of rules and accepted usages. Suppose you received the following memo:

> Publik hellth spectators will be visitating our planet on Juny 14. Last year we recieved a low rating because civiral employs were not following proper HiGene practices. If the plant does not pass inspekshun. Are hole operashun could be shut down by the state. Sense this akshun wood jiperdize everwon's job, weer enplumb-menting a new polusy to purtect all of us. Closed sircut camaras will be placed above the sinx in the restrooms, and employs who return to the wurkplace without first warshing their hanz will be sub ject to dismissile.

With some effort, it is possible to understand most of what the writer is saying in this memo, but the misspellings and other errors make it difficult to read. You might notice that in some cases the writer's spelling is closer to the actual sound of the words than the standard spelling ("inspekshun" = "inspection"). But since we are accustomed to sight-reading words, the phonetic spellings only make it more difficult to read. We have standardized spelling — even some of the most improbable spellings — in order to simplify reading. Although remembering the correct spelling of words can be frustrating at times, following standard spelling is necessary for us to communicate with each other efficiently. As well as making reading easier, following standard usage is important to establishing our credibility as writers. When spelling and grammar errors creep into our writing, we are likely to be judged as careless or even unintelligent. By checking our work carefully, we can help to establish ourselves as trustworthy and reliable sources of information.

Perhaps at some time in the past you have had a paper returned to you with comments and corrections all over it. You may feel that your grammatical skills are beyond help, that no one else has the same problems you do. In fact, the errors you have made are probably those common to most writers. By focusing on correcting the most common and the most glaring errors in your writing, you will immediately earn a much better reception for your work.

TEN TROUBLE SPOTS

A mechanic working on a car uses a trouble-shooting procedure to help find the problem. The mechanic knows that certain problems are more common than others and, naturally, looks for these first. You can use the following trouble-shooting procedure to find common mistakes in your own writing.

The 10 "trouble spots" discussed in this chapter are some of the most frequently encountered errors in college writing. They do not, of course, represent all the major errors that can be made in writing. Consult a dictionary or a handbook for additional information about correct usage. Your ultimate goal, however, is to internalize the guides to usage provided in reference sources. Good writers develop an "ear" for language based on their own reading. They become sensitive to current idioms and nuances of meaning. A writer's intuitive understanding of how the language works is much more intricate than even the most exhaustive reference manual. Reading through these "trouble spots" can help you further refine your own intuitive knowledge of how language is used.

Spelling

By far, the most common error in most people's writing is misspelling. This comes as no surprise since, according to several research studies, the average adult recognizes somewhere between 155,000 to 200,000 words. Few of these words are spelled phonetically; in fact, it is difficult to know exactly what the "correct" letter is for some sounds. The "uh" or "schwa" sound, for instance, can be represented by all the vowels and several vowel combinations.

"a" in CanadiAns (kuh-nay-dee-UHnz)

"e" in maidEns (may-dUHnz)

"i" in raisIns (ray-zUHnz)

"o" in reasOns (ree-zUHnz)

"u" in SUndays (sUHn-daz)

"ea" in ocEAns (oh-shUHnz)

"io" in lotIOns (loh-shUHnz)

For some people, spelling comes very easily. You may have known friends who could look at a list of new words and remember all of their spellings with no difficulty. For other people, spelling is a source of constant frustration. Words never look right on the page, even when they are spelled correctly. If you find spelling difficult, take heart; some of the most intelligent and creative people, including many great writers, have been horrible spellers.

If you have difficulty spelling — and nearly all of us get tripped up on some words — you can do several things to improve in this area. First, you can identify common words that give you problems. The word "receive," for instance, is frequently misspelled. However, this word conforms to the well-known rule "*i* before *e* except after *c*." Whenever someone makes note of a word you've misspelled, take a few moments to study the correct spelling and commit it to memory.

Before turning in a final paper, be sure to check all the words you think might be misspelled. Even if you are fairly sure a word is spelled correctly, check it against the dictionary spelling. If you are writing on a computer and have access to a spell checker, be sure to take advantage of this. You might also want to have a friend check your spelling, but your ultimate goal should be to proofread and correct your own work.

EXERCISE 10.1 Identifying Spelling Strengths and Weaknesses

The following list of words can help you identify your strengths and weaknesses as a speller. Identify all the misspelled words in the list and write the correct spellings for them. Check your spellings in a dictionary, and then rate yourself on the chart that follows.

February	seperate
freind	counselor
procede	consciousness
invisable	personel
payed	ratchit
occurrence	calluses
heighth	bookeeping
occasional	pageant
passable	obnoxous
bussing	nickle

20 = You are a confident speller and will be able to assist those with weaker skills.

18–19 = You are a strong speller, but need to proofread for those few words that do trip you up.

16–17 = Your spelling skills are average; don't let misspellings ruin the impression you want to make.

15 and below = Your spelling skills are weak; use great care in proofreading your final papers.

Spelling errors are even more difficult to detect in your own writing. Some writers proofread their writing by scanning from the bottom of the page to the top. In this way, they focus on spelling without being distracted by what the paper is saying. Try scanning through the following exercise from bottom to top.

EXERCISE 10.2 **Finding Spelling Errors**

The following paragraph contains 21 spelling errors. See how many of them you can find and correct.

Oliver Stone, one of the most impasioned of contemporary American filmakers, will no doubt be remembered for his controversial film *JFK* for quiet some time. Mingeling location scenes shot in Dallas with actual footage of the November 22, 1963 asassination, this director has chalenged the political establishment in a more direct manner than in any of his other endeavers foccussing on the 1960s. Though audiences may have been horrified by Charlie Sheen's loss of inocence in *Platoon* and though they may have been moved by Tom Cruise's retched existance in *Born on the Forth of July*, never have they been so directly addressed in a Stone movie as they are by Kevin Costner's sumary arguments during the last moments of *JFK*. Discrediting the Warren Commision's conclusions and implecating the CIA, the FBI, and the entire "military-industrial complex," Oliver Stone, whose illustrious carreer as the premier cinimatic expositér of the 1960s, may rise or fall with this exploretion of high-ranking, warmongering Washington military/intelligence officers and sordid, Mafia-afiliated New Orleans insurgents.

If spelling is not one of your strengths (and, as we pointed out previously, with many writers it is not), you will become increasingly appreciative of spell checkers, which are now incorporated into most word processing programs. Using the spell command, you can have a computer dictionary match every word in the document (or in a section of the document) to its list and tell you if it is included there or not; you can even build a personalized list of spellings not found in most dictionaries, such as your own name. Most writers using computers learn to depend on their spell checkers, and issuing the spell command usually becomes as automatic as saving the file.

There are, of course, some liabilities when writers rely excessively on this feature. These checkers cannot determine if a word is used correctly or not; they can only tell you if the word exists in their dictionaries. The programs cannot discern the difference between homonyms such as *there* and *they're*, and they will only stop at words that aren't included in their lexicon. In a few instances, dictionaries have been found to be faulty, allowing misspelled words to escape undetected. But, generally speaking, most spell checkers are a valuable resource, especially toward the end of the writing process.

A computer thesaurus is also being included with more and more word processing packages. The thesaurus works similarly to spell checkers, but instead of matching your words to a list of correctly spelled words, the program will match your words to a list of synonyms. You must not, of course, indiscriminately choose a synonym just because it has more syllables or sounds fancier. Make sure that your choice of vocabulary is appropriate for your audience and will achieve your purpose. You may already have the best word to express the tone and meaning you have in mind.

You may find it helpful to make a list of your own personal "spelling demons." (You might begin with the words you missed in exercise 10.1.) As you discover words that give you difficulty, add them to your list of practice words. In addition to your own spelling demons, be aware of these areas that often cause spelling problems:

When spelling two words that are frequently combined

He had *a lot* of work to do. (not "alot")
Liz did *all right* on the test. (not "alright")
There is *no one* I can trust. (not "noone")

When spelling one word that is frequently divided

He was *already* late. (not "all ready")
We were caught in a *snowstorm*. (not "snow storm")
How much *downtime* do you anticipate? (not "down time")

When spelling a word with a suffix

The insurance policy *paid* for all our expenses. (not "payed")

The newborn baby *cries* all night. (not "crys")

You are *truly* welcome. (not "truely")

Cocaine is a *controlled* substance. (not "controled")

You have many *desirable* qualities. (not "desireable")

That was a *judgment* call. (not "judgement")

When spelling a word that sounds like another word

You should *have* stayed until the fourth quarter. (not "should of")

The news was better *than* expected. (not "then")

The manager was *quite* pleased. (not "quiet")

When spelling a word with a sound that is lightly pronounced or unpronounced

Richards was a *candidate* for governor. (not "canidate")

The party was a complete *surprise*. (not "suprise")

An *arctic* cold front swept across the state. (not "artic")

The old-timers were *used* to the cold weather. (not "use")

The time has *passed* for talking about this problem. (not "pass")

When spelling a word containing *ie* or *ei*

We *believe* in her integrity. (not "beleive")

The Sioux *chief* approached the explorers. (not "cheif")

How much will the *freight* charges be? (not "frieght")

When spelling a word with one of these frequently confused endings

-able	-ible
inscrutable	visible
advisable	perfectible
indispensable	incredible

-ant	-ent
attendant	permanent
irrelevant	inadvertent
dominant	independent
defendant	correspondent

-le	-el
pickle	nickel
sickle	mackerel
shackle	laurel

EXERCISE 10.3 The "*I* before *E*" Rule

You probably have heard the spelling rule "*i* before *e*, except after *c*, or when sounding like *a*, as in n*ei*ghbor or w*ei*gh." Which of the following words can be correctly spelled applying this rule? Which are exceptions?

deceive	reprieve
thieves	weird
seize	brief
conceive	achieve
sleigh	either
relief	grieve
counterfeit	yield
vein	ancient
ceiling	weigh
science	friend

Word Choice

One of the most common errors in writing is choosing the wrong word for the meaning you intend. Many times the word you have chosen may sound much like the one you had in mind. Here are some examples taken from student writers:

All Christians believe in the *immorality* of the soul.

Children need a *since* of independence.

Sports Illustrated uses many pictures to *compliment* the articles.

I feel sorry for him because he has done the best he could and *know* one appreciates it.

Whoever has the lowest *role* [of the dice] must do the dishes.

Jazz is the only restaurant in town to extend the *flare* of a Louisiana kitchen.

In retrospect Kennedy's career was a glowing spot in American history. His death by no means *distinguished* that glow.

As these examples indicate, many of these problems stem from *homonyms*, words with the same sound, but different spellings and meanings. These are some of the most frequently confused homonyms:

to	too	two
there	their	they're
cite	sight	site

holy	holey	wholly
write	right	rite
affect	effect	
aisle	isle	
altar	alter	
bare	bear	
brake	break	
buy	by	
compliment	complement	
council	counsel	
course	coarse	
faze	phase	
forego	forgo	
it's	its	
passed	past	
peace	piece	
principal	principle	

The following pairs are not true homonyms, but their sounds are so similar that they are often confused:

accept	except
advice	advise
allusion	illusion
conscience	conscious
desert	dessert
lose	loose
personal	personnel
precede	proceed
predominant	predominate
weather	whether
were	where

Errors in word choice often result from using the specialized vocabulary of a particular group. As we begin learning a new field, we are confronted with many new terms. Consequently, it is not surprising to read of the "Spanish Imposition" (for Spanish *Inquisition*) or to be told that "Carrie Nation was a leading exhibition-ist" (for *prohibitionist*). Always carefully check specialized terms for meaning as you revise. You may need to consult a specialized dictionary or a glossary in your textbook for the meaning of some terms.

Probably all of us have been frustrated by spellings that seem to have little connection to the way the words sound. Why does *pneumonia* begin with a *p*? Why does *gnat* begin with a *g*? And why does *tough* end in *gh*? Was there a conspiracy of dictionary makers trying to make the language more difficult?

One reason spelling differs from pronunciation is that oral language is more changeable than written language. Our system of spelling has remained much the same that it was in Shakespeare's day, but our pronunciation of many words has changed drastically. The *gh* sound in words like *tough, rough,* and *enough* was once pronounced with a deep guttural sound like the German pronunciation of the final sound in *Bach*. That pronunciation has disappeared from the language, but the spelling remains. Vowel sounds have been particularly subject to change. At one time, the word *bite* would have been pronounced *beet*, and the word *house* would have been *hoose*. Pronunciation shifts continue to occur in our own time. The word *harass* was traditionally pronounced "HAIR-us," but is now often pronounced "huh-RASS."

Even if we desired to have a system of spelling that represented current English pronunciation, we still would have to decide whose pronunciation would be "correct." Does the proper pronunciation of *greasy* rhyme with *breezy* or *fleecy*? In different regions of the country, *thing* is pronounced *thang*, *girl* is pronounced *goil*, and *park* is pronounced *pock*. Is one region's speech preferable to another? Even if pronunciations are fairly standard for some words, what letter or letters should represent certain sounds? Should *cat* be changed to *kat*, or should *kit* be changed to *cit*? And assuming that such an overhaul could be undertaken, what would happen to books written in the "old" alphabet? Would all the books currently on our library shelves become unreadable for new generations? And would spellings continually change as new pronunciations became popular?

Given the difficulties of changing the spelling system, most people are content to stay with a system that, though flawed, is relatively stable. By accepting conventional spellings, we make the writing of people whose pronunciations are different from our own readily accessible. A truly phonetic language would cut us off from the contemporary English of Ireland as well as the historical English of Shakespeare and Milton.

By the way, if you held that there was a conspiracy of dictionary makers against phonetic spellings, you were partly right. At one time the normative spelling of *debt* was *dette*, and *receipt* was *receit*. During the Renaissance many scholars believed that the spelling of English words should conform to their Greek and Latin origins rather than to current pronunciation. Early dictionaries reflected these preferences, and spellings such as *debt* and *receipt* became standard. However, such decisions account for only a fraction of the spelling problems faced by contemporary writers.

EXERCISE 10.4 Finding Errors in Word Choice

Are the italicized words used correctly in these sentences? If not, consult with your Discovery Group and see if you can supply the correct word.

1. The use of the inverted *mordant* was one of the trademarks of the composer.
2. Each of the children vied to see who would be able to break open the pinyata.
3. Can newborn babies be addicted to *heroine*?
4. I found out that my best friend had been admitted into the hospital and had been diagnosed as having a myocardial *infraction*.
5. The mortgage company informed the homeowner that, due to the way in which the loan had been *amourized*, her loan payment amount would be increased by $50 per month.
6. Some cattle ranchers have found raising *lamas* to be lucrative.
7. The *denoumente* of the frothy comedy was entirely predictable.
8. Your point seems *irreverent* to our discussion.
9. The young man and woman, *ingenious* as newborn babes, were brought into the arena.
10. The Ohio River is one of the major *tribulations* of the Mississippi.

Use of the Comma

After spelling, the comma probably causes the most problems for writers. In general, the comma represents a pause when a sentence is read aloud. For the reader, a comma represents a division or break in the sentence. The comma helps the reader see at a glance what the main units of the sentence are.

Commas Before Coordinating Conjunctions   Many writers fail to place a comma before a coordinating conjunction. Notice the confusion that can result in reading a sentence when this comma is omitted:

The auditorium was crowded with singers and dancers warmed up in the lobby.

It would be easy to misread this sentence by assuming that both *singers* and *dancers* are the object of the pronoun *with*. In the following sentence, the comma helps to make clear that *dancers* is the subject of *warmed up* and not the object of *with*.

The auditorium was crowded with singers, and dancers warmed up in the lobby.

By placing a comma before a coordinating conjunction that joins two independent clauses, you can avoid this confusion. The coordinating conjunctions *and, but, or, nor, for, yet,* and *so* are used to join independent clauses. However, these conjunctions are also used to join other parts of the sentence:

He did not like turnip greens or buttermilk.

The conjunction *or* connects two nouns, and consequently, the sentence doesn't require a comma.

He did not like turnip greens, and buttermilk made him break out in a rash.

Here, the conjunction *and* joins two independent clauses, each with its own subject and predicate, and, therefore, the sentence does require a comma.

Commas After Introductory Elements   Commas are frequently used to set off introductory elements at the beginning of sentences:

Introductory subordinate clause

After you finish with my lawn mower, please put it away.

Introductory participial phrase

Jumping to his feet, the dog growled as we approached.

Introductory expletive

Well, I decided it was time for us to leave.

Introductory adverb

Consequently, we left our work unfinished.

Short prepositional phrases at the beginning of a sentence do not usually require a comma:

On the backroads we encountered many unusual people.

Commas are required when sentences begin with long series of prepositional phrases or when commas are needed to make the meaning clear:

Comma to set off a series of prepositional phrases

In the middle of his speech about the need for law and order, the mayor was interrupted by a group of hecklers.

Comma to prevent confusion

In the country, music is a part of life. (Without the comma the reader might run together "country" and "music.")

Commas to Set Off Nonessential Words and Phrases   Commas are often used to set off words and phrases within sentences that are not essential to the meaning. The commas are placed immediately before and after the nonessential element:

Interrupting words

Children, of course, can be a nuisance.

Appositive

Timur, a direct descendant of Genghis Kahn, was difficult to control.

Nonessential (or nonrestrictive) modifier

He destroyed the slide, which was made of concrete and reinforced steel, in a matter of minutes.

Some modifiers are essential. Such modifiers are often called *restrictive* because they restrict or limit the noun being modified.

The children who sang in the Christmas cantata practiced for weeks. (Because not all children sang in the Christmas cantata, the modifier restricts the meaning of "children" to a particular group.)

A 35mm slide which was projected on the screen upside down had the children laughing hysterically. (The adjective clause, "which was projected upside down," identifies the particular slide that created the hysteria.)

EXERCISE 10.5 **Practice in Using Commas**

Place commas where they are needed in the following sentences. Be prepared to explain the reason for the use of the comma.

1. As the bulls rushed through the streets spectators began to run after them.
2. The press insisted that the president had prior knowledge of the dictator's intention to invade the neighboring country but the president's press secretary denied this story.
3. As she peered inside her nose was visible to everyone in the room.
4. Fortunately the alarm had been turned on before the cashier left Friday evening.
5. On the elevators and throughout every hallway in the municipal building discussion was centered on the trial.
6. The chapel's only relic which had been in the alcove since 1843 suddenly disappeared.
7. Dr. Filia Marquez the personal physician of the major-general examined the medical records.
8. There is no question therefore that this request must be forwarded to the manager.
9. Although the drama was expertly directed and performed the playwright was not fully satisfied with the production.
10. Standing above the Santo Fermin canal from the Aquilo Bridge you may view the hill upon which Juan and Jorge made their arrangements.

Commas in a Series Another common use of the comma is to set off items in a series. Commas are placed between each item in the series, but not after the last item.

Series of nouns

The British, the French, the Canadians, the Americans, and other allied forces stormed the beach.

Series of verbs

> The engines coughed, sputtered, and wheezed.

Series of adjectives

> She had a small, sheepish grin.

Series of participial phrases

> The wind changed directions suddenly, shifting the mainsail, unbalancing the boat, and scuttling the crew.

Series of subordinate clauses

> Lincoln praised those who established a nation devoted to individual liberty, those who died at Gettysburg defending that noble ideal, and those who lived to carry on the fight.

Most writers place a comma before the conjunction that signals the end of the series although some style guides recommend that it be omitted.

Using commas in a series of adjectives can be tricky. Where would you place the commas in these sentences?

> The bouncy jazzy swinging music had a Latin beat.

> The well worn tape recording didn't do the song justice.

The first sentence needs commas to separate the adjectives. Thus, you would place a comma after *bouncy* and *jazzy*. The second sentence does not require a comma because *tape recording* is a compound noun and the adverb *well* modifies *worn*. Since there is only one adjective — *worn* — that modifies the noun, no commas are needed. An easy test for placing commas in a series of adjectives is to try the word *and* between the modifiers. If *and* sounds reasonable, you probably need a comma.

> We stood under a beautiful old fashioned gaslight.
> (You say, "We stood under a beautiful AND old fashioned gaslight." Since the *and* sounds reasonable between beautiful and old fashioned, you need a comma here. You would not say "old AND fashioned," so no comma is necessary after *old*.)

Thus, you would punctuate the sentence this way:

> We stood under a beautiful, old fashioned gaslight.

Other Uses of the Comma   The comma has many other uses. These are some of the ones you may encounter in your writing:

In dates

> March 3, 1978, is my birthday.

In addresses

> We sold our home at 218 Buena Vista Drive, Albuquerque, New Mexico, and moved to Seattle, Washington.

Before formal titles after a name

Richard Van Aken, R.N., was working the nightshift.

Tomas Hinojosa, Ph.D., presented the lecture.

Between a quotation and words attributing it to a particular source

Our manager said, "Anything less than your best is unacceptable."

"I only get angry with people I respect," sneered the politician.

EXERCISE 10.6 **More Practice in Using Commas**

Place commas where they are needed in the following sentences.

1. The senator the philanthropist and the vice-president met in the suite during the conference.

2. Because of his endeavors to bring understanding of Latin American culture because of his efforts to resolve the political turmoil and because of his sensitivity to the issues confronting the regime the director was awarded the highest honors.

3. The van went out of control on the ice-covered road turning 180 degrees sliding into the embankment and missing the precipice by inches.

4. The speaker's incisive pertinent remarks intrigued the audience.

5. The quarterback dropped back rolled to his right and threw the interception.

6. He had lived at 406 Senovia Drive Los Montes California during the summer of '67 and had worked as a construction worker throughout the following fall.

7. I will always remember the morning of March 16 1978.

8. Marta Cavendar Ed.D. will lecture concerning her work at the reservation.

9. "I find that explanation unacceptable" declared the investigator.

10. The sultry seductive vocalist took the stage.

Sentence Fragments

A complete sentence has a subject and a verb and expresses a complete thought. Most sentence fragments are "broken" sentences; that is, two parts of a sentence have been punctuated as though they were separate sentences. Here are some examples of broken sentences:

High on a trail in the Appalachias. We paused to take in the beautiful vista.

We had to abandon the trail after only three days. Because a bear had devoured most of our food during the night.

If you suspend your backpack on a rope from a tree limb. You can prevent some of the large animals from stealing your food.

Although our trip is over, we still have one souvenir. A great feeling of accomplishment.

Once you have recognized a sentence fragment, you can usually correct it by joining it with the main sentence.

High on a trail in the Appalachias, we paused to take in the beautiful vista.

We had to abandon the trail after only three days because a bear had devoured most of our food during the night.

If you suspend your backpack on a rope from a tree limb, you can prevent some of the large animals from stealing your food.

Although our trip is over, we still have one souvenir: a great feeling of accomplishment.

Some writers use sentence fragments intentionally. This is particularly true in advertising. Here is an example of the use of sentence fragments in an advertisement by a bicycle manufacturer:

The trail beckons you onward. *And upward*. All around you nature is at its finest. *Perfect in every detail*. Your Axis Team inspires you to go further. *Steeper. Faster*. You push your limits. And Diamond Back's ultimate mountain bike responds. *Beautifully*.

As this example indicates, a certain kind of energy is generated by the artistic use of sentence fragments. However, if you wish to use such fragments outside of advertising, keep the following principles in mind:

1. Some editors (and teachers) will not tolerate sentence fragments of any kind. Know whether artistic sentence fragments are permissible for your audience.

2. Not every sentence fragment is artistic. Don't try to excuse a broken sentence with a claim of artistic license.

3. Use sentence fragments sparingly. Like any rhetorical device, if you overuse fragments, they become less effective.

EXERCISE 10.7 **Eliminating Sentence Fragments**

Revise the following paragraph, eliminating sentence fragments.

We went to southwestern Colorado to learn more about the history of the Anasazi Indians. The amalgamation of tribes which lived thousands of years ago in the American Southwest. We had brought along a minimum amount of cash (approximately $150 each). Because we were going to spend only one night in a motel and camp during the rest of the trip. We hiked many miles. Covering close to 20 miles a day. Our entire club began to get tired and irritable on the third day. But the rewards were worth the effort. Although our trek was long and arduous. I will never forget the sight of the Mesa Verde cliff dwellings in the early morning sunlight on June 28.

304 EDITING FOR CORRECTNESS

Run-On Sentences

If you run together two or more sentences without punctuation, you have written a *run-on sentence*. Some writers and editors refer to this problem as a *fused sentence*, since the two halves of the sentences are fused together. Here are some examples of run-on sentences:

> Music is my whole reason for being it gives my life purpose.

> I waited in line overnight to get tickets I didn't get very good ones.

> A sonata is a musical composition written for one or two instruments a symphony is for a full orchestra.

> Jazz differs according to the region of the country where it originates St. Louis jazz is not New Orleans jazz.

Correcting most run-on sentences is simply a matter of adding the appropriate punctuation. You can correct run-on sentences in several ways:

1. Make two separate sentences.

    > Music is my whole reason for being. It gives my life purpose.

2. Add a comma and a coordinate conjunction to make a compound sentence.

    > I waited in line overnight to get tickets, but I didn't get very good ones.

3. Join two independent clauses with a semicolon.

    > A sonata is a musical composition written for one or two instruments; a symphony is for a full orchestra.

4. Join two independent clauses with a semicolon and an adverb followed by a comma.

    > Jazz differs according to the region of the country where it originates; obviously, St. Louis jazz is not New Orleans jazz.

Some run-on sentences are more difficult to correct. Sometimes we attempt to make a phrase modify both parts of a fused sentence:

> Deadheads roam the country following the Grateful Dead is one of the few remaining rock bands from the sixties.

> The Beachboys also have a loyal following at their concerts are fans of all ages that have come to see this legendary group.

Correcting this sentence requires changing the wording as well as adding necessary punctuation:

> Deadheads roam the country following the Grateful Dead, one of the few remaining rock bands from the sixties.

The Beachboys also have a loyal following at their concerts. Fans of all ages come to see this legendary group.

EXERCISE 10.8 **Correcting Run-On Sentences**

Correct the run-on sentences by adding necessary punctuation. In some cases, you may need to alter the wording to correct the sentence.

> San Miguel de Allende is a Mexican town of diverse inhabitants can be classified into four categories. The village of Indians comprises the first category this indigenous population primarily labor in the surrounding fields many times, though, other work must be sought. The second group of townspeople, the Mexican bohemian crowd, live in a strange demimonde defines their existence of meandering and often rum-induced visions. The foreign writers, painters, and retirees, of which the third group consists, subsist on either art or gardening, being their primary areas of interest, they are congenial and provide many medical and educational services to the Mexican and Indian segments of the population. The fourth category of resident to be found is the descendant of the colonist, living in splendor reminiscent of the days in which locally mined silver provided a lifestyle for barons made their fortune from the abundant natural resources found within the area.

Verb Problems

If you've ever tried to learn a foreign language, you know that using verbs can present special problems. Actually, verbs in English are simpler than in many other languages. Still, using the wrong verb is one of the most frequent and most noticeable problems in writing. In this section, we concentrate on three common problems: subject–verb agreement, irregular verbs, and verb tense.

Subject–Verb Agreement   Subjects must agree with their verbs in number: Singular subjects take singular verbs; plural subjects take plural verbs. With most regular verbs, singular and plural forms differ only in third person, as the following chart demonstrates:

	Singular	Plural
First person	I sleep	we sleep
Second person	you sleep	you sleep
Third person	he/she/it *sleeps*	they sleep

Failure to make third-person singular subjects agree with their verbs is one of the most noticeable and most frequently criticized errors in writing. Mistakes of the following kind will draw extremely negative reactions from most readers:

Incorrect

He *don't* work here.

She *weren't* feeling well today.

We *does* subscribe to cable television.

Correct

He *doesn't* work here.

She *wasn't* feeling well today.

We *do* subscribe to cable television.

Use special care in selecting the correct verb form for compound subjects. Subjects joined by *and* usually require a plural verb:

George Burns and Jack Benny *were* radio celebrities in the days before television.

The musical and the variety show *are* not as popular as they once were.

If the compound subject refers to a single item, it takes a singular verb:

"Bait and switch" *is* the technique of luring customers with a sale item and then turning their attention to more expensive merchandise.

The founder and guiding force behind the University of Virginia *was* Thomas Jefferson.

Law and order *depends* on an effective judicial system.

For subjects joined by *or, neither . . . nor,* or *either . . . or,* the verb must agree with the nearer subject:

Either drought or boll weevils *have* ruined the cotton crop every year.

Either boll weevils or drought *has* ruined the cotton crop every year.

Most indefinite pronouns take a singular verb:

Each of my friends *is* coming to the wedding.

Everyone *is* welcome at the reception.

Everybody *knows* where the Heartbreak Hotel and Wedding Parlor is located.

Some indefinite pronouns, such as *all, any, more, most, none,* and *some,* may be singular or plural depending on the context:

Some of my friends *are* known for their quirks.

Some of the food at the reception *was* spoiled.

If you are unsure whether an indefinite pronoun should be treated as singular or plural, consult a dictionary.

Collective nouns and terms of quantity require singular verbs when treated as a unit. When the members are treated individually, plural verbs are required.

Singular

The local theater group *is* planning a revival of *The Man Who Came to Dinner*.

The choir *has* been invited to perform in Vienna.

Plural

A large number *were* opposed to the renovation plans.

The faculty *have* been filing grievances against the new dean.

Irregular Verbs   Some of the most commonly used verbs in our language are irregular. The verb "to be," for instance, has these different forms in the present tense:

	Singular	Plural
First person	I *am*	we *are*
Second person	you *are*	you *are*
Third person	he/she/it *is*	they *are*

Most regular verbs form the past tense by adding *d* or *ed* to the base form of the verb:

We *listened* to the account manager.

The stock split *corresponded* with the company's twentieth anniversary.

Donnie *filed* the divorce papers on December 26.

Regular verbs use the same form for the past and past participle (the form used with helping verbs):

Present	Past	Past participle
We listen.	We listened.	We have listened.
I work.	I worked.	I have worked.

Irregular verbs usually change the base form of the verb in order to form the past tense. Many times the past and past participle are different for irregular verbs. Here are some common irregular verb forms:

Present	Past	Past participle
begin	began	begun
bring	brought	brought
build	built	built
burst	burst	burst

Present	Past	Past participle
catch	caught	caught
choose	chose	chosen
come	came	come
cost	cost	cost
creep	crept	crept
do	did	done
drink	drank	drunk
drive	drove	driven
fall	fell	fallen
freeze	froze	frozen
get	got	gotten, got
give	gave	given
go	went	gone
grow	grew	grown
hide	hid	hid
hurt	hurt	hurt
know	knew	known
lay (to put or place something)	laid	laid
lead	led	led
leave	left	left
lend	lent	lent
lie (to assume a resting position)	lay	lain
lose	lost	lost
pay	paid	paid
ring	rang	rung
run	ran	run
see	saw	seen
set	set	set
shake	shook	shaken
sit	sat	sat

Present	Past	Past participle
sleep	slept	slept
speak	spoke	spoken
sting	stung	stung
swim	swam	swum
take	took	taken
tear	tore	torn
throw	threw	thrown
wake	waked, woke	waked, woken
write	wrote	written

Most problems occur when we try to make irregular verbs conform to the regular pattern:

Incorrect

The shortstop *throwed* the ball to first base.

I *teared* off the coupon.

His finger *hurted* badly.

Correct

The shortstop *threw* the ball to first base.

I *tore* off the coupon.

His finger *hurt* badly.

Some problems are caused by modeling one irregular verb on the pattern of another:

You write . . .

I *have rung* the bell.

Pavarotti *sang* in the oratorio.

but . . .

I *have brought* (not "brung") the coffee.

After the unexpected shower, we *wrung* (not "wrang") out our clothes.

Problems also arise when we try to make regular verbs follow an irregular form:

Correct

They *sneaked* in through the back door.

The bottles in the back of our pickup *clinked* together.

After being asked several times, we *dragged* out our notebooks.

Incorrect

They *snuck* in through the back door.

The bottles in the back of our pickup *clunk* together.

After being asked several times, we *drug* out our notebooks.

EXERCISE 10.9 **Correcting Errors in Subject–Verb Agreement**

Correct the subject–verb agreement problems in the following paragraph.

> Everybody who studies European history become aware that imperial powers such as England, France, and Germany claimed vast lands in Asia and Africa during the eighteenth and nineteenth centuries. Spain, which had lay claim to an enormous empire in the sixteenth and seventeenth centuries, clinged to only a few of her former possessions. The Dutch and Belgian holdings, though they might not be considered a great empire, was of great importance to these countries. In 1800 Europeans controlled approximately 35% of the world's land surface. By the advent of World War I, that figure had rose to 84%. What was the motivations behind the growth of these empires? Certainly, the wealth that come from foreign colonies was one factor. A flourishing trade with China and India in the nineteenth century lead to England's tremendous wealth and power during that century. However, some colonies had did little to increase the wealth of the imperial power that controlled them. In some cases, lands in remote parts of the world was of strategic value. England, for instance, had took an interest in the Crimean, not because they believed their investment there would be payed back, but to halt Russian expansionism. The alliance of England, France, Turkey, and Sardinia were successful in stopping the Russian threat during the Crimean War, but at a tremendous cost. Both human life and money was wasted in this war. Another reason imperial powers tryed to accumulate colonies was for the prestige it give to them. This was particularly true of Germany, which begun colonizing Africa much later than the other European powers.
>
> The difficulties of maintaining an empire is still with us. The Falklands is a tiny group of islands off the coast of Argentina. When the Argentine military was wanting to enhance their prestige, they overtook these islands. England felt obligated to protect these colonies even though they seen little strategic or economic value in them. England won the war for the Falklands, but many people feeled it was a futile war. The Falklands illustrate how former colonies continues to be a deadweight hanged around the neck of a country.

Verb Tense Verb tenses vary from the simple ("I *misunderstood* his directions") to the intricate ("I *was being misunderstood* by my director"). Most tense problems result from needlessly shifting from one tense to another. In any piece of writing, there is always a dominant tense. When a dominant tense is not established, as in the following example, the writing becomes difficult to follow:

> In *As You Like It*, Rosalind and Orlando *fall* in love at their first meeting. Then the evil Duke *banished* Rosalind, and she *flees* to the Forest of Arden in the

disguise of a young boy. Orlando *left* when he *learned* that his brother *plans* to kill him. Because Rosalind *is disguised*, she *is* able to tease Orlando about his lovesickness, but in the end she *married* him.

When the verb tenses are made consistent, the paragraph is much easier to read:

In *As You Like It*, Rosalind and Orlando *fall* in love at their first meeting. Then the evil Duke *banishes* Rosalind, and she *flees* to the Forest of Arden in the disguise of a young boy. Orlando *leaves* when he *learns* that his brother *plans* to kill him. Because Rosalind is *disguised*, she *is* able to tease Orlando about his lovesickness, but in the end she *marries* him.

Of course, some tense changes are unavoidable as you switch from describing a past event to giving your commentary on that event (in present tense) or to predicting future events (obviously, in future tense). As long as you maintain a dominant tense, the reader will have little difficulty following your meaning.

EXERCISE 10.10 **Correcting Verb Tense Problems**

Correct the verbs in the following paragraph to maintain a dominant tense.

The symphony orchestra underwent many changes during the romantic period. The classic orchestra had been dominated by string instruments. A symphony that would be composed by Mozart in 1788 would have only a single flute and two French horns. Twenty years later, Beethoven's Fifth Symphony is performed with an expanded woodwind and brass section, and kettledrums provide percussion. By 1895 a Strauss symphony would be performed with a piccolo, an English horn, a bass clarinet, a contrabassoon, six trumpets, three trombones, a tuba, kettledrums, a snare drum, a bass drum, cymbals, and a triangle. None of these instruments were being used in Mozart's day.

Pronoun Problems

Although there are only a handful of pronouns in the English language, these words create numerous problems for writers. In this section, we consider three common problems: pronoun–antecedent agreement, pronoun case, and pronoun reference.

Pronoun–Antecedent Agreement   A pronoun stands in the place of a noun:

Because Jimmy Stewart has a unique way of talking, *he* is often imitated.

The noun replaced by the pronoun is the *antecedent*. In the preceding sentence, *Jimmy Stewart* is the antecedent for the pronoun *he*.

Just as verbs must agree with their subjects, pronouns must agree in number with their antecedents. The rules concerning agreement with compound nouns, collective nouns, and indefinite pronouns discussed in connection with subject–verb agreement also apply to pronoun–antecedent agreement:

Compound nouns

Harley-Davidson and Kawasaki are known for *their* different styles of motorcycles. (plural subject followed by plural pronoun)

Neither the Harley-Davidson nor the Kawasaki brand earned *its* reputation by building inferior motorcycles. (singular subject followed by singular pronoun)

Collective nouns

The team broke *its* own record for fumbles. (the team considered as a unit requires a singular pronoun)

The team brought *their* complaints to the coaches in a closed meeting. (the team considered as a collection of individuals requires a plural pronoun)

Indefinite pronouns

Each of the women gymnasts has *her* favorite event. (*each* requires a singular pronoun)

Even after the lecture, no one could make up *his or her* mind about the meaning of political correctness.

Many of the cyclists are competing in *their* final meet.
(*many* requires a plural pronoun)

Third-person pronouns must agree in gender as well as in number:

In *her* valedictorian address, Felicia challenged *her* classmates to be ethical as well as successful. (feminine)

Maury found out *his* car had been taken for a joy ride and nearly destroyed. (masculine)

The newspaper made *its* recommendations on the Friday before the election. (neuter)

When referring to groups of people, be careful not to exclude women:

Instead of . . .

An attorney must present *his* closing argument in vigorous language.

A scientist who receives the Nobel Prize always carries that distinction with *him*.

Use . . .

An attorney must present *the* closing argument in vigorous language.

Scientists who receive the Nobel Prize always carry that distinction with *them*.

Pronoun Case   Unlike nouns, pronouns change form when used as objects or subjects in a sentence:

Nouns

> *Vanessa* sent a letter to *David*.
>
> *David* wrote back to *Vanessa*.

Pronouns

> *She* sent a letter to *him*.
>
> *He* wrote back to *her*.

The form a pronoun takes when used as a subject (*she* or *he*) is the *subjective case*. The form taken by pronouns used as objects is the *objective case* (*him* or *her*). Pronouns may also be in the *possessive case* (for instance, *my*, *his*, *her*, *its*).

Most case problems occur when pronouns are used in compound expressions. Usually, by removing one part of the compound expression, the pronoun choice becomes clear:

> My friend and (*I* or *me?*) left before the trouble began. ("*me* left" is clearly wrong)
>
> My friend and *I* left before the trouble began.

When referring to yourself in a compound expression, mention yourself last:

> He gave the warning to *Tom and me* (not "me and Tom").

Also, do not use nonstandard forms of pronouns such as *hisself* or *theirselves*.

Pronoun Reference   Pronouns prevent the monotonous repetition of nouns when we write:

> Mike came into the room. Mike sat down at the desk. Mike took out Mike's notebook. The notebook was disorganized. Mike needed to organize the notebook.

But because readers must keep in mind what the antecedent is for each pronoun, writers must guard against vague or ambiguous pronouns.

Unclear

> The manager told Allan to clear up the mistake before *he* left for the day.

Revised

> The manager told Allan that he wanted the mistake cleared up before Allan left for the day.

Unclear

> We usually buy our produce at the farmer's market, but today *they* didn't have a good selection.

Revised

> We usually buy our produce at the farmer's market, but today the vendors didn't have a good selection.

Unclear

> The Federal Reserve Board decided to lower interest rates in order to spur investment, *which* was predictable.

Revised

> The Federal Reserve Board made a predictable decision to lower interest rates in order to spur investment.

Unclear

> We read about murders in the paper every day. It is time *they* did something about *it*.

Revised

> We read about murders in the paper every day. Our police department should do something to reduce the number of people being murdered.

Problems with pronoun reference are often difficult for a writer to find because the antecedent is usually obvious to the person who is writing. In order to find pronoun errors, read your own paper as though you were seeing it for the first time.

EXERCISE 10.11 **Correcting Pronoun Problems**

Revise the following sentences by changing pronouns or by clearing up vague pronoun references.

1. Everybody has their own opinion about the dangers of sex stereotyping.

2. A physicist must not let his preconceptions influence his observations.

3. The trophy was given to she and her teammates.

4. After watching the videotape, our squad saw theirselves in a new light.

5. My two cruises were enjoyable although the boat had to return to shore twice, my table companion got seasick during two dinners, and the captain almost had to cancel it.

6. Because his family had never really understood him, he tried to find it in his friends.

7. Should my supervisor request the letter, I will neither cooperate with it nor will I reveal the conversation between he and I.

8. We were unprepared for the weather and for the enemy resistance; therefore, me and my brigade were forced to retreat.

Modifier Problems

Modifiers are descriptive words or phrases. They may tell, for instance, what something looks like, what kind of thing it is, or how something is done. Here are some sample modifiers:

Adjective (modifies a noun or a pronoun)

> Leon is a *timid* student.

> Anna seems *boisterous*.

Adverb (modifies a verb, an adjective, or another adverb)

> Yuri plays chess *well*.

> The sacrifice of the queen was a *highly* unusual move.

Adjective phrases

> The original colors *of the painting* had been restored recently.

> *Ranging from anatomical drawings to the Mona Lisa*, the art of Leonardo da Vinci has been celebrated widely.

Adverb phrases

> The eagles soared *over the mountains*.

> I hesitated *to read the telegram*.

Most mistakes in the use of modifiers result from one of these three problems: confusing adjectives and adverbs, placing modifiers in the wrong position, using double negatives.

Confusing Adjectives and Adverbs   Most adverbs end in *ly* (*suddenly, boringly*). Be careful not to drop the ending of adverbs in your writing.

Incorrect

> The storm came up *real sudden*.

> He played *brilliant* on the drums.

Correct

> The storm came up *really suddenly*.

> He played *brilliantly* on the drums.

Good and *well* are the modifiers most often misused. *Good* is an adjective and should not be used when describing how something is done.

Incorrect

> The car ran *good* on the road.

> He sang *good* during the talent show.

Correct

> The car ran *well* on the road.

> He sang *well* during the talent show.

Placing Modifiers in the Wrong Position   If modifiers are separated too far from the words they modify, confusion may result. What problems might you have in understanding these sentences?

1. The children nearly ate everything that was put before them.

2. The ship sailed off slowly turning to the west.

3. None of the children will ever forget driving by the church, singing "99 Bottles of Beer on the Wall."

4. Formerly an astronaut on *Apollo 7*, Timmy eagerly listened to the speaker.

5. Failing to include the operator's manual, the computer had remained unused.

The first sentence suggests that the children only thought about eating their food. The sentence should read, "The children ate *nearly* everything that was put before them." Simply moving the adverb before the word it is to modify clears up the confusion.

In the second sentence, the adverb *slowly* might describe either how the ship sailed off or how it turned to starboard. Writing either "the ship *slowly* sailed off" or "turning *slowly* to the west" will clear up this confusion.

Assuming that the church members were not singing "99 Bottles of Beer on the Wall," the writer should move the modifier in the third sentence to clarify who is doing the singing: "None of the children will ever forget singing '99 Bottles of Beer on the Wall' as they drove by a church."

The fourth sentence also has a misplaced modifier. Timmy was not an astronaut on *Apollo 7*, so the modifier must be moved and the wording revised to fit the meaning of the sentence: "Timmy eagerly listened to the speaker who had been an astronaut on *Apollo 7*."

The final sentence is an example of a "dangling" modifier. No word in the sentence as it is currently written can be modified by the phrase "failing to include the operator's manual." In order to correct this sentence, the writer must supply a subject: "Because the manufacturer had failed to include the operator's manual, the computer had remained unused."

Using Double Negatives   One absolute taboo in writing is the use of the double negative. Virtually all readers react extremely negatively to such constructions as "He don't listen" and "It wasn't no use." You should also be careful not to use a negative with such adverbs as *hardly* and *scarcely*.

Incorrect

Some people *won't* listen to *no one*.

Leonard *couldn't hardly* hear the radio.

We *could scarcely* find *no one* who had seen the movie.

Correct

Some people *won't* listen to anyone.

Leonard *could hardly* hear the radio.

We *could scarcely* find *anyone* who had seen the movie.

Also, avoid awkward negative expressions such as "He hadn't not seen" and "I don't know but what."

Awkward

Donneva almost *never didn't do* her work.

I *didn't doubt but that* you were wrong.

Better

Donneva almost *always did* her work.

I *didn't doubt that* you were wrong.

or

I *doubted that* you were right.

EXERCISE 10.12 **Correcting Modifier Problems**

Revise the following paragraph by correcting the modifiers.

> Realizing the benefits of technology advances over the past few decades, it is real easy not to forget to dismiss some of the consequences of our recent innovations. Yes, I cannot but disagree that we have benefited from conveniences such as microwave ovens and automatic dishwashers which heat food quick. Even if they can be bought for less than $300, most people aren't willing to give up their health for an appliance. Until recent, almost nobody said nothing about the negative benefits of such waste substances as synthetical detergents and radiation have on our interdependently ecological system. As pollution has increased, suddenly we have become aware of the problem. Covered with scum and filled with poisons, most environmentalists believe our rivers are in desperate condition. But not only the environmentalist but also the average citizen has become frustrated with our increasing inability to speed up a slowdown in the rise of pollution or to counter the downward trend in gaining increased awareness about growing environmental health hazards and declining antipollution standards.

Capitalization

In order to use capitals correctly, you must distinguish between proper nouns and common nouns. Proper nouns are the names of particular persons, places, and things (John Dewey, Cleveland, the Biltmore Hotel). Common nouns are more general (an educator, a city, a hotel). In most cases the distinction between proper nouns and common nouns is obvious, but in some cases the choice depends on how the word is used in the sentence.

Capitalize

Aunt Selina came to visit.

She was a delegate to the *Democratic* National Convention.

Attendance was good at this year's *Dunwoody High School Spring Festival*.

Home Alone was one of the most popular movies of 1990.

We elected Akita Starnes as *Sophomore Class President*.

Atlanta is one of the largest cities in the *South*.

I took ENGL 411: *Contemporary British Literature* from *Professor Matthews*.

Do not capitalize

She is one of my favorite *aunts*.

This nation was founded on *democratic* principles.

Our *high school* has a *spring festival* every year.

I would never dare leave my child *home alone*.

Several *sophomores* ran for class *president*.

Birds fly *south* in the winter.

I don't think many *professors* could have made *British literature* interesting to me.

Remember to capitalize the first word, the last word, and all major words in a title. Do not capitalize articles (*a, an, the*), coordinating conjunctions (*and, but, or, nor, for, so, yet*), or prepositions (e.g., *from, with, between*).

"On the Road Again"

An Officer and a Gentleman

The Sound and the Fury

Desire under the Elms

"The Force That through the Green Fuse Drives the Flower"

EXERCISE 10.13 **Correcting Capitalization Problems**

Correct the capitalization errors in this paragraph:

Entering college after being a homemaker for several years can be a frightening experience. I can recall when I decided, at my Mother's suggestion, to return to College. I particularly remember the day in june when I enrolled. Just the thought of signing up for courses such as math, science, and english made me hesitate. Although I had done rather well in High School, my confidence in my academic abilities had fallen sharply over the years. As I stood in line on the day of Freshman Registration, I kept hearing the words to "Enter The Clowns" going through my head. I was thinking about giving up and going home until I met my Advisor. Her name was Dr. Garcia, a recent graduate from Florida international university. I really appreciated hearing encouragement from a fellow hispanic. I summoned enough Courage to submit my forms to the Registrar, but as I drove home, I was still shaking at the thought of my new undertaking and anticipating the worst. It was only after completing my Fall Semester and getting on the dean's honor roll that I realized that I would someday be able to go to Commencement and get my Bachelor's Degree.

Plurals and Possessives

Most nouns form their plural with *s* or *es*, but not all. Most possessives are formed by adding an apostrophe and an *s*, but not all. And then, of course, some nouns are plural and possessive. *How could anyone ever be confused about something as simple as using plurals and possessives correctly?*

Although plurals and possessives can present special problems, the guidelines given here cover most of the situations you will encounter.

1. The most common problem for writers is simply forgetting to include the apostrophe to show possession.

    As you proofread your papers, make it a habit to check whenever you add an *s* to the end of a word:

Plural

The *actors* were protesting homelessness.

I would like to earn a hundred *dollars* an hour.

Possessive

The *actor's* home was in Beverly Hills.

A *dollar's* value depends on how it was earned.

Some writers prefer to form possessives of inanimate objects with the preposition *of*: "The value of a dollar depends on how it was earned."

2. Don't add an apostrophe to a possessive pronoun.

Incorrect

We attended *his'* graduation.

The travel bag is *her's*.

The dog bared *it's* teeth.

Who's book is that?

Correct

We attended *his* graduation.

The travel bag is *hers*.

The dog bared *its* teeth.

Whose book is that?

Be careful not to confuse possessive pronouns with contractions:

Possessive

The dog bared *its* teeth.

Whose book is that?

Contraction

It's (it is) not safe here.

Who's (who is) coming to the movie?

3. Add an apostrophe and an *s* to form the possessive of singular nouns.

We read *Faulkner's* last novel.

We decided to try the *manager's* special.

I love *Keats's* poetry.

Do you understand *Camus's* position?

4. Plural nouns ending in *s* require only an apostrophe. Plurals not ending in *s* require an apostrophe and an *s*.

Plural

There were several *victims* in the drive-by shooting.

The *Thompsons* are our best friends.

The *children* were thrilled to see the snow falling.

The *Rodriquezes* have a collection of classic cars.

Possessive

What were the *victims'* rights in this case?

We enjoy sitting and talking on the *Thompsons'* porch.

We began to hunt for the *children's* gloves.

Have you seen the *Rodriquezes'* Pace Arrow?

5. Apostrophes are sometimes used to form the plural of letters, numbers, abbreviations, and words referred to as words.

Amanda puts hearts instead of dots above her *i's*.

You have too many *great's* in this description of the concert.

The apostrophe is frequently omitted when it is not needed for clarity.

The televisions and *VCRs* were stolen from the storage room.

The *1950s* were not as tranquil as many people believe.

EXERCISE 10.14 **Correcting Plural and Possessive Problems**

Correct the errors in plural and possessive forms in the following paragraph.

Entering todays job market, especially for applicant's with little or no recent experience in their field of interest, can be challenging. When you begin a career search, your first consideration should be determining your transferable skills. Are you handy with machine's and tool's? Do you enjoy working with people who's opinion you can influence or whom you can train or teach? Or would you rather work with numbers, following others instructions? Perhaps you are adept at the analyses and solution's of problems. Grades can be one indication of your interests, but having all As in a subject is not the only factor to consider. Whatever your aptitudes and ability's, if your willing to conduct a thorough search, you will find companys which can use your talents. Don't rely too much on a company's reputation or a recruiters' recommendation. If this is to be your lifes work, you should make sure its the right choice for you. Remember that the future is yours for the taking.

6. Consult a dictionary if you are not sure about the plural form of a noun, especially if it ends in one of the following letters:

Singular	Plural
-o	
studio	studios
cameo	cameos
piano	pianos
memo	memos
domino	dominoes
hero	heroes
-y	
key	keys
Wednesday	Wednesdays
party	parties
folly	follies
Bundy	Bundys
-f or -fe	
half	halves
sheaf	sheaves
chief	chiefs
roof	roofs
-us, -um, -on, -a, -is, *or* -us	
alumnus	alumni
medium	media
stadium	stadiums

criterion	criteria
vertebra	vertebrae
analysis	analyses
locus	loci

Also, remember that some words do not change in the plural form:

Singular	Plural
fish	fish
deer	deer
species	species

EXERCISE 10.15 **Forming Plurals**

Consult your dictionary for the plural form of the following nouns. If the dictionary lists more than one form, list all of them in the order they are given. The first form is generally preferred.

hoof	housefly
wharf	attorney
emphasis	colloquium
bronchus	moratorium
index	auditorium
radio	syllabus
tomato	cactus
cargo	elk
zero	axis
barrack	nucleus
formula	phenomenon
ninety	Swiss

SELF-EVALUATION

Although you should welcome suggestions from your teacher and your class-mates about how to correct the kinds of problems we have discussed in this chapter, you must ultimately assume responsibility for the work you do. The best way to feel confident about your work is to edit it carefully. One way to gain confidence in your editing skills is to perform your own self-evaluation. As you complete the self-evaluation checklist that follows, you will find ways that your sentence structure and word choices could be improved.

As you use the checklist, you will also be developing a sense of the areas where you are strongest and weakest. Every catcher in professional baseball keeps a "book" on the opposing batters. The catcher knows if a particular player has difficulty hitting an inside fastball or is a sucker for a change-up. By using the checklist, you will be developing your own "book" to avoid your most common errors.

Most of us who do a great deal of writing are aware of areas that cause us problems. I know, for instance, that I often have trouble spelling *occurrence* and *occasion*. That double *r* in *occurrence* never looks quite right to me, nor does that single *s* in *occasion*. Even when I think I have these words right, I often look them up just to make sure.

Use the following checklist as you work on editing your papers. Feel free to add your own trouble spots to the list.

Self-Evaluation Checklist

Manuscript form

1. Is my *heading* complete and correct?

2. Is the *title* of my paper well chosen?

3. Have I left adequate *margins* and used correct *spacing*?

4. Do all pages have the appropriate *headings*? Are they *numbered* correctly?

5. Have I corrected errors *neatly*?

Development

6. Is the *purpose* of the paper clear? Do I get off the topic in the course of the paper?

7. Does the *introduction* give the reader a reason to be concerned about my topic?

8. Do I have many short paragraphs? Should these paragraphs be *developed* further or *combined*?

9. Do the paragraphs link together smoothly? Are additional *transitions* needed?

10. Does the *conclusion* provide a sense of closure? Have all the questions raised in the paper been resolved?

Trouble spots

11. Have I checked the *spelling* of all the words that I might have misspelled? If I used a computer spell checker, have I checked the spelling of homonyms and other words that might be used incorrectly (for instance, *to* and *too*)?

12. Have I checked the *meaning* of words that I use infrequently to be sure that they are used appropriately?

13. Have I checked after *coordinating conjunctions* (*and, or, nor, for, so, yet*) to see if *commas* are needed to separate *independent clauses*?

14. Have I checked after *introductory phrases* to see if *commas* are necessary?

15. Have I checked to see if *commas* are placed before and after *nonessential phrases and clauses*?

16. Have I checked to see if *commas* are used correctly between items in a *series*?

17. Have I checked to see if sentences beginning with a subordinate clause (*because, if*, etc.) express a *complete thought*?

18. Have I read the paper aloud and listened for natural pauses that might signal that punctuation has been omitted and that a *run-on sentence* has resulted?

19. Have I examined my *subjects* (especially compound subjects, collective nouns, and indefinite pronouns) to make sure they agree with their *verbs*?

20. What *irregular verbs* are sometimes a problem for me? Have I used them correctly in this paper?

21. What is the *dominant tense* of my verbs? Have I shifted unnecessarily to other tenses?

22. Have I examined my pronouns to see if they *agree* with their *antecedents*, if they are in the *correct case*, and if they clearly *refer* to their *antecedents*?

23. Do I sometimes confuse *good* and *well* or omit the *ly* from adverb forms? Have I checked for these problems in this paper?

24. Does every *modifier* have a word, a phrase, or a sentence to modify? Have I placed modifiers near the words they modify?

25. Have I used *double negatives*?

26. Have I *capitalized* seasons (spring, summer, etc.), subjects (biology, socialism), or other common nouns (high school, seniors)?

27. Are *titles* of books, magazines, etc., underlined? Have the rules for capitalizing titles been followed?

28. Are *quotations* correctly punctuated?

29. Have I looked at words ending in *s* to see if they are *possessive* and require an apostrophe? Have I mistakenly used an apostrophe with the possessive form of personal pronouns (his, hers, its, etc.)?

30. If I have made *plurals* of words ending in *o, y,* or other special endings, are they correctly spelled?

A FINAL WORD ON EDITING FOR CORRECTNESS

Having looked at some common problems that confront writers, you may feel a little like a marine in a minefield, afraid that any misstep will create a disaster. Probably the worst thing you can do for your writing is to become overly conscious of errors that you make. Everybody makes errors. Learning to accept your mistakes and to work on the problem areas is fundamental to your growth as a writer. For one thing, if you can't accept your errors, you will avoid writing. And you can't get to be a better writer without writing—and writing a lot. Also, errors don't matter when you are writing a draft. You need to give yourself some space to think and to explore ideas without the pressure of expecting perfection as you do so. Finally, as you attempt different writing assignments and more challenging ones, you will find that there is always more to learn.

As I wrote this chapter, the U.S. Figure Skating Championships were in progress. My wife and I watched the best skaters in our country perform lovely and intricate maneuvers, and we watched several of them slip, tumble, and sprawl across the ice. But even when these skaters fell, we were impressed with how quickly they got back up and resumed their routines. It was clear that they knew falling was always a possibility and that they had trained to recover quickly and regain their poise. As a writer, you should strive to do your best possible work, but you must also understand that—in writing as well as in figure skating—making mistakes is a part of learning.

 THE CRITICAL MOMENT

As we have looked at the conventions of English spelling, punctuation, and usage, you may have encountered some practices that are quite unlike the ones used by your family and friends. In fact, using the "standard" English we have described here might make you feel uncomfortable around some people. They might interpret your change in language habits as an attempt to act superior to them.

In a sense, what we have described in this chapter is "blue business suit" English, the kind we use when writing a paper for a class, applying for a job, or in some other formal situation. Most of us also have a kind of "blue jeans" English as well. We may enjoy using the latest slang around our friends because it adds interest and vitality to our language. We adjust our language use to make us feel comfortable in the particular situation we find ourselves.

How would you respond to these questions about language conventions?

1. Is one kind of language right for all situations?

2. Is it wrong to use language that doesn't conform to conventions?

3. Is it hypocritical to use formal language if that isn't your customary way of speaking?

4. Should people always speak formally so that they won't embarrass themselves by using the wrong word in a formal speaking situation?

5. Do you ever make judgments about people based on the way they speak or write? Why do we make such judgments?

Editing for Style

A WRITER'S VOICE

Have you ever noticed how much we react to the tone of a person's voice? Sometimes our tone can totally change the meaning of our words. Think of the different ways we might say the word *fine* and the various meanings we could give the word:

A word showing approval

> Q: Did Michael's piano recital go well?

> A: He put on a *fine* performance.

A word showing unenthusiastic compliance

> Q: How would you like to go see *Adventures of the Last Aardvark?*

> A: Oh, that would be *fine*, I suppose.

A word showing sarcastic disappointment

> Q: Is something wrong?

> A: Oh, no, everything is just *fine*. I wrecked my car. My girlfriend left me. And somebody ran over my hound dog. But, really, I'm *fine*.

We establish a tone when we are speaking by the inflection of our voices and our facial expressions as well as by our choice of words. In writing, however, we establish a tone primarily by the words we choose. Writers may occasionally use exclamation points or italics as a way of indicating how a particular word or sentence should be read, but the words themselves are the primary means of conveying the writer's feelings to an audience. Although these words probably will be read silently, they still provide a clue to the writer's personality, feelings, and attitude toward the subject. We often refer to these attributes as the writer's *voice*.

Because words are so crucial to establishing a writer's voice, we must choose them carefully. Compare your reactions to these two paragraphs:

> According to your contract, "If the outstanding balance is not paid when due, the entire loan amount will become immediately payable. If not paid within 30 days, the property will be repossessed and the owner sued for collection fees, legal fees, and any amount not recovered through the sale of the property." Because you have been negligent in your payments, we will soon have to enforce these provisions of your contract. We will not be cheated out of our money by deadbeats like you. MAKE PAYMENT IN FULL IMMEDIATELY, or your automobile will be repossessed!

> We have not received payments on your loan for June or July. All accounts which are over 90 days delinquent are referred to a collections agency for further action. By acting now, you can avoid hurting your credit rating and having your car repossessed. Please call me at the number below to discuss your alternatives.

Both of these paragraphs have the same objective — to collect an outstanding debt. The writer's voice in the first paragraph is threatening, perhaps even belligerent. The writer of the second paragraph also indicates the seriousness of the situation, but the writer's voice seems more controlled and less judgmental. The first writer assumes that the customer is attempting to "cheat" the bank out of its money. The second writer does not attempt to assess blame. After all, the customer may have been on a long vacation, the mail may not have been forwarded after a move, or some other problem may have resulted in failure to pay. By showing firmness, but no malice, the writer of the second paragraph is striving to maintain good customer relations, even in a difficult situation.

Although many different "voices" are possible when writing, some of these are common enough to warrant special attention. The preceding examples are typical of what might be called an "institutional" style. In the Institutional Style, the writer is speaking on behalf of the organization that he or she represents. In contrast with the Institutional Style is the Personal Style, the language of personal letters and private correspondence. There is also the Scholarly Style, the kind of writing that is done for academic audiences, and the Literary Style, writing that is valued primarily for the experience it presents to the reader.

Before we discuss these various styles, certain preliminary explanations are in order. Each of these categories represents only general tendencies, not some absolute formula. Thus, there is not one Institutional Style, but many, each with its own unwritten rules and traditional structures. These varieties of style are quite apparent in academic circles. Historians, linguists, anthropologists, mathematicians, and every other specialty has its own stylistic conventions. However, even these varied groups share some common patterns.

Another common misconception is that some styles are "good" and others are "wrong." People frequently condemn institutional writing for being dishonest, personal writing for being simple-minded, scholarly writing for being pedantic, and literary writing for being obscure and frivolous. In fact, each style has its uses and abuses. One purpose in studying style is to be aware of the pitfalls of various kinds of writing.

Finally, these categories are not mutually exclusive. The letter, for instance, has long been considered an art form. Thus, a friendly letter might be considered personal writing or literary writing, or, in some cases, both simultaneously. A study of various styles is generally less useful for pigeon-holing writing samples than for understanding how a writer's voice becomes embodied in particular kinds of language.

Institutional Style

Institutional writing is primarily for transactional purposes; that is, it is writing to get things done—making plans, organizing meetings, proposing new ventures, assessing current activities, and conducting other transactions necessary for getting business done. Because of its transactional nature, institutional writing strives to be clear, direct, and purposeful. The following example, taken from a local phone book, is typical of this style.

Establishing South Central Bell service:

Call a service representative and provide the following information:

1. Complete street address (with apartment number, if applicable, or lot number of mobile home). Also, if you can provide the name and phone number of the person who lived there before you, it will help us respond faster to your request for service.

2. The type of home telephone service you want. See the listings on this page.

3. How you would like your directory listing to appear. Two people with the same last name living at the same address can have both first names listed.

4. Information about previous phone service.

5. Other credit information.

6. Social Security number.

Unfortunately, much institutional writing is neither clear nor concise. The following public notice is an example of writing that probably would confuse many of the people for whom it is intended.

BYTE-SIZE BULLETIN: STYLE ANALYSIS PROGRAMS

One of the fastest growing fields of software development for writers is in the area of programs that analyze style. Writers in both business and education are becoming increasingly aware of the benefits of having their documents scanned and critiqued by programs that detect the use of passive voice constructions, weak verbs, faulty punctuation, and other stylistic faults. And indeed these programs have their place, especially when you must write quickly and without the editorial comments of a colleague. Since we are so involved in what we are trying to communicate and must many times communicate our message quickly, stylistic finesse is sometimes sacrificed. Many style analysis programs can be issued a command to check our document for a certain style (such as what we've termed institutional, personal, scholarly, or literary), and a good style analysis program can help us gain a degree of objectivity, detect the use of ineffective grammar and sentence structure, and examine stylistic alternatives.

However, since these stylistic analysis programs are increasing in popularity, some writers have begun to rely too completely on the advice they receive. No matter how good a style analysis program may be, it does not replace a human being reading the text. It cannot ascertain the nuances a flesh-and-blood reader would perceive, and it cannot tell when a certain stylistic element is inappropriate; it simply can detect its presence within the document.

Style analysis programs are becoming more sophisticated and are allowing the writer to select an increasing number of areas to be checked and methods of checking them, but these programs will not take the place of your careful editing. Regardless of the program you may choose, make sure that you yourself (and preferably another reader) carefully analyze your document for style before presenting it to your reader.

PUBLIC NOTICE

ALL CREDITORS that hold any claim against Standard Insulations, Inc., formerly known as Standard Asbestos Manufacturing & Insulating Company, that wish to share in the Debtor's estate must file proofs of claim with the Clerk of this Court, 913 U.S. Courthouse, 811 Grand Avenue, Kansas City, Missouri 64106, on or before November 6, 1991, or be FOREVER BARRED from filing claims against the estate and from being treated as a creditor for the purposes of voting and distribution.

CREDITORS WHOSE CLAIMS ARE SPECIFICALLY LISTED ON THE DEBTOR'S SCHEDULES, WHICH SCHEDULES WERE FILED WITH THIS COURT ON SEPTEMBER 5, 1986 AND WHOSE CLAIMS ARE NOT LISTED AS DISPUTED, CONTINGENT OR UNLIQUIDATED AND WHO DO NOT DISPUTE THE LISTED AMOUNT OF THEIR CLAIM, MAY, BUT NEED NOT, FILE PROOFS OF CLAIM. CREDITORS WHO HAVE ALREADY FILED PROOFS OF CLAIM NEED NOT FILE AGAIN.

Those responding to this notice would need to understand the legal meaning of "creditor." In fact, the legal meaning runs counter to the common notion of credit as something owed to a lending agency. (People carry "credit" cards, not "debtor's" cards.) In addition, they would need to understand what it means to "share in the Debtor's estate." (Does it mean assume responsibility for the debts?) They would need to know what is meant by a "debtor's schedule." (Is this a list of amounts to be paid? a timetable for payment? both?) And they would need to know what "disputed, contingent or unliquidated" claims are. If the original claim has been disputed, should the creditor file again? Is this really a "public notice," or only a notice for the public with law degrees?

A few years ago I received a letter from an insurance company that read as follows:

> Attached to and made a part of the Contract or Certificate to which it is attached.
>
> The Variable Annuity Life Insurance Company is responsible for determining the qualified status of qualified domestic relations orders ("QDRO's") and for paying benefits in accordance with Chapter 76, Title 110B, Vernon's Revised Statutes.
>
> The effective date of this Endorsement is September 1, 1989.

After reading the first line several times, I finally decided that this was an addendum that was to be attached to my current policy. However, I am still in the dark about what QDRO's are, which ones are "qualified," and what benefits they might receive.

What these samples illustrate is that much institutional writing fails in its intended purpose. Writing that is vague, that uses unfamiliar terms, and that does not clearly state what response is necessary from the reader is not efficient or effective.

Personal Style

In the Institutional Style, the identity of the writer is often submerged. Policies are set by "the company" or "the department" rather than by individuals. The writer is given the authority to write because of her position within the company rather than as an expression of individual preferences or concerns.

Personal writing is an expression of self. As well as using the first-person pronouns *I* and *me*, the writer refers to personal feelings and experiences.

> I heard the news on Sunday morning. Donnie and one of his friends had been down at the river drinking. They decided to go into town and buy another six-pack. Donnie got the idea to sit on the headrest with his head sticking out of the sunroof. Deke, his friend, lay on the floorboard and pushed the gas while Donnie steered with his feet. Everybody laughed as they drove off.

Creative financing
Pre-owned automobiles
Handyman special
Free gift inside
Early bird offer

Do these phrases sound familiar? Most of us have been victims of irresponsible language—misleading sales promotions, distorted reporting, and even outright lies. One sign of an educated person is the ability to regard printed information with a healthy suspicion. Even when a writer strives for accuracy, mistakes have a way of creeping in, and obviously there are many unethical sources that have no concern for accuracy.

The words we use to describe our world help to shape our readers' perceptions and reactions. We will produce quite different responses if we describe a conflict as a "bloody war" or a "police action." On a personal level, we would recognize a difference between an "animated discussion" and a "bitter argument." When the welfare of our family, our community, or our nation depends on an accurate description of events, we need to take special care to describe people and events as accurately as possible.

Of course, the responsible use of language can be difficult to gauge. Falsifying information is clearly unacceptable, but what about trying to cast a negative situation in a favorable light? Every politician has a campaign manager who attempts to put the correct "spin" on the politician's actions. Corporations spend millions to project the right image to the public. Many people who would never deliberately cheat someone compromise themselves by writing slanted or distorted reports. They rationalize their actions by insisting that these reports are "just words." Ultimately, responsible use of language requires not only the ability to communicate clearly and effectively but also a strong sense of personal integrity.

A couple of miles down the road, Donnie lost control. The car flipped as it went off the road, and Donnie was thrown from the car. He died on impact. Deke lived long enough to crawl over to Donnie. However, it was hours before anyone discovered the car. In the meantime, Deke had bled to death.

I feel empty. I had known Donnie since third grade. You never think that the kid next to you with the Spiderman lunchbox is going to die in some terrible car wreck when he's seventeen.

I'm scared, too. You and I both know it could have been me instead of Donnie in that wreck. Of course, right now I'm as sober as a Baptist funeral, but I don't know what I'll be like next month or next year. I'm afraid of forgetting, and then Donnie won't have died for anything at all.

Some personal writing is never intended to be read by anyone. Many people keep a journal just to record their own thoughts and reflections on the events in their lives. Some personal writing goes on in informal letters and messages. Occasionally, personal writing may serve other functions; for instance, your boss may write you a personal note congratulating you on some achievement. Although the note is a genuine expression of your boss's feeling toward you as a person, such notes also help cultivate a sense of your individual worth and your importance in the organization.

Scholarly Style

Scholarly writing might easily be equated with academic writing. However, schools and academies are institutions, and a great deal of the writing that goes on in them is of an institutional nature — memos, correspondence, committee reports, and so on. Scholarly writing goes on in schools, but such writing is also produced by independent scholars and researchers with no academic affiliation. Whatever its origins, scholarly writing is distinguished by a concern for detail and precision, by a desire to acknowledge previous research on a topic, and by a commitment to expand the present bounds of knowledge.

Although most people understand the need to be continually exploring new frontiers of knowledge, the scholar is often a subject of derision. The scholar is portrayed as an ancient curmudgeon with no respect for students, as an absent-minded professor oblivious to the constraints of everyday life, or as a naif who falls victim to the pranks of his worldly-wise students. Five hundred years ago, Shakespeare parodied the stereotypical notion of the scholar in the figure of Polonius:

> My liege, and madam, to expostulate
> What majesty should be, what duty is,
> Why day is day, night night, and time is time,
> Were nothing but to waste night, day and time.
> Therefore since brevity is the soul of wit
> And tediousness the limbs and outward flourishes,
> I will be brief. Your noble son is mad:
> Mad call I it; for, to define true madness,
> What is 't but to be nothing else but mad?

As Polonius' speech indicates, the conventions of scholarly writing were already well established in Shakespeare's day. Scholars indulge in long prologues before reaching their subject (Polonius' discourse on night, day, and time), and scholars are always careful to define their terms (although Polonius' definition of madness is entirely circular).

In fact, scholars do provide extensive background as a way of providing a context for new information. A physicist who is studying the effect of impurities on semiconductors generally provides some background about prior studies in this field of research. By knowing what other scholars have learned, the physicist avoids repeating the work done by them and points the reader to other helpful sources. The ability to cite sources, as we discussed in chapter 8, is an identifying characteristic of the scholar's writing.

Scholars also try to provide precise definitions of the terms they use. Again, because of the desire for precision, scholars are sometimes accused of "splitting hairs," or being overly concerned about the meaning of words. But the need to make distinctions cuts to the heart of the scholarly enterprise. Observe how James Harvey Robinson in *The Mind in the Making* attempts to define concretely the idea of the "unconscious":

> The term "unconscious," now so familiar to all readers of modern works on psychology, gives offense to some adherents of the past. There should, however, be no special mystery about it. It is not a new animistic abstraction, but simply a collective word to include all the physiological changes which escape our notice, all the forgotten experiences and impressions of the past which continue to influence our desires and reflections and conduct, even if we cannot remember them. What we can remember at any time is indeed an infinitesimal part of what has happened to us. We could not remember anything unless we forgot almost everything. As Bergson says, the brain is the organ of forgetfulness as well as of memory. Moreover, we tend, of course, to become oblivious to things to which we are thoroughly accustomed, for habit blinds us to their existence. So the forgotten and the habitual make up a great part of the so-called "unconscious."

Perhaps no other attribute so well defines scholarly writing as the search for something new — a new discovery, a new theory, a new philosophical position, a new interpretation of an existing work of art. Of course, some scholarly writing attempts only to summarize and review what others have already said, but even in this particular compilation of sources there is the hope that some new understanding will be achieved.

Literary Style

The term *literature* is often used broadly to refer to any kind of writing (e.g., "the literature of science") or narrowly to refer to novels, poems, plays, and other forms of creative expression. Even in the latter sense, literature embraces a great range of styles, from Milton's epic poetry to Hemingway's spare prose. Whatever the form, the purpose of the literary artist always has been to provide readers with a rich, imaginative experience. Unlike in institutional writing, conciseness is not always a virtue in literary expression. When reading a good novel, the reader may wish it would go on forever. Unlike personal writing, literature generally attempts to be accessible to those outside the writer's own circle of friends. Unlike the scholar, the literary writer often works by nuance and association rather than by precise definition. A reader of poetry will recall Eliot's London as a place where "yellow fog . . . rubs its back upon the window-panes" and Frost's New Hampshire as a place of stone walls and birches and snowy woods.

The literary writer generally attempts to *show* the reader a meaning rather than to tell it. Compare these two methods of revealing character:

1. My brother is a great person. I mean we didn't always get along that well when we were kids, but we always cared for each other, and I always knew that he would be there for me when I needed him.

2. For some strange, perverse reason, I always wanted to be a flute player. I didn't know as a child that musical instruments were generally treated as gender-specific; but when I arrived in junior high school, I discovered that some unwritten code had determined that trombones and trumpets were for boys; flutes and piccolos, for girls. I had chosen to play the flute just because I liked the sound of it, and by the time I learned that I had made a fatal error in sexual identity, it was too late to change. So, throwing caution to the wind (in this case, woodwinds), I tried out for the junior high school band on the flute, and made it. Although I was teased about my instrument, I really didn't mind too much sitting next to all those girl flute players, especially Donna Murphy — but that's another story.

    One day I was on my way home from school when Mitch Kunkel and some of his friends stopped me as I was crossing the parking lot.

    "What's in the little box?" Mitch said, snickering and glancing back to his companions.

    "It's a flute, O.K.!" I said and tried to move on past them.

    "Hey, we got us a little Flute Boy here, guys," Mitch said, snatching the flute case from my hand and opening it up. "Why don't you play us something, little Flute Boy?"

    "Just give me back my flute." I could feel the color rising in my face. I wanted to punch Mitch, but in all probability I would have wound up hunting for my teeth in the gravel parking lot.

    "Well, maybe, I'll just play a little tune myself," Mitch chuckled. Fortunately, putting the flute together was a little too complicated for Kunkel, who was widely rumored to have failed an IQ test.

    I made a lunge for the flute, and Kunkel jerked it out of my reach. Next he began tossing pieces of it around to his friends.

    What Kunkel had not counted on was the appearance of my brother, Tommy, who had just gotten his driver's license the previous month. Tommy was coming by the school to pick me up and take me to practice. When he saw Mitch and his friends tossing around the flute, he figured out what was going on pretty quickly.

Tommy had lettered in weight lifting for three years, and though he was   10
not particularly big, he had been known to bend things, like golf clubs and
street signs, when he was angry. And he was really angry now.

I tried not to give it away when I saw Tommy sneaking up behind Mitch.
Suddenly Tommy performed what is known in weight lifting circles as a
"clean-and-jerk" with Mitch Kunkel as the dumbbell.

Mitch, who only moments earlier had seemed so menacing, was now the
laughingstock of Millard Fillmore Junior High School. Even in his anger,
Tommy had the decency not to drop Mitch in the gravel. Instead, he heaved
him into a nearby embankment.

I was relieved to be rescued by my brother. (Mitch never so much as gave
me a harsh look after that day.) But more than that, I was surprised. I guess I
had always known that Tommy loved me, but I saw it more in the way he
manhandled Mitch than in the expected filial duties of exchanging Christmas
gifts and playing card games together. Neither of us said anything to Mom
and Dad about the incident, and we seldom even discussed it ourselves, but
there was, from that day on, an unspoken bond of loyalty between my brother
and me, stronger than any blood oath that had ever been sworn.

It is not very efficient to tell a long story to illustrate the nature of a relationship,
but "telling" about the way you feel about your brother seldom has the same impact
as "showing" the nature of the relationship through a specific incident.

Each of the styles we have reviewed has its place. There is no "one" correct style
to be used in all situations. Every time you write, you will have to consider the style
that will work best for your particular writing situation — whether it involves institutional, personal, scholarly, or literary writing. Furthermore, you may find that
you are adept at one style of writing but have difficulty with another. As you
continue to develop as a writer, try a variety of different writing styles.

EXERCISE 11.1   Categorizing Writing Styles

Categorize the writing styles of the following passages as institutional, personal, scholarly, or
literary. Discuss with your Discovery Group what features you observed that enabled you to
place the writing in the category you chose.

1. Jane smiled feebly. She had just been asked a question for which she had no answer. Her
    life was largely a series of questions without answers, and a smile was her only defense.
    Normally, the question passed on to another student, like a storm passing overhead, but
    this teacher was different.

    "I'm expecting an answer, Jane," Mrs. March demanded. "Haven't you studied?"

    "Oh yes, ma'am," said Jane sincerely.

    "Then why don't you know the answer?"

    "Because I'm not very bright," said Jane smiling.

A wave of laughter passed through the class. Mrs. March reddened and went on to the next student.

2. Should the lessee fail to meet the terms of the above provision within the specified time of 60 days from the date of default, the property will return to the holding company and, within 30 days of confiscation, be rendered inaccessible according to the terms of Article IV.

3. You would love what I am seeing. Snow is deep around the cabin, and frost has swallowed up the windowpanes. I am deep in beauty. I don't think I realized just how pleasantly isolated I am until today. For some, this cabin might seem a prison; for me it's a place of freedom and independence. I want nothing more than to live simply and to be alone with my thoughts.

4. The delineation of the cycle of deforestation, presented in tabular form by Bacon, Johanison, and Hopkins, failed, however, to extend the theories of Matthison to the politics of Costa Rica and, therefore, did not present the complete rationale for the environmental practice.

5. I can't say exactly why I don't trust him. I can't explain it. Maybe it's the way he brushes his hair back. Maybe it's the crinkling around his eyes when I ask a question. I don't want to be overly suspicious, but I don't want to get sucked in either.

6. Phase III of the Juniper Project must be completed by April 17, 1994. Specific assignments will be given by Yolanda Jones, the project manager. A revised time schedule will be circulated to the project team within a week.

ESSENTIAL ELEMENTS

Given the variety of styles we have discussed, it might seem unlikely that any stylistic features are useful in all kinds of writing. Certainly, there are exceptions to every rule, but generally you will find that readers expect specific, vigorous, and imaginative language.

Specific Language

Whether you are describing *Ivanhoe* or a backhoe, readers will respond to specific language that provides the shape, color, size, weight, and feel of an object or the moods, mannerisms, expressions, and physical characteristics of a person. Note how adding specific language improves the quality of writing in each of the four styles we have discussed:

Institutional

Vague

I would like to order the yellow jacket I saw on page 334 of the catalog. I am enclosing a check for the amount.

Specific

Please send me the following merchandise listed as Item 6 on page 334 of your 1992 Fall-Winter catalog:

Item: Sunrunner Jacket

Stock Number: JLC02-2811

Color: Yellow (04)

Size: Adult Medium

I have figured the total cost of the merchandise as follows:

Sunrunner Jacket	28.99
8% Sales Tax (NJ resident)	2.32
Shipping and handling	3.00
TOTAL	34.31

I am enclosing a check for $34.31. Please deliver to the address above in 4–6 weeks.

Personal

Vague

I had a great time at the beach. I mainly just hung out. I had a really excellent time.

Specific

Crystal Shores is probably the best beach I've ever seen. The sand is soft, white, and seems to stretch on forever. The water is blue, really blue — not brown or green or some other earth tone. Best of all, the place isn't crowded. No screaming kids, no grandmothers with shopping bags full of books and baby oil, no wacked-out beach bums trying to relive 1969. It's the beach of my dreams.

You would like to know where it is? Not a chance. I'm not going to spoil a good thing.

Scholarly

Vague

Early photographs, called daguerreotypes, were printed on metal plates and have an "old-timey" look to them.

Specific

The earliest photographic process was called a *daguerreotype*, after the French painter, Louis J. M. Daguerre, who pioneered the method. The images were produced by coating copper plates with silver and then exposing them to the light. The process was slow. A single exposure could require up to an hour, depending on the available light. Daguerreotypes have a shiny surface and were often touted as "the mirror with a memory."

Literary

Vague

Everybody has heard that old song about the "flying trapeze." I think the trapeze is probably the best thing at the circus. I mean, those guys are really taking a risk.

Specific

Like a spider on a silken strand, the trapeze performer hangs suspended above the crowd. For the lion tamer and the trick rider, the glance is downward, but for the aerialist all eyes are turned upward, as in admiration, as in worship. He cleaves the air at dizzying speeds, waits for the perfect synchronous moment, and launches himself into a pair of somersaults, stretching out at the last moment to take the hands of the catcher. We marvel at the aerialist's skill and grace, but most of all, it is sheer nerve that we admire. For ultimately, the trapeze show is not about beauty; it is about death.

As well as specific language, many writing occasions require *concrete* language, that is, language which describes the way things look, feel, smell, sound, or taste. A stock number for an automobile part is specific, but it is not concrete. Observing that an apple pie was rated 9.2 by the judges is also specific without being concrete. Observing that the crust of the apple pie was "light, flaky, and tender" is concrete language. In contrast to concrete language is *abstract* language. Abstractions, like "politics" or "happiness," do not refer to any particular phenomenon. Obviously, both abstract and concrete language is necessary for communication, but frequently you will want to dramatize a point by using concrete language.

EXERCISE 11.2 Using Specific and Concrete Language

Rewrite the following sentences, making the language more specific and concrete.

1. New York is quite a place.
2. [A movie you have seen] was really good.
3. We couldn't start the car because something was wrong.
4. The house looked creepy.
5. You'll find that I'm very well qualified for the job.

Vigorous Language

The basic building blocks of sentences are nouns and verbs. In discussing specific language, we looked primarily at nouns. Instead of using abstractions or generalizations, we used specific nouns that referred to particular things and people. As we strive for vigorous language, we look primarily at verbs, words that express actions or conditions.

One of the most commonly used verbs in our language is *to be*. All the forms of *to be* are used simply to establish the condition or status of something.

George III *was* king of England during the American Revolution.

The Empire State Building *is* not the highest building in New York City.

My friends *were* helpful when I moved out of my apartment.

Because *to be* verbs do not express any particular action, they add little meaning to the sentence. A verb like *shove* expresses a definite action, but you cannot *was* or *were* anything. When possible, try to substitute a more active verb for the verbs of being. For instance, the verb *was* in the sentence about George III might easily be changed to a more active verb:

George III *ruled* England during the American Revolution.

Or you might put the information about the reign of George III into an appositive and proceed to tell something about the nature of his rule:

George III, king of England during the American Revolution, *tyrannized* the colonies by requiring them to pay various taxes and tariffs and by forcing them to provide food and shelter for members of the British army.

As this example illustrates, removing the *to be* verb often allows you to add more information to your sentence or to combine several sentences. Of course, *is, am, are, was, were,* and so on, can't always be removed from your sentences. Frequently, these verbs are used as auxiliaries to a main verb in order to express the appropriate tense.

The Toledo flight *was delayed* because of the snowstorm.

The last member of the relay team *will be swimming* freestyle.

Any remaining hopes that Hitler would restrain his ambition *had been crushed* by the invasion of Czechoslovakia.

As well as avoiding using a form of *to be* as the main verb in a sentence, you should select all of your verbs carefully. Use the verb that best matches the idea you want to convey to the reader.

Weak verbs

Hakam *held* the ancient scrolls carefully, *looking* for any sign of a forgery.

The Dodgers *fell* behind in the seventh inning.

More vigorous verbs

Hakam *fingered* the ancient scrolls carefully, *poring* over them for any sign of a forgery.

In the seventh inning, the Cubs *shelled* the Dodgers for 11 hits resulting in 8 runs.

EXERCISE 11.3 Using Vigorous Verbs

Change weak verbs to more vigorous ones in the following sentences.

1. That storm was one of the hardest to ever hit the West Coast.
2. Although Mr. Preston was a relatively short man, his demeanor was impressive.
3. The dissolution of the Soviet Union probably will be one of the top stories historians discuss when they look at the early 1990s.
4. Something smelled bad in the room.
5. We have been having an increased number of absences among the employees in this division, and we must make some determination of the reasons for this excessive absenteeism.
6. Although the eighties have been given the label of the "me decade," enough altruistic deeds were done during these years to make necessary a reappraisal of this popular view of the time period.
7. She made eye contact with him and then made lip contact with him.
8. Because Daphne was, at one time, an agent for both the United States and the Soviet Union, she was at considerable risk of disclosure with potentially lethal results.
9. Thank you for the opportunity to see the inside of your house. I found your furnishings and historical artifacts to be of great interest.
10. An objective examination of the causes of the Civil War seems to be less likely in the current political climate, which has created strong emotional reactions to those historians now dealing with the subject.

How you use verbs in a sentence also affects the vigor of your language. If the subject of your sentence is performing the action, you are writing in *active voice*.

Benito *scored* the winning goal.

However, you can rewrite this sentence so that the subject is no longer performing the action:

The winning goal *was scored* by Benito.
[The "goal" is not doing the scoring.]

When the subject is not performing the action, the sentence is said to be in *passive voice*. Frequently, the one responsible for the action is mentioned in a phrase beginning with the preposition *by* after the verb.

Our mailbox was destroyed *by* some juvenile delinquents.

The package was delivered on time *by* Federal Express.

However, many sentences written in passive voice do not mention the one responsible for the action at all.

Our mailbox was destroyed.

The package was delivered on time.

In some cases, passive voice is a natural choice. The writer may not know who destroyed the mailbox. Or it may not be important who was responsible for delivering the package. However, most sentences are more interesting and readable when written in active voice. An entire paragraph written in passive voice is nearly always dull.

The front of the office had been the scene of considerable damage. The door had been forcibly opened, and the windows had been broken by some heavy object. The investigator was given as much information as possible by the neighbor, but the crucial questions had not been broached. Sure, the adjacent walls had been inscribed with slanderous graffiti, but why were the street signs reversed? She had been presented with only enough information to make her agree to accept the assignment, and now she herself was being examined by one of her own supervisors. She had been acclaimed many times for her ability to withstand hostile interrogation, but now she was being doubted by those who had formerly trusted her.

EXERCISE 11.4 Using Active Voice

Change the following sentences from passive voice to active voice. Supply a subject for the action if one is not given. Discuss with your Discovery Group which of these sentences might be best left in passive voice.

1. He was given his trophy by the coach.

2. The government of the country had been transferred into enemy hands.

3. The last song was sung by me.

4. The formula has been found to be defective.

5. At approximately 8:32 p.m., the liquor store was robbed.

6. He was swayed by the opinions of his constituents.

7. I have never been so honored as I am this evening.

8. The prison bus had always been driven by Jerry.

9. The signal for retreat was given at 19:07, Wednesday, October 19.

10. The assassination attempt has been under investigation for six years.

Imaginative Language

Whenever you write, you are exercising your imagination. Imagination is required not only of poets and novelists but of nurses, chemists, real estate brokers, and store managers as well. Everyone who writes has to find language to convey ideas and experience, and this search requires imagination. Suppose you have to tell a customer about a new door that is in stock at your building supply store. The door looks like the drawing in Figure 11.1. What words would you use to describe this door? You could try a mathematical description: "In the upper left corner is a concave arc that is 22 mm long . . . ." Obviously, such a description would be long and, for most people, confusing. What is needed are a few words that will convey the general style of the door. You might use adjectives like *colonial, ornate, scrollwork,* and *elegant* to describe this kind of door.

Every day we encounter dozens of examples of language that work less by numerical description and more by a visual sense of the size, shape, and color of objects:

bell-shaped curve
mechanical arm
camel-colored coat
pencil-sized extrusion
volcanic temperatures
sugarcoat the bad news

Although imaginative language does make writing more vigorous and interesting, it also is a highly efficient way of communicating information. Observe the use of imaginative language as Annie Dillard describes flocks of starlings in *Pilgrim at Tinker Creek*:

Out of the dimming sky *a speck* appeared, then another, and another. It was the starlings going to roost. They gathered deep in the distance, flock *sifting* into flock, and strayed towards me, *transparent and whirling, like smoke*. They seemed to *unravel* as they flew, lengthening in curves, *like a loosened skein*. I didn't move;

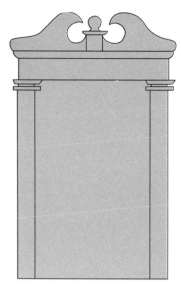

FIGURE 11.1: The Door

they flew directly over my head for half an hour. The flight extended *like a fluttering banner, an unfurled oriflamme*, in either direction as far as I could see. Each individual bird *bobbed* and *knitted* up and down in the flight at apparent random, for no known reason except that that's how starlings fly, yet all remained perfectly spaced. The flocks each *tapered* at either end from a rounded middle, *like an eye.* Over my head I heard a sound of beaten air, *like a million shook rugs, a muffled whuff.* Into the woods they *sifted* without shifting a twig, right through *the crowns* of the trees, intricate and rushing, *like wind.*

In this paragraph, Dillard conveys a visual impression through well-chosen verbs (*sifting, bobbed, knitted, tapered*) and through vivid comparisons ("like smoke," "like a fluttering banner"). In some cases, Dillard combines a physical description with a visual image. For instance, she tells us that the shape of each flock was "tapered at either end from a rounded middle," but the comparison to the shape of an eye immediately conveys the physical arrangement of the birds. This is a good example of the power of imaginative language to compress what could be a lengthy description into a few words.

EXERCISE 11.5 **Visual Comparisons**

After examining the shapes on the following page, think of a word or an expression that would quickly convey the shape to someone else.

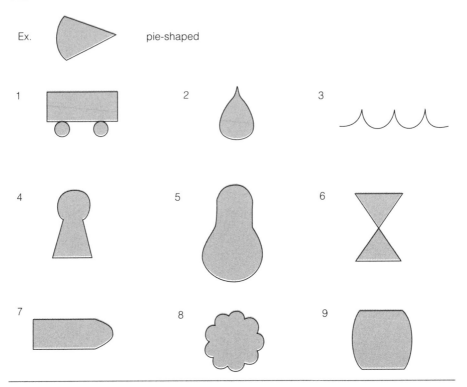

You may have noticed that many of the images used by Dillard begin with the word *like*. A comparison beginning with *like* or *as* is called a *simile*. Simile comes from the same root word as *similar*. However, in most similes, the objects being compared may have only a few features in common. For instance, if you call your boss a "grizzly bear," you don't mean that he is furry or likes to walk around on all fours. You probably are indicating that he has a mean disposition.

Sometimes you will make a comparison without using *like* or *as*. In this case, you will be using a *metaphor*. These are sample metaphors:

> When she smiled, *the sun broke loose and a thousand stars danced*.

> In the annual review our team's performance was *denounced, beaten, whipped, and held up on a pike as an object for public ridicule*.

> The bedroom where Arnold was sleeping rumbled *with the noise of an aging B-52*.

Because the comparison is implied rather than stated in a metaphorical statement, the writer of a metaphor assumes some risk of being misunderstood. Some readers might fail to realize that the noise of the B-52 in the preceding example refers to Arnold's snoring. Usually such metaphors are made clear by the context and by the absurdity of the literal meaning.

Reprinted by permission: Tribune Media Services

A fresh metaphor or simile can add interest and vitality to your writing; however, metaphors that are used too often are like jokes everyone has heard. Here are some clichéd metaphors and similes:

light as a feather
stiff as a board
scratching the surface
scraping the bottom of the barrel
food for thought
old as the hills
run like the wind
grow like a weed
throw caution to the winds
he would give the shirt off his back for you
they were running around like chickens with their heads cut off

Sometimes such clichéd expressions can be revitalized by changing a few words or putting them in a different context. Suppose in reading over a rough draft, you come across this sentence:

After coming in late for work three days in a row, Allan's *head was on the chopping block*.

The expression his "head was on the chopping block" is fairly predictable, one of the signs of a cliché. What are some other ways of communicating the same idea?

Change the wording

After coming in late for work three days in a row, Allan imagined his *career would soon be on the chopping block*.

Choose a different comparison

After coming in late for work three days in a row, Allan *waited quietly for the guillotine blade to fall*.

After coming in late for work three days in a row, Allan knew it was time *to empty out his desk drawers into a cardboard box.*

Use a literal explanation

After coming in late for work three days in a row, Allan knew he would be fired.

EXERCISE 11.6 Using Similes and Metaphors

Underline the similes and metaphors in the following paragraph. Discuss with your Discovery Group which are lively expressions and which are clichés.

> Our approach to Puerto Vallarta was one of the memorable experiences of the trip and will continue to stick in our minds. As we drove down from the jagged blades of the mountain's summit, we spied the little sleeping village resting between the dark, humid jungles with vine cords tightly twisted like overstrained muscles and the ocean glistening like Coronado's dreams of golden cities. The water was sparkling like a valley of diamonds as the sun set on the horizon like a red ball of flame. We could detect skiffs maneuvering in the shallow water close to the shore, making their way in and out, resembling tiny minnows searching for food. The only distracting object in our view was the central church's crowned apex, which stood out like a sore thumb.

EXERCISE 11.7 Avoiding Clichés

Replace the clichés in the following sentences with effective metaphors and similes or with literal language.

1. On that sweltering midsummer day, the humidity had risen by 30%, and it was hotter than a firecracker.

2. After heaving those boxes and unloading the cargo, I was tired as a dog and hungry as a bear.

3. The old house had a beautiful entrance, but the central hallway was uglier than sin.

4. He ran out of the jail doors like a bat out of hell.

5. This computer has many impressive features; however, it's as slow as molasses.

6. That child is as pretty as a picture.

7. We can no longer compete in this market since the other manufacturer is assembling components as fast as you can say "one, two, three."

8. She spends money like there's no tomorrow.

9. He would have given the shirt off his back to help his friend.

10. He was laughing like a hyena while he told me the story.

SENTENCE WORKOUTS

In revising your papers, you should begin by considering the entire work. Have you said what you intended to say? Have you accomplished your purpose? If you are satisfied with the overall content of your work, begin to examine individual paragraphs and sentences. The following examples and exercises represent a kind of tune-up for looking at the areas that may need attention in your own work.

Expand Dull Sentences

One of the secrets of good writing is to know how much detail to give the reader. If you provide too much information, the reader can become bogged down with meaningless information. If you provide too little, the sentence will often seem dull or simple-minded. Imagine a paragraph with no descriptive words.

> The circus is the world in microcosm. The circus is better than any other form of entertainment. Everyone likes the circus. Many enjoyable things can be seen at a circus. I admire circus performers.

Here is the treatment of this same theme by a noted essayist:

> The circus comes as close to being the world in microcosm as anything I know; in a way, it puts all the rest of show business in the shade. Its magic is universal and complex. Out of its wild disorder comes order; from its rank smell rises the good aroma of courage and daring; out of its preliminary shabbiness comes the final splendor. And buried in the familiar boasts of its advance agents lies the modesty of most of its people. (E. B. White, "The Ring of Time")

Notice that White expands the sentence through various means, not simply by piling on adjectives. For instance, in the first sentence he uses two adverb clauses: "as close to being the world in microcosm" and "as anything I know." The sentence also contains a strong visual comparison. Instead of merely saying that the circus is superior to other forms of entertainment, White says that it puts them "in the shade." One-word adjectives are used sparingly in this passage, but they are used effectively — *wild* disorder, the *good* aroma of courage, *preliminary* shabbiness, *final* splendor, and *familiar* boasts are all used to define nouns in important ways.

EXERCISE 11.8 **Expanding Sentences through Descriptive Detail**

Expand the following sentences by adding detail through descriptive words and phrases.

1. The town of Stonebridge was nearly hidden among the trees.

2. The potter pulled up the clay as she worked.

3. We heard the bells toll from a nearby church.

4. The fence leaned outward.

5. The weather created hazardous conditions.

Reduce Wordy Sentences

The failure to add descriptive detail can make your writing dull and ordinary. Too much detail, however, can make your writing confusing and difficult to read. Good writers are selective about the amount of detail they choose to include.

Overburdened sentence

The merry tune which was emitted from large loudspeakers on the side of the brightly decorated ice cream truck reminded me of similar music I had heard at the circus, and it seemed to me a sure sign that summer, my favorite of all seasons, had arrived.

Revised sentence

The raucous sound of the ice cream truck was a sure sign that summer had arrived.

Overburdened sentence

Only a handful of the really great actresses — names like Katherine Hepburn come to mind — have been able to play such a wide variety of roles, from high drama to low comedy, from aristocrats to ordinary people, and in all of these many different roles to have achieved such widespread critical acclaim and recognition from the most respected critics of our generation as Meryl Streep has in her distinguished acting career.

Revised sentence

Few actresses have played so many different roles or achieved such critical acclaim as Meryl Streep.

Of course, no one can say what is too much detail without some knowledge of the purpose for which you are writing or of the nature of your audience, but most writers and readers possess an intuitive sense of when a sentence has gone on too long and attempted to say too much and, thus, when it would have been better to have removed some of the detail from the sentence rather than for the sentence to continue on too long and begin to overwhelm the reader with unwanted or even repetitious material (as this sentence surely has!).

EXERCISE 11.9 Removing Unnecessary Detail

Shorten these sentences by removing unnecessary detail. Discuss with your Discovery Group why you chose to omit some details and retain others.

1. The overwhelming splendor of the room, with its vaulted ceiling rising for what seemed miles above him, its recesses dimly illuminated by hundreds of candles, and its heavy velvet draperies surrounding three of the four walls, seemed to intoxicate his mind and his emotions, causing him to reel as from the perfume of a thousand censers and sending him into a delirious euphoria which he had not experienced since three years ago when he was overcome by the beauty of the architecture which he had lovingly admired with such awe and had heroically strived to imitate with his entire being.

2. The word *biology* comes from two Greek words: *bios*, meaning "life," and *logos*, "the study of" (literally, "words about living things"), but in our own time it has come to take on a more specific meaning, that is, the science which explains the nature and origin of life in all of its myriad forms from the simple amoeba to the anatomy and physiology of human beings and other vertebrates.

3. Expounding upon the theoretical improbability of the proposed hypothesis, Bertrand raised his serpentine left eyebrow, straightened his French cuff adorned with emerald studs, gently pushed back his charcoal lock of hair which hung at a curved right angle over his pink-tinted, ivory forehead, and began to assert his own explanation of the failure of the endeavor which had so wrecked the family business and had thrown the entire Williams enterprise into the financial and emotional disarray in which all six family members so surprisingly and suddenly found themselves.

4. The wintry day, chilly and dismal, was the perfect time for this venture into the quest of the secret, the hidden knowledge of what lay just beyond the old, grey stone wall which had encapsulated her world for so long and which had fortified the psychological distance between her and the alien and foreign outsiders who had for so long intimidated her with their howls and shrieks of derision and who had thus imprisoned her in her own world of two acres, five trees, two sheds, and one house with a window which, although it possessed a view of the freedom which lay just over the river, had nevertheless taunted her with the impossibility of her escape.

5. The nuclear reactor, looming on the horizon like a primordial beast rising from the desert and plotting its destructive attack on all innocent surrounding plant and animal life, including prickly pear cactus and rust-colored roadrunner, resembled the monstrous and insensible robotic amalgamation of metallic materials which would signal the final apocalypse, the last bell for mankind.

Combine Related Sentences

As well as expanding and reducing sentence length in order to provide the right amount of information for the reader, we can also combine sentences to achieve the same effect. Frequently in writing a rough draft, we write sentences that contain needless repetition. By combining sentences, we can achieve a more economical and readable style. The following paragraph is typical of "rough draft" writing:

Discovery Draft

I had lived in the house on 24th Street all my life. In many ways this house was a part of me. It just didn't seem right to be leaving it. The house reminded me of many things I had done when I was younger. Every room contained a million memories. I had broken the glass in my bedroom window once. I was pretending to throw my new baseball when it slipped out of my hand. My dad had really been mad at me. The window was repaired now, but I could still see the broken glass the way it was. And I could still hear my father's tongue-lashing. And the kitchen floor would be just a kitchen floor to a stranger. But I remember when mom was six months pregnant and ran in to answer the telephone and slipped on some jello and went skating across the floor. At first I was scared, but mom started laughing. We knew everything was O.K. then. So when my parents started talking about selling the house, I felt bad. It was my house, too. It's almost as if they had decided to sell the family photo albums. I just couldn't believe they'd really do it.

Revised Version

I had lived in the house on 24th Street so long that it had become a part of me; I couldn't leave it now. Every room contained memories of my childhood. If I looked at the window in my bedroom, I remembered how I had shattered the glass when a baseball slipped out of my hand. I could still see the broken glass, still hear my father's tongue-lashing. If I walked into the kitchen, I could easily picture my mother, six months pregnant, slipping on jello and sliding across the floor. After a few silent moments, mom had started to laugh and soon the rest of us had joined in. Sell this house? They might as well auction off the family photo albums.

By combining sentences, the revised version reduced the total number of sentences from 18 to 8 with little loss of content. The result is a tighter paragraph that contains few unnecessary words and consequently is easier to read. Nearly every rough draft needs to go through a similar process of combining sentences and eliminating repetitive thoughts.

Sentences may be combined in various ways. In some cases a subordinating conjunction is used to show the dependent relationship of one of the sentences.

Separate

The weather was bad. The plane was late.

Combined

Because the weather was bad, the plane was late.

A coordinating conjunction indicates that both sentences are equally important.

Separate

I failed my algebra test the next day. I heard my son play his first recital that night.

Combined

I failed my algebra test the next day, but I heard my son play his first recital that night.

Sometimes an entire sentence can be reduced to a phrase or even a word and combined with another sentence.

Separate

California is famous for its beaches. It also is famous for its beautiful mountains.

Combined

California is famous for its beaches and beautiful mountains.

Separate

Spiro Agnew was vice-president under Richard Nixon. Agnew was famous for his colorful rhetoric. He once condemned the press for being the "nattering nabobs of negativism."

Combined

Spiro Agnew, vice-president under Richard Nixon, was famous for his colorful rhetoric, such as condemning the press for being the "nattering nabobs of negativism."

Separate

Tennyson wrote one of his most celebrated poems in remembrance of his friend Arthur Hallam. Hallam had died from drowning as a young man. The poem dedicated to Hallam is called *In Memoriam*.

Combined

Tennyson wrote one of his most celebrated poems, *In Memoriam*, in remembrance of his friend Arthur Hallam, who had drowned as a young man.

EXERCISE 11.10 Combining Sentences

Combine the following sentences into a single sentence. Make the sentence read as smoothly as possible.

1. Tom was one of my closest friends. He was a bright, serious young man when I first met him.

2. The Soviet Union no longer exists. Just a few decades ago, the Soviet Union was perceived to be one of the biggest threats to our national security.

3. Shakespeare wrote many historical dramas. One of his most patriotic dramas concerns the glorious reign of Henry V. Henry V defeated the French at Agincourt. He became a symbol of England's pride.

4. Tennessee Williams lived in New Orleans for many years. The ambiance of the city caused a psychological tension within him. His puritanical background was challenged by the life he found in New Orleans. His writings are influenced by this conflict.

5. The culture of the American Indian is replete with environmental concerns. Only recently has this culture been examined for its environmental message. Before, the American Indians were considered backward. Their culture is now seen as progressive in many ways.

6.   This coastal village relies on fishing as its primary industry. Sixty-nine percent of the workers living here are fishermen. Almost all of the other local businesses support the fishing industry. Fish products are a valuable source of income.

7.   *Snow White* should not be considered appropriate literature for children. We should not entertain impressionable minds with stories of haggard witches. This story concentrates on envy and death. Envy and death are not appropriate topics on which children's minds should be focused.

8.   My father was impressed by what his new computer could do. It could help him write letters. It could help him budget his income. It could help him organize his list of addresses. He was pleased with his purchase.

Clear Up Confusing Sentences

Sentences can be confusing for a number of reasons. The reader may be unfamiliar with the concepts being discussed and, therefore, be confused about the meaning of the sentence. For instance, if your readers are not trained in medicine, they may not immediately recognize *hematology* or *infarction*. Confusion also occurs when the reader has in mind a different context for the same word. If you have two friends named Felipe, you might easily confuse your readers if you refer to one of the Felipes without identifying which one. By supplying additional information, providing definitions, and identifying your subjects carefully, you can avoid these forms of confusion.

On the other hand, sometimes a reader is confused simply because a sentence is awkwardly worded. Most readers would puzzle over the following sentence for some time.

> Politicians have often been known to be cunning, dishonest individuals who seek personal gain without caring or respecting the rights of others whom they set out to attack while in the process of playing the shrewd using game of politics much like plays in sports.

If a reader struggles with a sentence because it contains difficult and complex ideas, the reward of understanding an important idea usually makes the effort seem worthwhile. But if a sentence creates confusion because it is awkwardly worded, many readers will become frustrated, and some will give up altogether.

Frequently, confusing sentences are the result of failing to read carefully what you have written. Had the writer of the preceding sentence read her own work carefully, she probably could have eliminated many of the problems. Sometimes confusion results from choosing the wrong word. See if you can spot the word choice error in this sentence:

> Companies should higher workers in compliance with equal opportunity laws.

Another frequent error results from placing a modifier in the wrong position. What confusion could arise in reading this sentence?

> Many students are dropping out of school which is believed to be caused by the use of drugs.

One of the most frequent problems is a failure to examine the "truth value" of a sentence. In the course of writing, all of us fall into the trap of making generalizations that will not stand up under scrutiny. How believable are the following statements? Would you accept them without additional evidence?

> I can honestly say that the day will come when all public school students will be required to wear uniforms to class, all the same without distinction of any kind.

> Integrity in today's society does not exist.

> The attitude of the adolescent is very narrow-minded and opinionated.

Obviously, it would be impossible to catalog all the different reasons that sentences become confusing. Ultimately, writers must become their own editors, able to see their own writing through another's eyes. When this happens, most of the confusion can be eliminated from any writing.

EXERCISE 11.11 Revising Confusing Sentences

Read the following sentences. Discuss with your Discovery Group what makes each of them confusing and how to eliminate such confusion.

1. Being overweight is a big problem for those of us who eat Brownie Buster Bellies perhaps even more so which is why so many people who don't have any self-control become overweight.

2. All the criminals within our prison system should be whipped and sentenced to hard labor because this would eliminate all the problems in our society and people would want to do better.

3. He was exhausted from his first day of work in the mines, which were totally unlike his village without fresh air and sunlight.

4. I feel that it is wrong to spend so much of our taxes on a country which enslaves such a large proportion of its citizens and banishes people who speak out against them, but it is necessary in order to promote freedom.

5. Blueberry cheese bars are my favorite dessert made with cream cheese and if you get fresh blueberries and make them real tangy with grated lemon rind and poured it all out into huge chunks of heaven.

6. Students of history that Thomas Jefferson was a slaveowner although he didn't believe in it and treated them well and set them free in his will.

Make Sentence Elements Parallel

If your sentence contains a series of words, phrases, or clauses, you should make these elements parallel. When sentence elements are parallel, they use the same grammatical form even though the words are different. Think of it as using the same cookie cutter on different dough. All the shapes will be the same even though the cookies are different. For instance, these two phrases are grammatically parallel:

in my house

at the zoo

and so are these:

cleaning the bathroom

ironing the clothes

but these are not:

reading the newspaper

having bought a magazine

Putting items in a series in parallel form makes a sentence easier to read and understand, as these examples indicate:

Series of nouns

Not parallel

We took beach balls, visors to keep the sun out of our eyes, and cold drinks.

Parallel

We took beach balls, sun visors, and cold drinks.

Series of adjectives

Not parallel

He was tall, tanned, and had a muscular physique.

Parallel

He was tall, tanned, and muscular.

Series of prepositional phrases

Not parallel

You could hear people discussing the Senate hearings everywhere — in hotel lobbies, some talked about it as they checked out at the grocery store, it was also the topic of discussion in neighborhood bars.

Parallel

> You could hear people discussing the Senate hearings everywhere — in hotel lobbies, in grocery stores, in neighborhood bars.

Series of participial phrases

Not parallel

> In my favorite part of the movie, a zebra runs through the department store and upsets some racks of clothing, and then knocks down some of the customers, and also, a row of televisions are destroyed.

Parallel

> In my favorite part of the movie, a zebra runs through the department store, upsetting racks of clothing, knocking down customers, and destroying a row of televisions.

Series of adjective clauses

Not parallel

> The man who had claimed to be fearless was also known to boast of his prowess with a gun, and was someone who had worn the sheriff's badge proudly, but he now cowered under the shadow of Black Bart.

Parallel

> The man who had claimed to be fearless, who had boasted of his prowess with a gun, and who had worn the sheriff's badge proudly, now cowered under the shadow of Black Bart.

Series of independent clauses

Not parallel

> Henchard came to Casterbridge in poverty; however, good fortune smiled on him and he became wealthy, but riches soon vanished, and in the end, he left the town with no more than when he had come.

Parallel

> Henchard came to Casterbridge in poverty; he made and lost a fortune; and he left as he had come.

Writers frequently use parallelism to organize several related thoughts. In the previously quoted passage about the circus, note how E. B. White uses parallelism to make three related points:

> Out of its wild disorder comes order;
> from its rank smell rises the good aroma of courage and daring;
> out of its preliminary shabbiness comes the final splendor.

In each clause, White argues that out of something bad ("disorder," "rank smell," "shabbiness") comes something good. Using the parallel structure allows White not only to make these points quickly but also to give them a dramatic flair.

EXERCISE 11.12 Adding Parallel Structures

Complete the following sentences by adding the suggested parallel structures.

1. The three activities the children seemed to enjoy the most were *when they got to go to the skating rink, the days we had movies for them to watch, and a game we played called "Steal the Bacon."* (Change to a series of gerundial phrases.)

2. The movie was marred by *a screenplay that was poorly conceived, the location was poorly chosen, and the actors didn't seem to care.* (Change to a series of nouns followed by adjective clauses.)

3. Johnson's proposal is *dangerous to our interests, lacks any real practicality, and I won't accept it.* (Change to a series of adjectives.)

4. The college was considering offering distance education programs for residents who lived outside a 100-mile radius because the programs would be beneficial *for the students, and they would also help the instructors, and even the school would profit.* (Change to a series of prepositional phrases.)

EXERCISE 11.13 Revising for Parallel Form

Revise the following sentences by placing the words, phrases, or clauses in parallel form.

1. The varsity quarterback, the halfback on the varsity team, and the athlete who played varsity defensive tackle went to the party after the game.

2. Believing that the owner's objections were unjustified and because he did not want the animal to suffer, Dr. Hopkins performed the operation the next afternoon.

3. The blue grape hyacinths covered the front yard, they were all over the backyard, and even the shadow boxes had blue grape hyacinths growing out of them.

4. All graduates should pay their diploma fee, and they should make sure that they have no outstanding fines, and a cap and gown deposit should be made.

Replace Nouns with Verbs

When a sentence becomes overburdened with nouns, it becomes dull and difficult to read. We often associate such writing with government and business publications. In fact, such language has been dubbed "bureaucratese" because it so often comes from various government bureaus and agencies. Here is an example of such writing:

American educational revitalization will mandate reform-based strategies that ensure maximum potential achievement of human resources.

Note the many noun phrases in this sentence: "American educational revitalization," "reform-based strategies," and "maximum potential achievement." Frequently, verbs are buried within nouns in such sentences. For instance, the nouns *revitalization* and *achievement* contain the verbs *revitalize* and *achieve*. By substituting verbs for nouns and replacing some of the abstractions with more concrete language, we get the following sentence:

American education can be revitalized through reforms that encourage all students to achieve their maximum potential.

By liberating the verbs hidden within nouns, you will produce a much more readable style.

EXERCISE 11.14 Liberating Hidden Verbs

What verbs are contained in the following nouns?

management

discussion

generalization

subscription

fulfillment

substitution

disturbance

simulation

assessment

formulation

EXERCISE 11.15 Replacing Abstract Nouns

Rewrite the following sentences, replacing abstract nouns with verbs.

1. The restoration of the historic building will be undertaken by a well-known architectural firm.

2. Please allow the evaluation process of the teacher's classroom performance to continue uninterrupted by commentary from the observers.

3. The flight crew's enjoyment of the educational game was a result of the special effects incorporated into the simulation of actual flight conditions.

4. The ramifications of the actions in this recommendation from the Senate have not been under investigation for a period of adequate time.

5. The inhabitants, even in their impoverished circumstances, lived a life of nonconfrontational simplicity and contentment.

6. The ratification of the resolution by members of the United Nations led to an outbreak of hostilities between the countries which had a contention over the disputed territory.

7. The general assembly's amendments to the report made by the committee were for the inclusion of fiduciary resources.

8. Reduction of the complications in the reapportionment process that were made by the steering committee will not affect the scheduled implementation of the procedure by the task force.

LEVELS OF FORMALITY

Although the decisions you make about sentence length and complexity will be governed by the specific purpose and audience for your writing, writers frequently distinguish formal and informal writing styles. Here are some of the features associated with these two styles:

Informal	Formal
short, direct sentences	long, complex sentences
common words	specialized vocabulary
concrete language	abstract language
use of contractions	no contractions
personal references ("I," "me," etc.)	no personal references
directly addressing audience ("you")	audience addressed indirectly ("the reader will observe . . .") or not at all

In practice, elements of these two styles are often fused. Much popular writing combines complex sentences and specialized vocabulary with personal references and a lighter tone. In general, the Institutional Style and the Scholarly Style lean toward a more formal style. The Personal Style is nearly always informal. The Literary Style may include elements of either formal or informal writing.

EXERCISE 11.16   **Identifying Levels of Formality**

Categorize the following passages as formal, informal, or a mix of the two styles. Identify the words or phrases that helped you place the passage in a specific category.

1. Communication and understanding are the two most important links between cats and their owners. It is obvious to sensitive and caring owners that their cats are aware when

the owners are unhappy or in ill health. Likewise, the cats respond with joyful play when the owner's mood is jolly. By understanding the cat's psyche, you are better able to open the pathways to a rewarding and fulfilling relationship — for you and for your feline friend. All you have to do is look at any situation from your cat's point of view. (Anita Frazier, *The Natural Cat*)

2. Initializing the network printer is a precautionary step to make sure WordPerfect is communicating properly with the network printer and that your printer is set up with the desired fonts. You can enable printer initialization for network printers by running WordPerfect with the {WP initials. If you have font files that can be downloaded from your computer to your printer, WordPerfect provides an Initialize Printer option from the Print (Shift-F7) feature. When you select the Initialize Printer option, soft fonts marked with an asterisk (*) in the Cartridges/Fonts/Print Wheels menu are downloaded to the selected printer. For more information about printing, see *Cartridges/Fonts/Print Wheels* and *Printer, Select* in *Reference*. (*Word Perfect Reference Manual*)

3. It was of the men, not white nor black nor red but men, hunters, with the will and hardihood to endure and the humility and skill to survive, and the dogs and the bear and deer juxtaposed and reliefed against it, ordered and compelled by and within the wilderness in the ancient and unremitting contest according to the ancient and immitigable rules which voided all regrets and brooked no quarter; — the best game of all, the best of all breathing and forever the best of all listening, the voices quiet and weighty and deliberate for retrospection and recollection and exactitude among the concrete trophies — the racked guns and the heads and skins — in libraries of town houses or the offices of plantation houses or (and best of all) in the camps themselves where the intact and still-warm meat yet hung, the men who had slain it sitting before the burning logs on hearths when there were houses and hearths or about the smoky blazing of piled wood in front of stretched tarpaulins when there were not. (William Faulkner, "The Bear")

4. The novel of eighteenth-century England was concerned with the comedy and tragedy inherent in the revolutionary social mobility which characterized the emergence of a middle class within the traditions of an older and more static class structure. On a scale unprecedented in human history, individuals were free to rise and fall within an existing class hierarchy. The novelist was exploiting the drama of individuals who had suddenly achieved a qualified freedom within a community that had become partially fluid. (David W. Noble, *The Eternal Adam and the New World Garden*)

5. Hereby, too, I shall indulge the inclination so natural in old men, to be talking of themselves and their own past actions; and I shall indulge it without being tiresome to others, who, through respect to age, might conceive themselves obliged to give me a hearing, since this may be read or not as any one pleases. And, lastly (I may as well confess it, since my denial of it will be believed by nobody), perhaps I shall a good deal gratify my own *vanity*. Indeed, I scarce ever heard or saw the introductory words, *"Without vanity I may say,"* etc., but some vain thing immediately followed. Most people dislike vanity in others, whatever share they have of it themselves; but I give it fair quarter wherever I meet with it, being persuaded that it is often productive of good to the possessor, and to others that are within his sphere of action; and therefore, in many cases, it would not be altogether absurd if a man were to thank God for his vanity among the other comforts of life. (Benjamin Franklin, *Autobiography*)

6. CLSHOST.BAT may be used to invoke the attachment program for a wide variety of hosts. The user should be familiar with the attachment interface program being used and have it configured properly before attempting to invoke it from the CLAS menu. It is recommended that the attachment program be installed on a Personal Computer with a hard disk and run from the hard disk rather than the network. The user should also determine if the attachment program being used is compatible with Novell NetWare and the network hardware being used. Hardware and/or software conflicts may exist in some cases. The following is provided as an example of attaching to the IBM SYSTEM/ 36 as a host using ENHANCED 5250 EMULATION (P/N 74X8402) as the interface program. The lines in the batch file may vary depending on the type and number of host sessions and the subdirectory where the program is installed. (International Business Machines Corporation's on-line ICLAS documentation)

EXERCISE 11.17 **Revising for Increased Formality**

Rewrite this informal paragraph in a more formal style.

I have called you jerks three times and have even written two letters, but you've never even had the decency to get back in touch with me. Are you so busy repairing your "well-built" houses for other suckers who bought them that you never have time to repair a measly crack which just happens to run all the way from the top of my ceiling to the baseboard of my living room? I didn't pay you guys $49,000 for this shack just to get ripped off, and I don't intend to let you continue to walk all over me. I'm going to contact a lawyer really soon if you don't send your drywall guy out here and fix my wall!

In recent years there has been a concerted effort to remove unnecessary technical language from government and legal documents. This "plain English" movement has helped to make information more readily accessible to a wider audience of readers. Some critics of the plain English movement have been concerned that substituting familiar words for the traditional term may only create more confusion. For instance, what is the appropriate equivalent term for *plaintiff* in a trial? We certainly don't use *plaintiff* in ordinary speech any more. We wouldn't want to use the word *complainer* instead, and the "one who is bringing the charges against the one who is being charged" obviously would be too cumbersome. In some cases, using the traditional term seems to be a necessary evil. Still, those employing plain English principles have managed to remove much of the tedious and confusing language associated with contracts and legal notices.

Consider these questions about matters of style:

1. Can all complex information be communicated using simple terms and ordinary language?

2. Do certain groups benefit from using language that the general public does not understand?

3. Can a specialized term sometimes be simpler than a plain English equivalent?

4. Would we be better off if everyone always tried to communicate using the simplest English possible?

5. If clichés are immediately recognizable and easily understood, why are people advised not to use them?

Index

Acknowledgments

Page 11 SHOE cartoon, 1-4-90. Reprinted by permission of Tribune Media Services. **Page 21** CALVIN and HOBBES cartoon. Copyright 1989 & 1992 Watterson. Reprinted with permission of Universal Press Syndicate. All rights reserved. **Page 34** HERMAN cartoon. Copyright 1981 Jim Unger. Reprinted with permission of Universal Press Syndicate. All rights reserved. **Page 51** CALVIN and HOBBES cartoon. Copyright 1989 & 1992 Watterson. Reprinted with permission of Universal Press Syndicate. All rights reserved. **Page 74** From "Los Angeles Against the Mountains" by John McPhee from *The Control of Nature*. Copyright © 1989 by John McPhee. Reprinted by permission of Farrar, Straus & Giroux, Inc. **Page 93** NANCY ® cartoon. Reprinted by permission of UFS, Inc. **Page 98** From "The Warrior Culture" by Barbara Ehrenreich, from *Time*, October 15, 1990. Copyright 1990 Time, Inc. Reprinted by permission. **Page 136** "One Perfect Rose" from *The Portable Dorothy Parker* by Dorothy Parker, Introduction by Brendan Gill. Copyright 1928, renewed © 1956 by Dorothy Parker. Used by permission of Viking Penguin, a division of Penguin Books USA Inc. **Pages 136 and 147** "A Narrow Fellow in the Grass" and "I Heard a Fly Buzz — When I Died" by Emily Dickinson. Reprinted by permission of the publishers and the Trustees of Amherst College from *The Poems of Emily Dickinson*. Thomas H. Johnson, ed., Cambridge, Mass.: The Belknap Press of Harvard University Press. Copyright © 1951, 1955, 1979, 1983 by the President and Fellows of Harvard College. **Page 140** "The Metal Smokestack" by William Carlos Williams: *The Collected Poems of William Carlos Williams, 1939–1962, Vol. II*. Copyright © 1962 by William Carlos Williams. Reprinted by permission of New Directions Publishing Corp. **Page 142** "Death Comes In Time" by Rachel Greer. Reprinted by permission of the author. **Page 145** "Out, Out —" by Robert Frost from *The Poetry of Robert Frost* edited by Edward Connery Lathem. Copyright © 1969 by Henry Holt and Company, Inc. **Page 148** "Incident" by Amiri Baraka from *Black Magic Poetry*, published by Bobbs Merrill 1964. Copyright © 1964 by Amiri Baraka (LeRoi Jones). Reprinted by permission of Sterling Lord Literistic, Inc. **Page 149** Excerpt from "Mirror," excerpt from "Sheep in Fog" from *The Collected Poems* by Sylvia Plath. Copyright © 1963, 1965 by Ted Hughes. "Mirror" originally appeared in *The New Yorker*. Reprinted by permission of HarperCollins Publishers Inc. **Page 150** "Traveling Through the Dark" by William Stafford from *Stories That Could Be True*, Harper & Row 1977. Copyright © William Stafford. Reprinted by permission of the author. **Page 151** CALVIN and HOBBES cartoon. Copyright © 1989 and 1992 Watterson. Reprinted with permission of Universal Press Syndicate. All rights reserved. **Page 152** "Selling Out," from *The Oranging of America* by Max Apple. Copyright © 1974, 1975, 1976 by Max Apple. Used by permission of Viking Penguin, a division of Penguin Books USA Inc. **Page 161** "The Lottery Ticket" by Anton Chekhov from *The Wife and Other Stories* by Anton Chekhov, translated from the Russian by Constance Garnett. Copyright 1918 by The Macmillan Company, renewed 1946 by Constance Garnett. Reprinted with permission of Macmillan Publishing Company. **Page 168** "Riding to Redemption Ridge" by Richard Schickel from *Time*, November 1, 1990. Copyright 1990 Time Inc. Reprinted by permission. **Page 169** "New Age Daydreams" by Pauline Kael from *The New Yorker* December 17, 1990. Copyright © 1990 Pauline Kael. Reprinted by permission of The New Yorker. All rights reserved. **Page 182** From "What is Vulgar" by Aristides (pseudonym for Joseph Epstein) from *The American Scholar*, Vol. 51, No. 1, Winter 1981/82. Copyright © 1981 by the author. Reprinted by permission. **Page 200** CALVIN and HOBBES cartoon. Copyright 1989 & 1992 Watterson. Reprinted with permission of Universal Press Syndicate. All rights reserved. **Page 218** From "Spare the Prod, Spoil the Child" by Dyan Machan from *Forbes* October 14, 1991. Reprinted by permission of *Forbes* Magazine. **Page 291** FRED BASSETT cartoon 11-1-89. Reprinted by permission of Tribune Media Services. **Page 345** MOTHER GOOSE & GRIM cartoon 6-10-91. Reprinted by permission of Tribune Media Services. **Page 359** SHOE cartoon 11-1-89. Reprinted by permission of Tribune Media Services.